A SHORT HISTORY

OF

ANCIENT CIVILIZATION

by

TOM B. JONES
Assistant Professor of History
University of Minnesota

HARPER & BROTHERS PUBLISHERS
New York and London

This book is dedicated to the memory of

PROFESSOR ALBERT A. TREVER

a fine teacher, a competent scholar,
and, above all, a true gentleman

CONTENTS

ILLUSTRATIONS

These plates, grouped together, follow page 176

EDITORIAL FOREWORD

By some turn of fate this foreword to a book about the beginning and development of civilization around the Mediterranean must be written as America watches a struggle in the same area to preserve some of the fruits of man's efforts to raise himself above the brute forces with which this sketch of ancient civilization begins. Names and places in the index to this volume march today across the headlines of the newspapers or come by modern magic to our ears. We hear voices on the spot telling of titanic struggles in lands where the fate of ancient peoples and of still more ancient issues were decided. The forty centuries that looked down from the Pyramids upon Napoleon's battalions and yet more centuries look out at us and our world from the pages of this book to comfort and command. Only the poor of heart will say it is but a tale that begins with primitive man, portrays his rise to great heights in culture and civilization, only to close as hordes of barbarians from the North were overwhelming the civilization that had been built up around the eastern Mediterranean and in the Italian and Greek peninsulas.

In this volume a young and competent scholar has brought into clear relief what the latest researches permit us to know of the lives and institutions of ancient peoples to whom we owe much in a living world. As he and his students study in a building that is a bit of Greek architecture translated to a midwestern campus, so all others who teach or study the volume will learn how much they live in a climate of civilized customs and thoughts and issues that had their beginnings and sometimes their perfect flower in the world called ancient and among peoples whose languages we call dead.

It has never been the purpose of forewords to the Harper

Historical Series to elaborate special features of the volume. It has been the hope, as volume after volume added to the established reputation of the series and of the venerable house that publishes them, that college teachers would expect and find in them the qualities of clarity, scholarship, good organization, and teachability. To that end maps, illustrations, selected bibliographies, and indexes have been freely used as integral parts. In none of these qualities or aids does this volume fall short.

Ancient history is not a simple straight-line story of successive nations. At points it is as complex in the contemporary and parallel development of different peoples as is modern history. Neither is it a static subject, for archaeology, epigraphy, ethnology, anthropology, and linguistics have poured streams of new facts and interpretations into the reservoirs upon which Grote and Gibbon drew. To be clear, accurate, adequate, and brief in a treatment of ancient civilization in any true sense of the word civilization is today no easy task. It takes a certain amount of intrepidity as well as sound scholarship to undertake it. If I had not thought my young colleague possessed them I should never have encouraged him to write the volume. With the end results of his labors before me I am glad to send this volume forth in the full confidence that its use will justify the thought and labor that have gone into it, the more because it is short rather than many-volumed.

GUY STANTON FORD

April 23, 1941

PREFACE

This is not an "ancient history"; rather, it is a brief account of the rise and fall of a civilization which had its origins in the Near East and reached its fullest development in the two Mediterranean peninsulas, Greece and Italy. Although most of the essential factual information required for beginning courses in ancient history will be found in this book, the main emphasis has been placed on the analysis of the causes of certain cultural developments and on the synthesis of the whole story of cultural growth and decline in antiquity. There has also been an attempt to put into practice the theory that a textbook should not aim at encyclopedic self-sufficiency, but that it should provide points of departure for reading and discussion.

The author is greatly indebted to a number of people who aided him in the writing and preparation of this volume. The late Professor Albert A. Trever of Lawrence College read the major part of the manuscript before his death, and his must be the credit for much that is worth while in this book. Then, too, there is no volume in this series which has not gained in effectiveness through the matchless editorial skill of President Guy Stanton Ford of the University of Minnesota. The author also wishes to acknowledge the help and encouragement rendered by his colleague, Dr. Rodney C. Loehr, and by his faithful students, Ida Kramer, Charles Sweet, and W. Donald Beatty.

Mr. Leonard Mason of the Science Museum in St. Paul very graciously permitted the use of his map of Ancient Athens (p. 164).

Tom B. Jones

University of Minnesota

A SHORT HISTORY

OF

ANCIENT CIVILIZATION

CHAPTER I

THE ORIGIN AND RISE OF CIVILIZATION

Civilization is not an easy word to define. At best, the term is abstract, and we use it in many different ways. The phrase "modern civilization," for example, might call to mind our great factories with their complicated machinery run by steam and electric power, our automobiles, airplanes, radios, and stream-lined trains—the products of the "machine age." One person might think of "modern civilization" in terms of our public school system, our democratic government, and the humanitarian interests of the modern period; another might think only of contemporary art, music, and literature. Since the word civilization will be used many times in the pages that follow, it seems desirable to find a definition for it before proceeding further.

Civili-
zation

Civilization may be defined in terms of another abstract word, culture. Thus it can be said that a civilization is a culture which has attained a degree of complexity usually characterized by urban life. What is a culture? A culture is the sum total of all the culture traits possessed by a given people at a given time. Culture traits or cultural items are the material things (tools, weapons, machines, clothing, etc.), the political and social institutions, the habits, customs, and ideas, the possession of which differentiates men from animals. Our "modern civilization" is an extremely complex culture made up of thousands of culture traits. Television, baseball, the fourth dimension, automats, prohibition, newspapers, movies, silk hats, "Paris models," marriage, divorce, communism, fascism, democracy, and countless other things are culture traits or cultural items. In less complex cultures the culture traits are not so numerous. Fifty thousand years ago, for example, the habitual use of a few simple tools and

Culture
and
culture
traits

1

weapons, a spoken language, the making of fire, a belief in the supernatural, and certain social customs comprised the meager cultural store of our ancestors.

There was a time, of course, when there was no culture; a time when only their physical appearance and structure served to distinguish our forebears from their near relatives, the great apes. How our ancestors acquired culture, and how culture became increasingly complex until the first civilizations arose are matters which will concern us first in this study of the history of civilization.

EVOLUTION AND CULTURE

Today the earth teems with hundreds of millions of animals which we call men. These erect, featherless bipeds are mammals; they fall into the same zoological *class* as whales, elephants, cows, dogs, and sheep; they belong to the same *order* (the primates) as monkeys and apes. "By applying the principle that structural resemblances point to a relationship one is forced to admit that man is an animal whatever else he may be. We have to call him a vertebrate, we cannot avoid calling him a mammal; there is, then, no reason why we should kick at having to call him a primate."[1]

Nevertheless, man is the only animal that possesses a culture; and, as we have already pointed out, it is his possession of a culture which clearly marks him off from the other members of the animal kingdom. Primarily, man's culture is based upon two things: his habitual use of tools and his articulate speech. In building up the material side of his culture as well as in making advances in its non-material or intellectual phases, man found his gift of speech invaluable; but just as important was his ability to employ tools.

In order to speak articulately and to become a tool-user man had to fulfill certain requirements: he had to have the proper vocal apparatus; he had to attain a high degree of intelligence, a good memory, manual dexterity, and a special type of vision. It is interesting to note that other animals

Side notes: Man as an animal · The only animal possessing a culture · Requirements for the creation of culture

[1] G. G. MacCurdy, *The Coming of Man*, New York, 1932, p. 11.

are equipped by nature in such a way as to fulfill some of these requirements—the elephant has a good memory, the monkey has manual dexterity, the parrot can talk—but man is the only animal that can fulfill them all. Extremely important, of course, is the fact that man's intelligence is superior to that of any other animal.

All the physical and mental essentials for the creation of culture were provided for man in the course of the evolutionary process by which he became man. In this modern era the theory of evolution is almost universally accepted. Although there are still gaps in our knowledge of the evolutionary chain, the evidence which scientists have collected is so overwhelming that further proof of the theory is hardly necessary. Why or how evolution occurs is subject to dispute, but that it has taken place is no longer questioned.

Evolution

Our particular variety of man, *homo sapiens,* is one of the more recent animals to appear upon the earth. *Homo sapiens* was not to be found in Europe before 25,000 years ago, although recent discoveries indicate that he appeared in northern Africa at a much earlier date. In Europe and elsewhere, however, *homo sapiens* was preceded by other types of men who were less manlike and seemed more apelike than he. None of these earlier types, as known to us today through their fossilized skeletons, can be called our ancestors with any degree of certainty; but somewhere far back in the chain of evolution these fossil men and our ancestors had a common progenitor. Even more remote was the divergence of apes and men. It should not be thought that we are descended (or ascended) from the apes, or they from us; it is simply that, at a certain point, apes and men became differentiated from a common stock and thereafter went their separate ways.

Homo sapiens

Fossil men

Man's rise to a position of terrestrial superiority was anything but meteoric. His prehuman history might be reconstructed as follows:

About 150 million years ago an amphibious quadruped deserted his home in the water for a new existence on land;

From am-
phibian
to tree
dweller

in the course of time he began to spend most of his life in the trees. This rather insignificant creature was important because he possessed one of the physical attributes necessary for manual dexterity: each of his four limbs terminated in five prehensile digits which might be used for grasping boughs and twigs. Many generations of life in the trees brought about changes in the physical structure of our hypothetical quadruped. He increased in size; while he used his hind legs more and more for support, his forelegs were employed for grasping and pulling himself along; he also acquired the habit of sitting on his haunches.

Physical
alterations

The sitting posture was productive of several physical alterations. First, it freed the forelimbs; they could be used for handling objects, particularly food. This encouraged hand-feeding, and hand-feeding led to a change in the snout-like form of the head: "A primitive land-dwelling quadruped mammal needs a projecting snout for touching things and conveying tactile impressions to the brain. The snout also serves as a food conveyor. A snout is useless on an arboreal animal. With its free and mobile forelimbs food is conveyed to the mouth and objects are brought into contact with the organs of smell and taste, or into the field of vision. Release of the hands from locomotor functions makes hand-feeding possible. . . ."[2]

Mental
develop-
ment

As the snout became less exaggerated, stereoscopic vision (the forward look of the eyes) was made possible, and the head change also allowed an increase in the size of the brain. An additional factor in the growth of the brain was the fact that the jaws, because of the new feeding habit, could be used for the mastication of food rather than for seizing and tearing; therefore they did not need to be so rugged and powerful as formerly, and in the young animals the period of cranial growth was prolonged. Not only did the brain increase in size, but the change from smelling to handling also developed new cerebral areas.

In the second place, the sitting posture brought an altera-

[2] *Ibid.*, p. 13.

tion of the thorax and collar bone that made for greater freedom of arm movement. The development of the arms, shoulders, and chest was further enhanced by a new method of locomotion in the trees: *brachiation,* swinging by the arms from branch to branch.

Brachia-
tion

It was only natural that the increase in the size of our hypothetical animal and his arboreal existence should effect a decrease in the number of offspring produced in a single litter. At the same time this led to a longer period of infancy and thus a longer period of learning for the young under the supervision of the parents.

More than one million but probably less than two million years ago, the animal that was to become man descended from the trees.[3] Now he was very dissimilar to the quadruped who had sought an arboreal refuge millions of years earlier. He was many times larger—this was certainly one reason for his descent to the ground—and he walked on two legs instead of four. The forelegs had become arms, and the forepaws, hands; the biped gait soon led to a specialization of the feet, and the toes began to lose their prehensile ability.

Descent
from the
trees

The erect walking posture produced further changes in the shape of the head which, because of the force of gravity, tended to become more spherical and less ellipsoidal. This increased the cranial capacity and made possible the enlargement of the portions of the brain connected with the functions of memory. Alterations in the head and throat paved the way for articulate speech.

New
physical
alterations

The picture which one must draw of the animal soon to become *homo sapiens* is not flattering. He was a man, but he was not yet a human being. He was hairy and probably walked with a stooped, shuffling gait. His features were coarse; he had no chin and very little forehead; his eyes peered from beneath heavy projecting (supra-orbital) ridges of bone. Prehuman man roved from place to place with a herd of his

Prehuman
man

[3] Some time during the period of arboreal existence the differentiation of men and apes occurred, and shortly after the descent from the trees (or perhaps before) the various types of men began to branch off from the parent stock.

fellows, gathering roots and berries and preying upon small animals which he ate raw. He himself was hunted by large carnivorous beasts; it has been suggested that the only reason he survived was that he was tough and stringy and made a very unsatisfactory meal—the carnivores preferred other animals and ate man only when there was nothing better to be had. The social life of the prehuman man left much to be desired. He was savage and unpredictable; he was promiscuous. The only law he recognized was the law of the pack; the group was supreme, and the individual could transgress none of its simple regulations and live to tell the tale.

Tools

Prehuman man eventually discovered that sticks and stones were more efficient in fighting than hands and teeth. The use of sticks and stones became habitual; from this, it was only a step to the selection of the more suitable sticks and stones. Then came, very naturally, the fashioning of these weapons to fit the need at hand. Thus, the use and making of tools was established upon a permanent basis; culture was born.

The "hand-made" brain

The effects of habitual tool-using were far-reaching. The use and manufacture of tools required certain physical essentials, principally agile, prehensile fingers; the so-called "opposable thumb" was also important. Manual dexterity (plus the constant use of the hands) increased mental ingenuity and brain power, and the growth of the brain paved the way for a superior capacity for remembrance and imitation. In the light of these considerations it will be seen how significant the adoption of the tool-using habit was for the mental development of our ancestors; someone has well said that man's brain is, in a sense, "hand-made."

Speech

It is believed that man began to speak almost simultaneously with the beginning of tool-using. Speech made explanation and instruction possible; ideas could be exchanged and experience consolidated. Consolidation of experience has great value; not only can knowledge be perpetuated, but serious pitfalls can be avoided. Let us suppose, for example, that a certain root or berry is found to be poisonous. Without speech it would be difficult to warn a person of the danger involved in eating the poisonous food; he would have to learn it by experience, and that experience would have little value for him if it proved fatal.

Slowly, imperceptibly, man became man—*homo sapiens*. When the final transformation occurred we cannot say; perhaps a date fifty to one hundred thousand years ago would be close to the true figure. Just before man became man he acquired a considerable forehead and chin; as he became man he lost his stooped posture and came into the possession of all the minor structural details that distinguished him from his prehuman forebears and his contemporaries, the manlike fossil men. An important difference between *homo sapiens* and the various types of fossil men was that *homo sapiens* was endowed with a larger and heavier brain; in other words, his mental capacities were probably superior to those of the others. The final transformation

After man became man his physical evolution practically ceased; at least, we can see no perceptible difference between *homo sapiens* today and *homo sapiens* fifty or one hundred thousand years ago. No mental or physical change is apparent. On the other hand, it might be argued that fifty or one hundred thousand years is only a fleeting moment in the evolutionary time scale, and, for all we know, new changes may take place in the future.

Today we recognize three main branches or races of men: whites, Negroes, and Mongoloids. Nevertheless, all are human beings (*homines sapientes*), and the obvious variations of pigmentation and predominant physical characteristics may well be environmental in origin. Moreover, it cannot be scientifically demonstrated that any one of these three races is superior or inferior to the other two. The point is that race has nothing to do with physical evolution. Race

From the first, *homo sapiens* had a culture; he had inherited it from his prehuman ancestors, and it is possible that he borrowed some culture traits from the contemporary fossil men. The Neanderthal race of fossil men, for example, who lived in Europe, Asia, and Africa during a period ex- Early culture

tending from about fifty to twenty-five thousand years ago,
manufactured stone weapons and implements, made fire by
striking flint and iron pyrites together, wore clothes, and
believed in spirits. Our human ancestors, living side by side
with this race, undoubtedly incorporated some of the Neanderthal culture into their own.

Eventually, however, the last of the fossil men became
extinct, and *homo sapiens* alone was left. Next, we shall see
how he added to the culture of his predecessors and created
civilizations.

THE EVOLUTION OF CULTURE

Cultural
evolution

Without too much inaccuracy one may say that the evolution of culture began when physical evolution came to an
end. True, the creation of culture antedated man as man;
but when man became man, his culture was anything but
complex, and it was not until later that cultural evolution
began to proceed at an accelerated pace.

In the past, it has been customary to divide the cultural
history of man into cultural epochs or ages: the Paleolithic

Cultural
ages

(Old Stone) Age, the Neolithic (New Stone) Age, the Bronze
Age, and the Iron Age. This system of classification arose
from the fact that the only remains of the activities of primitive men are of the material sort (stone weapons, etc.). In the
Old Stone Age hard stones were chipped or flaked into
appropriate shapes for use as knives, scrapers, and hammers.
In the New Stone Age a new technique for shaping stones—
grinding and polishing—was invented. In the Bronze Age
the stone artifacts gave way to those made from bronze (an
alloy of tin and copper); then, in the Iron Age, bronze was
in part replaced by iron.

On the whole, this system is not entirely satisfactory, since
the emphasis which it places upon the changes in materials

Alterna-
tive
termi-
nology

and techniques employed in what was really only one phase
of man's cultural existence tends to overshadow certain more
fundamental developments which were of greater importance
than the shift from the use of stone to that of bronze, or the

use of bronze to that of iron. In this book a different terminology will be employed. We shall speak of the Age of Primitive Culture, the Age of Agriculture, and the Age of Civilization.

The Age of Primitive Culture corresponds roughly with the Paleolithic Age. It begins with the origins of culture and runs down to the time (about 10,000 B.C.) when man first began to practice agriculture; this would also include what is sometimes called the Early Neolithic Age. The Age of Agriculture covers the Full Neolithic Age down to the rise of cities. The appearance of cities (about 3500 B.C.) begins the Age of Civilization; the Bronze Age began about the same time.

Correlation of the two systems

THE AGE OF PRIMITIVE CULTURE

In the Age of Primitive Culture man obtained his food by hunting and fishing and by gathering roots, berries, and nuts. His life was necessarily nomadic, since he had to rove with the animals upon which he preyed. In Europe the early part of this epoch coincided with the latter part of the Ice Age when successive glaciers produced a cold, disagreeable climate (until about 25,000 years ago). The Europeans of the Ice Age lived in caves; then, when the glacial period came to an end, they moved out into the open and often built temporary brush shelters. For the most part, however, man did not have any permanent dwelling or home.

The material aspects of primitive culture are well known. Weapons and tools were manufactured from stone, wood, bone, and horn; stone was shaped by flaking and chipping; bone and horn became increasingly popular in the latter part of the Old Stone Age. Of the weapons, the club and the fist-axe (a stone shaped to fit the hand) came first; the knife, the spear (in principle, a long-hafted knife), and the mace (a hafted fist-axe) followed; at the end of the period (in the Early Neolithic Age) the true axe and the bow were invented. There were numerous implements, among which

Primitive culture

were scrapers, drills, and needles. Clothes were made of pelts and hides; basketry and wickerwork were begun.

One of the most important of the primitive (probably pre-human) discoveries or inventions was the making of fire. Fire **Fire** provided warmth and a means of defense against dangerous animals; food could be cooked, and, as a result, some foods were made more digestible and formerly inedible plants and roots could be added to the diet. The potentialities of fire, however, were of greater significance than its actual uses at this time, for the chemical changes which it could produce were later to lead to the making of pottery and the smelting of metals.

The oldest extant remains of art date back to the entrance of the first members of the human race into Europe (about **Art** 25,000 years ago). On the walls of caves may still be seen primitive drawings of animals and men. The origins of art are obscure, but the development of primitive art was closely connected with various magical practices. In the beginning, it seems probable that men might have amused themselves by making rough sketches in the sand with sharp sticks or by molding figures in mud or clay. But the real turning point came when men began to think that by drawing pictures of animals, reciting certain incantations, or following definite, rituals they could overcome dangerous animals or increase the numbers of those that were essential (as a source of food) for man's existence. Cave art was realistic because man felt that it was necessary to reproduce the subject as accurately as possible in order to gain the maximum magical effect.

Magic Magic and supernaturalism were primitive inventions, and many interesting beliefs and practices were developed. Some men thought themselves the descendants of certain animals; others believed that, for example, by eating deer meat they could run more swiftly or by eating bear meat they could **Totemism** become more powerful. Hence, certain animals came to be associated with various groups of men; this is called *totemism*.

Men tended to interpret the natural world about them in terms of their social relationships, their dealings and contacts with other men. It was not surprising, therefore, that men **Animism** should believe that other living creatures were endowed with "spirits" like men themselves. Inanimate objects (trees, stones, etc.) were also thought to be the dwelling places of "spirits." This is called *animism*.

Death was something of a mystery. One wondered what became of the "spirit" when a man died. Perhaps death was like sleep when the "spirit" or "soul" left the body and wan- **Death** dered far afield. The spirits of great men might easily become "gods." Then, too, spectacular natural phenomena were un- **Gods** doubtedly possessed of divine spirits or gods: the wind, the lightning, the sun, the moon, and the stars.

Evil men should be buried so that their spirits would not walk abroad; perhaps all men should be buried in order that they might find eternal peace after dangerous and trying **Burial** lives. Naturally, the dead would find some solace in having their few poor possessions—their favorite weapons, perhaps —buried with them.

Tribal organization eventually replaced that of the pack. The chief was the man who was the cleverest hunter and the **The** best warrior. The old men, whose knowledge was the result **tribe** of accumulated experience, were the advisers of the chief. The elders were also the historians of the tribe; by word of mouth they passed on tribal traditions to the younger men— the great deeds of some long-dead hero, the story of the great drought, of the starving time when game was scarce and only powerful magic had saved the people from extinction.

In primitive society women occupied a subordinate posi- tion, yet it was they who were responsible for certain impor- tant cultural advances which took place at the end of the primitive period. While the men hunted and fished, made **Women** weapons, and fought the battles of the tribe, the women bore children, gathered roots and berries, and made clothes and baskets. From the food-gathering activities of the women and their basketry came three outstanding discoveries: (1) agriculture, (2) pottery-making, and (3) textile manufacture.

1. Undoubtedly, the women found it profitable to tend or

Origins
of plant
cultiva-
tion
protect young food plants; from this it was only a step to the
discovery of the part that seeds play in the cycle of growth.
The women began to make small garden plots, but their
activity along these lines was necessarily sporadic at first because of the migratory habits of the primitive tribes; this type
of cultivation is called garden culture or "hoe culture." Garden culture was begun late in the primitive period; subsequently (about 10,000 B.C.), agriculture was established upon
a more permanent basis, and then, of course, the Age of
Agriculture began. We shall return to this point later in
our discussion (see below, p. 13).

2. At any rate, the gathering of plant foods made necessary
the production of baskets in which to store and carry this
food. It was customary to fill the interstices of the baskets
with clay, and it was soon noticed that contact with fire trans-
Pottery formed the clay into a different and harder, insoluble material: pottery.

3. The invention of weaving, of textile manufacture, came
Textiles as an extension of principles already developed in basketry
and wickerwork. Whereas the discovery of pottery was certainly an accident, the invention of weaving implies the application of logical thought.

Nevertheless, the power of these new discoveries and inventions to effect economic changes was only potential. Primitive life, with its food-gathering economy and all its other
culture traits, might have continued indefinitely if it had not
been for important environmental changes which took place
in the Near East and northern Africa after the close of the Ice
Age. The European glacial period had had a corresponding
Environ- period in Africa and southwestern Asia, a period not of
mental extreme cold but of rather heavy rainfall. Afterwards, the
changes climate became much drier, and gradually the Sahara Desert
began to encroach upon the fertile north African coastal
region. Arid sandy stretches appeared where formerly a
luxuriant vegetation had flourished. As the desert advanced,
some tribes crowded together on the oases, and other groups
migrated northward to Europe or eastward to the valley of

the Nile. In Asia the enlargement of the Arabian Desert drove people to the banks of the Tigris and Euphrates or westward to Syria and Palestine. As a result of these climatic changes, two important things happened: (1) man domesticated animals, and (2) agriculture was established upon a permanent basis.

1. In the post-glacial period, animals as well as men sought refuge on the oases. The young animals were often captured and tamed. Some species were found amenable to domestication[4]—cattle, sheep, swine, and goats—but most of the others man could not tame. Domesticated animals were very useful because they provided a surer food supply than wild game; their hides and wool could be employed for clothing, and later some animals were used for draft purposes.

> Domesticated animals

2. The scarcity of game caused by increasing aridity enhanced the importance of agriculture, and man began to depend more and more upon plants for his food. The primitive "hoe culture" gave way to extensive agriculture. Many species of plants, especially the cereals, were now "domesticated."

> Agriculture

The domestication of plants and animals produced an economic revolution. Man became a food-producer, whereas formerly he had been only a food-gatherer. As we shall see, this economic revolution was to alter every phase of his existence and culture.

> The economic revolution

THE AGE OF AGRICULTURE

Agriculture is of vital significance in human history. Its adoption augmented and assured the food supply; this allowed an increase in population because it meant that more people could be fed. The birth rate rose automatically. In addition, since young boys and girls could labor in the fields, children became an asset rather than a liability.

> Significance of agriculture

> Population increase

---

[4] A domesticated animal is one which has become the tame companion or servant of man; it reproduces its kind in captivity. Primitive man had only one domesticated animal, the dog. In the glacial period the dog hung about the outskirts of the camp, and before long it became man's companion on the hunt. The dog also served primitive man as food.

The tribes that adopted agriculture gave up their nomadic life and became sedentary. Permanent homes were established, since the duties of cultivation and the harvest required man's constant presence. The houses were grouped together in villages because a concentration of the population provided mutual protection; the crowded living quarters also

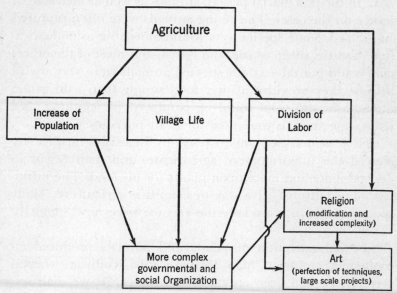

CHART I.—Results of the Adoption of Agriculture.

left more land free to be cultivated. Village life automatically increased the complexity of social and political organization. The tribal chief had many new duties; he had to become an administrator and a judge; in time, the press of affairs forced him to build up a staff of assistants with specialized functions. The growing importance of land brought a concept of private property; for the protection of property rights and the maintenance of order, regulations were made which ultimately became laws.[5]

[5] Perhaps this point should be elaborated. The first regulations were oral, of course. As they continued to be enforced through the ages, they became sanctified by tradition. In time, people began to feel that it was almost sacrilegious to transgress them. In the Age of Civilization, when writing was invented, these regulations were recorded and thus became laws.

Religion, as well as custom and habit, was affected by the adoption of the agricultural way of life. Even in the Age of Primitive Culture man had recognized that nature was more powerful than he; as we have seen, magic and religion **Religion** were employed by early man in an attempt to coerce nature. Obviously, in the Age of Agriculture man could be threatened by various natural difficulties which endangered his food supply: the rain might fail, destructive floods might ruin the crops, or a cloud of insects might destroy the harvest. Men felt that the gods alone had power to prevent such catastrophes; therefore they sought divine assistance when human skill and knowledge were of no avail.

The new life brought new concepts of the gods. The old hunting gods became the gods of the farmer; they were invested with new powers and functions. Sometimes new gods were created. In order to exercise the proper supernatural controls, man surrounded every simple technological act with ritual and ceremony. The planting of the crops was accompanied by rites which often involved human sacrifice; the ceremonies of the harvest, however, were more cheerful and free from tension. Nevertheless, the gods demanded attention; they must be continually propitiated and made happy with gifts.

It was also possible to bind mysterious powers to do one's bidding if the proper magic spells were recited and magical acts performed. In every community there were certain men **Magic** who appeared to have potent spells at their command. These were the medicine men, or witch doctors, and they were to become the first professional men of history.

A few of the material cultural items invented during the Age of Agriculture may be mentioned in order to illustrate the advance which was made in this period. Naturally, new implements and tools were developed for agriculture. In addition, the loom was invented, and there were improvements in pottery-making and other industries. The neolithic technique of stone-working was introduced; by this method **Material culture** stones were ground and polished into the desired shapes. This

technique was employed for the larger weapons and implements: axes, maces, mortars, pestles, etc. Often bowls and
other vessels were made from stone. Nevertheless, it should
be emphasized that the paleolithic methods of stone-working
were retained and used side by side with the neolithic technique. Last, but not least, an important invention of the Age
of Agriculture was the boat.

Agriculture was established upon its first and firmest
bases in the great river valleys of the Nile in Egypt, the
Tigris and Euphrates in Mesopotamia, and the Indus in

**The
great
river
valleys**
western India. In those regions there was a plentiful supply
of water, the climate was favorable to plant growth, the soil
was extraordinarily fertile and could be cultivated easily by
very primitive methods. The overwhelming importance of
agriculture in the great river valleys brought a shift in the
basic activities of the human inhabitants. Most men became
farmers, and hunting and fishing were transformed into

**Division
of labor**
specialized professions in which only a small group of the
population participated. As time passed, there was a further
specialization or division of labor when some men found it
profitable to give up farming and turn to trading and manufacturing. There were two reasons for the appearance of
traders and artisans:

1. Because farming tends to be a full-time occupation, the
farmers had little time to make weapons, implements, and

**The needs
of the
farmer**
utensils. As a result, certain men became artisans and manufactured the articles which the farmers needed; for these
articles the artisans received the products of the soil in trade
from the farmers. Then, too, there were certain basic necessities of life—flint, salt, etc.—which could be secured only
from regions some distance away. The farmers could not
leave their fields to procure these necessities, and therefore
a class of merchants and traders developed which made its
living, like the artisans, by supplying the farmers' wants.

**The agri-
cultural
surplus**
2. Because of the needs of the farmers, trading and manufacturing were bound to develop in any agricultural region
on a small scale; but in the great river valleys this develop-

ment was fostered and enhanced by another important factor: the agricultural surplus. The point is this:

In the great river valleys the soil was so fertile that at first, even though the population increased rapidly, it was possible to produce more food than could be consumed. In other words, there was an agricultural surplus. This meant (a) that it was not necessary for all to be farmers—some could turn to trading and manufacturing—and (b) that the agricultural surplus (the wealth of the farmers) provided the agricultural population with great buying power which stimulated progressive increases in the volume of trade and industry.

In view of these considerations, it is not surprising that the great river valleys soon forged ahead of other areas and became the home of the first civilizations. We shall now see how these civilizations developed.

THE AGE OF CIVILIZATION

About 3500 B.C. the culture of the river valleys reached a stage at which civilization began. The villages had grown into cities, and with the cities came all the complexities of economic, social, and political organization associated with urban life. The preeminence of Egypt, Mesopotamia, and the Indus Valley and the manner in which their civilizations were built up merit some consideration.

The division of labor which had originated in the Age of Agriculture ultimately became so marked that the artisans and traders became members of definite economic classes. **Trade** The growth of these classes was the natural outcome of environmental conditions which fostered the growth of trade in the Near East—with the growth of trade, there was a corresponding development of industry. Trade flourished in the Near East because it was possible to travel from Egypt through Syria to Mesopotamia without encountering any impassable natural barriers: high mountain ranges, extensive deserts, or broad seas. Moreover, the easily navigable rivers of the Near East—the Nile, Tigris, and Euphrates—simplified the problems of communication and transportation. Important also was the fact that no single division of the Near East was entirely self-sufficient; it was necessary to import many articles from other regions.

Towns and cities

Villages located at points where trade routes converged began to grow into towns and cities. As these towns and cities grew, further specialization of labor occurred. New industries sprang up; middlemen appeared who sold to urban and rural customers. New ways of living permitted an additional increase in population; in like manner, the growing volume of trade was paralleled by an increase in manufacturing which in turn opened up new opportunities for work. These new economic developments, like the earlier introduction of agriculture, produced an economic revolution and a new growth of population.

A second economic revolution

It cannot be emphasized too strongly or too often that the agricultural surplus was the foundation of the whole economic structure of the Near East. The agricultural surplus had made possible the developments already described; *but,* as the population increased as a result of the new opportunities for making a living in the towns, it at last became necessary to find some means of augmenting the production of food. The solution of this problem was provided by the irrigation of marginal desert lands, reclamation of swampy areas, control of the annual floods in the great rivers by means of dikes, canals, and reservoirs, and the supervision and direction of the efforts of the agricultural laborers. This solution involved an extension of the powers and functions of the government. In some areas this resulted in the regimentation of the agricultural population; everywhere the demands of the economic superstructure which had been built up in the towns necessitated alterations in the patterns of rural life and work. Undoubtedly, the changed situation contributed to the growth of the traditional antipathy between the country people and the city folk.

Agricultural developments

The basis of governmental control over agriculture and the means by which it was extended are interesting. The union of religion (or magic) and technology in ancient times has already been mentioned. In agriculture, magic and religion played an important part: the principal gods of the peasant village masses were agricultural deities, and the main religious ceremonies in the rural areas were those connected with planting, cultivation, and the harvest. The village chief, as the representative of his people before the gods, came to be a high priest who presided over these ceremonies. Thus, religion and government, "church and state," were combined, and through religion the state gained an additional means of controlling the people. Not only did his priestship give him added authority, but the close connection between religion and agriculture also allowed the village chief to direct agricultural activity when the occasion arose. *The government and agriculture*

Although we can see that the basis for the governmental control of agriculture was established in the Age of Agriculture itself, this function of the government was clearly not of major importance until the growth of cities produced a situation that demanded a great increase of agricultural activity. At this later date, the Age of Civilization had begun, and the former village chief, now the ruler of a large city, was in a much better position to exercise sweeping powers. City life had made governmental organization more complex; it had made necessary the growth of a bureaucracy. The growth of a bureaucracy meant that the head of the government became more and more remote from the common man, and the ruler seemed less and less human to those who had no real contact with him. The bureaucracy helped the ruler to take on that "divinity which doth hedge a king." This seeming divinity was enhanced by his high priestship. Some rulers were eventually considered the viceroys of the gods; others even went so far as to claim that they themselves were divine. Nevertheless, the heads of these theocratic states, whether they were viceroys of the gods or gods themselves, would not have great difficulty in ordering and arranging the lives and work of the simple peasants who lived in the country outside the cities. It is also significant that the control of *Theocratic government* agricultural activity gave the rulers control of labor, and the man power at their disposal might be employed for projects not even remotely connected with agriculture.

Theocratic states

The typical theocratic state of the Near East consisted of a large capital city (sacred to the chief god of the region) and the surrounding agricultural area dotted with rural villages and possibly some towns and small cities. The ruler was either a priest-king, the earthly representative of the principal deity, or else he was himself a god, perhaps regarded as the descendant of the deity. The growing complexity of governmental organization was paralleled by a similar development in religious organization, and priest classes came into existence. In some areas, it is possible that at first the priests were the only administrative officers of the king, but ordinarily in the historic period both religious and civil officials are found.

Class distinctions

Society was stratified, and class distinctions came to be extremely rigid. There were privileged, less privileged, and non-privileged classes whose origins were basically economic. Division of labor had brought the first classes—farmers, artisans, and traders—into existence. Then came the priest class which was supported by the gifts, later the tribute, of the workers. The priest class secured the favor of the gods and protected the people from supernatural enemies; for these valuable services the masses had to pay.

The nobles

In addition to these classes, there was also the nobility. Primarily, the nobility formed a warrior class. One might say that, just as the priest class protected the people from superhuman enemies, so the nobles protected them from human foes. On the other hand, it must be recognized that the origins of the nobility were much more varied and complex than those of the priest class. In some cases, the nobility were invaders who had conquered and subjected a native population. In other cases, the nobles were those who owned better land, or who had acquired more land, than their neighbors. In the early days before the great development of trade and industry, land was the chief form of wealth, and wealth meant power—both economic and political. Some of the nobility were the faithful servants of the priest-king—soldiers or bureaucrats—who had been rewarded with gifts of land or office; others might have been potential enemies whose friendship and allegiance were bought with gifts. Whatever their origins, the nobles were rich: they did not have to do manual labor; and they were warriors because they could afford suitable military equipment and had the leisure to learn the art of war.

Serfs and slaves also appeared with the coming of the civilized era. The regimentation of the agricultural masses **Serfs and** led directly to serfdom; the farmers, in many cases, became **slaves** bound to the soil and could be sold or transferred when the land changed hands. Slaves were captives of war and debtors. The scramble for a livelihood, which the new age with its complex economic problems had produced, made man power very important, whereas man himself (as an individual) tended to lose his identity unless he belonged to a privileged class. It was a vicious system. Its growth had been so insidious that it was not perceived until it emerged fully matured. Mankind has fought against it ever since, but with varied success.

The organization of priest classes was important for the growth of culture. In the first place, the priests were essen- **Priest** tially a leisure class; that is to say, they were freed from **classes** manual labor because they were supported by the economic **and** surplus created by the efforts of the rural and urban workers. **culture** Consequently, the priests had time for intellectual pursuits. In the second place, the business of the priests—religion— led almost automatically to new cultural developments. The priests were charged with the duty of ascertaining the correct periods for the sowing and harvesting of the crops; this brought the development of a calendar. The calendar was based upon the observation of astronomical phenomena; its creation and use led to the science of astronomy, as well as to the invention of the pseudo-science of astrology. The calendar, astronomy, and astrology fostered mathematical studies.

The priests were also healers; as physicians they relied heavily upon magic and supernatural forces, but they also learned much about herbs, drugs, and surgery.

Writing

In addition to the various mathematical calculations which the priests had to make in connection with their religious duties, there was the problem of the management of priestly estates and other wealth. The priests had to keep accounts of the gifts and tribute of the faithful, and their financial transactions had to be recorded. Then, too, there was a growing body of rituals, spells, charms, and traditions which was becoming so large that human memory could hardly retain all of it. These demands upon the mind, and particularly upon the memory, led to the invention of writing.

Development of writing

The invention of writing was a potentiality from the very moment that the cave men began to draw pictures on the walls of their caves; but it is a true proverb that "necessity is the mother of invention," and writing was not invented until there was a great need for it at the beginning of the Age of Civilization. The first writing was undoubtedly pictographic: a man drew a picture of a cow; his intention was to convey to the minds of those who saw the picture that this was a particular cow, but later a drawing of this type came to represent not *a* cow, but *any* cow. From this abstraction, it was possible to proceed to others: a man might be represented with his legs bent to convey the idea that he was running; this sign might be used ideographically as a symbol for the verb "to run." From this, it was only a step to phonetic writing in which sounds rather than ideas might be attached to signs. To represent the word "manifold," for example, one might draw the figure of a man, an eye, and a folded paper. With phonetic writing established, the use of signs for syllables and, finally, the alphabet (separate signs for separate letters) became potentialities.

Trends in writing

Certain trends in early writing are worthy of note. At first, with pictographic and ideographic writing, it was inevitable that hundreds of different signs should be employed; and those who used the signs were always careful to draw their figures as realistically as they could. Later, however, there was a tendency toward simplification; the number of signs was steadily reduced, and the figures themselves became conventionalized. Conventionalization was possible because

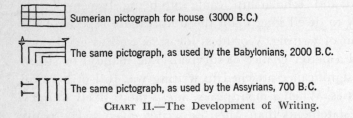

1. Hypothetical (for English language)

    eye

      Pictographic___eye
      Ideographic___to see
      Phonetic_____i, ai

    bee

      Pictographic___bee
      Ideographic___to buzz, to sting
      Phonetic_____be
      Alphabetic____B

| | two lines

      Pictographic___two
      Phonetic_____to, too

| | two lines, bee

      Pictographic___two bees
      Phonetic_____to be (verb)

2. Actual (Egyptian)

    eather

      Pictographic___feather (Egyptian word ma'at)
      Ideographic___truth   (Egyptian word ma'at)
      Phonetic_____y   (as an alphabetic sign)

3. Trend toward conventionalization of signs

    Sumerian pictograph for house (3000 B.C.)

    The same pictograph, as used by the Babylonians, 2000 B.C.

    The same pictograph, as used by the Assyrians, 700 B.C.

CHART II.—The Development of Writing.

people were becoming familiar with the signs and because it was desirable to write more rapidly. An example of conventionalization might be provided by a sign for "house." At first, the picture of a house would be drawn very carefully; later, this same sign might be simplified to a rectangle or even a straight line.

The development of an alphabet was not so easy as one might suppose. The evolution of writing was hampered by man's almost inherent conservatism. Innovation and change were resisted. Then, too, writing was felt to have connections with magic; perhaps the fact that writing was the invention of the priests contributed to this impression. In the systems of writing employed in the Near East, ideographic and syllabic writing were intermingled, and the scribes hesitated to discard the old ideographs. The business men, however, who eagerly embraced writing as an aid to their commercial operations, were more progressive; it was no coincidence that the alphabet first came into use somewhere in the Syria-Palestine region (in the late second millennium B.C.) where business was often considered more important than religion. It is true that the Egyptians had long before developed a series of alphabetic signs, but the predominance and conservatism of the Egyptian priests prevented the discarding of the old ideographs and syllabic characters.

The alphabet

The invention of writing meant that more knowledge could be preserved. The human memory had its limits, and written records provided an excellent substitute. Writing also made possible the widening of the horizons of abstract thought. The opportunities for intellectual activity were increased, and "scholarship" came into being. It seems hardly necessary to dwell long upon the unfortunate aspects of the invention of writing. Worthless ideas, as well as good ones, now had a better chance of survival. The magical or supernatural significance attached to writing was full of harmful possibilities. When a man speaks, one is more likely to question his statements than when he writes; even today, many people still feel that the printed word, by some magical process, cannot contain an untruth.

Importance of writing

Literature, of course, came into existence with the invention of writing. Folklore, myths, ballads, and traditions were now committed to writing in poetic and prose forms. Religious literature grew apace. The keeping of governmental

Literature

records eventually led to historical writing; the historic period may be said to begin about 3500 B.C.[6]

About 5000 B.C., in the transition from the Age of Agriculture to the Age of Civilization, man first began to use metals. **Metals** In the Near East copper, gold, and silver were to be found in a free state. At first, these metals were used only for ornaments and trinkets, but soon copper began to be substituted for stone in the manufacture of some implements. Then came the discovery, undoubtedly accidental, that when heated in the fire certain ores (containing copper and tin) produced a hard metallic substance—bronze. Bronze weapons and implements were superior to stone because they were not so brittle and could be reshaped. Bronze armor and implements became popular in the Near East about 3500 B.C. The introduction of iron did not come until two thousand years later; this was because iron ores were to be found only outside the civilized area, and also because iron was more difficult than bronze to produce.

Because of their value and their comparative scarcity, the metals became popular as media of exchange. As trade continued to increase, they were employed more and more in this **Money** capacity. Traders, and later their governments, adopted the practice of stamping various distinctive devices upon bullion to guarantee its weight and purity. Out of this custom came the invention of coined money—about the eighth century B.C.

Important inventions made early in the Age of Civilization were those of the plow and the wheel. The plow made possible greater agricultural production, and the wheel was important for the development of transportation. Moreover, the invention of the wheel led to new mechanical devices: the pulley, the cog, and the potter's wheel (by means of which more symmetrical pottery could be made).

The increase in the power of the rulers and the priest class and their control of vast resources of labor were important **Art**

---

[6] The period before 3500 B.C. is the *prehistoric* period; in other words, the prehistoric is an age which has no written records.

for the development of architecture, sculpture, and painting. The greatness of the kings and of the deities whom they represented seemed to demand a certain amount of ostentation. Consequently, large palaces and temples were constructed, and the technical problems which these buildings presented to the architects fostered the growth of a knowledge of engineering.

Sculpture

The development of sculpture and painting was closely related to that of architecture. The temples and palaces were decorated with relief sculpture which was painted with bright colors. Eventually, sculpture was divorced from architecture and became an art in its own right. It should not be forgotten, however, that the modeling of small figures in clay, stone, and metal also contributed to the evolution of sculpture.

Painting

Somewhat later than the separation of architecture and sculpture came the emancipation of painting from sculpture. The important thing to bear in mind, however, is that these three major arts were originally joined together, and that sculpture and painting are offshoots of architecture rather than independent developments.

Such were the origins of the earliest civilizations. It is significant that these first civilizations arose in the area which we shall call the Ancient Near East (see map, p. 31). From the Near East civilization spread eastward in Asia and westward to Europe. In European lands around the Mediterranean Sea the growth of culture was stimulated by commercial contacts with Egypt, Syria, and Mesopotamia. Until the Near East fell into cultural decay (about 600 B.C.), Europe lagged far behind the eastern peoples.

Thus far we have spoken of civilization only in the most general terms. Now it will be necessary to consider the individual civilizations of the Near East and those which appeared later in the area around the Mediterranean Sea. Before we leave the general topic of civilization, however, it will be instructive to examine the general laws which seem to govern cultural growth.

THE PRINCIPLES OF CULTURAL EVOLUTION

1. As we have seen, cultural development has been basically dependent upon the course which was taken by man's physical evolution, for physical evolution provided man with certain mental and physical traits and abilities which made possible the creation of culture. Physical and cultural evolution

2. All culture traits may be traced back to very simple origins, to what might be called primary inventions and discoveries. Elaboration and adaptation of these simple traits produced new cultural items; a good example of this point is provided by the spear which is, in principle, a knife with a long handle. Simple traits (and more complex traits) might often be combined to produce new items; the combination of the bow with the arrow (again, an elaboration of the knife) made a more effective weapon; later, of course, there was a further elaboration with the invention of the catapult. Similar developments occurred, and still occur, not only in the case of material culture, but also in social, economic, religious, and intellectual fields. Simple origins Elaboration

3. Culture tends to accumulate. In the Age of Agriculture, for example, man retained many of the culture traits invented in the Age of Primitive Culture. Moreover, providing environmental and economic conditions remain favorable, the accumulation and growth of culture tend to be accelerated. Clearly, the more culture traits a given group possesses, the more will be the opportunities for combination and elaboration. It is an elementary mathematical fact that one can make more combinations and permutations with fifty numbers than he can with five. Accumulation

4. In ancient times, the growth of culture within a given area was greatly dependent upon environment and geographic location. Environment not only encouraged or limited cultural growth, but it also determined very largely the course which cultural evolution was to take; Esquimaux do not invent ice boxes or fans, nor do the inhabitants of tropical countries invent central heating or skiis. Climate, Environment

soil, natural resources, and topography are factors which must always be taken into consideration.[7] We have seen in the Near East how an environment favorable to primitive agriculture was important for the rise of civilization, and how the situation as regards topography and natural resources affected the growth of trade. Culturally, trade was important because it brought the various geographic divisions of the Near East into contact with one another; the traders took out with them (and brought home) culture traits which had little or no connection with their commercial dealings. In other

Cultural interplay

words, trade made possible a cultural interplay which greatly stimulated the growth of civilization. Culture traits were exchanged, and in the countries into which they were introduced they received new adaptations and elaborations.

Diffusion

5. The passage of a culture trait from the area of its origin into a new area is called diffusion. The process of diffusion is important because it makes possible increased cultural complexity in civilized areas, and also it facilitates the growth of culture in regions which might otherwise remain backward because of unfavorable environmental conditions. In ancient times, this was especially true of Europe; the Europeans were immeasurably indebted to the Near East for many of the culture traits which later helped to make up "European civilization."

A stone dropped into a quiet pond produces a series of ripples which travel in concentric rings farther and farther from the center of the disturbance until they lap the shore. The action of diffusion is similar to this; a culture trait tends to spread from its center of origin to the far corners of the earth. This point may be illustrated by the story of tobacco:

The use of tobacco, a discovery of the pre-Columbian Indians of the New World, was a culture trait carried back to Europe by the Spaniards about the beginning of the sixteenth century. The trait spread across Europe and Asia

---

[7] In modern times, man's conquest of nature has somewhat decreased the importance of environmental factors.

and was carried by the Russians (in the eighteenth century) to the Alaskan Esquimaux, who had not known of tobacco until that time.

6. The growth of culture is, in a sense, automatic. Given certain conditions, certain developments are likely to take place. The laws of accumulation and acceleration operate without man's conscious knowledge. Man created civilization without being aware of what he was doing. The instincts which drove him in search of food and shelter provided the motivating force for the creation and elaboration of culture. Moreover, stronger than the individual man were the demands of society, the group. *Automatic growth of culture*

In view of these considerations, it must be admitted that man was allowed, by the mere force of circumstances, little self-determination—by either his natural or his social environment. Then, too, it is obvious that when culture, especially in its non-material aspects, attained a certain degree of complexity it was no longer the servant of man, but his master. The tail began to wag the dog, and it has done so ever since.

We began this chapter by speaking of modern civilization, and we may end it in the same way. The great indebtedness of our culture to earlier cultures defies complete evaluation. One has only to consider a few of the many culture traits which we have inherited from our ancestors—and from peoples not related to us. Fire and funerals are part of our primitive heritage; agriculture and boats go back to the Age of Agriculture; the ancient Mesopotamians gave us our astronomy, our division of the day into hours, and our seven-day week (originally sacred to the sun, moon, and five major planets—we still speak of Sunday and Monday); logic we owe to Socrates, and much of our language stems from Greek and Latin; algebra came from the Arabs, firecrackers from the Chinese, and tobacco from the American Indians. *Our indebtedness to the past*

Our civilization is built upon foundations provided by cultures of the past; without those foundations, modern civilization could not have been created.

CHAPTER II

THE CIVILIZATION OF THE ANCIENT NEAR EAST

The Ancient Near East

We shall now turn to a consideration of the civilizations of the Ancient Near East, the first civilizations in the history of the world. The Ancient Near East (or Ancient Orient) is the name which we shall give, quite arbitrarily, to an extensive region stretching from the Nile Valley in Egypt eastward to the Indus Valley in India. As a cultural area, the Ancient Near East should include Egypt, Syria, Palestine, Crete, Cyprus, Asia Minor, Mesopotamia, Assyria, Iran (Persia), and the Indus Valley. The three great river valleys of the Nile, the Tigris-Euphrates, and the Indus were centers of origin and diffusion from which culture traits spread to other parts of the Near East that might be designated as intermediate and peripheral areas. As a result of this diffusion, the intermediate and peripheral areas increased their cultural stores until they reached the level of civilization. Although there were individual local differences that distinguished the civilizations of the various areas of the Near East from one another, there was, nevertheless, a fundamental underlying unity of culture which permits us to speak also of *the* civilization of the Ancient Near East.

Chronology

In the history of the entire region which we shall discuss in the following pages, it is possible to make certain chronological divisions:

1. About 3500 B.C. there were civilizations in Egypt, Mesopotamia, and the Indus Valley which enjoyed an extremely prosperous and flourishing existence down to about 2000-1800 B.C.

2. Then, as the result of a series of barbarian invasions, the first half of the second millennium B.C. in the Ancient Orient

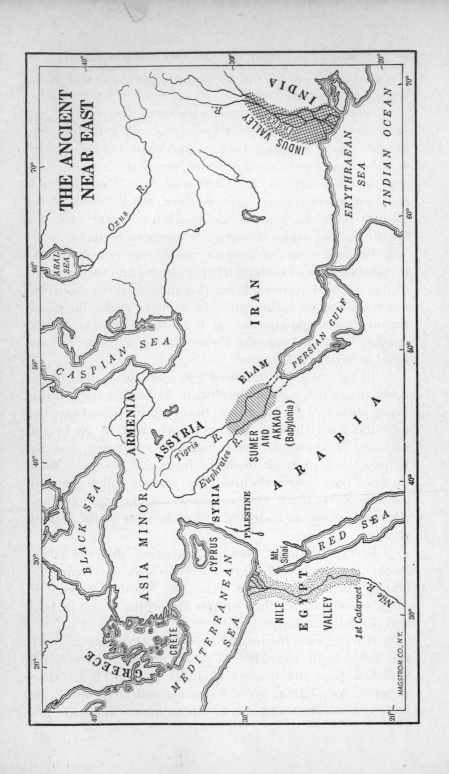

THE ANCIENT
NEAR EAST

INDIA

INDUS VALLEY R.

ERYTHRAEAN
SEA

INDIAN OCEAN

Oxus R.

ARAL
SEA

IRAN

CASPIAN SEA

PERSIAN GULF

ELAM

ARMENIA

ASSYRIA

Tigris R.

Euphrates R.

SUMER
AND
AKKAD
(Babylonia)

ARABIA

BLACK SEA

ASIA MINOR

SYRIA

CYPRUS

PALESTINE

Mt.
Sinai

RED SEA

MEDITERRANEAN
SEA

CRETE

GREECE

NILE

EGYPT

VALLEY

1st Cataract

Nile R.

HAGSTROM CO., N.Y.

was marked by a decline in the political predominance of the three major culture areas.

3. About 1600 B.C., however, a nationalist revival in Egypt produced a wave of imperialism; Syria and Palestine were brought under Egyptian control, and until 1350 B.C. Egypt was the most powerful state in the Near East.

4. In the meantime, the Hittites of Asia Minor had also built up an empire; as Egypt declined, the influence of the Hittites increased, and in the thirteenth century B.C. the Hittites gained political control of northern Syria.

5. Between 1200 and 1000 B.C. another series of barbarian invasions destroyed both the Hittite empire and the remnants of that of the Egyptians. From this time down to about 750 B.C. there was no really extensive territory under the domination of a single state in all the Ancient Orient. It was during this period that the Phoenicians and Hebrews flourished in Syria and Palestine.

6. In the years that followed 750 a new state, that of the Assyrians, arose and accomplished the unification of the major portion of the Near East. In their great period (745-612 B.C.) the Assyrians built up an empire that, at its height, included Mesopotamia, Syria, Palestine, and Egypt. Assyrian influence was also felt in Asia Minor and on the Iranian plateau. But Assyria declined, for reasons which we shall consider later; there were revolts among her subjects, and the empire came to a violent end at the close of the seventh century.

7. For a little more than a half-century after the fall of Assyria, a number of large states divided the Near East among themselves. There were the Neo-Babylonians in Mesopotamia, the Lydians in Asia Minor, the Medes in Iran, and the Saites in Egypt.

8. After 550 B.C. the meteoric rise of the Persians (formerly the subjects of the Medes) produced an empire which stretched from the borders of India through Iran, Mesopotamia, Asia Minor, Syria, Palestine, and Egypt to Cyrene in northern Africa and the European area around the Bos-

porus known as Thrace. The Persian empire continued to exist until the fourth century B.C. when it was conquered by Alexander the Great.

With this chronological outline in mind we may proceed to a description of the individual civilizations of the Ancient Near East.

THE TIGRIS-EUPHRATES VALLEY

Some time before 3500 B.C. the Age of Civilization began in the lower Tigris-Euphrates Valley. Then the Persian Gulf extended two hundred miles farther to the northwest than it does today, and the two great rivers did not converge but emptied into the gulf through separate mouths. During the Age of Agriculture Semites[1] from Arabia and highlanders from the north had settled on the broad alluvial plain at some distance northwest of the gulf, although the first civilization to appear was the creation of later invaders, the Sumerians, who came from the east and settled at the head of the gulf perhaps about 5000 B.C. The Sumerians drained the swamps and built cities, and their culture was soon borrowed by the earlier peoples who had established themselves farther inland. The land of the Sumerians—at the head of the gulf—was called Sumer, whereas the territory occupied by the earlier settlers—around modern Bagdad—was called Akkad. The combined area of Sumer and Akkad—in other words, the lower Tigris-Euphrates Valley—was later known as Babylonia.

Early settlers

Sumerians

Sumer and Akkad together did not occupy an extensive territory; but the fertility of the soil in this region made possible the support of a large population once agriculture was established on a large scale and the labor of the peasants was brought under governmental management to construct canals for flood control and irrigation. The geographic position of Sumer and Akkad was favorable for the development of trade; the commercial routes from east to west and north to south passed through the plain. Moreover, the lower valley

Economic conditions

[1] People who spoke various Semitic dialects.

was not self-sufficient; its inhabitants needed to import many things, principally stone and metals.

The political history of Sumer and Akkad was almost predetermined by topography. Political unification of the area was not difficult because of the lack of any natural divisions

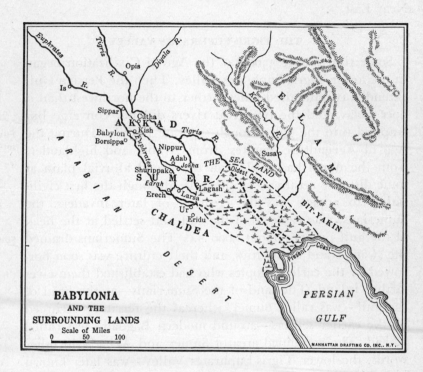

BABYLONIA
AND THE
SURROUNDING LANDS
Scale of Miles
0   50   100

within the plain itself; on the other hand, the absence of any defensible frontiers plus the richness of the plain made it easy and tempting prey for invaders. Later we shall observe similar environmental influences at work in shaping the course of religious, artistic, and intellectual history in this region.

Early civilization By 3500 B.C. the civilization of Sumer and Akkad had almost achieved maturity. The plain was dotted with cities; agriculture, trade, and industry were thriving; a knowledge of metal-working and writing was common, and monumental works of architecture were being constructed. Society had already become stratified, and slavery had been introduced. The civilization created by the Sumerians had been adopted by the people of Akkad where the predominant element had become Semitic.

In this age the city-state was the largest political division, and each city-state constituted an independent nation. The government of these states was theocratic; each was thought to be the property of a particular local god whose earthly representative, a high priest (patesi), was the ruler of the city and its surrounding territory. The principal cities were Ur, Lagash, Erech, Eridu, Nippur, Sippar, Umma, and Akkad, but there were many others. Theocratic states

The city-states were often at war with one another. Sometimes the victor in these struggles would incorporate the territory of the vanquished with its own; as time went on, various strong states were able to create short-lived empires through their conquests. Before the middle of the third millennium B.C. the Sumerians enjoyed political as well as cultural supremacy; but about 2650 B.C. the Semite king from the northwest, Sargon of Akkad, built up an empire which stretched from the Persian Gulf to the Mediterranean. Although Sargon's empire could not be long maintained by his successors and disunion once more prevailed, the old Sumerian predominance which he had overthrown could never be completely restored, and the Semitic element gained more and more in strength and numbers at the expense of the Sumerians. At the end of the third millennium B.C. a wave of Semitic invaders, the Amorites, conquered all of Sumer and Akkad. The most important of the Amorite kings, the famous Hammurabi (c. 1950 B.C.), made the city of Babylon his capital, and the old territory of Sumer and Akkad was henceforth called Babylonia. Empires Sargon Hammurabi

Under Hammurabi the civilization of the lower Tigris-Euphrates Valley reached its peak. Politically, the whole area was unified; as a matter of fact, the empire of Hammurabi extended up the Tigris into Assyria and as far west as the

Mediterranean coast. The city of Babylon was not only the capital of this great realm, it was also a center of cultural life.

Baby-lonian civilization
The Babylonian civilization was founded upon that of the Sumerians. In the time of Hammurabi the economic and social structure, technology, art, literature, religion, intellectual outlook, laws, and the system of writing all were derived from Sumerian origins. The Semites of Akkadian times and Hammurabi's own Amorites had adapted some of these culture traits to their own needs and had made some elaborations; but the principal difference between the Babylonian civilization and that prevailing a thousand years earlier was that the language in Hammurabi's day was Semitic instead of Sumerian and the old Sumerian people themselves had become so thoroughly assimilated by their Semitic conquerors as to be indistinguishable. True, the Semites had introduced a few new gods and some new moral and ethical concepts regarding family life; but compared with the great body of culture already created by the Sumerians, these things were insignificant.

Society
Babylonian society was composed of three main classes: the upper class, the commons, and the slaves. In the upper class were the feudal landholding nobility, the hierarchy of civil and military officials, and the priests. In the early Sumerian period the priests had been all-powerful under the theocratic regimes, but with the successive conquests and unifications of the valley the kings had found it profitable to set up a lay aristocracy beside the priest class. The commons were subdivided into several groups according to their varying economic positions. The rich merchants, the craftsmen, the scribes, and other professional men formed a bourgeoisie, whereas the city and rural laborers and the small landholders constituted a proletariat. At the bottom of the social structure were a large number of slaves and a few serfs.

Slavery
The slaves were recruited from captives of war and debtors. A man might pledge his wife or his children, or even himself, as security for a loan; failure to repay the loan within the time specified in the contract meant slavery for the person

thus pledged. Nevertheless, the slave enjoyed some legal protection. The buying and selling of slaves as a speculative venture was discouraged by the government. The slave could acquire property, engage in trade, marry a free woman, and eventually (with good luck) buy his freedom. One method of emancipation was the adoption of the slave into his owner's family. On the other hand, the slave was not legally a person; he was only a thing, a chattel. His master might treat him as well or as badly as he pleased. Slaves were branded; escape was not easy, for once a slave ran away from his master every free man was his enemy. The law provided severe penalties for the man who assisted or harbored a fugitive slave.

The position of women in Babylonia was hardly what one would expect in an Oriental society. The women were quite independent; they could own property and participate in **Women** legal proceedings in the courts. The married woman had a favored position in the home, for she had equal power with her husband over the children, and her rights were protected by law and defined by a marriage contract. In a sense, the Babylonians were monogamous; a man took only one wife, and, although he might have a number of concubines, the rights of his wife took precedence over all other claims. If a woman did not choose to marry, she might pursue a socially accepted career as a temple prostitute.

Babylonian government was a highly organized bureaucracy under the headship of the king and his chief ministers. The principal functions of the government were national defense, the collection of taxes, the direction of agricultural produc- **Government** tion (chiefly through the construction and maintenance of canals and irrigation ditches), and the administration of justice. Both civil and ecclesiastical courts existed, and the king might receive final appeals. There were professional judges whose tenure depended upon good conduct in office; it has been said that every priest might act as a judge. In the various small districts of the kingdom were royal appointees who acted as policemen; there were also foremen or overseers who directed the digging of canals and ditches. The policemen and the overseers were given lands for their support; these lands constituted small fiefs which could not be sold or transferred.

Law

An important source of information regarding Babylonia in the time of Hammurabi is the famous law code drawn up by the order of the king himself. The code was based upon previous Sumerian compilations to which were added some typically Semitic provisions regulating family life and morals. The laws contained in the code deal with seven broad subjects: personal property, real estate, trade, business relations, the family, injuries, and labor. To us today the general tone of the criminal code of Hammurabi seems harsh because of its insistence upon retaliation in kind; the guiding principle was "an eye for an eye, a tooth for a tooth." The law was definitely a class law; men in the same class received equal treatment, but when a poor man injured a noble he received a much heavier penalty than did a noble who injured a poor man. On the other hand, civil law was in an advanced stage and reflected the economic progress which the Sumerians and Babylonians had made. Typical of a capitalist society was the fact that private property was regarded as more sacred than human life itself.

Land

The economic life of Babylonia was surprising in its complexity. Land was held by the crown, by the temples, and by private persons. The small freeholder did not become extinct, although the land tended to pass into the hands of the nobility and the priests. Many of those who worked the temple lands were serfs or slaves, but on other holdings tenant farmers were numerous. The tenants might be either renters or share-croppers. Large landowners increased their holdings by purchases, but sometimes we find a rich man persuading an elderly farm couple to adopt him as their son; in return, he arranges for the cultivation of their land and provides them with a living, and when they die he becomes their heir.

Industry

In industry each craftsman had his own shop and belonged to a craft guild. The apprentice system was universal; the apprentices were adopted as sons by the master craftsmen.

There were also artisans, especially weavers, who worked in the palaces and temples; they received board and wages.

Trade and commerce were carried on over wide areas. Babylonian traders sent their goods to India in the east and to Syria and Egypt in the west; they also penetrated the hills **Trade** to the north of the valley. Gold, silver, and copper were used as media of exchange, and the widespread use of the Babylonian system of weights and measures throughout the Near East is adequate testimony of the economic predominance of the Tigris-Euphrates cities. The merchants might also be bankers who supplied agents with money or stock for trading ventures in foreign lands. The agent returned to the merchant a fixed share of his profits. Caravans and ships might be hired by agents to transport their goods to and from Babylonia. Like private individuals the temples engaged in trade and banking; many of the temples were very rich, and often a hard-pressed ruler would extort forced loans from them.

All kinds of complicated business transactions are known. Goods were sold on credit, promissory notes were common, and loans were made by the temples and private persons at high interest rates. Interest rates ordinarily ran about 25 per cent per month. Thousands of commercial and legal contracts inscribed on clay tablets have survived. Sales, loans, rentals, partnership agreements, receipts, transfers of property, and wills are only a few of the subjects with which they deal. Each transaction was recorded by a scribe, and the par- **Business** ticipants and their witnesses affixed their seals. The courts of law were crowded with litigation involving economic affairs; quarrels between partners, difficulties with collections, breaches of contracts, suits over inheritances, and forged wills were matters submitted for judicial settlement.

Babylonian art was greatly influenced by environment. The lack of good wood and stone made it necessary for the people to use mud bricks for their buildings, since clay was plentiful **Archi-** in the valley. Most of the public edifices were built upon high **tecture** platforms because of the numerous floods. In every city was

the zikkurat, the temple mound, a high terraced tower with
the sanctuary of the municipal god at its peak. The priests
and temple workers had their quarters in an enclosure at
the foot of the zikkurat; these included sleeping rooms, workshops, archives, stables, breweries, etc. The column and the
true arch were used in architecture. Bricks were baked in the
sun; sometimes walls of mud brick were covered with bi-
tumen to protect them from moisture. Kiln-baked bricks
were impervious to the dampness, but they could not be
made in large quantities because the scarcity of fuel made
the expense of their manufacture prohibitive. Glazed bricks
in bright colors were often set into the walls in attractive designs, and in the interiors of the buildings the walls were
covered with painted stucco.

Some of the kings imported marble, granite, porphyry,
and limestone for their palaces. Cedar and other aromatic
woods were employed. There were cedar doors mounted on
sockets of bronze that "creaked like the thunder bird who is
judge in heaven." Bronze, lapis lazuli, and gold dust were
often used for decorative purposes; mulberry trees were
planted in the gardens.

Although the deficiency of stone prevented its common
use in sculpture, on occasion both soft and hard stones were
Sculpture worked by the artists; limestone, steatite, gypsum, alabaster,
diorite, and porphyry were favored.

"Because all stone had to be imported into the lower river
valley the influence of material on style is particularly strong
in the case of Sumerian sculpture. . . . From the very beginning therefore the true Sumerian sculpture in stone is
timid in execution, and the limitation which their material
imposed on its earliest exponents gave rise to a tradition that
was never quite outgrown."[2]

On the other hand, the artists excelled in the use of gold,
silver, and copper and in the carving of small semi-precious
stones. From the Sumerian period comes a magnificent bull's
head of gold with a beard of lapis lazuli; the little gold and

[2] C. L. Woolley, *Development of Sumerian Art,* London, 1935, pp. 87-88.

silver donkey from the pole of Queen Shub-ad's chariot, and the handsome gold, silver, and lapis-lazuli statuette of the "ram caught in a thicket" give us a more than adequate idea of Sumerian skill.[3] We do not have abundant evidence for Babylonian art in the age of Hammurabi, but we receive the impression that there was a marked decline in sculpture.

Babylonian technology was far in advance of science, although the priests, who monopolized the work in the latter field, did make some advances. Arithmetic and the simpler geometric principles were known; astronomy was employed for the creation of an adequate calendar and for "studies" in astrology. Time was kept by means of sundials and water clocks. The seven-day week (in which each day might be assigned to the sun, moon, and the five major planets) and the twenty-four-hour day (divided into twelve double hours) were Sumerian contributions to later ages. **Tech-nology**

The Babylonians recognized the existence of many gods, spirits, and demons. In Sumerian times each city had its own major god and various minor ones. As the plain was unified politically, the worship of certain municipal gods spread from city to city, and the gods were given places in the Babylonian pantheon to correspond generally with the political positions held by their home cities; for example, Hammurabi made his god, Marduk, the head of the whole company of divinities. There were sun gods, moon gods, and gods identified with the major planets; likewise there were water gods, storm gods, and other divine personifications of natural phenomena. **Religion**

One of the most important deities was the goddess Ishtar, identified with the planet Venus. Ishtar was a mother goddess, a goddess of life and fertility, and also of love. At the beginning of winter each year Ishtar was thought to descend into the underworld in search of her dead consort, Tammuz. During her absence, vegetation decayed and life was dormant. In the spring, Ishtar returned from the underworld, and the season of plant growth began.

[3] *Ibid.*, plates 34, 35, and 36.

The Babylonians and Sumerians took a gloomy view of life after death. The underworld was called "the land of no return"; the dead were huddled together in a huge cave, naked, bound hand and foot; clay was their only food. A number of pessimistic myths dealt with the impossibility of attaining an everlasting life which was in any degree desirable; only the gods were thought to be fortunate in this respect.

Divination One matter of particular interest to the Babylonians was divination; they wished to ascertain the will of the gods or to learn what might be expected in the future. They believed that the movements of the heavenly bodies, the behavior of birds and animals, and dreams might be interpreted in such a way as to throw light on future events. They also engaged in the interesting practice of hepatoscopy or liver divination, in which the seers studied the livers of sacrificial sheep for various abnormalities which were supposed to indicate favorable or unfavorable auspices for the future. It was generally believed that the liver in man and the animals was the abode of the soul and the emotions. Although later thinking placed the soul in the heart, jealousy and anger were still connected with the liver. Thus the Assyrian king, Esarhaddon, says, "I roared like a lion; my liver was aroused."

Literature Religion and literature were closely related; most of the Babylonian and Sumerian literature, especially the myths and legends, dealt with religious subjects. Creation and flood legends similar to those later incorporated into the Old Testament were early committed to writing. There were magical texts for the exorcizing of demons, and numerous prayers, psalms, and laments. In addition to historical inscriptions, business records, and medical and mathematical texts, many letters by governmental officials and private persons have been found. Interesting, too, are maps and city plans sketched on large clay tablets.

Writing Writing was a Sumerian invention. It began in a pictographic stage, but soon passed on to ideographs and syllabic signs. The carefully drawn signs of the early period became conventionalized. Because the characters were incised on clay tablets with a sharp point, they tended to assume a wedge-shaped form; thus we call this type of writing *cuneiform*. The Semites took over the Sumerian signs and adapted them to their own language; throughout the history of the cuneiform script there was a steady reduction of the number of characters employed.

The Babylonian phase of this history came to an end about 1750 B.C. when the power of the plainsmen was broken by the attacks of northern invaders. These invaders, principally the Hittites and the Kassites, spoke languages which were related neither to the Sumerian nor to the Semite. The **Kassites** Kassite tongue belonged to the great family of languages, the Indo-European, which includes Greek, Latin, Persian, German, and others; the Hittite language was also distantly related to these Indo-European languages. The Hittites created a great empire in Asia Minor, whereas the Kassites conquered Babylonia and made Babylon their capital for the next six centuries.

THE INDUS VALLEY

Far to the east of Babylonia lies the Indus Valley, a region in which another great civilization flourished contemporaneously with that of Sumer and Akkad. Unfortunately, we know **Chro-** very little at present about this Indian culture, because it **nology** was discovered in comparatively recent years (1923) and much detailed information as well as precise correlations with Babylonian history is lacking. We can say, however, that the Indus civilization was in existence before 3000 B.C., and that it survived until after 2500 B.C. when the Indo-European-speaking Aryans invaded India. The Aryans, in other words, played a part in Indian history similar to that of the Kassites in Babylonia.

The Indus people were farmers, herdsmen, and traders. They cultivated the rich valley and produced wheat, barley, **Economic** cotton, and other crops. Their domesticated animals were **life** chiefly cattle and sheep, although it has been suggested that they had the elephant as well. There was an exchange of products with the surrounding country and also with Babylonia; Indian pottery and seals have been found in Sumerian cities.

Cities Two cities of the ancient Indian civilization have been excavated: Harappa in the north and Mohenjodaro in the south. Though far inland at present, Mohenjodaro was once a seaport. The Indian cities seem to have been large and well planned; their streets were laid out in rectangular checkerboard patterns, and adequate provision was made for sanitation and drainage. Because of the lack of stone, as in Babylonia, the buildings were of mud brick and kiln-baked brick. They were set on platforms because of the danger from floods. The private houses were usually two stories in height; the roofs were flat.

Art Although the Indus people made good pottery and their metal workers were skillful in using gold, silver, copper, and lead, such sculptural remains as have been found indicate an inferiority to Babylonia in this respect. From the sculpture, however, it is possible to get some idea of the appearance of these early Indians. They were bearded, and the common costume consisted of a kilt and a shawl.

Writing A system of writing—as yet undeciphered—was in use. About 300 different signs were common, and it is thought that they were given syllabic values. The script appears on seals similar to those in use in Babylonia.

It is admittedly difficult to evaluate the importance of the Indus Valley civilization. At present, it is generally assumed that it was one of the major culture centers, and that it should be classed with Egypt and Babylonia. As our knowledge of the Indus Valley is increased by subsequent archaeological investigation, however, we may find that this early civilization was less important than has been supposed. In that case, we should have to class it with the Cretan culture as an intermediate area of diffusion rather than a center of cultural origin.[4]

[4] See below, p. 87.

EGYPT

Ancient Egyptian history and culture were largely the product of the peculiar Egyptian environment. In antiquity Egypt consisted only of the Nile Valley (north of the first cataract) and the Delta. The valley is a narrow, deep trench only a few miles wide and about 600 miles long; on either side of it is the desert. In this region there is little or no rainfall, and the Nile Valley itself would be desert land if it were not for the river. Every summer, however, the Nile is in flood; it overflows its banks and inundates the valley. As the waters recede, the rich silt carried down from the equatorial highlands is deposited upon the land of the valley. In ancient times, before modern methods of control were applied to the river, fertilizer was unnecessary because of the annual renewal of the soil by the flood deposits. Moreover, wherever water could be obtained, the desert soil would bear crops. *The valley*

The Delta is unlike the valley. It has considerable rainfall and is inclined to be swampy; this was probably also true of the valley itself before the climatic changes which took place at the end of the glacial period. The amazing thing about ancient Egypt, however, was that although the distance from the first cataract to the Mediterranean edge of the Delta was 750 miles, the total area of habitable land was only about 10,000 square miles. *The Delta*

An important factor in the development of Egyptian culture was the isolation of the country and its ordinary freedom from invasion. To the east and the west lay the desert, to the north was the Mediterranean Sea, and to the south equatorial Africa. An ancient author remarked that Egypt was fortified by nature, and history proved the correctness of his statement. Egypt could be invaded only from the north through the Delta and from the south down the Nile Valley; this southern entrance, however, was somewhat protected by the cataracts of the upper Nile. As a result, once Egypt gained political power and unity, it was difficult for neighboring peoples to *Isolation* force their way into the country and subdue its inhabitants. In the prehistoric period, however, before Egypt was unified into a single large state, invasions were less difficult. Consequently, the Egyptians, when they became a definite national group, were the descendants of a mixed people: Semites from the northeast, Libyans from the northwest, and Negroes from the south. These diverse groups were fused in Egypt into a hybrid, yet decided, physical type which persists in that country even today. Egyptian culture, like the Egyptian people themselves, was drawn from numerous sources before the country was politically unified; after unification, however, the intrusion of foreign elements was less frequent, and the culture evolved in the historic period was as distinctly "Egyptian" as the people themselves.

**Uni-
fication**

The Nile River not only provided Egypt with its fertility, but it was also a factor in unifying the country. In the prehistoric period a number of independent communities were to be found along the banks of the Nile at the points where the cliffs receded from the river and the valley widened out. Before 5000 B.C. there were forty or more of these separate states—the Greeks called them nomes. The Nile, however, as a main highway, connected these communities with one another, and it was inevitable that unification should take place. By 5000 B.C. two large kingdoms had been established; one was in the Delta, and the other included the whole valley south of the Delta down to the first cataract. Then, about 3500-3400 B.C., the kingdoms of the Delta (Lower Egypt) and the valley (Upper Egypt) were combined into a single state.

**Economic
develop-
ment**

The economic development of Egypt was, of course, dependent upon the fertility of its soil and the nature of its resources. The amazing fertility of the valley made possible the growth of a large population and produced an agricultural surplus which in turn led to a complex economic and social structure. Moreover, Egypt was more self-sufficient than the Tigris-Euphrates region. Egypt had an abundance of clay and good stone. Gold was to be found near Koptos, and

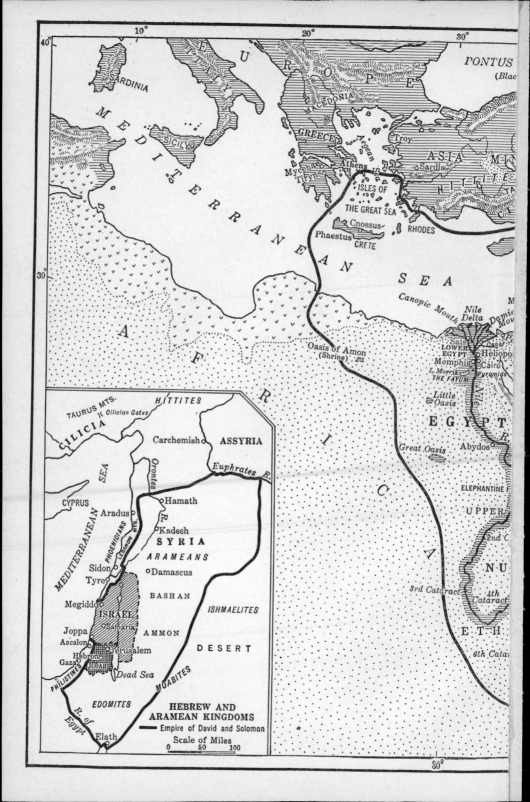

HEBREW AND
ARAMEAN KINGDOMS
—— Empire of David and Solomon
Scale of Miles
0   50   100

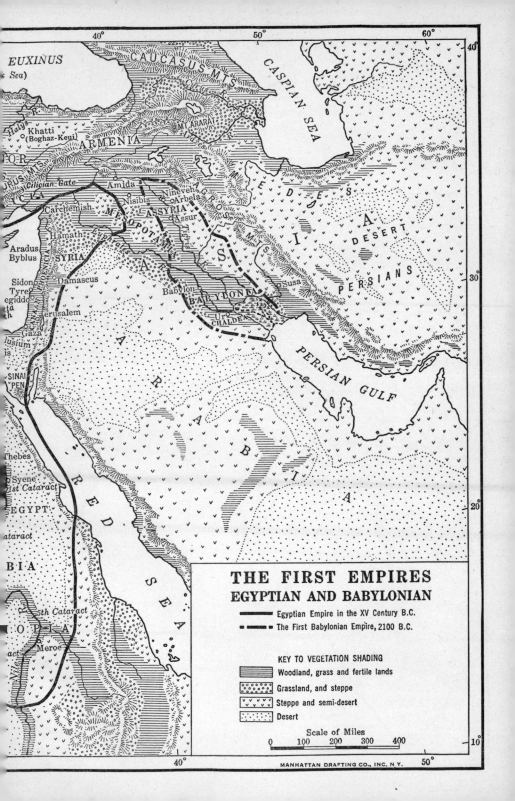

THE FIRST EMPIRES
EGYPTIAN AND BABYLONIAN

━━━━━━━━ Egyptian Empire in the XV Century B.C.
━ ▪ ━ ▪ ━ The First Babylonian Empire, 2100 B.C.

KEY TO VEGETATION SHADING

Woodland, grass and fertile lands

Grassland, and steppe

Steppe and semi-desert

Desert

Scale of Miles

0   100   200   300   400

MANHATTAN DRAFTING CO., INC. N.Y.

copper could be secured from nearby Sinai. What Egypt lacked was timber; as a result, the problem of gaining access to the "cedars of Lebanon" exerted a great influence upon Egyptian economic and political policies. The fact that Sinai and Lebanon lay to the northeast was important; it forced Egypt to turn in the general direction of Mesopotamia, and the trade connections which the Egyptians formed in Sinai, Palestine, and Syria brought them into contact with traders who had come west from Babylonia. Cultural interchange with the Tigris-Euphrates region was thus facilitated.

Environmental influences were also at work in the case of Egyptian political evolution. In Egypt the absolute necessity for irrigation and the conservation of water brought extreme governmental centralization and the strict regimentation of the agricultural population.

Political evolution

Perhaps the development of Egyptian civilization can be clarified if we compare and contrast the situation in Egypt with that in Babylonia. Both regions were fertile, but Egyptian agricultural production was dependent upon getting water to the soil, whereas in Babylonia the problem was to keep the floods from washing the soil away or destroying the crops. Political unification and governmental centralization were essential for maximum agricultural production in Egypt, whereas in Babylonia, although unification and centralization were easily accomplished, they were not at all essential. The isolation of Egypt fostered an independent cultural development, but the ease with which Babylonia could be invaded meant that foreign influences were frequently exerted. Then, too, the central position of Babylonia, as well as its lack of self-sufficiency, paved the way for the growth of trade, whereas the remoteness of Egypt and the abundance of its resources prevented trade from becoming as important as in Babylonia. Thus, Egypt remained a predominantly agricultural country; at least, it appears so when we compare it with Babylonia.

Comparison with Babylonia

Last of all, the situation as regards church and state was different in Egypt and Babylonia. In Babylonia, the early

patesis and the later kings were the viceroys of the gods; in Egypt, the rulers themselves were considered gods. This is easily explained when we remember that the unification of Babylonia came only after a long city-state period during which the theocratic viceroy tradition was firmly established. In Egypt, on the other hand, the unification of extensive areas came very early; and it was much easier for the ruler of a large area to acquire divine attributes than it was for a ruler whose territory included only a few square miles. Moreover, the early growth of a trading class in Babylonia hampered the apotheosis of the priest-kings, whereas the simple farmers of Egypt were far more likely to acquiesce in such a procedure.

In Egypt the historic period begins about 3500-3400 B.C. with the unification of the Delta and the valley. From this time down to about 1100 B.C. Egypt enjoyed an independent existence and a position of some political importance in the ancient world. The era from 3500 to 1100 B.C. in Egypt included three periods in which Egyptian cultural and political influence reached high peaks: (1) The Old Kingdom (2900-2500 B.C.); (2) the Middle Kingdom (2000-1800 B.C.); and (3) the New Kingdom (1580-1100 B.C.).

1. Under the Old Kingdom (Dynasties III-VI) Egypt enjoyed internal peace and prosperity. Adequate evidence of the wealth and power of the rulers of the Fourth Dynasty are the royal tombs, the great pyramids. Egypt traded with Sinai, Phoenicia, and the Sudan, but there was no real effort to extend political control to areas outside of Egypt proper. After 2500 B.C. came an age of decentralization in which the royal power declined and the nomes became almost independent under the rule of various noble families.

2. In the period of the Middle Kingdom, the Pharaohs of the Twelfth Dynasty, who came from Thebes in Upper Egypt, restored national unity by curbing the power of the nobles. Trade was built up with the outside world, and Egyptian political influence was extended south of the first cataract. After 1800, however, decline once more began. On

this occasion, the decline was not due so much to internal disintegration as it was to foreign invasion. The movements of the Indo-European-speaking peoples which we have observed in connection with Babylonia also affected Egyptian history. The Indo-Europeans did not come to·Egypt, but they disturbed the desert Semites who in turn invaded Egypt. In the Delta, a dynasty of these Semitic invaders, the Hyksos (Shepherd Kings), ruled Lower Egypt for perhaps a century.

3. The New Kingdom (Dynasties XVIII-XX) began with an Egyptian nationalist revival which resulted in the expulsion of the Hyksos. The Pharaohs of the early Eighteenth Dynasty were soldiers who made Egypt a militarized and centralized state. The Hyksos had done much to destroy the feudal nobility, and the new Egyptian dynasty completed **New Kingdom** this process by exalting the Egyptian middle class to a position of civil and military importance. Army officers and bureaucratic officials were henceforth drawn from the bourgeoisie. After the Hyksos were driven out, the nationalism of Egypt became imperialistic, and in the fifteenth century B.C. the Egyptians acquired territory in Syria and Palestine. By 1400 Egypt was a world power without any close rival; other nations sought her friendship, and none dared to oppose her. Trade with foreign countries reached its highest peak.

This halcyon age could not last. The Hittites of Asia Minor had been increasing in strength, and their determination to gain a foothold in northern Syria could not be long denied. Moreover, there came to the Egyptian throne in 1375 B.C. a religious visionary, Ikhnaton, whose sole interest lay in the new theology, the cult of the universal sun god, **Ikhnaton** with which he was completely preoccupied. The affairs of the empire were neglected while Ikhnaton tried to impose his religious beliefs upon the Egyptian people. The Hittites weaned the Syrians from their allegiance to Egypt while Egypt was torn by religious dissension. When Ikhnaton finally died, much of Syria had been lost.

Later rulers tried to revive the imperial glories of the

Eighteenth Dynasty, but it was too late. The great Rameses II, who reigned in the first half of the thirteenth century, was forced to sign a treaty with the Hittites which conceded to them the northern half of Syria. By 1200 B.C. a new wave of Indo-European invaders broke across the Aegean and eastern Mediterranean lands. The Hittite kingdom was swept out of Asia Minor, and sea raiders from the north harassed the coast of Egypt. Libyan tribes invaded the Delta from the west. Rameses III was forced to defend his country against these foreigners, both the Libyans and the sea raiders, at the beginning of the twelfth century.

The twelfth century in Egypt saw the end of the New Kingdom. Nationalism and imperialism had spent their force, and the Pharaohs had to depend upon mercenary soldiers to fight their battles. The expense of maintaining a mercenary army impoverished the government. Moreover, to gain divine favor, the rulers had given more and more land to the temples until, at last, the throne itself actually had little land left for its support. Constant pressure from outside enemies, combined with the increasing decline in royal revenues, led to a collapse about 1100 B.C.

We may now turn to a consideration of Egyptian civilization as it developed in the period from 3500 to 1100 B.C.

In prehistoric Egypt it seems likely that each nome had its own ruler whose monarchical position was an elective one; but by the time of the Old Kingdom the national monarchy had become hereditary. Moreover, the ruler was recognized as the son of the national god and therefore as a god in his **Peraa** own right. The ruler's name was regarded as sacred and not to be employed except on extraordinary occasions; it was customary to refer to the ruler simply as Peraa, Great House. Pharaoh is, of course, a corruption of the Egyptian word.

The god-king of Egypt was an autocrat who headed the administration of justice and economic life, commanded the army, and was the chief religious representative of the nation. **Govern-** Despite the unity of the state which the position of the king **ment** expressed, the fact that Egypt was really a dual kingdom could not be concealed. The ruler wore a crown which combined the symbols of kingship of Upper and Lower Egypt; it was composed of the cap worn by the old kings of the valley and the uraeus (the serpent diadem) of the Delta. The administration of Egypt was often divided into two parts. Sometimes the king would direct his attention to either Upper or Lower Egypt, leaving the administration of the other portion to a prime minister. During the Middle Kingdom the problem was solved by the co-regencies by means of which the kings associated the crown princes with themselves in the administration. Then, under the empire, there were two prime ministers, one for the Delta and the other for the valley.

The once-independent states, the nomes, were made units of administration in the historic period. Under the Old Kingdom royal appointees from among the nobility governed the nomes. The fact that these governorships were allowed to become hereditary was disastrous for the rulers of the Old Kingdom, for some of the noble families consolidated their positions so firmly that they became more or less independent of the Pharaohs and a feudal age ensued in which the government of Egypt was subject to a baneful decentralization. It was not until the time of the New Kingdom that the national government was able to remedy this defect and bring the nomes once more under central control.

Egypt remained throughout its history an essentially agricultural country. All the land was considered as belonging to the king, and he might give it to his subjects. The ruler directed agricultural production; as we have seen, the close **Agriculture** connection between agriculture and religion and the position of the Pharaoh as god-king made this development possible. The agricultural population was regimented, and the majority of the peasants were transformed from freeholders into serfs. Egypt was a country of large landholders. The land not directly held by the crown was turned over in large blocks to the nobles and the priests. Every temple possessed vast holdings which contributed to its support; in the latter part of the imperial era, most of the best lands in Egypt were in the hands of the priests.

In order to keep agricultural production at high levels, continuous cooperative work was necessary. Canals and irrigation ditches had to be kept in perfect condition. After the annual floods the whole land had to be resurveyed because the flood waters obliterated the landmarks. A huge bureaucracy was built up to perform these duties, collect the taxes, and take the census of the inhabitants and their possessions. Taxes were paid in kind, and the rural population was subject to forced labor. It has been well said that the economy of Egypt was essentially a plantation economy.

Plantation economy

Industry and trade flourished in Egypt, but never attained the importance in economic life that they did in Babylonia. Artisans were to be found in the workshops of the king and the nobles; there were also independent artisans in the towns. There were metal workers, potters, weavers, jewelers, brewers, and workers in many other crafts. Mummification (see below, p. 56) required skilled artisans, and thus provided employment for many people. The ethics of the mummifiers often left much to be desired; bodies were not carefully wrapped, and sometimes fake mummies were made up—in one case the supposed mummy of a baby "consisted of an old man's skull for bulk and a thigh bone for length."[5]

Industry

Egyptian traders penetrated equatorial Africa, controlled the commerce of the Red Sea, made their way into Palestine and Syria, and sailed the eastern Mediterranean. Egyptian products have been found in Asia Minor, Cyprus, Crete, Greece, and Italy. The principal exports were pottery, glass, stone and metal work, textiles, and jewelry. Egypt imported wood, copper, pottery, spices, ivory, and slaves.

Trade

Egyptian society, like that of Babylonia, was stratified. The royal family, the nobles, and the priests formed the upper class. There was a middle class of traders, artisans, scribes,

Society

[5] W. M. Flinders Petrie, *Social Life in Ancient Egypt*, New York, 1923, p. 29.

and other professional men. Most of the rural population were serfs, and there were also, of course, slaves.

The life of the nobles was one of culture and refinement. They had fine palaces with gardens and ponds. The labor of their serfs and slaves provided them with adequate incomes and leisure time. Except when a noble served in the army or held some official position, he could devote himself to his games and amusements. Hunting, fishing, and fowling were very popular. Lions and hippopotami were the game of the more courageous hunters; birds were often killed with throwing sticks. One of the most famous accounts in Egyptian literature deals with the elephant hunt which Thothmes III conducted in northern Syria. In this case, one of the elephants nearly turned the tables on Thothmes himself, and the Pharaoh narrowly escaped death when one of his generals intervened and cut off the elephant's trunk. **The nobles**

The Egyptians of the upper classes wore waistcloths, cloaks, and leather sandals. They shaved their heads and wore wigs. It was customary to paint the eyebrows black or green, and the nails henna. Metal bracelets and necklaces were worn by both men and women. **Costume**

In Egypt there were domesticated dogs of several breeds, and by 2000 B.C. the cat had also been domesticated. Fish were kept in the ponds adjoining the palaces. Beer and wine were popular beverages; they were sipped through tubes made of metal. The common musical instruments were the flute and the lyre; there was also the sistrum, the sacred rattle.

Although Egyptian writing and art had begun to develop before the period of the Old Kingdom, the first great advances were made when that age began. Literature, architecture, and sculpture attained their first real importance. Under the Old Kingdom the canons of Egyptian art and literature were established. After this, no more important advances were made except for a brief period during the reign of Ikhnaton when art and literature were temporarily freed **Cultural history** from the bonds of convention by the religious movement which he originated.

In the field of art, the Egyptians are perhaps best remembered for their architecture. The spectacular results which they achieved were due to the prevalence of good building stone in Egypt. The pyramids and the great temples and palaces could not have been built if stone had not been available. Moreover, because the Egyptians built in stone, they favored the use of the column and lintel, whereas the Babylonians, who used bricks, were prone to employ the arch. The Egyptians knew the true arch as early as the Old Kingdom, but it was easier for them to use the column and lintel.

Architecture

The pyramid, so popular under the Fourth Dynasty, was impressive in appearance, but really very simple in principle. Far more impressive than mere appearance is the significance, both social and economic, of the pyramids. The pyramids were royal tombs. Their construction was begun during the lifetime of the king for which each one was intended. The largest of the pyramids at Gizeh covered some thirteen acres and was constructed of over two million blocks each weighing about two and one-half tons. It is said that it took 100,000 men twenty years to complete this structure. The inference which we may draw concerning the wealth and power of the Pharaohs of the Fourth Dynasty is nothing less than staggering. One man was rich enough and had authority enough to order 100,000 men to work for twenty years to build his tomb!

Pyramids

In their own way, the great palaces and temples of the Middle and New Kingdoms were spectacular, too, with their gigantic stone columns and labyrinthine rooms. The architecture of Egypt is always characterized by a massive and monumental style which dwarfs the architecture of all other ancient civilizations.

Egyptian sculpture, like the architecture, is always on the grand scale. It is a peculiarity of the sculpture that no matter how small or minute a statue may be in actual size, it gives the impression of being large in concept—it appears to be a

Sculpture

copy of some colossal original. Sculpture began in Egypt as an adjunct of architecture, but by the time of the Old Kingdom it had emancipated itself and become an independent art. The Egyptian artists worked in both hard and soft stones with equal success; they also used bronze and gold. Although it became customary to adhere quite strictly to certain formal conventions, the sculptors did manage to raise portraiture to new heights. Comparisons of royal statues with their corresponding royal mummies show the most accurate delineation of the subject.

Painting was even more dependent upon sculpture than sculpture upon architecture. Sculptured figures were usually painted in bright colors to make them appear more lifelike, **Painting** and Egyptian painting got its start when it was used to decorate the relief sculpture of the tombs and temples. The Egyptians were not successful with perspective or shading, but their works do have a lively, distinctive quality which makes them very pleasing.

The artisans who dealt with the lesser arts acquired great skill in working with difficult materials. The pottery, textiles, and stone and metal work of the Egyptians were highly prized in antiquity. Their jewelry and furniture were especially desirable.

Early religion in Egypt was totemistic. In each of the nomes the chief god had the form of an animal—a crocodile, hippo- **Religion** potamus, jackal, etc. In the historic period the religious cults might be grouped into two categories: state and popular. The state cult was a formal religion. The kings were thought to be the sons of certain national gods. Before the Old Kingdom the ruler was considered the son of Horus, the hawk god; under the Old Kingdom Horus was replaced by Ra, the sun god. Then, in the time of the Twelfth Dynasty, Ra was combined with Amon, the chief god of Thebes, and the national deity was henceforth known as Amon-Ra. Throughout Egyptian history, however, the old animal gods remained dear to the hearts of the masses and were never replaced in popular affection by the state gods.

Immortality

An agricultural country like Egypt naturally paid much attention to its fertility cult; but the important thing was that, because of the peculiar climatic conditions, the fertility cult led the people to a concept of immortality, something unknown to the Babylonians. The dryness of Egypt retarded decay, and the fact that the bodies of the dead decomposed fairly slowly heightened the primitive concept of death as a kind of sleep. Osiris, the fertility god who died—yet lived again—became the symbol of everlasting life.

Mummification

The Egyptians believed that as long as the body of a dead man was preserved, his soul might continue to inhabit it. This gave rise to the practice of mummification, and the Egyptians developed great skill in preserving their dead. It should nevertheless be noted that they were aided by the climatic conditions of their country; mummification would have been much more difficult in a land where there was more rainfall.

The ka

The body was thought to be the dwelling place of a soul called the *ka*. After death the *ka* had to appear before the god Osiris to be tried for its mundane sins. A righteous life on earth had immortality as its reward. Since the after-life was lived in the tomb it was necessary to make provision for the soul's comfort. Food and drink were placed in the tombs, on the walls were painted pictures of everyday life, and many of the personal effects of the dead man were laid at his side.

Ikhnaton

In the fourteenth century B.C. an interesting chapter in the history of Egyptian religion was added by the "heretic" ruler Ikhnaton, the first monotheist. Ikhnaton conceived the idea of the sun god, Aton, as the sole and universal deity of the world. He apparently became fanatical in his desire to secure recognition for his deity. He tried to uproot the older established priesthoods in Egypt; the priests of the other gods were persecuted, and the name of Amon, the state god of his fathers, was erased from the monuments.

His importance

Ikhnaton failed to gain his objectives. He encountered great opposition from the priesthood, which was firmly entrenched, and his highly spiritual religious concepts awoke no response among the masses. The principal effect of the new religion was felt in art and literature where for a brief period the artists and writers broke away from the formal conventions which had been established under the Old Kingdom and reveled in a new freedom that expressed itself in realism and naturalism. Some of the best works of sculpture and painting as well as many of the great hymns and psalms date from this age.

This seemingly strange development in Egyptian religion may be explained rather simply. The creation of the Egyptian empire had made it possible for the Egyptians to realize somewhat the extent of the world which lay beyond the borders of Egypt proper. The empire gave rise to concepts of universalism, and the sun, whose rays shone everywhere, naturally became the symbol of these ideas. Ikhnaton, highly sensitive (and, as some believe, insane), was also in a position to put these feelings of universalism into terms of definite action. **Empire and universalism**

One of the most distinctive features of Egyptian culture was the system of writing. The writing began with a pictographic script which developed through ideographic and syllabic stages to an alphabet. The important point, however, was that the Egyptians, when their writing reached the alphabet stage, refused to discard the older pictographs, ideographs, and syllabic characters, but used all their signs together in what seems to us a magnificent hodgepodge. A word might be represented very simply by an ideographic character, or it might be spelled out with syllabic or alphabet signs; on the other hand, one commonly finds a word phonetically rendered and followed by an ideograph for the word itself.[6] **Writing**

There were three main varieties of the Egyptian script, the types of writing called hieroglyphic, hieratic, and demotic. The hieroglyphs were carefully drawn pictures which were descended, so far as appearance was concerned, from the early pictographs. Hieratic writing was like the hieroglyphic except that in the former the characters were drawn in a more cursive or running hand. The demotic was an extremely cursive

[6] See the chart on p. 58.

and more simplified type of writing which developed in the first millennium B.C. after the close of the imperial period. The Egyptians carved their writings on stone or inscribed them on metal; where such media were used, the characters were hieroglyphics. More common, however, was the use of a paperlike material made from the pulp of the papyrus plant and also called papyrus. Although hieroglyphs were written

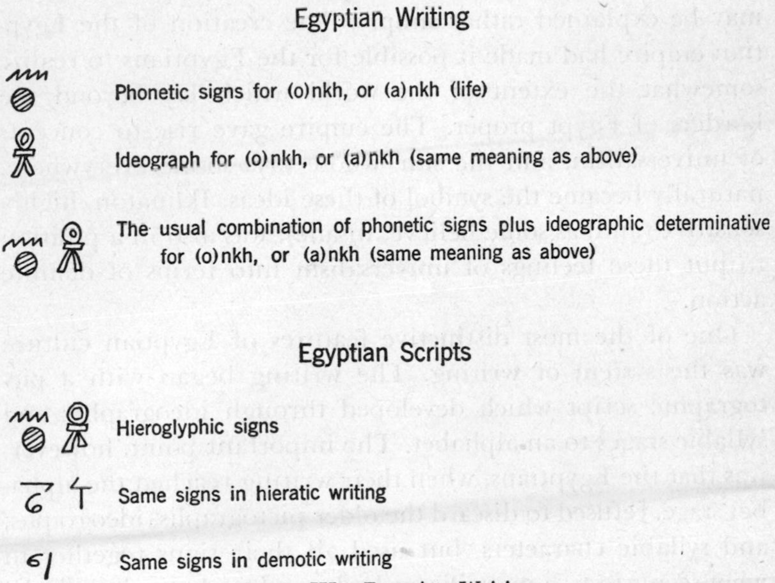

Egyptian Writing

Phonetic signs for (o)nkh, or (a)nkh (life)

Ideograph for (o)nkh, or (a)nkh (same meaning as above)

The usual combination of phonetic signs plus ideographic determinative for (o)nkh, or (a)nkh (same meaning as above)

Egyptian Scripts

Hieroglyphic signs

Same signs in hieratic writing

Same signs in demotic writing

CHART III.—Egyptian Writing.

on papyrus, it was more convenient to employ the cursive hieratic script for this medium.

Literature   Egyptian literature was much more varied in character than the literature of Babylonia. Although magical and religious texts (the Pyramid Texts and the Book of the Dead), hymns, and psalms are common in Egyptian literature, there are also other types of writing. There are narratives of adventure and travel, love songs and banquet songs, accounts of military campaigns, prophecies, proverbs, and treatises on medicine, mathematics, and science in general. There is much didactic literature, the work of teachers who lay down principles of conduct and discuss moral questions. We have copies of model letters written by schoolboys which deal with various subjects.[7]

Egyptian science stressed the accumulation of factual material rather than the formulation of general laws and principles. Much was known about architectural engineering and surveying. The mathematicians worked out methods of performing the fundamental arithmetical operations, although they never found a really satisfactory way to deal with fractions. There was a considerable knowledge of general medicine and surgery; but in chemistry, metallurgy, and other kindred fields knowledge was technological rather than scientific.

Science

We have now completed our survey of the civilizations of the three main culture centers of the Ancient Near East. Although environmental conditions produced individual variations in each of the three areas, it is possible for us to see a certain unity of culture when we look at the broad general outlines of the civilizations of the great river valleys. Each was founded upon an agricultural base. Upon the agricultural base arose a superstructure of trade and industry. Common culture traits were cities, sculpture, architecture, writing, theocratic government, class stratification, and a knowledge of metal-working. In each there was a governmental bureaucracy and a complex religious organization. Slavery and serfdom were common to all three.

Our uncertainty about the exact position of the Indus Valley civilization has already been noted; it must always be borne in mind that we may eventually have to class this civilization as an intermediate one on a par with that of Crete, a civilization which we shall describe later.[8]

In the next chapter we shall observe how culture was diffused from the major centers to other areas of the Ancient Near East.

[7] For translations of the literature, see A. Erman, *The Literature of the Ancient Egyptians,* London, 1927.

[8] Actually, the description of Cretan culture might have been included in this chapter, but it seems most convenient to use it as a point of departure for our study of Greek culture.

CHAPTER III

THE CIVILIZATION OF THE ANCIENT NEAR EAST
(Continued)

Cultural
diffusion
from
Babylonia

One of the earliest areas to receive cultural stimulation from the Tigris-Euphrates Valley was that which lay generally to the north and west of the valley—Assyria, Armenia, Asia Minor, and Syria. Naturally Assyria and Syria were the regions first affected; it will be remembered that Syria was included in the empire of Sargon of Akkad and that Assyria was a province of Babylonia in the time of Hammurabi. Nevertheless, Assyria and Syria were too close to the Tigris-Euphrates center and too much under its political domination to develop distinctive civilizations in the early period; they simply borrowed traits from the Tigris-Euphrates Valley and made no important additions of their own. Thus it was the more remote areas—Asia Minor and Armenia—which, although they were influenced by the Tigris-Euphrates culture later than Assyria and Syria, first created new civilizations. Their cultural development began in earnest after the Indo-European invasions that destroyed the Babylonian kingdom of Hammurabi's successors. Of these new civilizations we shall discuss only the most important, that of the Hittites.

THE HITTITES

Hittites

The Hittites entered Asia Minor, possibly from southeastern Europe, late in the third millennium B.C. Imposing themselves as a ruling class upon the native population, they gradually extended their political control over practically all of Asia Minor. Their strength increased as Babylonia fell to the Kassites and Egypt was disrupted by the Hyksos invasion. Expansion outside of Asia Minor was blocked, however, in the period from 1600-1400 B.C. by the rise of the Egyptian empire. Moreover, the kingdom of the Indo-Europeans known as the Mitannians, situated on the upper Euphrates, separated the Hittites from Mesopotamia. Ultimately, the Mitannians were crushed between the Hittites on the west and the rising power of Assyria in the east. When Ikhnaton came to the Egyptian throne, the Hittites began to make gains in northern Syria. From this time down to about 1200 B.C. they enjoyed the greatest period of their history.

The Hittite empire was a feudal state ruled by the Great King of the Hittites and his vassals. Its first capital was located in central Asia Minor at the site of modern Boghaz-Köi. The Great King was a hereditary monarch whose chief functions were those of war leader and high priest. He was assisted and advised by a council or assembly of the Hittite nobles. **Government**

The nobles formed a ruling caste recruited from the Hittite invaders and their descendants. The native population occupied a subordinate position. It has been said that there was a middle class of soldiers, workers, merchants, and farmers, but the workers or artisans were low in the social scale, and many of the rural laborers and farmers were definitely serfs. **Society**

Agriculture and grazing flourished in Asia Minor, and there were also considerable industry and trade. The Hittites controlled the most extensive deposits of iron in the Near East; this was one of their main sources of wealth. They were the first people of the Near East—possibly the first in the world—to work iron. **Economic life**

The Hittites borrowed much from Babylonia. They adopted the cuneiform system of writing; their law codes were based upon Babylonian originals although they were not so severe. In religion and art they were also borrowers, but their independence was somewhat more marked in these fields than in others. At Boghaz-Köi, as well as at other important Hittite cities, have been found the remains of massive stone fortifications and public buildings with foundations **Culture** of stone and walls of brick. Monumental relief sculpture in stone and sculpture in the round, both in stone and in metal, was produced by the Hittite artists. Human figures, lions, and double-headed eagles were favorite subjects. Hittite art is "portentously heavy, solemn, and, while markedly independent and inventive, conventional."[1]

Religion

Our knowledge of Hittite religion needs much amplification. Throughout Asia Minor the people worshiped an earth mother (a fertility goddess) and a sky god. In the Hittite state religion a sun goddess was very important, and there was also a moon god. The Great King, as high priest, stood at the head of the state cult and performed religious rites of major significance.

The people

The Hittites were predominantly a mountain people. They wore round, sometimes pointed, caps, short tunics, and high boots with upturned toes. The faces of some of their sculptured figures have almost a Mongolian caste. We know, however, that the Hittite conquerors spoke a language that was distantly related to the Indo-European tongues.

Phrygians

Shortly after 1200 B.C. Asia Minor was invaded by the Phrygians, an Indo-European group who destroyed the Hittite empire and drove the Hittites down into northern Syria and the upper Euphrates Valley. There the survivors, called the Neo-Hittites, feebly maintained themselves for a few centuries.

SYRIA AND PALESTINE (1200-750 B.C.)

Decline of the great states

After 1200 B.C. the Ancient Near East entered upon a period of confusion and chaos. As we have seen, the Phrygians overthrew the Hittites, and the power of Egypt was broken by internal dissension and the external pressure exerted by the sea raiders. In Babylonia a nationalist revolt brought the Kassite dynasty to an end, but the short-lived Babylonian kingdom which was then set up had little influence beyond its own borders. This general impotence of formerly strong nations was especially important for devel-

[1] *Cambridge Ancient History*, Vol. III, p. 153.

opments in Syria and Palestine where a number of small states now enjoyed a brief period of independence.

The region of Syria and Palestine is rough and moun- **Syria and** tainous; among its mountains lie valleys and plains. It is **Palestine** bounded on the north by the Taurus Mountains of Asia Minor, on the northeast by the upper Euphrates, on the east by the Arabian desert, and on the west by the Mediterranean Sea; it is separated from the Egyptian Delta by a strip of desert country. The character of the terrain naturally fostered the creation of small states, and the poverty of the soil precluded the growth of a large population. It was not surprising that the people of the coast soon turned to trade and industry as a means of supplementing their agricultural income.

Before 1200 B.C. Syria and Palestine had constituted a no man's land which had been at the mercy of the stronger **Foreign** states of the Near East. Between 3000 and 2000 B.C. the **domina-** Akkadians, Egyptians, and Babylonians had successively **tion** dominated Syria and Palestine both politically and economically. The first and third groups wanted an outlet to the Mediterranean, whereas the Egyptians, as we have seen, desired the cedars of Lebanon. In the second millennium B.C., Syria and Palestine were included in the Egyptian empire; then, after Ikhnaton's reign, the Hittites controlled northern Syria.

The inhabitants of Syria and Palestine were, after 3000, mostly Semites who came in from the desert to the east; wave **Semites** after wave of these people swept into the country. The Amorite forefathers of Hammurabi had invaded northern Syria before conquering Babylonia. Later, other Semitic groups—Canaanites, Aramaeans, etc.—arrived in Syria and Palestine. In the period of independence (1200-750 B.C.) which we are about to discuss, four groups were especially important: (1) the Phoenicians, (2) the Aramaeans, (3) the Philistines (who were not Semites), and (4) the Hebrews.

The Phoenicians.—The Phoenicians lived on the Mediterranean coast of Syria in a number of monarchical city-states,

**Phoe-
nicians**

principally Tyre, Sidon, Beirut, and Byblus. Of these states, Tyre assumed the most important position after 1000 B.C. The Phoenicians were traders and manufacturers whose naval power enabled them to control the Mediterranean until about 750 B.C. They carried the products of the Near East to Greece, Italy, and Spain. They established trading posts in northern Africa; their largest and most flourishing colonies were Carthage and Utica in Africa and Gades (Cadiz) in Spain. It was probably the Phoenicians who were the first to sail out into the Atlantic, and they were the first to bring tin from the British Isles. They sold their metal work, glass, dyes, and textiles to the inhabitants of all the Mediterranean lands.

**Diffusion
of culture**

Culturally, the Phoenicians were important for the part they played in the diffusion of the culture traits of the Near East to the Mediterranean world. Under their influence less advanced groups acquired a knowledge of technology and art. They also spread the Babylonian system of weights and measures. The alphabet, although not invented by the Phoenicians,[2] was adopted by them and carried to the Greeks and the people of Asia Minor.

Aramaeans

The Aramaeans.—The center of Aramaean power was the Syrian city of Damascus which lay inland at a point where caravan routes from the east and south converged. Like the Phoenicians, the Aramaeans were traders, but they conducted their activities on land instead of on the sea. The commercial influence of the Aramaeans can be seen in the fact that their language, Aramaic, became widespread throughout the Semitic-speaking portions of the Near East.

Philistines

The Philistines.—The Philistines were not Semites. They were sea raiders from southern Asia Minor who, after having been repulsed in an attack upon Egypt in the twelfth century, settled in cities on the Palestinian coast south of the Phoenicians. The famous Gaza was the most powerful of their five monarchical city-states. The Philistines formed a ruling caste which dominated the native population. Their

[2] See above, p. 24.

chief significance lies in the introduction of their art and religion into Syria and Palestine.[3]

The Hebrews.—The early history of the Hebrews is uncertain. They were a group of wandering desert tribes who entered Palestine some time after 1400 B.C. Some of the Hebrews may have gone to Egypt with the Hyksos, but by 1200 B.C. they returned to the north to join their fellows in the "Promised Land." Because of their cultural and economic poverty and their lack of unity the Hebrews fell easy prey to the Philistines and were dominated by them until the latter part of the eleventh century. Then, under the leadership of Saul and David, the Hebrews shook off the Philistine yoke and created a national state with its capital at Jerusalem. Solomon, the son of David, was the most opulent of the Hebrew rulers. His kingdom was typically Oriental in its display of wealth and luxury. The building of the temple at Jerusalem, the development of trade relations with Red Sea ports and with the Phoenicians, the alliance with the Tyrian King Hiram, and the extent of the royal harem are well-known facts in the story of Solomon. After his death (*c.* 930 B.C.), the kingdom split up into two parts: the Israelite kingdom with its capital at Samaria in the north, and the Kingdom of Judah centering about Jerusalem in the south.

The chief cultural contributions of the Hebrews were, of course, in the field of religion. Their ideas of monotheism and much of their theology and ethics were later used in the formation of Christianity and Mohammedanism. Their sacred book, which we call the Old Testament, is one of the world's greatest literary works. The individual books or writings of the Old Testament are products of various periods; some of the earliest go back to about 900 B.C., and the latest may be dated about 200 B.C. The Old Testament received its final form late in the first century A.D.

As far the student of ancient history is concerned, two points should be remembered: Hebrew religion was many

Hebrews

Solomon

Cultural contributions

---

[3] The Philistines were related to the Minoans of Crete, and their culture was very similar to that of the Minoans. See below, Chap. IV.

centuries in the process of growth, and the cultural importance of the Hebrews was manifested only when their political
power had long since disappeared. To the other peoples of
the Near East, The Hebrews of the pre-Christian era seemed
a small and insignificant group, hardly deserving of notice.

The rise of the Assyrian empire brought to an end the
independence of Syria and Palestine. The Aramaeans and
then the Phoenicians fell before the hosts of Assyria, and in
722 B.C. Sargon II carried off the Israelites into captivity. The
kingdom of Judah was conquered about 586 B.C. by the
Babylonian king, Nebuchadrezzar (see below, p. 72).

ASSYRIA

Up the Tigris, northwest of ancient Sumer and Akkad,
lies the country of Assyria, a region of rolling hills with an
area of less than 10,000 square miles, bounded on the south
by the Mesopotamian plain and on the other three sides by
rough mountainous country. Assyria, with fertile land, adequate rainfall, and good stone, early attracted the desert
Semites with the result that the Assyrians of the historic
period were predominantly Semitic and therefore closely
related to the Akkadians and Hammurabi's Amorites. On
the other hand, the Assyrians, unlike the Semites of the plain,
were never subjected to the enervating influence of a hot
climate and easy living. They were a hill folk, chiefly farmers
and herdsmen, whose life was not without its difficulties;
they had to work hard to eke out an existence, and they were
surrounded by enemies who coveted their lands. In their
contest with nature and their struggles with their foes, the
Assyrians became a hardy and vigorous people, well qualified
to dominate their softer cousins who dwelt in Babylonia.

In the age of Hammurabi, Assyria was made a province
of the Babylonian empire, but the Assyrians regained their
independence when the Kassites came. Under ambitious
kings, Assyria enjoyed a period of political power and territorial expansion between 1300 and 1100 B.C., but struggles
with the mountaineers of the north halted this development

*The
Assyrians*

*Military
history*

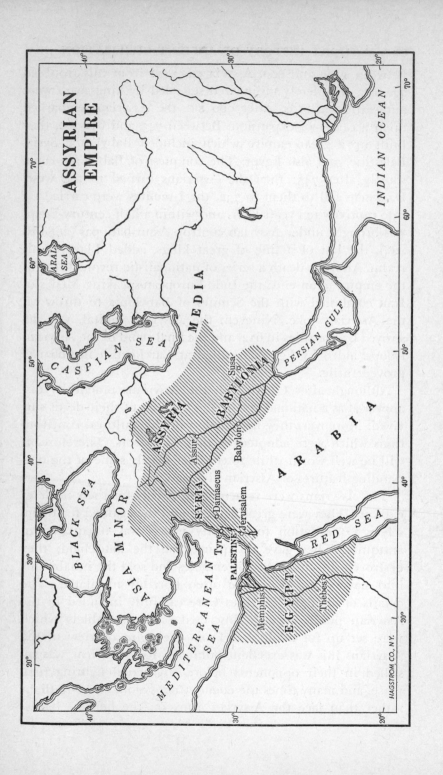

ASSYRIAN EMPIRE

ARAL SEA

INDIAN OCEAN

CASPIAN SEA

MEDIA

PERSIAN GULF

Susa

BABYLONIA

ASSYRIA

Assur

Babylon

ARABIA

BLACK SEA

SYRIA

Damascus

Jerusalem

ASIA MINOR

Tyre

PALESTINE

RED SEA

MEDITERRANEAN SEA

Memphis

EGYPT

Thebes

HAGSTROM CO., N.Y.

between 1100 and 900. Assyria emerged from this troubled age as a completely militarized state led by kings who were autocratic warlords. After 900 B.C. the Assyrians embarked upon a career of expansion. Between 745 and 612 B.C. they built up a great empire which included Babylonia, Syria, Palestine, and also Egypt. The conquest of Babylonia came shortly after 745; then the Assyrians turned to the west: Damascus fell to them in 732, the Israelites were carried off into captivity ten years later, and within a half-century Egypt was brought under Assyrian control. Assur-bani-pal (668-626 B.C.), the last of a line of great kings, added Elam to his realm. After his death a series of nationalistic revolts brought the empire to an end: the Indo-European-speaking Medes of Iran combined with the Semites of Babylonia to throw off the Assyrian yoke. Nineveh, the Assyrian capital, was destroyed by the allies in 612, and the final stand of the Assyrian troops, aided by Egyptian allies, at Carchemish in 606 B.C. proved futile.

Although after Carchemish the Assyrians practically disappeared as a national group, the memory of their deeds survived. Moreover, they had made valuable cultural contributions which were adopted by their successors. Therefore, it will be well worth while to consider briefly some of the outstanding features of Assyrian civilization.

The Assyrians were remembered chiefly for their military exploits. They were great fighters, and they gained for themselves a reputation for ferocity which was unequaled in antiquity. They gave no quarter on the battlefield; they destroyed the cities of their enemies and sold the inhabitants into slavery; captives were often horribly mutilated. The details of all these cruelties were carefully included in the Assyrian public records, inscribed on stone tablets which were set up for all to see. From the point of view of the Assyrians this was excellent publicity, for great fear was instilled in their opponents before any actual fighting took place, and many times the enemy troops would take to flight rather than face the Assyrian army on the field of battle.

The
Assyrian
army

Moreover, the Assyrian military organization was far superior to that of any of their contemporaries. Every able-bodied Assyrian male was a soldier; no citizen escaped military service at some time in his life, and, if necessary, all the citizens could be called out for a campaign. The army was well balanced. There were mounted cavalry as well as charioteers, and there was a large body of foot soldiers. Bowmen and slingers provided the artillery. The Assyrians also made great advances in the art of siegecraft; their engineers invented efficient machines for destroying the walls of heavily fortified towns. In short, the Assyrians in their heyday were almost irresistible.

The Assyrian empire was better organized than any that had preceded it. It has been said that the provincial system of government was invented by the Assyrians, and it certainly was passed on by them to their great successors, the Persians. At the head of the state were the king and his ministers; below them was a hierarchy of lesser officials who were kept in line by strict supervision and espionage. The conquered territory was divided into provinces, and these divisions were kept small in order that no governor might gain too much power. All the empire paid tribute, but in distant territories native client princes were intrusted with administration rather than Assyrian officials. Garrisons were stationed throughout the empire to forestall revolts. A novelty in administration was the granting of municipal charters to large cities. **Imperial organization**

Assyrian society was composed of three classes: the nobles, the middle class of professional men, craftsmen, and traders, and the proletariat of laborers and farmers. Agricultural serfdom was widespread, and there were large numbers of slaves who were captives of war. The Assyrians followed a policy of transplanting captive populations from their homes to other parts of the empire—the treatment of the Israelites provides a familiar example of this policy. It was felt that by moving the defeated groups into unfamiliar surroundings, the danger of revolt was lessened. **Society**

Culture

The underlying basis for Assyrian civilization was Sumero-Babylonian. Religion, law, art, and technology were borrowed from the people of the lower Tigris-Euphrates Valley; in addition, the cuneiform system of writing was adapted to Assyrian needs. Nevertheless, the Assyrians also borrowed from the Egyptians, the Hittites, and other western peoples. Furthermore, they were not content merely to borrow; they made adaptations and elaborations of earlier culture traits. In architecture and sculpture, stone was used much more than in Babylonia. Although mud bricks and kiln-baked bricks were employed for the walls of Assyrian buildings, the foundations and columns were of stone, and the arch was more common than in Babylonia. Assyrian reliefs and sculptures in the round are considered by some modern authorities to be superior to earlier works by other Oriental peoples; the Assyrian sculptors were only moderately successful in dealing with the human form, but their animal figures were superb. Palaces were large and impressive. There was a lavish use of metals and valuable wood in addition to stone. Paved roads and aqueducts were also built.

Literature

The Sumerian and Babylonian contributions to astronomical knowledge and to literature were preserved by the Assyrian kings who ordered the study and translation of ancient texts. Assur-bani-pal had a large library of cuneiform tablets; his collection was discovered by modern archaeologists, and it has proved invaluable in amplifying our knowledge of the earlier literature. The specifically Assyrian contribution to literature was in the field of history, for in the records of their campaigns they attained new heights of vivid description and narration.

Religion

In the religious field the Assyrians took over much of the Sumero-Babylonian practice and theology. The national god of Assyria was Assur who was represented not by a statue in human form but by a winged disk which was carried on a standard before the army. Babylonian influence is shown by the fact that Assur came to be identified with Hammurabi's Marduk. Fundamentally, however, Assur was a cruel and exacting deity who gloried in war and bloodshed. It is emphasized over and over again that the basis of Assyrian religion was fear, and the whole tone of religious thinking was rather gloomy.

On the other hand, Assyrian medical practice represented an advance over the Babylonian. The Assyrians had an extensive knowledge of drugs and herbs, and progress was made in surgery. Less dependence was placed upon spells and incantations for the cure of disease.

Medical science

The decline and fall of Assyria can perhaps be explained by the failure of the Assyrians to find a top-ranking place for themselves in the economic structure of their society. They were content to feed upon their subjects through the tribute which they demanded, and the middle class and proletariat of the Assyrian citizens never entered whole-heartedly into trade and industry. The Assyrians remained an agricultural people and left trade and industry to their subjects. The immediate cause of the collapse of the empire was provided by nationalistic revolts of Assyrian subjects. This collapse could not be prevented because the Assyrians themselves had probably greatly declined in numbers. The sturdy peasantry which had fought in the earlier campaigns had been largely wiped out by the losses suffered in almost continuous warfare, and the Assyrian ruling class, having exhausted this valuable source of soldiers, could not get the same results with armies composed of allies and mercenaries. Undoubtedly, Assyria itself was as populous as ever in the seventh century, but its inhabitants were foreigners who had been transplanted thither as captives of war, and they did not have the vigor, the loyalty, or the military training of the old peasant stock.

Reasons for Assyrian decline

It may perhaps help the student to remember the Assyrians as a people who might be called the "Romans of the Ancient Near East." They were, like the Romans, a hardy rural people surrounded by enemies who threatened their national existence. Both the Romans and the Assyrians adopted an aggressive policy of defense by means of which they con-

The Romans of the Ancient Near East

quered their neighbors and created empires. Both were not so much creators as adapters, elaborators, and carriers of culture. Both were, in their national traditions, practical rather than theoretical in their approach to life; they tended to be builders rather than dreamers.

THE SUCCESSORS OF ASSYRIA

The fall of Assyria ushered in a period of local independence in the Near East much like that which followed the disintegration of the Hittite empire. The chief powers in the Near East between 600 and 550 B.C. were the Neo-Babylonians (or Chaldeans) of Mesopotamia, the Saites of Egypt, the Lydians of Asia Minor, and the Medes of Iran.

Neo-Babylonians

The Neo-Babylonians controlled the Tigris-Euphrates Valley, Assyria, and the Syria-Palestine region. The great king Nebuchadrezzar (604-562 B.C.) drove the Egyptians from Syria and Palestine and carried off the Jews into their "Babylonian captivity." It was also he who built the famous "Hanging Gardens," a great zikkurat covered with trees and shrubs to simulate a mountain. Neo-Babylonian culture was an archaizing culture; it contributed little to the cultural store of the Ancient Near East because Nebuchadrezzar and his contemporaries were chiefly interested in trying to recreate the glories of Babylonia's past.

Saites

Egypt was ruled by the Twenty-Sixth (or Saite) Dynasty. The Saite rulers were native princes who had been vassals of Assyria in the time of Assur-bani-pal. In the seventh century they reunited Egypt, and, when the Assyrian empire fell, they gained complete independence. Like the Neo-Babylonians, they tried to revive the classical culture of their native land, a culture which was in the case of Egypt that of the Old Kingdom. The Saite Pharaohs were heavily dependent upon mercenary soldiers, and during this period the Greeks began to come to Egypt as soldiers and traders.

The Lydians of Asia Minor were an indigenous group who capitalized upon the fall of the Phrygian empire. The first Lydian kings appeared at Sardes in the eighth century

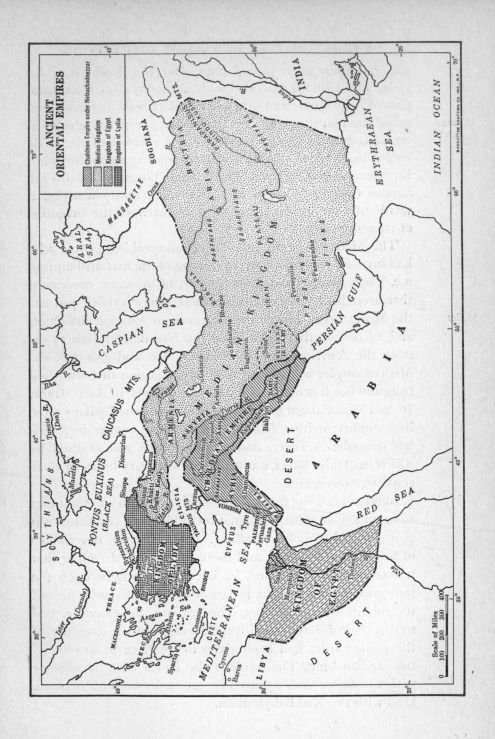

ANCIENT
ORIENTAL EMPIRES

Chaldean Empire under Nebuchadnezzar
Median Kingdom
Kingdom of Egypt
Kingdom of Lydia

B.C., but their great period came after the downfall of Assyria. The Lydians extended their authority over the central part of Asia Minor and over the Greek cities which had been established on the Aegean coast. Lydian prosperity was based on a geographic position that allowed control of the trade routes from Mesopotamia and Iran leading to southeastern Europe and the Aegean. The Lydian kings, especially the famous Croesus (560-546 B.C.), were notoriously wealthy; it was hardly an accident that the Lydians were the inventors of coined money.

Lydians

The Medes were an Indo-European-speaking people who had invaded Iran about the beginning of the first millennium B.C. Their coming was probably part of the same movement that brought the Phrygians into Asia Minor. About 700 B.C. the Medes began to free themselves from Assyrian influence, and, of course, they later aided the Neo-Babylonians to destroy the Assyrian empire. Between 600 and 550 B.C. the Median empire was extended to cover a region that stretched from the borders of India to the Halys River in Asia Minor. In Asia Minor about 585 B.C. the Medes and the Lydians came into conflict; neither felt strong enough to engage in a serious struggle, however, and a compromise was reached by which the Halys River was made the boundary between their respective territories.

Medes

In retrospect, the first half of the sixth century B.C. appears to be an age of cultural stagnation. This static condition was also reflected in political affairs. There were no movements of forceful imperialism, and there was a general feeling that it was better "to live and let live." Relations between the four great powers became progressively more friendly toward the middle of the century. The Lydians, for example, had settled their differences with the Medes, and the daughter of the Lydian ruler had been given in marriage to the son of the Median king. The Lydians also had a friendly alliance with the Saites and, apparently, an understanding of some kind with the Neo-Babylonians.

THE PERSIANS

The peace which was just beginning to settle down upon the Ancient Near East was rudely shattered in 550 by the rise of a new nation, the Persians. The Persians were a group of Indo-European-speaking tribes who lived in the southern part of Iran. They were related very closely to the Medes and were Median subjects before they embarked upon their career of imperialism. About 553 the Persian tribes under the leadership of Cyrus, king of Anshan (Susa) and grandson of the Median king, revolted against their Median masters. They rapidly gained control of the Median empire and then undertook military operations against the Lydians and the Neo-Babylonians. Croesus the Lydian fell before the conquering Cyrus about 546, and the Neo-Babylonian kingdom became subject to the Persians in 539. The last ten years of Cyrus' life were spent in bringing the eastern provinces of the old Median empire under Persian control. Cambyses, the successor of Cyrus, achieved the conquest of Egypt in 525 B.C.

<small>Cyrus the Great</small>

Although the death of Cambyses (c. 521 B.C.) was accompanied by revolts and disorders throughout the empire, a new dynasty was soon established by the famous Darius I whose descendants were to rule the empire until its conquest by Alexander the Great in the third quarter of the fourth century B.C. Darius himself restored order, defeated his rivals for the kingship, and gained possession of European Thrace. As we shall see later, he also attempted the conquest of Greece.

<small>Darius I</small>

The Persian empire was the largest of the Oriental empires of the pre-Christian period. It included all the territory which had been held by Assyria, plus other possessions in Iran, Armenia, Asia Minor, and Thrace. The rapid growth of the Persian empire was due to the superior military organization of the Persian army; but also important was the fact that two thousand years of continuous warfare, of conquest and reconquest, had completely broken the spirit of the inhabitants of the civilized areas of the Ancient Near

<small>Persian empire</small>

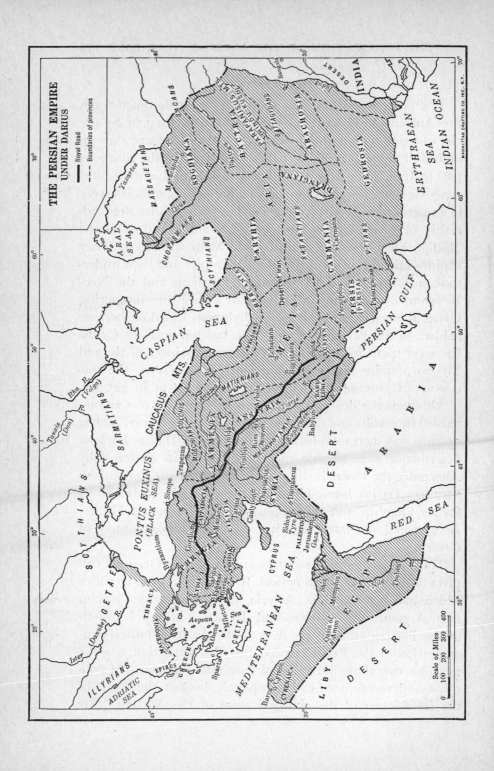

THE PERSIAN EMPIRE
UNDER DARIUS

— — — Royal Road
— — — Boundaries of provinces

East. The great masses of the population had become indifferent to changes of masters; to the common people it made little difference who ruled them, since they could expect heavy tax burdens and relentless exploitation whether native kings or foreign invaders were in the saddle. The only opposition to Persian expansion, therefore, was provided by the upper classes who were not numerically powerful and who depended upon mercenary soldiers for protection. The Persian host of the early days, on the other hand, was a national army of nobles and yeomen, and it was not surprising that they could overcome their opponents; certainly, the advantage of a nationalist psychology was on the Persian side.

At its height, in the fifth century B.C., the Persian empire had a population of perhaps thirty million; the Persians themselves did not number more than 500,000. The proportion of rulers to subjects was thus about 1 to 60, and this fact explains why Persian expansion stopped when it reached a certain point—the Persians could not easily hold in subjection a larger population. True, they could call upon their subjects for military aid, but they did not dare to arm any large body of native troops in any given area because of the danger of revolt.

At the head of the Persian state was the king, an hereditary monarch, who was assisted and advised by a council of his nobles. For the administration of the empire an extensive **Administration** bureaucracy was developed. The chief ministers were appointees of the king; they were of noble birth, and often they were members of the royal family. The empire was divided into provinces or satrapies. The civil administration of a satrapy was in the hands of an official called a satrap, but the military forces were commanded by an independent general in order that too much power might not be concentrated in the hands of one person. Royal investigators and spies kept the king informed of the conduct of his officials. Persian garrisons might be quartered in important towns. The king allowed the natives to retain their local governmental forms in most cases, since he was chiefly concerned with the collection of revenue and the defense of his realm and had no real interest in supervising local affairs which did not relate to his main objectives. An admirable system of post roads and a fast messenger service kept the king well in touch with the affairs of his empire.

Wealth

The Persian kings were very wealthy. The tribute which flowed into the royal coffers was paid in gold and silver, and amounted to perhaps twenty-five million dollars annually. Taxes were paid in kind; their monetary value greatly exceeded that of the tribute in precious metals.

The monarchy

The native masses regarded the Persian king as a god, whereas the Persians themselves looked upon him as a divine-right ruler possessing attributes of divinity. The establishment of the bureaucracy contributed to the remoteness and inaccessibility of the monarch. At the court he was surrounded with ceremony and his person was sacrosanct. The Persian queen was only one of many wives in the royal harem, and often Persian politics were complicated by antagonisms and rivalries within the royal household.

Culture

The Persians were the cultural heirs of the Babylonians and Assyrians. They borrowed the cuneiform script and used a simplified version of it for writing their own language. Their sculpture was influenced by that of their Semitic predecessors, and later by Greek art. Nevertheless, Persian sculpture can stand on its own merits; the sculptured figures of animals, especially of lions and horses, were magnificent. Persian architecture retained the Babylonian practice in that the palaces were built upon raised platforms. The Persians, however, were unlike the Babylonians in their use of the column. They had access to good stone, whereas the Babylonians did not, and thus the column was much more practicable in Persia than in the Tigris-Euphrates Valley. Persian columns were tall and slender, quite different from the heavier column favored by the Egyptians.

Religion

The lower classes among the Persians were polytheistic and addicted to many rude superstitions; their religion contained many animistic elements in which natural phenomena and fire played an important part. There was a priest caste known as the Magians. Chief among the deities were Mithra, the sun god, and Anahita, a mother goddess.

On the other hand, the Persian nobility and the royal family came under the influence of a religious reform movement which had been inaugurated (some time before the accession of Darius I) by the famous Zoroaster. Zoroaster was a **Zoroaster** monotheist who chose as his deity Ahura-Mazda, the god of light. Ahura-Mazda was the leader of the forces of truth and light as opposed to the superstition and darkness of other religions and gods headed by the Persian counterpart of the devil, who was called Ahriman. Zoroaster thus conceived of life as a struggle between light and darkness, or good and evil. He emphasized as the chief virtues truth, morality, and bravery. Nevertheless, Zoroastrianism, like Judaism, did not exert as great an influence at its inception as it was to exert at a much later period (see below, p. 341).

NON-MATERIAL ASPECTS OF THE CIVILIZATION OF THE ANCIENT NEAR EAST

As far as material culture is concerned, the common features of the civilizations of the Near East should now be clear. This community of material culture traits was also paralleled in non-material fields, and it was particularly true of social thought and of speculation about the world and its origins.

In the literature of the Egyptians, Sumerians, Babylonians, Assyrians, Hebrews, and Persians one finds a unanimity of opinion in respect to what was considered proper and improper social behavior. Most of these precepts of conduct are identical with those to which we subscribe today—partly **Common** because the Christian society of the modern western world **social** relies heavily upon the Old Testament, and partly because **precepts** these precepts are based upon good common sense and would be practical for any society.

The didactic writers of the Ancient Near East urge their fellow men to avoid boasting, lying, drunkenness, and over-

Behavior

bearing manners; to keep from injuring others by either word or deed. Humility, guarded speech, truthfulness, temperance, moderation, self-control, and kindness are virtues to be cultivated. Men are told to honor their parents, to be kind to their social inferiors, and to succor the weak and unfortunate. Murder, robbery, sharp dealing, and sexual abnormality are condemned in all societies. Very early in Egypt and Babylonia, the idea was developed that the gods will punish the sinner— either in this life (according to the Babylonians), or in the next (according to the Egyptians). Everywhere, the virtuous woman, the good wife, is extolled.

Hard work

Among the common people, there was a universal feeling that hard work was a virtue, and idleness a vice. Honest toil, though unproductive of great wealth, was preferable to ill-gotten gains. On the other hand, we often find writings that express a deep pessimism regarding the uncertainties of life. Wealth may easily be lost, life and work are futile, and so on. More than once the cynic advises his contemporaries "to eat, drink, and be merry."

Education

Few questioned the value of education as a means of gaining worldly success. An Egyptian teacher said: "Be not a foolish man, that hath no instruction." The point was a good one, for an educated man who came from the lower classes might hope to better himself by becoming a scribe, a priest, or an official. Some even valued knowledge for its own sake— like Assur-bani-pal, who had "a large ear for learning."

Responsibilities of the ruling class

There was a morality for the royalty and the nobility, too. Their responsibilities to society lay in providing justice and good government. Often, a ruler leaves behind a testament in which he lists his accomplishments—his upright administration of justice, his piety, his solicitude for the common people and for economic welfare. In Egypt and Persia there were also didactic writings on the duties of the rulers. Frequently, there is evidence that the nobles possessed a social consciousness. In the inscription of Henku the Nomarch, for example, we find:

"I gave bread to all the hungry. . . . I clothed him who

was naked. . . . I never oppressed one in possession of his property. . . . I was a benefactor to the nome."[4]

As yet, we know very little about the study of philosophy in the Near East. Undoubtedly, however, people as civilized as the Egyptians and the Babylonians did engage in philosophical speculation. We do, as a matter of fact, know something of their explanations of the origin of man and the universe. **Philosophy**

In both Babylonia and Egypt, men believed that originally there was no dry land—only water. According to one Babylonian myth, it was the gods who first created dry land and brought man into existence. In another myth from Babylonia, the primeval waters were envisioned as the dwelling place of the dragon Tiamat (chaos). Tiamat was slain in a battle with the gods. Her body was cut in half; one half became the earth which floated upon the waters beneath it, and the other half was elevated to form the sky and support the waters above which occasionally seeped through in the form of rain. After heaven and earth were thus created, plants and animals were devised by the gods. In Egyptian mythology, the grandchildren of the sun god, Keb and Nut, formed the earth and the sky. Nut rested both hands and feet upon the earth (her brother, Keb) and her torso constituted the heavens. A similar Egyptian belief postulated the sky as a cow goddess whose hooves rested upon the earth. **Origin of the universe**

The Babylonians believed man to be half animal and half divine; his intelligence differentiated him from the animals, and his inability to attain immortality separated him from the gods. Once, they said, man lived like the animals, but the gods taught him how to domesticate plants and animals, and thus man was able to become civilized. **Man**

With this brief survey of the cultural history of the Near East in mind, we may now turn to a consideration of the rise of civilization in the lands which border on the Medi-

[4] J. H. Breasted, *Ancient Records*, Chicago, 1906, Vol. I, p. 126.

terranean Sea. Much of the culture of these lands was borrowed from the Near East—a point which should never be forgotten—but there were elaborations and additions to this culture which altered its appearance. The Greeks and the Romans, who were responsible for many of these changes, will claim our main attention in the succeeding chapters.

CHAPTER IV

THE EASTERN MEDITERRANEAN REGION
(to 1200 B.C.)

The fall of the Assyrian empire was symbolic; it marked the end of a chapter in the history of civilization, for the Assyrian was the last of the truly great Oriental empires of the pre-Christian era. Political and cultural leadership soon passed from the hands of the ancient Oriental peoples to the young and vigorous Indo-European-speaking Greeks and Persians. In 600 B.C. cultural progress in the Ancient Near East was almost at a standstill; the dead weight of custom and tradition, of reverence for past glories, was an obstacle to further advance. The Ancient Near East no longer looked forward; instead, men looked backward to the "good old days." This tendency is shown most clearly in the archaism of the Saites in Egypt and the Neo-Babylonians in Mesopotamia; when these groups gained their independence from Assyria, they made pathetic efforts to re-create the greatness of the past, especially by reviving old forms of art and literature. It is difficult to explain in simple terms this cultural and intellectual bankruptcy. The ancient Oriental peoples might be likened to miners who have exhausted the possibilities of a rich vein of ore and lack the initiative to search for a new lead.

The cultural bankruptcy of the Ancient Near East

But the culture which the Egyptians, Babylonians, and their neighbors had created did not become extinct; it was preserved in the Near East, and, what is more important, it passed by a process of diffusion into an adjacent region to the west, a region which we may call the Eastern Mediterranean, where it formed the basis for a new civilization, that of the Greeks.

The Eastern Mediterranean region includes Crete, Cyprus,

The Eastern Mediterranean

the islands of the Aegean Sea, the western coast of Asia Minor, and the southeastern portion of Europe (Greece, Macedonia, and Thrace). The early inhabitants of these lands borrowed their culture mostly from the Ancient Near East, but environmental conditions in the Eastern Mediterranean precluded the establishment of a civilization identical with that of the Egyptians or Babylonians. Instead, the ancient Oriental culture was so adapted and elaborated that it was given a new and certainly different interpretation.

The Greeks

The Greeks, who will be discussed in detail later, were invaders, rather than aborigines, of the Eastern Mediterranean. They did not make their appearance in the region before 2000 B.C.; although their importance in it increased after 1400 B.C., their unquestioned predominance was not established in Eastern Mediterranean affairs until about 1200 B.C. Prior to the arrival of the Greeks a Bronze Age civilization had been created in their future homeland. Before we can consider the Greeks, we must speak of their cultural forerunners.

Pre-Greek civilization

The pre-Greek phase of Eastern Mediterranean civilization provides a connecting link between the Greeks and the peoples of the Ancient Near East. The center of this early culture was the island of Crete. Even before 3000 B.C. the Cretans, or Minoans as they are usually called,[1] were in touch with Egypt, Syria, and Asia Minor. As a matter of fact, Crete was a part of the Ancient Oriental cultural province; its Bronze Age civilization was contemporary with the great period of Egypt and Mesopotamia, and the foundations of Minoan culture were derived from the Near East even though the Minoans did not follow closely the traditional pattern of the Ancient Oriental culture.

The Cretans

The first inhabitants of Crete seem to have come from North Africa, and it is probable that a few immigrants also came from Asia Minor. Most of the prehistoric Cretans were a short, slender, dark people of the Mediterranean branch of

---

[1] Minoans: the subjects of Minos. Minos was the legendary king of Cnossus, the most important Cretan city.

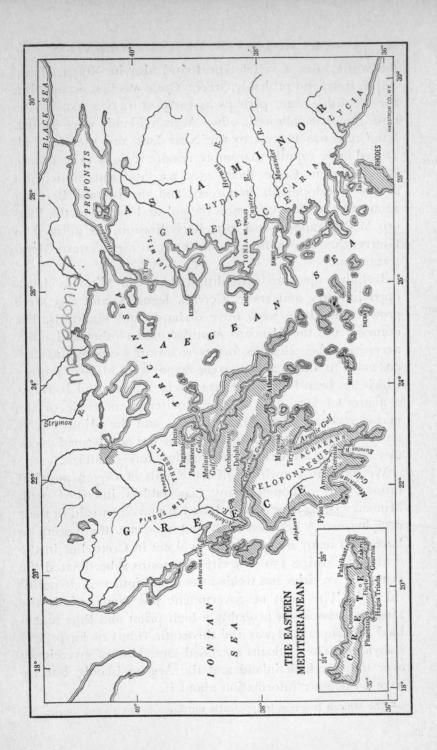

BLACK SEA

PROPONTIS

Hellespont

ASIA MINOR

Macedonia

Troy MTS.

IDA MTS.

Hermus R.

LYDIA

Cayster R.

MT. TMOLUS

Macander

IONIA

CARIA

LYCIA

RHODES

Ialysus

CHIOS

SAMOS

Cos

AMORGUS

THERA

MELOS

THRACIAN SEA

AEGEAN SEA

LESBOS

Strymon R.

THESSALY

Peneus R.

Iolcus

Pagasae

Pagasaean Gulf

Malian Gulf

Orchomenus

Delphi

Corinthian Gulf

Athens

Mycenae

Tiryns

Argolic Gulf

ACHAEAN

Eurotas R.

PINDUS MTS.

G R E E C E

PELOPONNESUS

Achelous R.

Amyclae

Gerenia

Alpheus R.

Pylos

Messenian Gulf

Ambracian Gulf

IONIAN SEA

THE EASTERN MEDITERRANEAN

CRETE

Palaikastro

Cnossus

Dicte

Zakro

Gournia

Phaestus

Hagia Triada

HAGSTROM CO. N.Y.

the white race, a racial type found also in North Africa, Spain, Italy, and probably Greece. Crete was first occupied in the Neolithic Age, perhaps as early as 10,000 B.C. In the centuries that followed, other Aegean islands were settled, but Crete was nearest to the Near East and therefore advanced more rapidly than more remote regions. The Bronze Age begins in Crete about 2500 B.C. and thus anticipates similar developments in Greece and the islands. Between 2200 and 1400 B.C. Crete was the cultural center of the Eastern Mediterranean, and from it civilization was diffused to Greece, the Aegean Islands, and even to the Western Mediterranean.

Cretan economy

Building upon an agricultural base, the Minoans developed industry and trade. Cereals, legumes, and flax were grown, and there were olive orchards and vineyards. For domestic use the Minoans manufactured clothes and other necessities; their chief exports were bronze weapons and various metal products, as well as the magnificent Minoan pottery which has been found in Egypt, Syria, Greece, and Italy. As a matter of fact, most of the Mediterranean trade of the period was carried in Minoan ships, and the Minoan navy seems to have been so powerful that it was not deemed necessary to fortify the Cretan cities against foreign attack.

We have no knowledge of the details of Cretan political history, for, although many clay tablets inscribed with Minoan writing have survived, we have no clue to aid in their decipherment.[2] Between 2200 and 1500 B.C. there seem to have been many independent city-states in Crete, but in the century following 1500 the city of Cnossus subordinated the other Cretan cities and welded the island into a single political unit. The form of government was monarchical; the king at Cnossus was probably a high priest and thus resembled in a superficial way the theocratic rulers of Egypt and Babylonia. The Minoans exercised some kind of sovereignty over the Greek mainland and the Aegean islands, but we have no definite information about it.

Chronology

[2] The Minoan language is apparently unrelated to any known tongue.

During its great period Crete was a populous land whose inhabitants were vivid and colorful. Cretan fresco paintings depict these people as small and wiry, with amazingly slender waists. The men were deeply tanned and wore few clothes, usually only a waistcloth and sandals; the women had wavy raven hair and white skins and wore very elaborate costumes; their low-necked dresses had full skirts with many flounces and ruffles. The impression of the Cretans which we gain from their art is one of gayety and light-heartedness; the bright colors which they employed, and the freshness and life of their frescoes and vase paintings show these people to have been observant, sensitive, and very close to nature. *Appearance of the Cretans*

Perhaps, however, the Cretan religion gives a truer picture of the temperament of the people than does the art, for in the religion the joyousness of some festivals and ceremonies was contrasted with other, more sinister, rites that demanded human sacrifice; there were gods of the underworld, the serpent was a sacred creature, and the Cretans undoubtedly believed in ghosts. The bull played an important part in their religion; representations of bulls' horns have been found in numerous shrines, and the dark legend of the Minotaur (a beast half-human and half-taurine) was connected with Cnossus. Then there was the ritual of bull-leaping: athletic young men and women would enter an enclosure in which was kept a ferocious untamed bull; when the bull charged at them the athletes would seize his horns and vault over his back. It was a dangerous trick; often the vaulter was impaled upon the horns or trampled under the animal's hoofs. One can imagine the savage thrill which the watching holiday crowd received when such an accident occurred. The Minoans seem to have worshiped an agricultural deity, the so-called Great Mother, whose devotees were also found in Asia Minor and other parts of the Near East. Trees, pillars, and stones were often considered sacred. *Religion*

In some ways the Minoan civilization was similar to that of the Indus Valley. Both cultures were located at the extremes of the then civilized world; both borrowed culture traits *Comparsion with other civilizations* from the Fertile Crescent. In neither the Indus Valley nor Crete did the aristocratic or theocratic elements gain absolute control over the life of the people as they did in Mesopotamia or Egypt; the individualism and freedom of the Indus and Minoan cultures seem to indicate the predominance of a middle class or bourgeoisie.

Art

In the arts the Minoans excelled the people of the Indus Valley. Minoan art did not follow the colossal tendencies of Egypt and Mesopotamia, neither was it hampered by the traditionalism which exerted such an influence upon the art of the Near East. Environmental conditions in Crete did not necessitate extreme governmental centralization and regimentation, nor was there an opportunity for the growth of a powerful priest class. Minoan artists were able to take advantage of the knowledge of technique which Egyptian and Mesopotamian artists possessed, but they were not bound by the conventions that were imposed upon mainland artists.

Architecture

Minoan palaces were low, rambling structures with many rooms and corridors oriented about numerous open courts. The famous Palace of Minos at Cnossus covered an area of approximately six acres; it was the result of the combination of several separate buildings which had stood facing a large plaza. Stone, brick, and wood were the materials used by Minoan architects; pavements, foundations, and some walls were built of stone; the upper courses of the walls were of brick, and wood was employed for columns and lintels. The Minoan column was unusual in shape because it tapered downward instead of upward. The walls of the rooms and corridors in the palaces were often decorated with fresco paintings. Domestic architecture was not pretentious in the Minoan period. The houses were one- or two-story buildings with no windows on the ground floor; the roofs were probably flat. The houses were huddled close together and faced upon very narrow streets. The Minoans built carefully with a view to permanence; remains of their paved streets and roads may still be seen in Crete.

Minoan sculpture was not monumental. The examples of

Minoan work which have survived are small and rather **Sculpture**
delicate. Stone, metal, terra cotta, and ivory were the principal materials. Jewelry was made of hard stones, bronze,
copper, gold, and silver; rings, seals, bracelets, necklaces, and
a few other trinkets have been found. The pottery was su- **Pottery**
perbly made, and its decoration excelled that of the pottery
of the Near East. The fine clay at the disposal of the Minoan
potters made possible the manufacture of vases of fine smooth
texture and eggshell thinness. The style of decoration varied
in different periods from monochrome to polychrome, from
geometric to naturalistic and finally to conventionalized patterns. Marine and floral motives were very popular. Some
vases were made of stone by a technique borrowed from
Egypt; both hard and soft stone were employed. A favorite
material was a soft, soapy stone called steatite which could
be easily carved in fairly high relief. It is possible that steatite
vases were often covered with thin sheets of gold.

Painting was less dependent upon sculpture than had been **Painting**
the case in Egypt. The frescoes of the Minoan period were
painted upon wet mortar, and the work had to be completed
before the mortar dried. The amazing results which the
Minoan painters obtained in executing a whole painting
within the space of a few hours is sufficient proof of their
skill. When the painter made mistakes, however, he could not
erase them, and the results were sometimes amusing; for
example, there are paintings of bulls with several heads and
numerous tails.

The economic situation in Crete was such that rigid class **Society**
distinctions did not develop. Wealth and property were distributed much more evenly among the population than in
Egypt or Mesopotamia. Farmers, artisans, and traders seem
to have formed a middle class; though there must have been
nobles and priests, they never gained the predominance which
similar classes acquired in the Near East. There appears to
have been slavery in Crete; at least, Negroes were brought
over from Africa.

All things considered, the Minoans, in the period of their

Everyday
life

greatness, must have been a happy and prosperous people. They were inveterate sportsmen, fond of boxing, wrestling, fencing, and hunting; singing and dancing were common; the discovery of a gaming board in the ruins at Cnossus indicates an interest in less strenuous amusements. The Minoans had most of the common domesticated animals; moreover, the horse was introduced into Crete about 1600 B.C., and the cat seems to have been imported from Egypt. Wild bulls were caught with nets, a hazardous undertaking.

Appraisal
of Minoan
civilization

The cultural indebtedness of the Minoans to the Ancient Near East was considerable. The signs used in their writing and many of their art motifs and techniques were derived from Egypt, as were some of their religious practices; the system of weights and measures was Mesopotamian in origin; Mesopotamian cylinder seals were common in Crete. Minoan gems often bear representations of mythological animals— winged quadrupeds, creatures with human bodies and animal or bird heads, etc. These ideas also represent borrowings from the East; as a matter of fact, the Minotaur appears on Babylonian seals. Nevertheless, Minoan civilization was important because it foreshadowed future cultural developments; it provided the first illustration of what might happen when the civilization of the Near East was transplanted into a European environment and released from the baneful influence of traditionalism.

The
end of
Minoan
supremacy

About 1400 B.C. the political influence of the Minoans was abruptly terminated. The palace at Cnossus was destroyed either by an earthquake or by invaders. The political center of the Eastern Mediterranean was transferred from Crete to the Greek mainland, and governmental supremacy passed from the hands of the pre-Greeks into those of the Greek invaders.

Greece
before
the
Greeks

In order to understand what happened, we must consider the prehistory of Greece itself. Before 10,000 B.C. there were probably no human beings in Greece. After that time, men of Mediterranean stock began to filter into the country, possibly from Asia Minor. Subsequently, Greece became divided into two cultural provinces: the north was influenced by the Danubian area, and the south was connected with Crete. Between 2500 and 2000 B.C. the Minoans began to exert a greater cultural influence over southern and central Greece. Fairly large towns—probably Cretan trading posts—grew up at Athens, Mycenae, Pylos, Thebes, Orchomenos, and a few other places, but the people of the mainland continued to be mostly farmers and herdsmen.

In the second millennium B.C. groups of invaders from the north began to penetrate Greece: these were the Greeks. We do not know much about the Greeks save that they were a pastoral people with a slight knowledge of agriculture; they spoke an Indo-European language (Greek) utterly unlike the ancient Mediterranean speech of the Minoans and their contemporaries on the Greek mainland. The first Greek invasions came about 1800 B.C.; a number of the pre-Greek towns and villages were sacked at this time, but apparently there was no large movement of the population. The Greeks simply settled down, established themselves side by side with the older peoples, and began to absorb the culture of the region. A second wave of invaders, in which the participants were more numerous, arrived in Greece about 1600 B.C. These might well be the Greeks whom Homer called the Achaeans. The Achaeans were powerful enough to dominate the older population in Greece; Mycenae and the other centers of Minoan influence became Achaean strongholds, and about 1400 B.C. the Achaeans seem to have conquered Crete. The rise of the Achaeans inaugurates a new cultural epoch called the Mycenaean Age; its title is derived from the importance which Mycenae now assumed in political and cultural life. The Achaeans themselves are often called Mycenaeans, and we shall use the two terms interchangeably.

Greek invasions

Mycenaeans

The Mycenaeans flourished between 1400 and 1200 B.C.; this was the heroic age of Greece, and sagas of the deeds of the Mycenaean warriors were later employed as the basis for the epic poems of Homer and his contemporaries. Mycenaean political influence was extended over the islands of the

The Mycenaean world

Aegean and the coasts of Asia Minor; some Hittite inscriptions apparently refer to the Achaeans. In the Mycenaean world the feudal monarchy was the prevailing type of government. The king was chiefly a war leader. He and his nobles with their retainers formed the army. Most of the fighting was done by the nobles who hurled spears from their swift-moving chariots or sometimes dismounted to engage in individual combats on foot. The retainers were archers and pikemen who probably played no important part in the battles of the heroic age.

Myce-
naean
culture
Mycenaean culture might be described as basically Minoan with an addition of certain northern elements introduced by the Achaean invaders. The Achaeans incorporated the Minoan religion into their own, and they took over much of the technology of their predecessors. On the other hand, climatic conditions on the Greek mainland led the invaders to retain their own style of dress; Mycenaean clothes were heavier and more voluminous than those of the Minoans. The ruling class of the mainland was taller and more heavy-set than the Minoans; the wearing of beards was fashionable. The use of bronze helmets and greaves, round shields, and heavier swords was typical of the Mycenaean armament.

Archi-
tecture
Architectural styles changed. The Mycenaean palace was strongly fortified; it was really a citadel which included the king's mansion as well as the dwellings of his followers. The typical Mycenaean building was the megaron; it consisted of a vestibule or antechamber which opened into a pillared hall. In the center of the hall was a large hearth which provided heat for the entire room; the smoke from the fire was drawn up through a hole in the roof. The Mycenaeans used the gabled roof instead of the flat roof of the Minoan house. The interior walls of the megaron were decorated with frescoes and friezes just as those of the Minoan palaces had been.

Remains of Mycenaean palaces and fortifications have been found at Mycenae, Tiryns, Athens, Thebes, Orchomenos, and many other sites in Greece. The individual stones used in the

walls of the fortifications were very large; they weighed several tons each. This type of masonry was called Cyclopean
because the later Greeks believed that only the Cyclopes, a
race of giants, could have raised these huge blocks into position. Not only were the fortification walls high, but they were
also very thick. At Tiryns, for example, there were arched

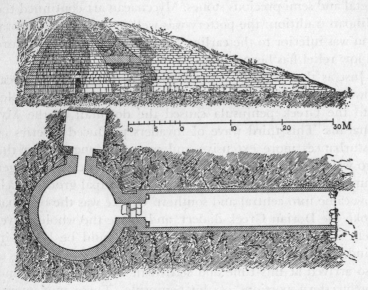

CHART IV.—Corbeled Arch and Beehive Tomb. (From Fowler and Wheeler,
Greek Archaeology.)

passageways running through the walls. The Mycenaeans did
not know the true arch (with its keystone); their arch was
the false or corbeled arch.

The Mycenaean tombs became rather elaborate. During
the period in which Mycenae was increasing in influence
(after 1600 B.C.) the deceased kings and nobles were buried
in shaft graves; these tombs, as their name implies, were deep **Tombs**
shafts sunk perpendicularly into the ground or cut into living rock. In the great period, the tholos or beehive tomb was
popular. The tholos tombs were circular stone buildings
shaped like a beehive; they were constructed underground,
usually in the hillsides. Inclined shafts sloped down to the

tombs and afforded easy access. The domed roofs of the beehive tombs were corbeled like the Mycenaean arch.

Art

Gold, silver, copper, and bronze were common in the
Mycenaean period. Gold masks were sometimes placed over
the faces of the dead. The table service of the rich was of
gold and silver. There was an abundance of jewelry made of
metal and semi-precious stones. Mycenaean art continued the
Minoan tradition; the pottery was well made, but its decoration was inferior to the earlier vase painting. Some sculpture
in low relief has been found.

**Dorian
invasion**

Just as the Achaean invasion had destroyed the political
power of the Minoans, so a new movement of Greek peoples
into the Greek peninsula caused the downfall of the Mycenaeans. This third wave of invaders produced a series of
disturbances more extensive and more prolonged than the
two waves which had preceded it, probably because a larger
number of people were involved. The principal group which
now came into central and southern Greece was the one that
spoke the Dorian Greek dialect, and hence the whole movement is called the Dorian invasion. It should be borne in
mind, however, that groups speaking other Greek dialects
also arrived at this time and settled in the west-central and
northwestern portions of the peninsula. These movements
continued from about 1200 to 1000 B.C., and the confusion
they caused brought an economic and cultural regression.
This was a transitional epoch bridging the gap between the
Mycenaean epoch and the period known as the Greek Dark
Ages.[3]

The Greek invasions were paralleled in time and character
by other movements elsewhere in the ancient world during
the second millennium B.C. The arrival of the first wave of
Greeks was more or less contemporary with the sack of Babylon by the Hittites, the establishment of the kingdom of the
Indo-Europeans known as the Kassites in Mesopotamia, the
arrival of the Aryans in India, and the penetration of Italy by
peoples who brought a Bronze Age culture. The Dorian wave

[3] The Dark Ages began about 1000 B.C. and came to an end about 750 B.C.

coincided with the overthrow of the Hittites by the Phrygians (an Indo-European group), the attacks of the sea raiders
upon Egypt, the settlement of the Philistines on the eastern
shore of the Mediterranean, and the invasion of Italy by
iron-using tribes. It will be remembered that the tradition
of the sack of Troy, the city located in northwestern Asia
Minor, dated that event shortly after 1200 B.C.; recent archaeological excavations have confirmed this date.

CHAPTER V

GREEK CULTURE (1200-500 B.C.)

As we have seen, the so-called Dorian invasion brought to an end the Mycenaean period in Greece. The Dorians were a migratory pastoral people whose culture was far less complex than that of the Mycenaeans. When large groups of these barbarians poured into Greece within a short space of time, there was no opportunity for a cultural assimilation like **The Dorians** that which had taken place when the earlier Greeks had come in contact with Minoan civilization; the Dorians by sheer weight of numbers dragged the other inhabitants of Greece down to their cultural level. Thus, the coming of the Dorians had an effect upon Greece similar to that which the barbarian invasions of the Christian era had upon the Roman empire.

Moreover, at this time the Greek world was isolated from the civilization of the Near East. The Hittite civilization had been eclipsed by the invading Phrygian hordes, while Egypt and Syria were harassed and weakened by the attacks of the sea raiders. As a result, the commercial and cultural interplay which might have fostered an immediate revival of civilization in Greece was not possible. Mycenaean trade relations were disrupted by invasion, piracy, and local warfare; the towns dwindled to villages, and political separatism was the **Conditions in Greece** order of the day. From trade and industry men were forced to turn back to agricultural and pastoral pursuits. Conditions were made more chaotic by the fact that the invasions displaced large sections of the pre-Dorian population; many groups deserted Greece for the coast of Asia Minor. Southern Greece (the Peloponnesus) became a Dorian stronghold,[1] and most of the non-Dorians who remained there were reduced to agricultural serfdom by their Dorian conquerors.

[1] There were also some Dorians who settled in central Greece.

With the Dorian invasion Greece reverted to an Age of Agriculture; but in the period between 1000 and 750 B.C. (the Greek Dark Ages) cultural evolution began anew, and the first steps were taken toward the creation of classical Greek civilization. It is interesting to note that the Greeks of the Dark Ages built the new culture upon foundations very similar to those which had been used by the Minoans two thousand years earlier. One should qualify this statement, however, by pointing out that many technological and religious traits developed in the Minoan-Mycenaean period were retained by the Dorians and their contemporaries; in addition, the Dorians were an iron-using people and introduced iron weapons and implements into Greece. The fact that Greece and the Aegean were almost completely isolated from the Near East during most of the Dark Ages was important, for the political and cultural independence of the Greeks during this period produced a situation in which environment became the most powerful force guiding the evolution of the new Greek culture.

Cultural evolution begins anew

THE GREEK ENVIRONMENT AND ITS INFLUENCE

Greece is a rugged, mountainous country; nestled among its mountains are small valleys and plains. Nature has divided the land into a number of small compartments, and in the Dark Ages each of these compartments tended to become the home of a distinct group of people who set up a tiny independent state. In other words, political separatism is inherent in the Greek environment; the disturbed conditions produced by the Dorian invasion aggravated this situation. In many cases, at the beginning of the Dark Ages, there were several separate political divisions even in the tiny valleys and plains themselves; but when more peaceful times began to prevail, naturally unified areas were consolidated. Ordinarily, in each valley or plain there was one town whose location was more favorable than that of the neighboring towns and villages. A harbor town, or one which had good natural defenses, was likely to become the capital of the

Environment and political evolution

surrounding territory. Athens and Corinth were good examples of this latter type: each had a natural citadel—the Acropolis at Athens and the Acrocorinthus at Corinth—where the people might take refuge in time of danger.

The small size of the Greek states was important for future developments because in the early period no one state was powerful enough to conquer the others. Moreover, the divine or theocratic monarchy of the Near East was a type of government which could not flourish in a small country whose population was not large. The fact that everyone tended to know everyone else rather intimately made it quite unlikely that a man's contemporaries, who had grown up with him from childhood, would ever think him eligible for divine honors. This situation thus led political evolution in the opposite direction from autocracy, and was favorable to the growth of more democratic governmental forms.

Democratic tendencies

The common political unit in Greece was the city-state, just as it was in the early history of the Near East; but the *polis* (the Greek term for city-state) continued to be the unit of government throughout the classical period in Greece, whereas in the Near East the city-states were consolidated into kingdoms and empires. Here again we may see the influence of environment, for the various large regions of the Near East were geographic units, but in Greece there was no unity of this kind. As we shall see, attempts were made to consolidate the city-states and to create empires in Greece, but none of these efforts met with more than temporary success until the whole peninsula was conquered by the Romans.

The polis

Since Greece is a peninsula, it has a long coast line, and no region is far removed from the sea. It is not surprising, therefore, that the Greeks became sailors. Everything favored this development: the Mediterranean and the Aegean have no tides; during the summer months the winds are steady and dependable; the Aegean is crowded with so many islands that not even the most timid seafarer need worry about getting out of sight of land. Also important was the fact that the Greek rivers were small, shallow, and usually swift,

The seaward outlook

therefore not suitable for navigation; as a result, the Greeks were forced to learn how to sail on the sea. This was fortunate because it might otherwise have been difficult for them to make the transition from river navigation to that in open water—certainly this difficulty beset the Egyptians and Mesopotamians who never became good sailors.

The seaward outlook of Greece was necessarily toward the east and south, for in the north the peninsula joined the European continent, and much of the west coast bordered on the Adriatic Sea which, because of its winds and currents, was avoided by most Greek navigators. To the east was the Aegean, easy to sail; the Aegean became a kind of Greek lake, and it acted as a unifying force in welding the east coast of Greece and the west coast of Asia Minor into a single cultural province. To the south, the Mediterranean **Greece** afforded access to Crete, Syria, and Egypt. Consequently, **faces** when there was a revival of cultural influence in the Near **east and** East in the time of the Assyrian empire, Greece was immediately affected because of its geographic relation to the Aegean and Mediterranean. This was very important for the cultural and political history of Greece; the point can be emphasized by comparing the positions of the Italian and Greek peninsulas. Italy faced the west (because of its inhospitable Adriatic coast on the east), and the Italian peninsula was not especially open to influences emanating from the east. The situation was exactly reversed in Greece, and Greece was able to forge ahead culturally under stimulus from the Near East, whereas the cultural growth of Italy was long delayed.

Other factors in the Greek environment were the climate, soil, and natural resources. The cold, rainy winters influ- **Other** enced architectural developments even in the Mycenaean **environ-** Age; the megaron with its sloping roof and "central heat- **factors** ing" was better adapted to the Greek climate than was the drafty, flat-roofed Minoan house. The soil of Greece was moderately fertile, although not more than one-fourth of the total land area was cultivatable. The middle slopes of the hills were covered with valuable forests, but the hill tops were mostly bare rock. However, when the Greeks began to cut off the timber, either for wood or to make more land available for agriculture, serious erosion occurred; in the end only the plains and valleys could be cultivated, whereas in the beginning it had been possible to raise crops on the lower slopes as well. On the middle slopes grazed the cattle, sheep, and goats. The goat, "man's worst servant," contributed much to the deforestation of Greece because its nibbling destroyed the second growth which might have replaced the virgin timber cut down by its masters. The Greeks had an abundance of fish and game to supplement their cereals and vegetables. They were also blessed with a climate and soil suitable for the vine and olive culture. As in Egypt, good stone was available; without Greek marble and limestone, classical architecture would have been impossible. Greece, moreover, had what Egypt sadly lacked—good timber. The Greek clay was excellent and permitted the making of fine pottery, tile, and terra cottas. Last of all, the peninsula contained silver, copper, iron, and gold. The Greeks were fortunate in the possession of their timber, stone, clay, and metals, for when agricultural production began to decline— as the result of erosion and soil exhaustion—they were able to develop trading and manufacturing and provide the means to buy food from abroad.

GREEK ECONOMIC HISTORY AND POLITICAL EVOLUTION

Political institutions in the Dark Ages

When the Greeks came to Greece their government was monarchical. In the Dark Ages each Greek state was headed by a king who was chosen from an hereditary royal family. The king was commander-in-chief of the army, high priest, and arbitrator of disputes. Except in time of war when his power was slightly greater, he was limited in his actions by public opinion, and by the *gerousia* (council of the old men) which he was supposed to consult on all occasions. In reality, the king enjoyed just as much authority as the forcefulness of his personality could gain for him. There was a popular assembly, the *ecclesia*, which consisted of all men able to serve in the army. The *ecclesia* could vote in the affirmative or the negative on questions submitted to it by the king, and when a candidate for the monarchy was selected by the *gerousia*, the choice could be accepted or rejected by the *ecclesia*.

The social organization of the Greeks was arranged upon a patriarchal basis. The smallest social unit was the family which consisted of all the male and unmarried female descendants of a common living male ancestor. Thus a family might be headed by a great-grandfather, and the group would include his wife, all his sons and their wives and children, his unmarried daughters, his grandsons, and so on. When the patriarch died, the family would split up into several parts, and the patriarch's sons would become the heads of new families of their own. Groups of families which traced their descent from a common (but long-deceased) male ancestor formed a social unit much larger than the family: this was the *genos* or clan.

Social organization

After the invasions were over and the Greeks settled down upon the land, the adoption of the agricultural way of life began to have its effect. The population increased, and specialization of labor gradually appeared. At the same time, certain families, or even whole clans, became more and more influential in governmental affairs. These people were those who possessed more land, or better land, than others. In some cases they might have inherited plots of land at the bottom of a valley; land thus located became more and more valuable as the hillsides began to erode (as a result of deforestation) and much soil was washed down into the valleys leaving the slopes uncultivatable. In the Dark Ages, land was the chief form of wealth in Greece, and the possession of this wealth meant political power. Thus, the large landholders came to have more and more influence; they became the nobles or aristocrats (the "best" people).

Landed aristocracy

The holders of small or unprofitable plots of land sometimes sought the protection of the aristocrats; they might even sell their lands to the aristocrats and become tenant farmers. The aristocrats, backed by their clients (those who had sought their protection) and their tenants, began to exert pressure upon the kings. Military and executive powers were taken from the kings and given to elected magistrates drawn from the aristocratic faction. Eventually, the functions of the king were reduced to those connected with his high priestship; even the high priestship, in many cases, became elective. The *gerousia* was transformed into a council of the nobles and wielded most of the real political power; the councilors were usually the representatives of the most powerful clans. While the *gerousia* gained power, the *ecclesia* declined because fewer and fewer of the common people could afford to equip themselves for the army. Greek government thus changed from a limited monarchy to an oligarchy, a type of government in which only *the few* participate.

From monarchy to oligarchy

From this brief description of developments in Greece between 1200 and 750 B.C. it will be seen that the over-dependence upon agriculture and grazing which characterized Greek economy for four and one-half centuries was productive of dire results. With the steady decline in the fertility of the soil and the concentration of the best land in the hands of a few people, Greece was faced with the problem of over-population. The landless had no means of making a living, and the tenants were becoming little better than serfs. Even more serious was the fact that, as a result of the economic developments, the very group that had profited by the changes in land tenure, the nobles, was also in control of the government and the administration of justice. Naturally, the oligarchic aristocrats did not concern themselves with the problems of the masses until the latter became desperate and threatened revolution. Then, and then only, did the governing class begin to consider possible reforms.

The crisis of the eighth century B.C.

For the Greek reformers of the eighth century B.C. there were two possible solutions: (1) a redistribution of the land in order that the common people might be able to support themselves, or (2) a program of colonization in foreign lands

Possible means of reform

to relieve over-population in Greece. In most states the poverty of the soil made redistribution impractical; then, too, the aristocracy did not seriously contemplate sharing its wealth with the masses. Most of the Greek states therefore resorted to colonization.

Thus far we have considered only the history of the mainland Greeks; but before we can carry this account further, we must retrace our steps to observe the fate of the Greeks who had deserted the Greek peninsula for the coast of Asia Minor. The experience of the Asiatic Greeks in the period 1200-750 B.C. was much different from that of their peninsular cousins. Furthermore, it was the Asiatic Greeks who were able to supply the answer to the problem of over-population. **The Asiatic Greeks**

The Greeks who settled on the western coast of Asia Minor and on the adjacent Aegean islands were divided into three large linguistic groups. The southernmost Asiatic Greek settlements had been founded by peoples of Dorian **Dorians** stock who had crossed over from the Peloponnesus some time before 1000 B.C. North of the Dorians were the Ionians who were, perhaps, the descendants of the Achaeans or My- **Ionians** cenaeans; at least, they preserved some Mycenaean traditions in art and dress. Still farther north were the people who spoke the Aeolic Greek dialect. The Ionians and Aeolians **Aeolians** were groups which had been driven from their Greek homes by the Dorian invasion. City-states had been established by these Greeks in Asia Minor and the islands; among the Asiatic coast states were Ephesus, Miletus, and Halicarnassus, and in the islands were Mytilene, Chios, and Samos. After 800 B.C. these states engaged in increasing trade with the back country of Asia Minor and with Syria. When the rise of Assyria in the eighth century interfered with the commercial activities of the Phoenician cities, the Asiatic Greeks fell heir to the carrying trade which had been monopolized by the Phoenicians. Even before the decline of Phoenicia, as a matter of fact, trade had brought prosperity to the Asiatic Greeks. The growth of business encouraged the adoption of writing; an alphabet was borrowed from the Phoenicians and adapted to the Greek language. Increasing contacts with the Near East led to the borrowing of many other culture traits; the art, religion, and intellectual life of the Asiatic Greeks were greatly enriched by these new acquisitions. Naturally, the growth of culture among the Greeks in Asia Minor soon began to have an effect upon the people of mainland Greece; we shall return to this point later (see below, pp. 119 ff.).

One aspect of the commercial activity of the Asiatic Greeks was particularly significant: they began to follow the Phoenician custom of establishing trading posts or colonies. These trading posts were located on the coasts of backward cultural regions inhabited by non-Greeks, especially in the northeastern Aegean and the Black Sea. Some of the mainland Greek states on the eastern coast of Greece, or on islands near that coast, began to find similar ventures profitable—Corinth and Chalcis were outstanding examples.[2]

Trading posts

From the idea of the colony as a trading post it was only a step to the idea of the colony as a means of relief for overpopulation. Within a short time after the first colonial trading posts were established, the hard-pressed Greek mainland states began to send their surplus populations to new homes outside of Greece.

The great age of Greek colonization extended from 750 to 550 B.C. As we have seen, there were two main motives for colonization: (1) the establishment of commercial connections, and (2) the relief of over-population. The first motive was more common among the Asiatic Greeks and the states of the Greek mainland which had close connections with Asia Minor, whereas the second motive was characteristic of the colonizing activities of the majority of mainland Greeks. Colonies were established all around the Black Sea, along the passage between the Black Sea and the Aegean, on the northern Aegean coast, in Cyrene in Africa, in southern Italy, in Sicily, and in what is now southern France and northeastern Spain. Northern Africa (west of Cyrene) and southern Spain

Colonization

---

[2] Both Corinth and Chalcis soon extended their activities to the western Mediterranean also.

constituted a Phoenician sphere of influence which the Greeks were not allowed to penetrate. In central and northern Italy, the powerful Etruscans prevented the establishment of Greek colonies.

Ordinarily, the Greek colonies were harbor towns; few of the settlements were located at any distance from the coast. Plots of land were distributed among the colonists for culti- *The* vation, and trade was built up with the interior. The fact *colony* that the Greeks did not attempt to settle the back country made relations with the natives more cordial than would have been the case if extensive conquests had been attempted. The colonists rarely had close political connections with their mother city (the metropolis); instead, the settlers governed themselves. At first, their governments tended to be democratic rather than oligarchic; this is typical of a frontier society. Later, however, when the colonies became older and more mature, an unequal distribution of land and other forms of wealth paved the way for oligarchies, and there were bitter struggles between the rich and the poor.

The chief relations of a colony with its metropolis were of a commercial nature; naturally, there was also a close bond *Colony* of religion, custom, and sentiment between the colony and *and* the homeland. As a matter of fact, when the Greeks left the *metrop-* Aegean and came in contact with non-Greeks, obvious dif- *olis* ferences between Greek culture and language on the one hand, and that of the natives on the other, led to a feeling of "racial" unity among all Greeks no matter from what city they came. The Greeks called themselves Hellenes (Hellas was the Greek term for Greece itself); all non-Greeks were classed as barbarians, people whose language had a strange sound.

Through colonization the over-population of the Greek mainland was somewhat relieved. Moreover, the planting of *Effects* colonies had far-reaching economic effects. It was natural that *of colony* trade should be stimulated, but, in addition, many of the *planting* mainland states turned to manufacturing; this was also true of the Asiatic Greeks. Textiles, pottery, and metal work were

manufactured for the colonial market, and there was an increased demand for Greek wine and olive oil. The growing importance of trade and manufacturing led the mainland Greeks to adopt two new culture traits: writing and the use of money.[3]

Agricultural changes

The great landholders were pleased with the new economic developments. They began to concentrate on the production of olive oil and wine; they sold these commodities abroad, and bought foreign wheat and other foodstuffs at lower prices than they could afford to produce them at home. They invested their profits in trading and manufacturing ventures; they bought more land, or else lent money to the poor farmers and then took over the land when the farmers could not pay off their mortgages.

On the other hand, the small farmer found himself in an increasingly unfavorable position. He could not compete with the low prices of foreign foodstuffs. He had little or no legal defense against the encroachment of the politically powerful large landholder. The new money economy also

The small farmer

wrought hardships. Interest rates were high; 12 per cent interest was considered moderate in this period, and usually the rate was in excess of that figure. There is little question that the large landholders took advantage of the ignorance of the poor peasants and indulged in sharp practices when they lent money. The only security that the farmer could give for a loan was his land, or he could mortgage himself and his family; in the latter case, failure to pay the mortgage meant slavery. The farmers could not give up agriculture and become artisans because they had had no training. In many states in mainland Greece the majority of the artisans were Asiatic Greeks or foreign non-Greeks who had settled in the towns or who had been brought in as slaves to work in the shops.

As one might expect, the growth of trade and industry was accompanied by an increase in the size of the Greek cities. In the cities a class of business men and artisans began to appear.

[3] For the origin of money, see p. 25.

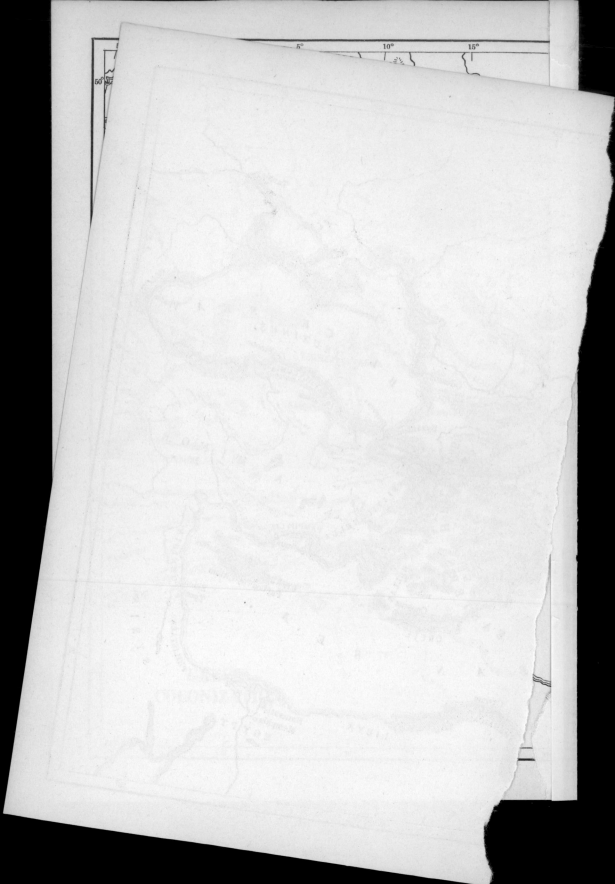

Many of the traders and manufacturers were wealthy; the A new middle class introduction of the money economy meant that land ceased to be the only source of wealth in Greece. The newly rich began to demand a voice in the government, and it was undoubtedly the business men who agitated for the codification of the law. Greek tradition has it that the common people wanted the law set down in writing, but it was the merchant and industrial group, rather than the masses, which was literate. The first Greek law codes date from the second half of the seventh century B.C.

The codification of the law, however, was not enough. The oligarchic forms of government were also attacked. The traders and artisans were wealthy enough to equip themselves with the heavy armor worn by the Greek infantry. Thus, they could serve in the army, and, according to traditional Greek practice, all those who served in the army were Timocracy eligible to take part in governmental affairs. The result was that oligarchy gave way to timocracy, a type of government in which the individual's participation varies in proportion to his wealth.

Nevertheless, there were few instances in which timocracies were established without revolution and bloodshed. In many cities there arose popular leaders who led the middle class, Tyrants or in some cases the masses, in rebellion against the aristocrats. Often these popular leaders themselves gained and held political control; these were the "tyrants." In those days the word tyrant did not have the harsh connotation that it now has. A tyrant was usually a kind of political boss who adhered strictly to the constitutional forms of his city-state; the tyrant rarely held any state office; he remained behind the scenes and directed operations through the duly elected magistrates who, he was careful to see, were his own henchmen. The general policy of the tyrants was to break the power of the aristocrats through confiscation and banishment, to foster trade by founding colonies and by making alliances with other states, and to alleviate the suffering of the masses by creating opportunities for work through large state building programs and by dividing the lands of the aristocrats among the poor agricultural population. The business men and small farmers acquiesced in the rule of the tyrants because of the numerous benefits which tyranny had to offer. Often when the tyrants seemed to have outlived their usefulness to the state, they would be overthrown by revolution; then timocracies would be established.

Tyrannies were common in Greece and Asia Minor during the seventh and sixth centuries B.C. There were tyrants, for example, at Corinth, Argos, Sicyon, Athens, Mitylene, Miletus, and Samos. Many of them were famous as patrons of art, literature, and learning. They attracted sculptors, poets, and philosophers to their cities because of the financial inducements they could offer.

The Greek Renaissance   The period from 750 to 500 B.C. is sometimes called the Greek Renaissance because of the cultural growth which took place in those two and one-half centuries. Our information about Greek political and military history in this age is more extensive than for the Dark Ages; Greek history may be said to begin with 750. In Greece the city-states which were most important were Argos, Aegina, Corinth, Megara, Sicyon, Chalcis, Thebes, Sparta, and Athens. Argos was strong in the eighth and seventh centuries; probably this was partly due to a survival of Mycenaean prestige; the rise of Corinth and Sparta in the sixth century brought a decline of Argive power. Aegina, Corinth, Megara, Sicyon, and Chalcis were great trading cities; their rise more or less paralleled that of the Asiatic Greek cities. The importance of Thebes was due to her hegemony of the cities of the Boeotian plain which made her a power in central Greece. The states about which we have the most information, however, are Sparta and Athens, whose influence, though not felt strongly in Greece until the sixth century, was to determine the course of Greek history in the classical period (the fifth and early fourth centuries). We shall therefore consider the rise of Athens and Sparta in some detail.

ATHENS

Archaeological investigation has disclosed that, although
Athens was one of the more important centers of the Mycenaean civilization, the city lost much of its early prestige
after the Dorian invasion and the coming of the Dark Ages. **Athens**
At the opening of the historic period (750 B.C.) Athens was **backward**
almost completely out of the main current of events in the
Greek world. She did not take part in the great movement
of colonization, nor were her people greatly affected by the
numerous foreign influences that produced such radical
changes in the more progressive Greek states at the beginning of the Greek Renaissance.

Although the geographic location of Athens would not
have prohibited her early participation in the trade and com- **Geographic**
merce of the Aegean, it is certain that several other Greek **location**
cities were in a much more favorable position. The island
city of Aegina, for example, commanded the entrance to
the Saronic Gulf and acted as a middleman for trade which
might have gone directly to Athens. Corinth in the Peloponnesus, later a bitter rival of Athens, was situated so as to control the western trade route through the Corinthian Gulf and
also serve as a terminus for goods from the East. Moreover,
Corinth had many colonies that naturally preferred to trade
with their mother city. As a result, Athens remained for
centuries a backward little country town, and the land of
Attica was devoted to agricultural pursuits. The indifference
of the Athenians to trade and commerce was shown by the
fact that they continued to use the open Bay of Phalerum
as a harbor until the fifth century, overlooking completely
the advantages of the Peiraeus, their natural seaport.

Attica was not a particularly rich agricultural region, but
it was not without other resources. Silver, for example, was **Resources**
to be found at Laurium. Moreover, there was an abundance
of good stone; the limestone of the Acropolis was used early
for building purposes, at a later date the Peiraic limestone
(poros) was quarried for the foundations of almost all the

great temples, and the marble of Mount Pentelicus was popular in the classical period. Nevertheless, before 550 B.C., the only natural resource extensively exploited by the Athenians was the excellent clay of Cape Kolias, far superior to any other in Greece. Most of the early pottery, however, was made for the home market; it did not play any considerable rôle in foreign trade until the Athenians fell into step with the rest of the Greek world. Until the middle of the sixth century B.C., the Athenian resources of stone, silver, and clay were only potential factors in the development of Athenian commerce and art.

Economic situation

At the opening of the sixth century B.C. the Athenians were faced with a situation which necessitated a radical departure from their traditional agricultural economy. Most of the arable land had become concentrated in the hands of a few families who by virtue of their wealth monopolized the government. A large majority of the once free population of Attica had been reduced to serfdom, and many of those who had escaped that harsh fate were without any means of sustenance. The soil had lost much of its former fertility, so that even if it had been distributed equally it would not have been capable of supporting the entire group.

Government

The evolution of Athenian government had been typical of a mainland Greek state. The original limited monarchy had been transformed into an oligarchy in which the aristocratic council (called the Areopagus) was all-powerful. The kingship had been abolished, and the functions of the king had been divided among annually elected magistrates who were, of course, members of the aristocratic group. In the last quarter of the seventh century Athenian law had been codified, but this afforded little relief for the economic situation.

Solon

The prospect of a civil war between the landed and the landless forced the upper class to seek a compromise. About 594 B.C. Solon, an aristocrat whom the common people trusted, was given power to make reforms that would relieve the tension. Solon devised a new constitution for Athens

which embodied political, judicial, and economic changes.
Oligarchy was exchanged for timocracy. The citizen body
was divided into four classes in which membership was determined by wealth. The richest citizens were enrolled in the   Timocracy
first two classes; they were eligible for election to the magistracies and for membership both in the old council of the
Areopagus and in the new council (the Council of the Four
Hundred) which Solon created.[4] The third census class set up
by Solon was likewise eligible for the Council of the Four
Hundred; members of this class, which might be called the
Athenian middle class, were also allowed to hold minor state
offices. The fourth class, the poor farmers and the city proletariat, had the right to participate with the other classes in
the *ecclesia*, the popular assembly, an elective and legislative
body. A huge tribunal, with a membership of 6000 citizens
drawn from all classes, was established as a supreme court
to consider appeals from the decisions of magistrates which
involved the death penalty or heavy fines.

Solon's economic reforms more than justified his reputation for sagacity and far-sightedness. He freed the debt slaves,
canceled the mortgages on their lands, and abolished the institution of debt slavery, but he realized that this was only the
first step in the economic rehabilitation of Attica. Mere
subsistence agriculture was no longer practical; Attica could
not be agriculturally self-sufficient,[5] and therefore it was necessary to find a way to purchase food from abroad. To this
end, Solon tried to build up exports which could be traded   Economic
to foreign countries in return for wheat and other agricul-   reforms
tural products. He saw that the land of Attica was one of the
few regions in Greece in which olive trees grew well. Therefore, he forbade the export of any farm products except
olive oil. Naturally, when the citizens realized that they

[4] The entire citizen body of Athens, like that of many other Greek states,
had long been divided into four groups called *phylai*, or tribes. In Solon's
new council each of the four tribes was represented by one hundred annually
elected councilors; thus the group was known as the Council of the Four
Hundred.

[5] Solon did try to increase agricultural production by introducing better
methods of farming.

would be allowed to export only olive oil, they concentrated upon olive culture with the result that Attica soon became a leading producer of olive oil, and those who possessed olive orchards enjoyed considerable prosperity. In addition, Solon encouraged the Athenians to turn from farming to the more profitable fields of commerce and industry. A law was enacted that no son who had not been taught a trade should be compelled to support his father, and Solon further stimulated the development of industry by offering citizenship to foreign artisans on condition that they settle permanently at Athens to ply their trades. The introduction of foreign artisans was helpful to the native Athenians because it enabled them to study the methods of the newcomers. The first major industry to develop at Athens was pottery-making; the growth in the manufacture of pottery paralleled the rise of Athenian exports of olive oil, for the oil was shipped in pottery containers. Last of all, it was Solon who instituted an Athenian system of coinage. Previously, the Athenians had used coins minted at Aegina. The creation of a local currency freed the country from the commercial domination of the more prosperous Aeginetans and assisted the development of Athenian trade with foreign countries.

Unfortunately, Solon's reforms only created new problems for the Athenians. No one was completely satisfied. The aristocrats thought that he had gone too far, whereas the common people were of the opinion that he had not gone far enough. The next quarter of a century was a period of political instability and occasional anarchy. By 560 B.C. three factions were engaged in a battle for the control of the Athenian government: the landed aristocrats continued to form a powerful group; opposed to them were the owners of small unproductive farms and those citizens who were still without land; a third party, composed of the new group of artisans and traders brought into existence by the commercial expansion of Athens, was also making a strong bid for a share in the government. The second faction—the poor citizens—

Party strife

was by far the largest, and it secured the most able leader, Peisistratus, son of Hippocrates.

Three times between 560 and 545 B.C. Peisistratus attempted to overthrow the government. When his third attempt met with success, he became the virtual head of the Athenian state, although he held no office except the unofficial one of tyrant. This position of supremacy Peisistratus retained until his death in 527, after which his sons, Hippias and Hipparchus, succeeded him. Hipparchus was assassinated in 514 B.C., and Hippias was finally driven from Athens by a popular uprising about 510 which brought the tyranny to an end and paved the way for the establishment of democratic government.

Peisistratus

It must not be thought that the period from 545 to 510 B.C. in Athens—the Age of the Tyrants—was characterized by repression and brutality. On the contrary, Peisistratus himself proved to be a benevolent despot who was able to solve most of the economic problems that beset Attica. By giving the Athenians a stable government and freedom from internal strife he made it possible for them to follow along the lines of commercial and industrial development already marked out by Solon. Peisistratus continued to encourage the production of olive oil (and also wine) which could be traded abroad for wheat, and he reformed the Solonian currency so that it was even better adapted for foreign trade. There is little doubt that the business men, many of whom were foreign-born, soon came to support Peisistratus when they saw that he was breaking down the traditional Athenian policy of isolation by making political alliances with foreign powers which were proving decidedly helpful to foreign trade. Peisistratus performed another valuable service to Athens when he broke the power of the landed aristocrats by wholesale banishments and confiscations; by giving many of the confiscated lands to poor citizens, he retained the enthusiastic support of his proletarian followers.

The Age of the Tyrants

In the second half of the sixth century B.C. Athens was more prosperous than she had been for seven hundred years.

Prosperity

Athenian olive oil, wine, and honey were exported to all parts of the ancient Mediterranean world. Since these products were, as we have seen, shipped in Athenian pottery containers, the distribution and quantity of this pottery in foreign lands serves as an index to the volume of Athenian trade. The quality of the Athenian pottery was so superior to that of other cities that it was soon in great demand, and the Athenian potters capitalized upon the popularity of their wares by producing many different types of vases for this new foreign market.

Pottery

We are better informed about the Athenian potters and their work than we are about any of the other craftsmen of Athens. The products of the metal and textile workers have long since disappeared, but the pottery provides evidence which was not destroyed so easily. Moreover, it was in their pottery that the Athenians first developed a style of art that could be called distinctive of their city. The Attic black-figured style of vase painting is contemporary with the Age of the Tyrants, and thus the effect of the great prosperity and commercial expansion of Athens upon the pottery industry is very clear. With an incentive to make pottery, it was inevitable that the Athenians should excel the other Greeks in this art, since, as we have noted, the Athenians had the best clay in Greece at their disposal.

Building program

The sixth century also saw the beginning of an interest in the major arts at Athens. In order to divert the minds of the citizen body from his tyranny Peisistratus embarked upon an extensive program of public works; as a result, the appearance of Athens was greatly improved. An aqueduct and a public fountain were built; a propylum or gateway was constructed at the entrance to the Acropolis. Down in the southeastern part of the city work was begun on a gigantic temple of Zeus; this project was not completed until seven centuries later.

Foreign artists

The important thing for us to note, however, is that these artistic projects were carried out under the supervision of foreigners, principally Ionians from Asia Minor and the

Aegean islands. Sculptors from the island of Chios dominated
the scene at Athens in the Age of the Tyrants; there was no
real native Athenian school of sculpture, and those who
aspired to become artists copied the Chian style.

The tyranny of Peisistratus and his sons gave Athens her
start on the road to political, economic, and artistic greatness,
and when Hippias was expelled in 510 B.C. the movement
which his family had begun went on of its own accord. It is
possible that his flight led to an exodus of the foreign artists.
At any rate, by 500 B.C. the Athenian sculptors had freed
themselves from the Chian influence and had gone a long
way toward evolving a distinctive Athenian style. It was
probably not a coincidence that Antenor, the first noted
Athenian sculptor, produced as one of his early great works
the statues of the Tyrannicides, Harmodius and Aristogeiton,
the patriots who killed Hipparchus and made the position
of Hippias insecure.

Conditions at Athens were very unsettled for about two
years after the expulsion of Hippias. The aristocrats made
an effort to regain control by calling in aid from Sparta, but
their designs were thwarted by the popular leader Cleisthenes
(who was himself an aristocrat). Once in power, Cleisthenes **Cleisthenes**
instituted new reforms at Athens. In principle, he upheld the
Solonian timocracy, but he made certain changes in it. The
traditional four tribes were deprived of their political significance, and ten new tribes were created with the object
of breaking up old geographic and party groupings; the new
tribes were also made the basis for a military reorganization.
Each of the ten tribes now elected a general who took charge
of the tribal military contingent, and from each of the tribes
were chosen fifty councilors who participated in a new council—the Council of the Five Hundred, or the *boule*—which
replaced the Solonian Council of the Four Hundred. The
Athenian people as a whole were also given a means of controlling state policy through the establishment of a new institution called ostracism. In any given year, if it seemed advisable, the Athenians might go to the polls to cast their

ballots for the man considered "most dangerous to the state." The winner of this—we might say—*un*-popularity contest had to leave Athens and go into exile. The Athenian ostracism was the reverse of the modern vote of confidence, but it served its end equally well.

Summary

This was the political evolution of Athens in the sixth century. The Athenian government, through the work of Solon, Peisistratus, and Cleisthenes, followed a course which was to lead in the fifth century to democracy. Solon substituted timocracy for oligarchy; Peisistratus strengthened the middle class by attacking the aristocrats and fostering Athenian trade and industry; Cleisthenes weakened old traditions and factions, and also gave the Athenian masses a powerful weapon, ostracism.

SPARTA

Early history

Sparta, which was to become the principal state in the Peloponnesus in the sixth century, boasted an unusual history. Down to the last half of the seventh century, the growth of Sparta was much like that of other mainland states. The region of Laconia, in which Sparta was located, had been fairly prominent in Mycenaean times. Probably even before the Dorian invasion much of the pre-Greek population had been reduced to a status of agricultural serfdom, a process which the Dorians completed. Sparta was a town formed by a union of five villages in the Dark Ages. It was the center of a fertile agricultural region; nature had also provided iron deposits, good clay, and an abundance of building stone. The people of Laconia exported their iron and their pottery; the Laconian pottery was popular with the Greeks in Cyrene who traded their silphium and other products in return for it.

Political evolution

Early Spartan political and economic evolution was typical. The landed aristocracy became very powerful and dominated the council. The kingship was not abolished, but, probably as a compromise measure to satisfy one particularly powerful clan, a second royal family was added to the one already in existence. Thus Sparta had two kings, one from each of these families, and in this way a kind of collegiate magistracy came into being. One king acted as a check upon the other.

Just before the extension of Spartan commercial relations took place at the end of the eighth century B.C., the Spartan aristocrats invaded the country of Messenia which lay to the west, divided up the agricultural land, and made serfs of the inhabitants. About 650 B.C., however, the Messenians revolted, drove out their Spartan overlords, and invaded Laconia itself.

The Messenian revolt precipitated a crisis in which the very existence of Sparta was at stake. Complete destruction was averted only when the Spartan aristocrats called upon the common people for aid. The Messenians were then defeated and reduced to their former position of servitude. Nevertheless, the Spartan nobles paid dearly for their victory, for the commons demanded sweeping reforms which included a redistribution of wealth and more popular participation in the government. *Messenian revolt*

Accordingly, a settlement was made, and a new system was instituted at Sparta. The object of the system was to preserve the *status quo*; this involved both the situation as regards the equal distribution of wealth and also the position of the subject population. To achieve the first end, private ownership of land was abolished; the land belonged to the state, and each Spartan citizen was given a plot for his support. This land was worked by a number of serfs (helots); the citizen himself was free to devote his time to civic duties. *The Spartan system*

The civic duties of the Spartan were largely military. The helots of Laconia and Messenia outnumbered the Spartans at least ten to one. To keep them in subjection it was necessary for Sparta to become an armed camp. Beginning at the age of seven the Spartan males were trained as soldiers. Strict standards of discipline and physical perfection were maintained. Newborn children who were in any way deformed were destroyed. The Spartan girls as well as the boys were given physical training in order that they might bear healthy children. Comfort and luxury were forbidden. The *Spartan training*

Spartan boys were not allowed to wear shoes; they had only one garment for both winter and summer so that their powers of endurance would be developed; they were deprived of sufficient food and were expected to steal from the helots to learn resourcefulness. Dancing and sports were emphasized because they fostered muscular coordination. The Spartans thus became the best soldiers in Greece, but their intellectual and cultural development ceased completely. Trade declined; as a matter of fact, money, or even the possession of silver and gold, was forbidden the citizens.

Helots

Not only were the helots held in check by the military machine, but there was also a secret police force which spied upon them continually. Any helot who showed a spirit of independence was immediately assassinated. Every year a declaration of war was issued against the helots so that any Spartan could legally slay an obstreperous serf. The helots could not escape, for around the territory in which they lived was a ring of communities inhabited by a population (also subject to the Spartans) known as the *perioeci*. The *perioeci* had their own local governments and were allowed to engage in trade; but their foreign relations were controlled by Sparta, and they were expected to furnish contingents for the army.

Perioeci

Peloponnesian League

Control of the internal situation in Laconia and Messenia was not enough, however, to preserve the *status quo* in Sparta. Some of the other states of the Peloponnesus feared the growth of Spartan power. It was essential that Sparta dominate the Peloponnesus because an attack upon Sparta by a hostile state might precipitate a helot revolt. Argos was Sparta's principal rival, and, in order to prevent the Argives from becoming dangerous the Spartans (in the sixth century) built up a confederation called the Peloponnesian League which included all the states of the Peloponnesus except Argos and a few cities along the Corinthian Gulf. The rich and powerful city of Corinth, of course, was only too glad to find an ally to side with her against Argos.

The Spartan governmental organization was unique. The

two kings were retained, and the council continued to be the **Government** monopoly of the old aristocratic clans. The popular assembly, however, had the power to elect five magistrates called *ephors* (overseers) who kept close watch over the kings. Two of the *ephors* always accompanied the kings when a military campaign was conducted outside of the country; the *ephors* could fine the kings or force them to abdicate in favor of other members of the royal families. The *ephors* also watched over public morals, presided at the meetings of the council and assembly, and acted as judges.

It is easy to see why progressive Athens and reactionary Sparta were to become rivals in the fifth century. The Spartans always favored oligarchic governments, whereas the Athenians, menaced by oligarchic jealousy, were willing to aid in the establishment of more democratic governments in Greece. Then, too, the trade rivalry between Athens and the Spartan ally, Corinth, was another source of discord. Thus the seeds were sown for the bitter struggle that was to ruin Athens, Sparta, and many of the other Greek states and finally to bring an end to Greek independence.

THE CULTURE OF ARCHAIC GREECE

The increasing complexity of Greek economic and social life which was evident from the late Dark Ages (850 B.C.) on was accompanied by the rise of Greek art, literature, and **Archaic Period** philosophy. The art of the Greek Renaissance (750-500 B.C.) is often called archaic, and there is no reason why we cannot apply the same term to all the cultural aspects of the period. Thus, we may refer to the Greek Renaissance as the Archaic Period of Greek history.

No thinking person would ever insist that "history repeats itself"; yet it is clear that we can draw certain parallels be- **Parallels with the history of the Near East** tween the rise of civilization in the Near East and that in Greece. If we call the Dark Ages the Greek Age of Agriculture, we cannot but see that the rise of trade and industry at the end of the Dark Ages brought Greece into an Age of Civilization which began with the Archaic Period. The growth of cities, the introduction of slavery, the adoption of writing (which led to the development of literature), and the rapid evolution of architecture, sculpture, and painting in Greece all have counterparts in the cultural history of the Near East.

Indebtedness to the Near East

At the same time, it is necessary to emphasize the extent to which the Greeks were indebted to the Near East. We shall have occasion to observe many instances in which cultural items borrowed from the Near East played an important part in the foundation of Greek art, religion, philosophy, science, and literature. The cultural effects of the unification of the Near East by Assyria were certainly felt in Greece as well as in the Near East. Moreover, cultural diffusion was one of the important results of the commercial activities of the Phoenicians; and the Greeks, through their overland trade with Mesopotamia and their direct sea trade with Egypt and Syria, were able to learn much from the inhabitants of those lands.

In our discussion of the culture of the Archaic Period we may well begin with Greek religion, since that particular phase of Greek life was closely connected with (and provided a stimulus or a starting point for) art, literature, and philosophy.

GREEK RELIGION

It is difficult to present a simple picture of Greek religion; the whole subject is tremendously complicated because of the many elements which the Greeks borrowed from other peoples and because there were innumerable variations of worship and religious practice among the several Greek states. In the Dark Ages Greek religion was a combination of elements imported into Greece by the Greeks themselves and of various features of the religion of the Neolithic inhabitants and the Minoans. In the period of the Greek Renaissance, there were borrowings from the religions of the Near East. In Greek religion there was an ancient and underlying substratum of totemism, animism, and magic which the anthropomorphism of the later Dark Ages failed to conceal.

Totemism

Undoubtedly the owl of Athena, the eagle of Zeus, and the other companions of the classic Greek deities had once been worshiped as divinities. Early animistic beliefs, to quote only **Animism** a few examples, would account for the sacred groves, springs, and rivers to which many references are made in Greek literature. Anthropomorphism, however, had produced a goddess, Athena, whose familiar was an owl; it was responsible for the river gods, the nymphs, and the dryads. Sympathetic magic pervaded Greek ritual and ceremony. The Greeks be- **Magic** lieved that man might coerce or supplicate the gods; he might also make a contract with them, and if he kept his part of the bargain, the gods must do likewise. Sacrifices were pleasing to the Olympians; to them were dedicated the first fruits of the harvest. The gods also looked with favor upon athletic contests and upon literary competitions.

The Greeks seem to have carried polytheism to extremes. The individual had his own personal gods; the farmer, the herdsman, the artisan, and the sailor looked to certain deities for aid. The family had its protecting spirits of the hearth **Polytheism** and the doorway; births, marriages, and funerals were accompanied by domestic rituals. There was also the state religion; each city had its own peculiar god or gods whose worship was the subject of public festivals and ceremonies. Although the Greeks never questioned the power or the existence of foreign gods (the gods of the barbarians), certain deities were nevertheless recognized as belonging especially to all the Hellenes or Greeks. Zeus, Apollo, Hera, Artemis, Athena, and the other Olympians were thought of as Greek gods. The festivals and games in honor of Zeus at Olympia, Apollo at Delphi, and Poseidon at Corinth were attended by Greeks from every state; in other words, they were Pan-Hellenic.

The Greeks practiced divination. They sought to interpret dreams and the flight of birds. A favorite means of foretelling **Divina-** the future was to examine the entrails of animals and fowls; **tion** this custom the Greeks had borrowed from the people of the ancient Near East. There were also centers of prophecy where oracles inspired by the gods gave answers to those who sought advice regarding future conduct. Most famous and least fallible was the oracle of Apollo at Delphi. There the priestess, the Pythia, transmitted the god's messages to Greeks and non-Greeks who came from far and wide to obtain a glimpse into the future.

The Greeks, like other people, sought immortality. Their ancient cults—those of the state, the crafts, or the home—did not offer them hope of everlasting life, and therefore they turned to a new cult which was imported from the Near East. The wine and fertility god, Dionysus, became the Greek counterpart of the Mesopotamian Tammuz and the Egyptian Osiris. According to legend, Dionysus had been slain, yet he had risen from the dead and had gained immortality. The rites of the Dionysiac worship were wild revels that took place at night deep in the forests. Dancing to the accompaniment of drums and cymbals, the devotees of the god worked themselves into a frenzy. In their emotional intoxication they seemed to gain the immortality of the god himself. The worship of Dionysus was transformed into a disciplined religion by the followers of the legendary poet and musician, Orpheus. They devised sacred writings, prophecies, and hymns which were transmitted to their converts after impressive rites of initiation. The Orphic theology was based on the idea that a man's body was the prison of his soul, that the soul was being punished for sin in a previous existence. By pure living after initiation, the soul might be cleansed and liberated for eternal happiness.

Immortality

Orphism

Religion in Greece, as in every other ancient land, was all-pervasive. Certain conditions in Greece, as we shall see, made religion the source of the artistic and intellectual activities for which the Greeks became famous.

Along with the religion of the Greeks went their mythology. The primary purpose of a myth is to offer an explanation to questions that naturally arise concerning the gods, the universe as a whole, and even man himself. We have already had occasion to observe the comprehensive supernaturalism which pervaded primitive society everywhere;

Myths

thus, when a question admitted of no obvious answer, the reply which one received usually involved an explanation in terms of the supernatural. A myth is an hypothesis; in ancient times it occupied the place now held by modern scientific explanations and theories. Each of the Greek states, as might be expected, had its own collection of local myths; but a "national" mythology for all Greeks was provided by the Homeric poems and the works of Hesiod (see below, p. 125).

PHILOSOPHY

The making of myths was the first intellectual occupation of the Greeks, and Greek philosophy was the descendant of mythology. In its first stages Greek philosophy was an attempt to explain the universe without recourse to supernaturalism. It cannot be emphasized too strongly that this early philosophy was not an independent development; it drew its inspiration from ideas and theories already present in Greek mythology and from hypotheses of the same nature as those which were part of the religions of the Near East. It was no coincidence that Greek philosophy arose in Asia Minor at a time when there were increasing contacts with Egypt, Syria, and Mesopotamia. Then, too, the adoption of writing which had occurred only a century before (c. 750 B.C.) now made it possible to express abstract ideas that could not have been adequately developed through oral intercourse.

Origins of philosophy

The first of the Greek philosophers was Thales of Miletus, who lived at the beginning of the sixth century B.C. Thales was interested in mathematics, astronomy, and physics; he owed the fundamentals of his knowledge to the Egyptians and Babylonians with whose scientific learning he was well acquainted. He tried to explain the universe in terms of a basic element, water, by expounding the theory that water was the source of all other matter. Thales envisioned the earth as a flat disk floating on water, and he also thought that the sky was enveloped by water. There is marked similarity between this concept of the universe and that of the Babylonians, who thought that the earth and the sky were composed of the two

Thales

halves of the body of Tiamat and that there was water both below the earth and above the sky (see above, p. 81). The hypothesis of Thales was likewise very close to the explanation of the universe offered in the theology of the Orphic cult:

"In the beginning there was a primal undifferentiated unity, called by the Orphics 'Night.' Within this unity the World Egg was generated, or, according to some accounts, fashioned by Ageless Time (*Chronos*). The Egg divided into two halves, Heaven and Earth. . . . In physical terms, the upper half of the Egg forms the dome of the sky, the lower contains the moisture or slime from which the dry land (Earth) arose."[6]

Anaximander, the successor of Thales, denied that water was the prime element; instead, he postulated some undefined material which he called "the unlimited." The universe evolved out of the separation of opposites in which "the Hot" moved outward away from, and "the Cold" moved inward toward, a central nucleus. Since, under this theory, the points farthest from the earth possessed the highest temperatures, it was natural to suppose that the sky was surrounded by a sphere of flame. A second pair of opposites was produced when the fires of heaven dried the earth; thus, land and water, "Dry" and "Wet," came into being. Anaximander believed that:

"The elements . . . encroach and prey upon one another. The Hot draws up moisture to feed the heavenly fires, and the cold earth, in its turn, claims warmth and rain. . . . The first living things were generated out of moisture evaporated by the sun. Man, like the other animals, must have been a fish-like creature, which later took to the land. This traffic of the elements was to Anaximander the work of 'injustice,' of encroachment and self-assertion on the part of hostile 'opposites.' "[7]

Again it is possible to see the parallels between the Orphic

6 *Cambridge Ancient History*, Vol. IV, p. 536.
7 *Ibid.*, Vol. IV, pp. 540-541.

cosmogony and philosophical speculation. Night, Chaos, and the Unlimited are the same in principle; Tiamat, the World Egg, and Hot and Cold all form heaven and earth by the process of separation; and the sundered opposites then reunite to generate life. Moreover, all this dualism reminds one strongly of the contemporary theology of the Persian Zoroaster with its emphasis upon the war between light and darkness, truth and falsehood, and good and evil (see above, p. 79).

A third philosopher, also like Thales and Anaximander an inhabitant of Miletus, was Anaximenes. He identified the Unlimited with air, and he held that the thinning or thickening of the air produced all visible forms. This was really the starting point in the evolution of an atomic theory which became popular at a later time. **Anaximenes**

A school of philosophy more religious and mystical than that of the Milesians was founded by Pythagoras of Samos, who established himself in southern Italy in the latter half of the sixth century B.C. Pythagoras was a mathematician who came to believe in the divinity of numbers and the transmigration of souls. The members of the cult-society which he established ate only certain foods and wore only linen. Through purification and contemplation, "by following God," man might free his soul from his body, and his soul would become immortal. **Pythagoras**

It is easy to see the similarity of Pythagorean and Orphic beliefs. The Pythagoreans also stressed the conflict of good and evil, and light and darkness, just as Zoroaster had done.

LITERATURE

The earliest literature of the Greeks was in the form of epics and sagas dealing with the deeds of the Achaeans, the great heroes of the Mycenaean age. These sagas were transmitted orally by the *rhapsodes*, the singers of the Dark Ages. It was probably in the ninth century B.C. that an Asiatic Greek poet, Homer, composed the famous Iliad. The Iliad, like many of the other sagas, has as its background the siege **Homer**

of Troy, but its principal subject is the "Wrath of Achilles."
It is possible that Homer was also the author of the Odyssey,
the story of the wanderings of Odysseus, although there are
many indications that the Odyssey is the product of a period
somewhat later than that of the Iliad. Both the Iliad and the
Odyssey are valuable sources on the social and governmental
institutions of the Greek Dark Ages.

About 800 B.C. another poet, Hesiod, whose father had
migrated from Asia Minor to Boeotia, produced two long
poems, the "Works and Days" and the "Theogony." The
Hesiod   "Works and Days" is a didactic poem addressed to Hesiod's
brother, Perses. Hesiod emphasizes the value of hard work;
he feels that farming is the best occupation, and his prefer-
ence reflects the rural point of view of agricultural Boeotia.
The "Works and Days" contains detailed information for the
successful management of a farm; in addition, Hesiod gives
certain precepts for conduct, and he lists religious prohibi-
tions or taboos and lucky and unlucky days of the month.
Justice, neighborliness, industry, and fair dealing are the
chief virtues in his moral code.

The "Theogony" provides a genealogy of the gods. Hesiod's
account of the creation of the world has a familiar ring: "First
was created Chaos . . . then broad-bosomed Earth . . . and
Earth first bore the starry Heaven . . . that he might cover
her."

Like the Iliad and the Odyssey, the poems of Hesiod portray life in the Greek Dark Ages. His verses describe Greece
in the transition period just before the historic era dawns.
In them we see the specialization of labor which has taken
place even in backward Boeotia, and we can also see how
the landed nobility have risen to a position of political influence and how they control the administration of justice.

The Greeks of the historic period held Homer and Hesiod
in high esteem. Their poems were committed to memory by
educated people and were quoted when questions concerning
theology or morality arose. It has been well said that Homer
and Hesiod provided the Greeks with a bible, for these two

poets formulated concepts of the gods and set up standards of behavior which were accepted by the Greeks of every city.

Homer and Hesiod were the greatest poets of the Dark Ages, but they were not the only ones. Other Greeks composed epic poems and "Homeric Hymns," although their verses survive today only in fragmentary form.

The opening of the historic period was marked, as we have seen, with a quickening of the tempo of Greek life and an increasing complexity of political, social, and economic organization. These developments, together with the introduction of writing, were productive of changes in Greek literature. The epic style of Homer and Hesiod and their simple hexameter verse were largely replaced by new forms and meters. The poets turned to the elegy, the iambic, and the personal and choral lyric. **New poetic forms**

The recitation of an elegy was often made to the accompaniment of a reed pipe or a flute; the elegaic form could be employed for many purposes. In the seventh century B.C. Callinus of Ephesus wrote martial elegies to inspire the Asiatic Greeks in their struggle with the invading Cimmerians; Tyrtaeus likewise roused the Spartans who participated in putting down the Messenian revolt. Solon's elegies embodied his ideas for reforms at Athens, whereas Theognis of Megara used similar forms to vent his political hatred upon tyrants and the proletariat; Mimnermus of Ionia wrote love elegies. The sharper iambic verse was well suited to satire; it was employed by the famous soldier of fortune, Archilochus of Paros, and the later and more philosophic Simonides of Amorgos. **The elegy** **Iambic**

The lyric was sung to the accompaniment of a lyre or cithara. Alcaeus and Sappho of Lesbos, who lived in the sixth century, were two of the foremost exponents of the personal lyric. The lyric was well adapted to the expression of emotional states, especially love. Another Ionian, Anacreon of Teos, was famous for odes which dealt chiefly with the themes of love and wine. **The personal lyric**

The choral lyric was employed for religious purposes when

groups of trained singers sang marriage, processional, or victory hymns; there were also funeral dirges. An Asiatic **Choral** Greek named Alcman was famous in the seventh century for **lyric** the choral works he composed at Sparta.

The earliest prose writers appeared in the sixth century. Many composed genealogies of the gods and men, the first form of historical writing in which the Greeks engaged; these writers were called the *logographoi*. Hecataeus of Miletus **Prose** wrote the first Greek treatise on geography in which he described the world as he knew it. It is possible that Aesop's Fables also date from the sixth century.

From this brief survey of the philosophy and literature of the Archaic Period, it will be seen that the Asiatic Greeks surpassed all others in numbers and activity in these fields. This was due partly to their proximity to the Near East and partly to the favorable economic conditions which existed in Asia Minor during the eighth, seventh, and early sixth centuries. The conquest of Lydia and the Greek coastal cities by Persia, however, forced many Greeks to migrate to the Greek mainland and the Western Mediterranean. They naturally carried their culture and their ideas with them, with the result that they stimulated cultural activity among the Greeks of the mainland and the west. Thus, in the fifth and fourth centuries, Greece, southern Italy, and Sicily became the centers of cultural growth.

ARCHAIC ART

The religious life of the Greeks provided the main stimu-**Religion** lus for the development of their architecture and sculpture. **and art** The temple was the first and most important type of building to be devised by the Greeks of the Archaic Period, and their first sculptural efforts were devoted to cult statues. Thus, in a general way, the history of the development of art in Greece parallels that of the Near East.

The first Greek temples were wood and mud brick structures erected to shelter cult statues from the elements. Their plan resembled very closely that of the Mycenaean megaron

with its portico leading into a square or rectangular chamber. Temples
From these simple origins more complex arrangements were
developed. Columns were added to the façade of the portico;
the portico was sometimes duplicated at the rear of the

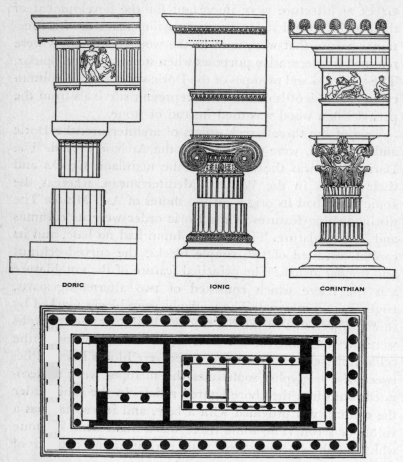

DORIC   IONIC   CORINTHIAN

CHART V.—Top figure: The Greek Orders of Architecture (courtesy, University Prints); lower: The Ground Plan of the Parthenon (from Robb and Garrison, *Art in the Western World*, Harper & Brothers).

temple; later, the inner chamber might be subdivided into a
number of rooms, and the temple might be given a colon-
nade which ran around the four sides (see chart V). In the
seventh century stone began to supplant the earlier wood

and mud brick materials; limestone, and finally marble, came into use. The Greeks, who like the Egyptians had plenty of good stone, preferred to use the column and lintel rather than the arch. Nevertheless, the wooden origins of Greek architecture were important for the development of their architectural styles, because various features of a functional nature that were used in the wooden buildings were retained for decorative purposes when stone became popular. The triglyphs and metopes of the Doric style, and the column capitals and dentils of the Ionic represent survivals from the period when wood was used instead of stone.

Two of the three Greek orders of architecture, the Doric and the Ionic, were developed in the Archaic Period. The Doric order was the product of the mainland Greeks and their fellows in the Western Mediterranean, whereas the Ionic order had its origin on the shores of Asia Minor. The distinguishing features of the Doric order were its columns and its entablature. The Doric column had no base, and its capital consisted of two simple blocks: the curved echinus and the flat abacus. The principal feature of the entablature was the frieze which consisted of two alternating parts, triglyphs and metopes. The triglyphs were blocks marked by three projections; in the old wooden buildings the triglyphs were the sheathing for the ends of the ceiling beams of the cella (inner chamber). The metopes were blocks inserted between the triglyphs; sometimes the metopes were undecorated, but often they bore figured reliefs. In the Ionic order the column was provided with a base, and its capital was a volute or scroll. The Ionic frieze was a plain band of stone which might be decorated with a continuous pattern of reliefs.

The roofs of the Greek temples were sloping, and they were covered with terra cotta tiles. Bright colors, principally red and blue, were often applied to the exteriors to make a contrast with the white marble. Beneath the gabled roof of the façade of the Greek temple was a triangular space formed by the two raking cornices (the lines of the roof) and the horizontal cornice; this was the pediment which, in the Doric order, was often embellished with sculpture in the round.

In the Archaic Period some rather large temples were constructed. The Ionic temple of Artemis at Ephesus was especially impressive, and in Sicily and southern Italy a number of huge Doric temples were built. The temple of Olympian Zeus which Peisistratus planned to construct at Athens would have equaled these in size.

The Greek sculptors employed wood, limestone, marble, ivory, and various metals, principally bronze. Both solid and hollow casting of metals became common in the Archaic Period; a technique for hollow casting was developed in the sixth century. Decorative sculpture advanced with the evolu- Sculpture tion of temple architecture, whereas substantive sculpture (sculpture in the round) evolved from the demands for cult statues and for statues of victorious athletes. Three main types of figures were produced over and over again by the early artists: the *kouros*, a nude standing male figure which might represent a god or an athlete; the *kore*, a draped standing female figure representing a goddess; and, finally, draped seated male or female figures which represented gods or goddesses. This repetition of types was important because continuous practice with a limited number of subjects made for mastery of material and gradual improvement of technique. The first statues were crude and stiff; the use of the law of frontality was reminiscent of Egyptian practice, for undoubtedly the Greek sculptors owed much to the Egyptians. Eventually, the Greek artists broke away from the bonds of convention; their work began to show close observation of anatomy, and they began to portray drapery in a more realistic fashion.

The Asiatic Greeks were most proficient in the making of female figures. A distinctive style, characterized by a careful attention to detail, was developed by the sculptors of Chios; Styles their female figures had oblique eyes, and the lips were curved in a pleasant but vacuous smile. The artists of the

Peloponnesus specialized in athletic figures which were generally short and stocky.

Stone sculpture was colored with red, blue, brown, and black. Bronze statues were often given eyes of paste or colored stone to make their appearance more lifelike. Sometimes the bronze figures were gilded.

We do not know much about early Greek painting because no examples of it have survived. There seems to have been a continuation or a revival of the Minoan-Mycenaean tradition of mural frescoes, and the literary sources tell us that a certain Kimon of Kleonai (*c.* 500 B.C.) invented foreshorten-

Painting ing and paid much attention to the portrayal of anatomy and drapery. It is possible to gain some idea of the progress of painting by observing the advances that were made in contemporary vase painting; for here an absorbing interest in anatomy and drapery is evident during the last quarter of the sixth century.

It would not be entirely inaccurate to say that vase painting was one of the major arts of Archaic Greece. A number of cities developed distinctive styles of decoration, but the

Vases best work, from about 550 onward, was done at Athens. The Attic black-figured style consisted of black silhouettes painted against the natural red background of the baked clay; interior details were indicated by incised lines filled with white. After about 520 B.C. the Attic red-figured style became popular; in this the background was covered with a black glaze and the figures were produced by an outline technique in which brownish lines were applied to the red clay. Many of the potters and vase painters signed their names to vases which they considered especially fine work. The names of more than fifty artists who made the black-figured ware are known, and the names of the red-figured artists are even more numerous.

Amazing as the developments in Archaic philosophy, literature, and art may seem, they constituted only a promise of the things that the Greeks were to accomplish later.

CHAPTER VI

GREEK CIVILIZATION (500-362 B.C.)

In the period between 500 and 362 B.C. the city-state civilization of Greece attained its fullest development. The Athenians of the fifth century were able to create the democracy for which the sixth-century reforms of Solon, Peisistratus, and Cleisthenes had paved the way; Greek art, literature, and philosophy rose to new heights. Nevertheless, we shall see that by 362 B.C. the city-state, as a dominant political institution, was on the decline, although the civilization which it had made possible was facing an even more brilliant future.

The fifth century opened with an invasion of Greece by the Persians. For two decades the independence of Greece hung in the balance, but the Greeks, united under the leadership of Sparta and Athens, finally managed to repel the invaders. After the great victories which removed the Persian threat to mainland Greece, the Spartans, whose domestic situation did not permit an aggressive foreign policy, resigned their hegemony in favor of the Athenians. The latter then formed a league of maritime Greek states with the object of carrying the war into Asia Minor and freeing the Asiatic Greeks from the Persian yoke. Shortly before the middle of the fifth century, the Athenians took steps to reduce their allies to the position of subjects. The result was the creation of a fairly large Aegean empire with its capital at Athens; the economic benefits that accrued from the empire made possible Athenian democracy and the flowering of Athenian culture. The Spartans, however, were drawn once more into Greek politics by the demands of their more commercially-minded allies whose prosperity was being undermined by Athenian economic imperialism. Sparta and her allies on the one side, and Athens and her empire on the

133

other, engaged in a series of conflicts which were brought to a conclusion with the complete collapse of Athens at the end of the fifth century. After this, the Spartans, partly because they had become imperialists and partly as an extension of their sixth-century Peloponnesian policy, began to force their rule upon all of Greece. The movement of reaction against Sparta was led by Athens and Thebes; by 370 B.C. Spartan power had been broken, and during the next eight years a Theban imperialist movement also rose and collapsed. By 362 B.C. all traces of Greek unity had vanished, and there was no Greek state powerful enough to force unification upon the others. As a result, the exhausted Greeks fell easy prey to the newly risen Macedonian kingdom of the north.

The numerous conflicts of the period summarized above were caused partly by the traditional separatism and desire for local independence that were the heritage of the Dark **Causes** Ages, but more fundamental issues were involved. The capi- **of Greek** talist system had produced within each city-state an antag- **discord** onism between the wealthy minority which held most of the agricultural and industrial property and the poverty-stricken masses who agitated for a redistribution of land and other forms of wealth. Overlying this economic conflict was a corresponding battle between two political philosophies: oligarchy and democracy. The rich naturally favored a restriction of the franchise, whereas the poor desired greater participation in the government in order that they might gain their economic ends. These party struggles disrupted domestic peace and often cut across city-state lines, for the oligarchs or the democrats of one city often aided the members of the corresponding party in another city. Thus, civil wars frequently led to "international conflicts." Then, too, the policy of the Persians, after their failure to subjugate the mainland Greeks, involved continual interference; the Persians wished to keep the Greeks divided and weak, for if the Greeks united they were sure to attack the Persian holdings in Asia Minor. Therefore, if any one Greek state threatened to become too strong, the Persians were always ready to give financial and military support to the other Greek cities.

With these points in mind we may turn to a brief survey of Greek history in the period between 500 and 362 B.C.

GREEK HISTORY (500-362 B.C.)

In a previous chapter (III) we traced the rise of the Persian empire from its beginnings under Cyrus the Great (c. 550 B.C.) down to the European conquests of Darius in the two decades preceding 500 B.C. After the fall of the Lydian kingdom of Croesus (546 B.C.) the Asiatic Greeks had become Persian subjects; in most of the Greek cities of Asia Minor, local tyrants were set up to rule as the representatives of the **Persian** Persian king. The Persians also gained a foothold in Thrace, **aggression** and they undoubtedly hoped to extend their rule over the Aegean islands.

Where was the Persian advance to end? Although the Persians already possessed more territory than their small ruling caste could hold conveniently, it was felt that further conquests were necessary. As long as the malcontents of Asiatic Greece could flee across the Aegean to a safe refuge in Greece proper—where they could make plans for organizing rebellions in Asia Minor—the Persian control of the Asiatic Greeks would be uncertain. Therefore, the next logical step of the Persian government appeared to be the conquest of Greece itself. Moreover, the Persians felt that there were certain scores with Athens and Sparta which ought to be paid off. Hippias, the Athenian tyrant, had fled to Asia Minor and had asked the Persians to reinstate him at Athens. A Persian request to the Athenians to take Hippias again as their ruler had been refused in a manner which was far from polite. In addition, the Spartans had been the allies of Croesus; even though they had not sent aid to Croesus when Cyrus attacked him, the Persians bore them a grudge.

The immediate cause for war between the Persians and the Greeks was provided by the so-called Ionian Revolt, an uprising of the Asiatic Greeks which began about 499 B.C.

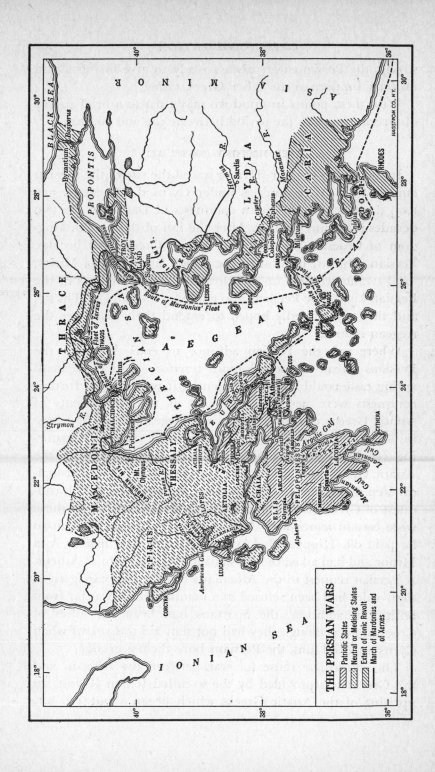

THE PERSIAN WARS

- Patriotic States
- Neutral or Medising States
- Extent of Ionic Revolt
- March of Mardonius and of Xerxes

HAGSTROM CO., N.Y.

The Ionians were dissatisfied with their tyrants, they disliked The Ionian Revolt the high Persian taxes, and they had suffered economic reverses; in the closing years of the sixth century the prosperity of Ionia had declined because of the competition provided by Phoenician, Carthaginian, and mainland Greek traders. The revolt was put down by Persia, but the fact that Athens and the Euboic city of Eretria had aided the revolutionists gave the Persians an excuse to attack Greece.

King Darius sent two successive expeditions against the Greeks. The first, in 492 B.C., proceeded no farther than The Persian wars Macedonia; it had to turn back when its fleet was destroyed by a storm off Mount Athos. The second expedition sailed directly across the Aegean to Euboea; Eretria was besieged, and a Persian force was landed upon the plain of Marathon in Attica about twenty miles northeast of Athens. A battle ensued between Persian and Athenian forces, and the defeated Persians had to withdraw (490 B.C.).

Before another invasion of Greece could be organized, Darius died. His successor, Xerxes, made elaborate preparations for the third and most serious attempt to subjugate the Greeks. In 480 a large army and fleet departed from Asia Minor. Macedonia, Thessaly, and central Greece capitulated; Athens was also taken. Led by Athenians and Spartans, the Greek fleet offered a final desperate resistance at Salamis; on this occasion, Greek strategy was successful, and much of the Persian fleet was destroyed. Xerxes withdrew hastily from Greece, leaving behind him, however, a large land army which continued to operate in central Greece. In 479 B.C. at Plataea in Boeotia, just over the border from Attica, a final contest was held. Once again the Persians were defeated, and Greece was forever freed from the threat of Persian overlordship.

The Greeks were not satisfied with driving the Persians from Greece; instead, they planned to follow up their advantage by attacking Asia Minor with the idea of liberating the Ionian cities. The military leadership of the Greeks had thus far been given without much question to the Spartans, but after 479 the overbearing attitude of the Spartan generals in the field antagonized the Greek contingents from the other states whom they commanded. The Athenians, on the other hand, were popular even though their position was subordinate to that of Sparta. Moreover, the home government at Sparta was not in sympathy with the aggressive foreign policy advocated by the ambitious Spartan generals. When the other Greeks intimated that they preferred to be led by Athenians rather than Spartans, the Spartan government withdrew its troops and commanders with little protest.

The
Delian
League

In 477 B.C. the Athenians organized a naval confederation known as the Delian League. The states which were interested in carrying on hostilities against Persia became the allies of the Athenians. Each state was to contribute a definite quota of ships and men (or a money equivalent), and operations were to be conducted under Athenian leadership. The object of the league was to free the Ionians, to prevent a revival of Persian imperialism directed at Greece, and to acquire enough loot from Persian territory to pay the expenses of the war. In 468 B.C. the league forces gained another great naval victory which swept the Persians from the seas and completed the liberation of most of the Asiatic Greeks.

In 468 it seemed to many people that the Delian League had served its purpose and might well be disbanded. The Athenians, on the other hand, argued that the setback suffered by the Persians was only temporary; peace had not been concluded and the Persians had not acknowledged the independence of the Ionian cities; as a matter of fact, the Persians had continued to assess the Ionian tribute even though they were not able to collect it, and the assumption was that at some time in the future an accounting would be demanded. The Athenians said that it would be unfair for the allies to withdraw from the league, thus leaving Athens to provide protection for all at her own expense.

The
Athenian
navy

The real basis for the Athenian desire that the league should continue, however, was that the league had been a profitable venture for Athens. Many of the allies had preferred to pay money into the league treasury at Delos rather than risk ships and men. As a result, it was the Athenian navy which had borne the brunt of the fighting. Money from the treasury had been used to finance the Athenian operations, and much had been spent in improving and enlarging the Athenian navy which had become the most powerful in Greece.

Moreover, the whole situation was closely tied up with domestic politics in Athens itself. Whereas in the Greek army the fighting was done by those who could afford to buy armor and weapons—the upper and middle classes—in the Greek navy the rowers were ordinarily recruited from the citizen proletariat. The fact that Athens had become a naval rather than a land power meant that the proletariat had become very useful. The Athenian proletariat capitalized on its important position to demand an increasing share in the government with the result that Athenian democracy came into existence. The navy, which was essential to the continued political predominance of the lower classes and to their financial support, could not be maintained at full strength without the funds which the league provided; and therefore, the league, in one form or another, must be continued.

As early as 468 a movement of secession from the league was on foot among the allies. The Athenians, however, argued that the treaties of alliance that had been made in 477 were eternally binding and might not be abrogated. When various states attempted to secede, they were attacked and overpowered by Athens; once in control, the Athenians made subjects of their rebellious allies. Control of their foreign relations was vested in the Athenian government; usually the states were forced to accept new constitutions which set up democratic forms of government similar to those of Athens. Athenian garrisons might be stationed in the chief cities; desirable lands might be given to colonists sent out from Attica, and tribute was imposed upon the subject states. Eventually nearly two hundred cities were made subject and

The Athenian empire

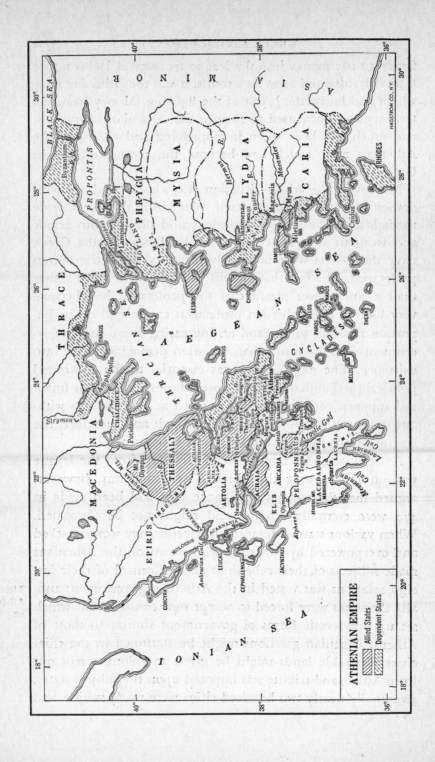

ATHENIAN EMPIRE

Allied States

Dependent States

tributary to the Athenian government, and only a handful of the former allies retained their original status.

Athenian imperialism reached its peak during the period from 461 to about 445 B.C. The democratic party at Athens under the leadership of Pericles was in the ascendant, and an attempt was made to include central Greece in the empire as well as the coastal and island cities. Aegina, Megara, and Boeotia were added just before the middle of the century.

The political and commercial expansion of Athens, however, aroused Corinth, Sparta, and the other Peloponnesian states. Corinth especially had suffered commercial reverses because of the monopoly of trade that the Athenians were building up in the Aegean and Black Sea regions. Sparta was on the whole indifferent to commercial developments, but the increasing prevalence of democracies menaced the traditional oligarchic system which it favored. The Peloponnesians attacked the Athenians in central Greece, the most vulnerable part of the empire. By 445 B.C. the Athenians were forced to sue for peace, for they were no match for the Peloponnesians on land. A treaty was signed by which the Athenians gave up their holdings in central Greece but retained their maritime possessions; peace was to endure for thirty years. Another reason for the Athenian failure, in addition to the weakness of their army, was the fact that, simultaneously with their conflict with the Spartans and their allies, hostilities against the Persians had been continued. The Persians had been attacked in Asia Minor, Cyprus, and Egypt. Against the Persians, the Athenians had met with only minor successes and with a number of serious losses. As early as 448 B.C., a truce had been made with Persia so that the Athenians might concentrate on enemies in Greece, but this arrangement came too late to save the land empire.

The first conflict of Athenians and Peloponnesians

The period from 445-431 B.C. was one of armed peace. Both Athenians and Peloponnesians realized that their previous conflict had decided nothing and that a continuation of the struggle was inevitable. Athenian imperialism was by no means dead, although it had been somewhat chastened. The

The armed peace (445-431 B.C.)

Peloponnesians felt that only the complete destruction of
Athenian power would remove the threat to political and
commercial independence. After 435 a number of political
crises occurred which led to increasing tension, and the long-
expected hostilities were begun.

The Great Peloponnesian War, as it is called, lasted twenty-
seven years. The first phase of it covered the decade 431-421

**The
Great Pelo-
ponnesian
War**
B.C. In this period, neither side won any permanent advantage. There was no common battlefield upon which the naval
strength of Athens could meet the land forces of the Peloponnesian League. The Peloponnesians could lay waste the land
of Attica, but they could not capture the strongly fortified
cities of Athens and Peiraeus which were connected by the
famous Long Walls. The Athenians could retaliate by raiding
the territory of their enemies by sea; and, through the control of the sea, they could disrupt Peloponnesian commerce
in the hope that economic strangulation might bring the foe
to their knees. At the opening of the war, Athenian chances
of success were very strong, but the death of Pericles robbed
the Athenians of their only really competent leader. The exhaustion of both sides, after ten years of sparring, finally led
to a cessation of hostilities in 421.

In the following years, the rise of the ambitious and un-
scrupulous Alcibiades at Athens brought a renewal of the
war. Alcibiades angered the Spartans when he half-persuaded
Athens to support Argos in a war with Sparta (c. 418 B.C.).
Then he evolved a plan for the conquest of Sicily by Athens.
After the Athenian expedition sailed for Sicily (415 B.C.),
Alcibiades was attacked by enemies at home who secured his
dismissal as one of the commanders of the expedition. The
whole affair ended in dismal failure when the people of
Syracuse, aided by Sparta, destroyed the entire Athenian force
in 413 B.C.

In the meantime, Alcibiades fled to Sparta and encouraged
the Spartans to renew the war with Athens. Without going
into the complicated details of this second phase of the war,
we may note that Sparta, aided by Persian money and ships,

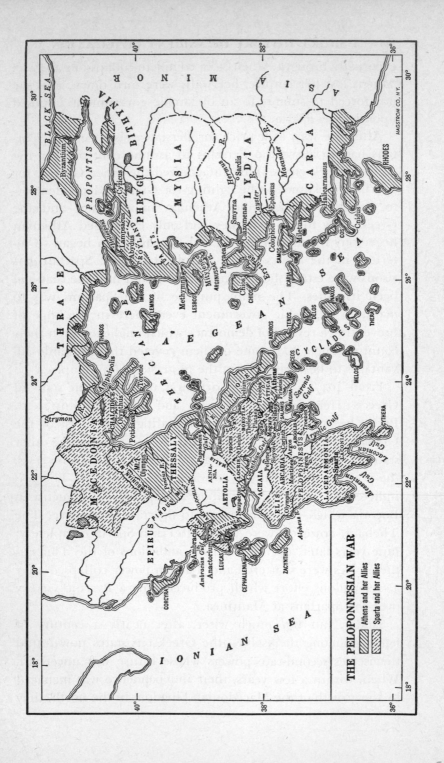

THE PELOPONNESIAN WAR

Athens and her Allies
Sparta and her Allies

eventually brought Athens to a complete collapse in 404 B.C. Athens lost her empire, her walls were torn down, and she was forced to submit to an oligarchic government imposed upon her by Sparta.

After the war, as a price for Persian assistance, the Spartans had to allow the Persians to assume control over the Asiatic Greek cities. This antagonized the other Greeks, for Sparta had claimed to be fighting for Greek independence— to free the Greeks from Athenian imperialism—and the Greeks now found that they had only exchanged Athenian hegemony for that of Sparta and Persia. Sparta began to interfere in the affairs of the mainland Greeks; Spartan garrisons were established in many cities, even in those that had been its allies. The main purpose of the Spartans was to maintain oligarchic government everywhere in the hope of preventing a revival of democracy which might threaten their country. Then, too, some of them coveted the economic advantages to be derived from the possession of an empire.

Spartan rule

From 404 to 372 B.C., Sparta was the dominant state in Greece. Her autocratic policies and her friendship with Persia became more and more irritating to the rest of the Greeks, and at length, Thebes, Athens, and some of the other states combined forces; after a number of military reverses, the power of Sparta began to wane. In 371 B.C. the Thebans inflicted a crushing defeat upon the Spartans at Leuctra in Boeotia which brought an end to Spartan dominance. The Thebans, however, were unable to crush Sparta completely; nine years later, the imperialistic ambitions of the Thebans themselves were shattered and Theban power collapsed after a tremendous effort which produced only a Pyrrhic victory over the Spartans at Mantinea.

Spartan decline

Sadder, but not much wiser, after nearly a century of fighting among themselves, the Greek city-states now found themselves second-rate powers whose future was uncertain. When, within a few years, their independence was menaced by the growth of the Macedonian kingdom in the north, they had little strength to combat the almost complete political eclipse which, it is to be feared, they richly deserved.

ECONOMIC AND SOCIAL LIFE

We have already seen that the Persian conquest of the Asiatic Greeks resulted in a shift of the economic, political, and cultural center of the Greek world to mainland Greece. This development took place in the closing years of the sixth century B.C. In the fifth century, after the unsuccessful attempts of the Persians to conquer Greece, the rise of Athens and the creation of the Athenian empire made that city the commercial and cultural capital of the Greek world. As Athens rose, there was a corresponding decline of her economic competitors—Corinth, Chalcis, Megara, and Aegina. On the whole, however, the economic life of the Aegean was stimulated because of certain benefits which were conferred upon it by the creation of the Athenian empire: (1) the Athenian navy was able to suppress piracy, and (2) the cities of the empire were forced to use a uniform currency, that of Athens. Both the suppression of piracy and the introduction of a uniform currency were most helpful to the growth of trade. Thus, although it was certainly the Athenians who gained the greatest economic advantage from their empire, other states in the Aegean area also enjoyed an increased prosperity.

General developments

The long Peloponnesian War undoubtedly injured agriculture, especially in Attica where the fields were ravaged and the vines and olive trees cut down; moreover, trade and commerce were seriously disrupted while the war was in progress. Nevertheless, the fourth century witnessed rapid recovery in all fields of economic activity, even though mainland Greece had to face increased commercial and industrial competition from the Greeks in Sicily and southern Italy. Then, too, the fourth century was characterized by a number of new developments. The Greek city-states had more and more difficulty in managing their public finances; this was partly an aftermath of the Peloponnesian War, partly the result of the numerous interstate conflicts of the first half of the fourth century, and partly due to the frequent civil wars which broke out in many of the states. Apparently, the division between the small group of the very rich and the increasing multitude of the very poor was becoming more marked; the struggles between the oligarchs and the democrats were, as we have seen, the political expression of economic discontent. Another result of the Peloponnesian War and the subsequent Greek conflicts of the fourth century was the appearance of large numbers of professional (or mercenary) soldiers, men who lacked the opportunity, or did not wish, to return to peaceful occupations. During the fifth century there had been evident an increasing specialization of labor, and this tendency was even more marked in the fourth century. Last of all, after 400 B.C. private banking first assumed considerable significance and financial operations of all kinds became more complex.

Agriculture

The importance of agriculture varied in different areas of Greece. In Boeotia and the Peloponnesus, where the soil was fertile and a fair amount of good land was available, the inhabitants were not compelled to import large quantities of foodstuffs—if, indeed, it was necessary to import any. But where the industrial population was large and the land was not rich, as at Athens, Corinth, and Megara, self-sufficiency was out of the question. The small farmers of Attica could supply their own needs, and there were truck gardens around Athens that produced vegetables for the city market; but wheat and barley had to be brought in from southern Russia to supply the city population. This was probably also true at Corinth and other large cities.

Methods

Greek agricultural methods were rather primitive in the fifth century. The use of fertilizer was not common; usually the fields were allowed to lie fallow in order to recuperate. In the fourth century, the soil was renewed by planting leguminous crops at intervals.

There was some specialization of agricultural production, particularly in areas where certain products were intended

for export. In Attica, for example, there was great emphasis
on the production of wine and olive oil, with the result that
much land was devoted to vineyards and orchards. On the   Special
island of Thasos, to cite a similar case, there was considerable   crops
concentration on viniculture, for Thasian wines were
popular.

Along with agriculture went grazing. The sparse vegetation
made the raising of sheep and goats more practical than cattle
raising. The sheep were kept for food and for their wool,
whereas goats' milk and cheese were universal Greek foods.
In many regions of Greece cattle were so scarce that hides   Grazing
became important imports. Horses were raised in Thessaly
and on the island of Euboea. Occupations of minor importance in areas outside the urban centers were charcoal-burn-
ing and bee-keeping.

Trade and industry were the most significant features of
Greek economic life. Metal work, textiles, weapons, armor,
pottery, lamps, marble, furniture, olive oil, wine, and honey
were exported from the Greek manufacturing cities in return   Trade
for foodstuffs, some Oriental luxuries, and great quantities of
raw materials from all the corners of the ancient world.
Wheat and barley came from Russia, Cyrene, and Sicily;
timber and hides came from Macedonia and Thrace; fish was
brought from the Black Sea, dates from Phoenicia, and
papyrus from Egypt. The Phoenicians secured tin from the
British Isles; metals came from Cyprus, Asia Minor, and
Thrace. Wool was imported from Asia Minor; flax, from
Egypt and Cyrene. Phoenicia sold to the Greeks its metal
work, glass, and textiles; Egypt, its ivory and perfumes.

Much industry and trade was carried on with borrowed
capital. Rich landowners might invest capital in some industrial or commercial venture; in the fourth century the bankers lent the depositors' money for similar purposes. A ship-
owner might trade on his own initiative, but more often he   Capital
leased his ship to carry cargoes. A rich man frequently set
up one of his slaves or freedmen in a shop to manufacture
some product. It was considered bad form for a gentleman

to engage in manufacturing or trading. In Athens, therefore, a large proportion of the industry and trade was carried on by slaves, freedmen, or aliens (free non-citizens).

Banking

The ancestor of the Greek banker was the money changer. In a world where there were many different coinage systems, the money changer, who sat at his table in the marketplace and exchanged the coin of the realm for foreign currency (at a nice profit), was essential to the conduct of trade. About 500 B.C. the Athenian money changers became pawnbrokers as well; they lent money when valuables were deposited with them as security. They also received deposits of money which were then invested in industrial or commercial ventures in the form of loans. Before these private bankers appeared on the scene, the temples made loans to governments and private individuals, just as they did in the Near East. The ordinary rate of interest was about 12 per cent.

Industry

Although it was customary for the Greek family to make its clothing and some of its coarse domestic pottery in the home, by the sixth century B.C. industrial shops and even factories had appeared in the cities. These establishments grew larger and the work of their employees became more specialized in the fifth and fourth centuries. In the shop of average size would be found the master craftsman and perhaps a dozen slaves and free workers; the largest factory about which we have any information was a shield factory which had 120 slaves. In the large cities all the shops devoted to one craft would be concentrated in a certain quarter; the same thing was true of those which sold food or other commodities; fish, vegetables, flowers, fowls, etc., would be sold at different stations in the marketplace. In the small manufacturing establishments, goods manufactured at the rear of the shop would be sold by the proprietor at the front entrance. In well-ordered factories, specialization produced an ancient version of the modern assembly line; in the production of pottery, for example, certain men prepared the clay, others molded the vases, still others made the bases, rims, and handles, and a special crew watched over the oven; specialists, of course, applied the painted decoration.

The Greek governments often concerned themselves with business and other economic affairs. We have already seen something of the activities of Solon and Peisistratus at Athens —how they made reforms and issued regulations to improve the condition of agriculture, industry, and trade. Commercial treaties were often negotiated, and frequently two governments were able to improve the trade relations of their citizens by the adoption of identical systems of currency. In the fourth century, the government of Thasos sought to regulate its wine trade. Speculators were discouraged: they were forbidden to buy up the harvest of a whole vineyard in advance. State inspectors saw to it that wine jars contained the specified amounts, and Thasian ships were not encouraged to carry foreign wines. Government in business

The Greek laborer may best be discussed in connection with the general topic of Greek social organization. The Greek nobility and the commons were never, after the close of the Dark Ages, divided by a rigid caste system such as one finds in the Ancient Near East. The principal social divisions in Greece were rather those of the citizens, the aliens (metics), slaves, agricultural serfs (like the helots), and special groups like the Spartan *perioeci*; there was no priest class. Society

The citizens were the full-fledged members of the city-state who could vote and hold office; they also enjoyed special privileges and exemptions. Citizenship was highly prized, and it was rarely given to outsiders. Sometimes foreign rulers or foreigners who assisted the state in some way were given civic rights; occasionally an alien might be adopted into a citizen family, or a government might, like Athens in the time of Solon, offer citizenship to alien artisans. In 451 B.C., however, the Athenians restricted citizenship to those who could prove that both parents had been Athenian citizens. Citizens

In Athens, and in other industrial and commercial centers, there were large alien populations. Each alien or metic had to have a citizen sponsor (*prostates*) who could represent him Aliens in the law courts. Aliens were required to pay a head tax and to render military service. They had no political rights, and they could not acquire land.

Captives of war, the victims of slave raids, and some criminals provided the slaves of the fifth and fourth centuries. Slaves were used in domestic service, mining, and industry, **Slaves** but not much in agriculture. The most intractable slaves were relegated to the mines where the unspeakable conditions under which they worked soon brought their lives to an end. The Athenian aristocrat Nicias had a thousand slaves whom he rented out for mining; from them he derived an income of better than ten thousand dollars a year. Slaves might hope for manumission at the death of their masters; sometimes slaves were set up in business by their masters and managed to make enough money to buy their freedom. An emancipated slave became a freedman whose former master was his patron; the patron was the legal protector of the freedman, but the freedman owed certain obligations to his patron.

In the preceding chapter (V) a discussion of helots and *perioeci* was presented; hence it should not be necessary to say more about these special classes. Helots, or agricultural serfs resembling them, were to be found in Laconia, Messenia, Crete, and Thessaly.

Most of the Athenians and some of the other Greeks felt that the only respectable form of manual labor was farming. In the country citizens, slaves, and serfs worked together. In the city, on the other hand, the artisan and the trader were mostly recruited from the slave class and the alien group. **Labor** Some citizens did engage in these activities, but they were looked down upon by others. Sculptors, architects, and painters were generally classed as manual laborers in the fifth century, and only a few very famous artists were thought to be socially above shoemakers or potters. As far as we can determine, architects at Athens received the same wages as the laborers whom they supervised. Building inscriptions from Athens and Eleusis show that citizens, slaves, and metics all worked together; the combined numbers of slaves and

metics exceeded those of the citizens in the proportion of five
to two.

Most of the Greeks, except perhaps a few wealthy citizens
or metics, lived in what we should consider extreme poverty. **Greek**
Their food was simple: wheat and barley were made into **life**
porridge or loaves of bread; they ate vegetables, cheese,
onions, figs, olives, and fruit; they ate fish more often than
mutton, pork, and beef. Wine was almost always diluted with
water. Greek private houses were built of mud brick; they
were not large, and they did not contain much furniture. In
cold weather, individual rooms might be heated, most inade-
quately, with braziers filled with coals. In the fourth century,
people with more than average incomes began to build larger
and more permanent houses and to live in comparative
luxury. In fifth-century Athens, however, a display of wealth
in any form was considered bad taste.

In Greek society men occupied a favored position. They
had complete freedom, whereas the women had almost no
freedom at all. While the men engaged in politics, lounged
about the marketplace, or exercised at the wrestling ground
or *palaestra*, the women were confined to their houses. The
one major event in a woman's life was her marriage, and **Men and**
even that was arranged for her by her prospective husband **women**
and her father; ordinarily, she would not be consulted. After
marriage, the woman was supposed to keep her house in
order and bear children. She usually left the house only to
attend some religious festival.

There were, of course, "other women." These were the
hetaerae, the courtesans, mostly aliens. The *hetaerae* were
usually skilled entertainers; some of them were well educated **Hetaerae**
and able to meet the men on equal intellectual terms. Men
found them much more interesting than their wives, many
of whom did not even know how to read or write.

In addition to the entertainment that the *hetaerae* were
able to provide, the men found pleasure in banquets, drink-
ing bouts, and simple games. The chief sports were boxing, **Amuse-**
wrestling, running, jumping, cock-fighting, and chariot-rac- **ments**

ing. There were professional athletes who participated in the national games. The mention of them calls to mind certain epigrams concerning their abilities: the epigram about the boxer whose competitors erected a statue to him because he never hurt any of them, and the numerous epigrams about runners who were mistaken for statues. There was also the runner who started in a race in one year, continued on around the course until the race was run in the second year, and still came in last.

Greek children, outside of Sparta, led fairly happy and normal lives. One must not forget, however, that the exposure of infants was practiced by all Greeks. Above all, the **Children** Greek wanted sons; daughters were a burden, and, if a husband could not be secured for them, they became liabilities. Thus, female babies were more likely to be discarded by their parents than the males.

Girls, if allowed to live, were rarely formally educated. They were taught to cook and sew and to perform other domestic duties. Boys, on the other hand, were given more attention. The son of poor parents might be apprenticed to **Education** a master craftsman. A boy who came from a rich family would be sent to a private school. His education would begin when he was six or seven years old and would continue until his fourteenth year. Reading, writing, and arithmetic were taught, of course. The best literature was read and memorized—the works of Homer, Hesiod, Solon, Theognis, and Pindar. Vocal and instrumental music was included, and the boys learned to play the lyre and the flute. There was also much emphasis upon physical exercise. The aims of Greek education were to produce good citizens who were well grounded in national traditions (and thus patriotic), who subscribed to a high standard of morality, and who possessed certain social graces. Boys who were just emerging into manhood were given military training by the state; they were taught military formations and the use of weapons.

A more advanced sort of education than that offered by the private schools might be gained from attending the lectures of the itinerant philosophers known as the Sophists who appeared in large numbers in the fifth century. For a rather **Sophists** large sum, one of these teachers would give a series of lectures in which he explained how to be successful in politics or the law courts. The Sophists specialized in rhetoric, oratory, and "practical" politics. Sophistic teaching fostered individualism and skepticism; its appeal was largely directed to the man who wanted to "get ahead" in the world. Conservatives looked upon the Sophists as dangerous to society, for these teachers often scoffed at tradition and religion. Later, we shall have occasion to observe the importance of the Sophists in the development of Greek philosophy (see below, p. 177).

GOVERNMENT

One of the most interesting cultural contributions of Athens was the creation of the democratic form of govern- **Democracy** ment. This was not the work of a moment, but the result of a long evolution which reached its climax in the fifth century in the years between 461 and 429 B.C., the so-called Periclean Age. Moreover, it is important always to remember that the Athenian democracy was largely the product of Greek economic developments, the Persian wars, and the creation of the Athenian navy and empire. Without the Athenian navy, which gave the proletariat a political lever, and the Athenian empire, which provided the means to pay Athenian citizens for their participation in the government, the democracy could not have been brought into existence. Before we consider the operation of the full-blown democracy, it will be necessary to review briefly its evolution in the pre-Periclean period.

In the Dark Ages, the monarchical form of government had existed in Athens. There was a king, a council (called the Areopagus), and the assembly (*ecclesia*). Between about 750 B.C. and the time of Solon, the Areopagus had become the stronghold of the landed aristocrats who had abolished the kingship and reduced the power of the *ecclesia*. The powers of the king were divided among elected aristocratic magistrates called archons. One archon was a general administrative officer for Attica, another was commander-in-chief of the army, and another was high priest. About 620 B.C. the threat of sedition forced the nobles to allow the codification of the law; it is probable that at the same time six junior archons, the *thesmothetae* (or keepers of the laws), were added to the original three magistrates.

In 594 B.C., the economic and political crisis brought the reforms of Solon, and the Athenian government was transformed from an aristocratic oligarchy into a timocracy. The citizen population was divided into census classes according to its wealth; the members of the two upper classes were eligible for election to the major magistracies, and those of the third class could hold minor offices; the three upper classes could be elected to the new Council of the Four Hundred, and all citizens were allowed to participate in the *ecclesia* and the *heliaea* (the great court of appeal). The Areopagus was henceforth composed of ex-archons; it was called the "Guardian of the Laws," exercised supervision over the magistrates, and also acted as a court of justice.

The tyranny of Pcisistratus was not productive of any constitutional changes, but the persecution of the landed aristocrats made it possible for the business men to gain increased participation in the government; in other words, the business men who fulfilled the financial qualifications for office were able to step into positions formerly held by the aristocrats. Under Cleisthenes, the creation of the ten new tribes, the Council of the Five Hundred, and the board of ten generals had the effect of disrupting old traditions and breaking down prejudices. The introduction of ostracism enabled the masses to eliminate political leaders who were oligarchically inclined.

The period of the Persian wars was notable for conditions favoring the development of the democracy. The almost continuous state of war which existed during the first three decades of the fifth century made the ten generals the most important officials of Athens. To save themselves from the Persian conquest, the Athenians were forced to elect the best and most capable men available without regard to financial standing. The archonships, mere civic offices, paled into insignificance before the predominance of the generals. After the wars, the creation of the empire and the difficulty of holding it increased the importance of the generals. Even as early as 487 B.C., however, the ancient authors tell us that the archonship was filled by lot (sortition); in other words, the duties of the archons were concerned with routine matters, and it made little difference who filled these posts as long as the incumbents satisfied the financial qualifications stipulated by law.

Moreover, when the Athenians built up a strong fleet in the period of the Persian wars, the proletarians, who could not afford to equip themselves for the army, suddenly became valuable to the state as rowers for the ships. Naturally, the new significance of the proletarians gave them a lever with which they could pry concessions from the government. Last of all, the creation of the empire brought revenue to Athens which could be used to pay public servants. As a result, persons who could not have afforded to take time from the business of earning a living to participate in governmental affairs now found it worth while to do so. **Navy** **Empire**

The final steps in the creation of the democracy came at the opening of the Periclean Age when the leaders of the proletarian party, Ephialtes and Pericles, secured the passage of laws which deprived the Areopagus of most of its power (462 B.C.). The Areopagus had, of course, declined with the archonship, for it was composed of ex-archons. The Areopagus lost its guardianship of the laws and its supervision of the magistrates, these functions being turned over to the Council of the Five Hundred, the *ecclesia*, and the *heliaea*. **Ephialtes and Pericles**

In 461 B.C. Ephialtes was assassinated by his political opponents. His associate, Pericles, then became the leader of the democratic party at Athens, a position which he held almost without interruption until his death in 429. During this **Pericles** period the Athenian democracy attained its fullest development and its most efficient operation.

We shall now examine the governmental machinery of Periclean Athens with special reference to the executive, legislative, and judicial departments and the organization of the empire. Then we shall attempt to ascertain the aims and purposes of this government and to evaluate it in terms of its success in attaining its ends.

The chief officials of the executive branch of the government were the ten generals. They were elected annually by the citizen body; there was no legal barrier to the same person **Generals** holding successive generalships—Pericles was chosen as a general on many occasions. The generals had charge of the army, the fleet, and the empire. Theoretically, the generals all had equal power; but a man like Pericles, who possessed a strong personality and great political prestige, might easily influence his colleagues to do as he wished.

Almost all the other officials in Athens were chosen by lot instead of being elected. Although the archons were important as civic administrators and judges, their prestige did not match that of the generals. There were also minor officers who made up various governing committees or boards and **Other** performed certain duties: the prison board, the police commissioners, the supervisors of the market, the state contractors, and the boards of treasurers for the important temples. The *Hellenotamiae*, the treasurers of the Delian League, became the treasurers for the Athenian empire. Usually each committee or board consisted of ten members—one member chosen from each tribe by lot—and a secretary.

In the legislative and deliberative branch of the government were the *boule* (Council of the Five Hundred) and the *ecclesia*. Fifty councilors were chosen by lot each year from each of the ten tribes. The full council of 500 members ordinarily met four times a month; at these meetings the *boule* considered legislation to be laid before the *ecclesia* for enact- **Boule** ment, discussed military, naval, defense, imperial, and financial problems, and scrutinized the acts of the magistrates.

When the full council was not in session a committee of fifty remained on duty night and day to act in any emergency. All the members of this committee belonged to the same tribe and were its representatives in the council; each month the committee was changed, the representatives of the various tribes succeeding one another in rotation.

All Athenian citizens eighteen years of age or over were members of the *ecclesia*. This assembly met from one to four times a month; an attendance of 6000 constituted a quorum. The members of the *ecclesia* discussed, amended, and ratified *Ecclesia* or rejected legislative proposals submitted to it by the *boule*. The *ecclesia* received foreign emissaries, elected the generals, and alone had the power to grant citizenship. It was also the body that voted on ostracism.

During the Periclean Age the *heliaea*, the Areopagus (as a court for homicide), and other special courts continued to function, but more important were the jury courts, the *Justice* *dikasteria*. The growth of the empire had increased the judicial business which had to be transacted at Athens, for the Athenians required all major cases arising in the subject states to be tried there. Each year a panel of 6000 jurors was drawn from the Athenian citizen body. From this panel juries of 201, 501, and similarly large numbers were drawn to try individual cases. The archons were usually the presiding magistrates; trials began at sunrise and had to be completed by sunset; the defendant had to plead his own case, although he might hire someone to write his defense for him.

The *dikasteria* were a more significant factor in the government than one might suppose. The introduction of pay for jury service during the Periclean Age meant that the poor of the city of Athens were provided with some means of support. The daily wage was small, and rich men or small farmers outside of the city would not be much attracted by it; but the unemployed of Athens were naturally anxious to offer themselves for jury duty. Through the courts the proletariat gained considerable political power. "The courts were in almost perpetual session; their jurisdiction extended to every aspect and department of public life; and from their decision there was no appeal."[1]

As a result of the transformation of the Delian League into the Athenian empire, nearly two hundred states were reduced from the position of allies to that of subjects. The "contribution" that the allies had paid for the support of military operations against Persia became the "tribute" which was now paid to Athens. A few of the original allies re-

Empire   mained faithful to Athens and managed to retain their freedom, but the other states were forced to turn over to Athens the conduct of their foreign relations and to submit to the establishment of democratic constitutions drawn up by the Athenians. As we have seen, the subject states had to bring many lawsuits to Athens for trial; they were also bound by Athenian commercial regulations. In some cases, Athenian garrisons were sent to the subject cities; often, fertile lands in the subject states were given to Athenian military colonists, the *cleruchs*. From this it is clear that, although the empire was productive of certain economic benefits to the subject states (the suppression of piracy and the adoption of a uniform currency), there were many just reasons for dissatisfaction.

With the details of Athenian domestic and imperial government in mind, we may now attempt an evaluation of it.

First, we ought to summarize the general features that were characteristic of the Periclean democracy. A major aim of the system was to secure the participation of all the citi-

Characteristics of Periclean democracy   zens in the government. This was accomplished by throwing open the various branches of service to the entire citizen body; the three upper census classes could hold any office, and the only office not open to the fourth class was the archonship. The use of the lot was based on the theory that any man was capable of filling any position. The practice of rotation in office—forbidding successive terms in the same position—made it possible for a greater proportion of the

[1] *Cambridge Ancient History*, Vol. V, p. 112.

citizens to engage in public service; the use of the committee
—to perform certain tasks which might have been performed
by one official—was another method of gaining the end
sought by rotation. The introduction of payment for service
in the *dikasteria* and the *boule* enabled even the poorest
citizens to participate.

There was some attempt to insure honest and efficient government and to fix responsibility. The personal qualifications
of candidates were considered; auditors examined the accounts of officials and committees; officials were liable to im-
peachment, and the general conduct of the government was
carefully scrutinized. Maladministration might be punished
by fines, exile, or execution.

The greatest benefits of the democracy were enjoyed by
the masses—it might even be said that this was the main purpose of the whole system. The tremendous power of the
ecclesia in which the masses secured preponderance by mere
weight of numbers, the composition of the juries, and the
use which was made of imperial revenues—the tribute was
used to pay the rowers in the fleet, the court fines to pay the
jurors—all tended to benefit the common people more than **Benefits**
any other group. The military *cleruchies* scattered through- **to the**
out the empire helped to relieve over-population at Athens, **masses**
and Pericles also sponsored a colonization project at Thurii
in Italy. Finally, the state expenses that could not be met by
the imperial revenues were provided for by revenue extracted
from the metics and the rich citizens. The rich citizens were
liable for the *liturgies*, the expensive public services which
were financed by individuals. A wealthy man might be re-
quested to build and equip a warship, to pay for the training
of a chorus for one of the Dionysiac plays, or to provide a
feast for all the members of his tribe. It would not be fair
to subject these features of the Athenian system to criticism,
for they were the methods by which the chief end of a democracy might be gained—that is, the greatest good to the greatest number.

Faults of the democracy

On the other hand, the Athenian democracy in operation displayed certain faults which outrage modern notions of the ideal democracy.

First, the Athenian citizen body was a very limited group. Only about half of the inhabitants of Attica were citizens; the rest were metics and slaves. The Athenians of the Periclean Age had no idea of extending citizenship to others; instead, they tried to reduce the numbers of those eligible for its privileges and exemptions.

Second, the democracy was dependent upon imperialism and economic exploitation. The Athenian citizens were really a group of 170,000 oligarchs who derived their financial support from 2,000,000 subjects. The enjoyment of democracy by each Athenian citizen was made possible by the labor of twelve subjects of his government.

Last of all, although the point cannot be pressed, one might question whether the Athenian democracy in the Age of Pericles was actually a democracy. It is very doubtful whether the Athenian people had much to do with the formulation of fundamental governmental policies. Pericles was not a dictator, but he and his clique certainly directed the government. The masses seem to have exercised their own initiative only when they wanted something that was of special benefit to them; and as long as Pericles kept them happy and satisfied he could propose and secure ratification for other projects which he himself favored. It might even be said that the democracy functioned most efficiently when it was under the partial dictatorship of Pericles; for after his death, when less able men were in the saddle, the proletariat took the bit in its teeth and was responsible for many ghastly mistakes.

These criticisms should not be construed as an indictment of democracy as a system. Democracy never received a fair trial at Athens, for one very necessary element for the success **Reasons** of democratic government was lacking: an intelligent, well-**for** educated citizen body. Contrary to a belief which is wide-**failure** spread today, the Athenian citizen body was neither intelligent nor well educated; at least, it was not educated for the task that it had to fulfill. We know that only a small group of Athenians ever received any formal education; only a minority knew how to read and write. Furthermore, it may well be asked whether the system of formal education in vogue at Athens would have helped the citizens to operate their government even if education had been available to all. It is often said that the opportunity for the actual participation of large groups of citizens in the government was an education in itself. It is true that most of the citizens well understood the workings of their governmental machinery, but that is beside the point. It is perfectly possible to understand how a machine works, but it is another thing to know what to do with it. The real point is that the Athenians were not sound judges of policy, although Pericles claimed that they were. Socrates later demonstrated clearly that none of his contemporaries understood, or were able to think clearly about, matters of ethics, society, and economics. Precise knowledge of these things was not available to the Periclean Greeks. As a matter of fact, if we were perfectly honest, we should have to admit that we today are not much better informed.

The subsequent history of Athenian government need not concern us here. The oligarchic government which the Spartans forced upon the Athenians at the end of the Peloponnesian War was overthrown when Athens regained her independence. Democracy was restored, and it was retained during the fourth century with only minor modifications.

Elsewhere in Greece, government varied from extreme oligarchy to moderate democracy. There were frequent revolutions in the city-states during the fourth century, and the government of individual states was altered when the oligarchs or democrats rose or fell in power. The most common governmental form was the timocracy, although some of the Greek states in the west fell into the hands of tyrants who occasionally established monarchies.

GREEK ART

The period from 500 to 350 B.C. constitutes the classic period of Greek art. In this century and a half the Doric and Ionic styles of Greek architecture reached their highest development, and the peak of Greek achievement in sculpture was attained by Phidias and Praxiteles. Advances in painting were made which paved the way for the perfection of the art (so far as the Greeks were concerned) by Apelles (*c.* 335 B.C.).

In the fifth century it was still the temple that received the major attention of the architects; but there was a growing interest in city-planning and the construction of public buildings other than temples which became more marked in the fourth century. In the fifth century, for example, the famous Hippodamus of Miletus revised the plan of the Peiraeus and later laid out the streets of the Periclean colony of Thurii in Italy. Council chambers, city halls, and stoae (colonnaded porches) began to make their appearance. In the fourth century, gymnasia, stadia, and theaters with stone seats were built in a number of cities.

In discussing Greek architecture of the classic period our interest naturally centers on Athens, where Pericles inaugurated a great building program that made his city the most beautiful in the ancient world. As we have seen, the empire had placed huge economic resources at the disposal of the Athenians. The position of Athens as an imperial capital seemed to Pericles and his followers to necessitate a certain degree of ostentation in order that the subjects as well as the enemies of Athens might be suitably impressed. At the beginning of the Periclean Age few of the buildings which had been destroyed by the Persians in 480 B.C. had been restored; most of them had been purposely left in ruins as a reminder of Persian barbarity. The Periclean generation, however, was less bitter than its predecessors, and the unsightly ruins offended civic pride. Moreover, both contractors and workmen must have enthusiastically supported a building program that had obvious financial possibilities for them.

Architecture

Periclean building

The principal structures erected during the Periclean Age were the Parthenon, the Propylaea, the temple of Athena Nike, the Odeum (music hall) of Pericles, and the temple of Hephaestus; the Erectheum was built shortly after Pericles' death. The Parthenon and the temple of Hephaestus were in the Doric style; this style reached its fullest development in the Parthenon. High above the city on the Acropolis, with its magnificent sculptural decoration planned by Phidias, the Parthenon in all its glory impressed the Greeks with its beauty and dignity; it was a monument to the greatness of Periclean Athens, and even today its majestic ruins conjure up visions of a mighty past. It was constructed of Pentelic marble; its pediment groups dealt with two famous Athenian legends, the birth of Athena (the eastern façade) and the contest between Athena and Poseidon for the possession of Attica (the western façade). Around the cella ran an Ionic frieze **Parthenon** showing the Panathenaic procession, the parade which culminated in the presentation of a new garment to the statue of Athena. Inside the temple was the gigantic gold and ivory statue of Athena, the work of Phidias.

The temple of Hephaestus was down in the agora or marketplace north of the Areopagus. This temple is sometimes **Temple of** erroneously called the Theseum because its metopes depict **Hephaestus** episodes in the life of that hero. It is important today because it is one of the best preserved temples in the Doric style.

The Propylaea (Gates) constituted the monumental entrance to the Acropolis; both Doric and Ionic columns were employed in its construction. The ceilings were richly cof- **Other** fered; in one wing was a famous gallery of paintings. The **buildings** temple of Athena Nike was a small but very handsome Ionic temple situated on a bastion adjoining the Propylaea. The Erechtheum was another Ionic temple sacred to Athena and Erechtheus (a legendary Athenian king); in its south porch, figures of maidens (caryatids) were substituted for columns; under the north porch were three depressions in the limestone rock which were supposed to be the marks of Poseidon's trident. The Odeum of Pericles was located at the

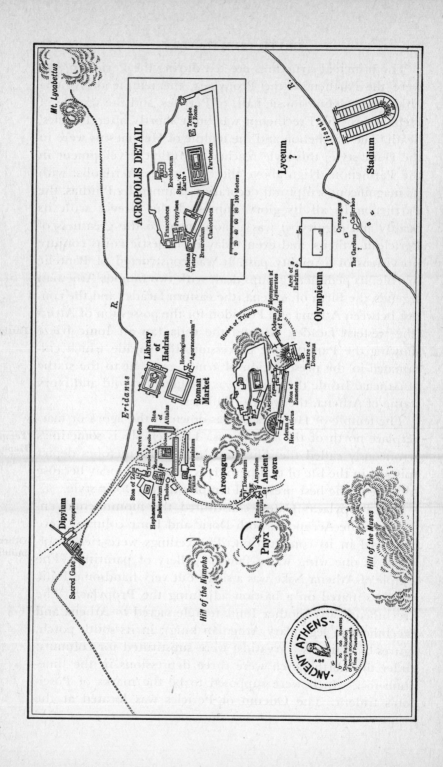

ACROPOLIS DETAIL

Temple of Rome
Erechtheum
Parthenon
Stat. of Ath.
Pinacothees
Propylees
Athena Victory
Brauronion
Chalcotheca

0 20 40 60 80 100 Meters

Mt. Lycabettus

R.

Ilissus R.

Stadium

Lyceum ?

Cynosarges
Callirrhoe
The Gardens ?

Arch of Hadrian
Monument of Lysicrates

Olympieum

Street of Tripods
Odeum of Pericles
Theatre of Dionysus
Stoa of Eumenes
Odeum of Her. Atticus

Eridanus

Library of Hadrian

Horologium
'Agoranomium'

Roman Market

Stoa of Attalus

Temple of Apollo
Temple of Zeus
Tholos
Metroon
Bouleuterium
Hephaesteum
Stoa of Zeus
Temple of Twelve Gods
Dionysus
Amyneion
Enneacrunus
Eleusinium
Enneacrunus ?

Areopagus

Ancient Agora

Dipylum
Pompeium

Sacred Gate

Pnyx

Hill of the Nymphs

Hill of the Muses

ANCIENT ATHENS

0   100 quarters
Shewing location
of known monuments
of time of Posidonus

southeastern foot of the Acropolis; it had a conical wooden roof, "like the tent of Xerxes," or, as some people unkindly said, "like onion-headed Pericles."

After the Persian wars, Athens was equipped with massive fortifications that rendered the city impregnable—the Greeks of the fifth century were notably unskilled in siegecraft. The Peiraeus was also fortified, and Cimon (471-461 B.C.) super- **Fortifi-** intended the building of the famous Long Walls which con- **cations** nected Athens with the Peiraeus and made the two cities into a compact defensible unit.

Although much more might be said of Greek architecture in the classic period, we must content ourselves here with only a brief mention of three important buildings: the temple of Zeus at Olympia, the temple of Artemis at Ephesus, and the Mausoleum. The temple of Zeus at Olympia was a **Temple** large Doric structure erected about 450 B.C. It contained a **of Zeus** colossal gold and ivory statue of Zeus, the work of Phidias. **at Olympia** The temple of Artemis at Ephesus was erected about 350 after a fire had destroyed another temple on the same site; it was in the Ionic style, and its size was extraordinary, for it covered an area of 340 by 160 feet. The Mausoleum, which also dates from about 350 B.C., was a funeral monument to Mausolus, the king of Halicarnassus. "The building con- sisted of four chief parts: a base or podium forty-two Greek feet high, supporting an Ionic peristyle also forty-two Greek feet high, which in turn was surmounted by a pyramid of the same height, and the whole was crowned by a . . . four- horse chariot, in or beside which two colossal statues, ten feet high . . . may have stood."[2]

At the opening of the fifth century there were distinctive schools of sculpture in the Peloponnesus, Athens, and south Italy. At Argos, Sicyon, and Aegina Peloponnesian sculptors and their pupils created mostly statues of victorious athletes distinguished by short, stocky figures. Calamis at Athens **Sculpture** was famous for his statues of horses; either he or his con-

---

[2] H. N. Fowler and J. R. Wheeler, *Greek Archaeology*, New York, 1909, pp. 178-179. The statues were those of Mausolus and his wife, Artemisia.

temporary, Pythagoras of Rhegium, may have made the famous bronze charioteer which was found at Delphi.

The sculptured works of the fifth century are characterized by their dignity, simplicity, and grace; the archaic stiffness **Style** of the figures was gradually overcome, and the representation of men and animals in both stone and bronze was considerably improved. Solutions were found for problems connected with the representation of drapery. The statues of divinities produced by fifth-century artists, particularly Phidias, influenced all future thinking about the actual appearance of the gods and goddesses. After Phidias created his Athena and his Olympian Zeus, few people could conceive of these divinities in any other form.

Three sculptors of the fifth century are deserving of special mention: Myron, Phidias, and Polyclitus. Myron, an Athenian who flourished about 475 B.C., was especially famous for his statues of athletes and animals. His Discus Thrower is **Myron** well known to us today; he also made a statue of a runner in full career, and a statue of a heifer so true to life that it deceived cattle in the fields.

We have already mentioned the Athena and the Zeus of Phidias. Phidias was another Athenian; his work was done between 450 and 425 B.C. He and his pupils were distin-**Phidias** guished for their *ethos*, dignity and simplicity, a characteristic which may well have had its inspiration from the majesty of Pericles and the Athenian empire. Idealism was the keynote of Phidian sculpture; even his figures of men and women seem to represent people who are something more than human.

Polyclitus lived at Argos at the end of the fifth century. He devoted himself chiefly to the statues of athletes, although **Polyclitus** he did produce a gold and ivory statue of the goddess Hera. Polyclitus evolved mathematical formulae for the ideal proportions of the human body, and his statue, the Doryphorus (Spear Bearer), exemplified his theories in practice.

Technically, the sculptors of the fourth century were superior to those of the fifth; but in many cases this very facility of execution proved their undoing, for many of these later artists were concerned with displaying their own cleverness, and they lacked the sincerity and personal modesty that had contributed so much to the success of their predecessors. Some artists, however, like Praxiteles and Scopas, managed to escape this pitfall. The fourth century saw the rise of portraiture in sculpture, the development of devices to express emotion, and some improvements in the representation of drapery. Fourth-century style

Two famous names in Greek sculpture in the first half of the fourth century are Praxiteles and Scopas. Praxiteles combined a perfection of technique with a greatness of concept which make his work, in the opinion of many people, the greatest of ancient times. His Cnidian Aphrodite and his Hermes and Dionysus are too well known to require comment. The grace of his figures and his rendition of drapery were never excelled by later artists. Scopas gained recognition when he discovered a way to express emotion in the faces of his statues by parting the lips and setting the eyes very deep in the head. He was one of four sculptors chosen to work on the sculptural decoration of the Mausoleum. Another artist, Lysippos, is generally mentioned in connection with Scopas and Praxiteles, but most of his work was done after 350, and we shall include him with the sculptors of the Hellenistic Age (see Chapter VII). Praxiteles Scopas

Polygnotos, the Phidias of painting, came to Athens after the Persian wars at the invitation of Cimon. Like Phidias, Polygnotos was noted for his *ethos*. He was also the first to give his murals perspective and depth; the colors he employed were white, red, ocher, and black, and thus he is called a four-color painter. Two of his most famous paintings were entitled "The Descent of Odysseus to the Lower World" and "Troy Taken." Polygnotos and painting

Painters who worked in the late fifth and early fourth centuries were Apollodorus, Zeuxis, and Parrhasios. Apollodorus was called the "shadow painter" because of his mastery of light and shade; Zeuxis was noted for his violent contrasts of color, and Parrhasios for lightness and gaiety.

LITERATURE

It should never be forgotten that literature is a cultural form that is greatly influenced by its political, social, and economic environment. In the history of Greek literature we have already seen how the epic, the natural product of a patriarchal and aristocratic society in which a knowledge of writing was not widespread, was superseded in the Archaic Age by the iambic, the elegy, and the personal and choral lyric. In a bustling commercial and industrial milieu where individualism was rampant and there was a considerable knowledge of writing, the iambic, elegy, and personal lyric were naturally popular. Thus, it is not surprising that we find these forms in Asiatic Greece in the period between 750 B.C. and the Persian conquest. Likewise, the choral lyric, a form well suited to the expression of national unity, was especially popular in mainland Greece where the state rather than the individual was more important; it will be remembered that the choral lyric flourished at Sparta where the state was dominant.

Literature and environment

When the Asiatic Greeks were brought under the Persian yoke and the mainland Greeks were threatened with conquest by the Persians, individualism was subordinated to the group (or the state). The natural result was that after 500 B.C. the iambic, elegy, and personal lyric declined, whereas the choral lyric reached its highest point in the first half of the fifth century in the skillful hands of Pindar of Boeotia, and the Greek drama, which had evolved as a special form of the choral lyric, became important.

The city-state influences literature

Another feature of the development of literature after 500 B.C. was the increasing use of prose. Whereas philosophy, political propaganda, history, and the like had previously been couched in poetry, in the fifth century writers on these subjects turned to prose as a more suitable medium for conveying their ideas. All this certainly indicates a wider use of

Prose

writing and a growing reading public; at the same time, it is quite probably connected with the rise of democracy and the increasing commercial and industrial life which had much to do with the rise of law courts and litigation, for oratory—which was encouraged by democratic forms of government and the courts—naturally helped to lead people away from poetry toward prose as a means of expression.

This is not to say that the Greeks no longer composed poetry, but we know little about poets who wrote in the period between 450 B.C. and the age of Alexander the Great, for contemporaries rarely mentioned them and only fragments of their works have survived.

Pindar, who brought the choral lyric to perfection, was born in Boeotia in the latter part of the sixth century and **Pindar** died shortly after 450 B.C. Of aristocratic extraction and sympathies, he had little feeling for democracy. He was considerably inspired by the glorious victories of the Greeks over the Persians, but most of his poetry which has survived consists of victory odes written for the various Pan-Hellenic games.

The most significant literary development of the fifth century was that of the drama. Unfortunately, this subject can be discussed only in connection with the drama at Athens, **Drama** since we know little of the Greek drama elsewhere. The drama owed much to two earlier literary forms, the epic and the choral lyric. It took its subject matter from the former, and it evolved out of the latter.

Greek tragedy originated with the choral songs honoring the wine god, Dionysus. These songs dealt with episodes in **Tragedy** the life of Dionysus, and they were sung by choruses of men dressed in goatskins (to represent satyrs). It became customary for the leader of the chorus to punctuate the songs of the chorus with what might be called dramatic recitatives; thus, he eventually became an "actor." The tragedy or "goat-singing" of the Athenians was given great encouragement by Peisistratus in 534 B.C. when he established annual dramatic contests in honor of Dionysus. This custom continued; when the drama reached its more or less completed form in the fifth century, the usual procedure was to select the works of three tragic and three comic writers for performance. The dramatists were much limited at first by having to deal only with subjects which related to Dionysus, but they evaded this restriction by composing trilogies (sets of three related plays) on other mythological subjects, and attaching a fourth play—a satyr play—which established a connection with Dionysus. In a sense, each part of a trilogy would correspond to one act in a modern play.

Athens produced three great writers of tragedy: Aeschylus, Sophocles, and Euripides. Aeschylus (525-456 B.C.) was the **Aeschylus** first of this group. He added a second actor and managed to solve the many difficult problems connected with reducing the chorus to a subordinate position. The plays became a series of episodes in which the action of the piece took place, and these episodes were separated by choral songs; it might be said that the choral songs were like the triglyphs separating the episodic metopes of a Doric frieze. The plays of Aeschylus were majestic in concept; their theme was usually the struggle of human endeavor against the irresistible force of fate or the will of the gods. Aeschylus seems to have preached that sin is always punished by suffering. He repeats the gloomy Greek warning of Solon to Croesus, "Count no man fortunate until his death."

The works of Sophocles (496-406) were somewhat more **Sophocles** sophisticated than those of Aeschylus. Sophocles added a third actor, inaugurated the use of painted scenery, and devised plots which were more complex than those of his predecessors. Sophocles was a product of the Periclean Age; his tragedies partook of the same spirit, or *ethos*, that characterized the sculpture of Pericles and the painting of Polygnotos. His characters are idealized, but they are more human than those of Aeschylus. Sophocles stressed moderation and self-control; he did not believe that immutable laws arranged man's life, but he felt that, although the gods often intervened in human affairs, one might shape his own destiny within certain limits.

Euripides (480-406) was clearly affected by the changed conditions which prevailed in Athens after the death of Pericles when the irresponsible citizen masses held sway. He **Euripides** was a realist in that he depicted human beings as they are in everyday life, but he also bowed to popular demands for sensationalism by presenting striking scenes and brilliant speeches. Euripides had little respect for the traditional Athenian attitudes toward the gods and society, and he was distinguished for his skepticism and his rational approach to human problems. Undoubtedly, he was much influenced by the contemporary sophistic teaching.

Athenian comedy sprang from the Dionysiac revels with which the country folk honored the wine god. From the rustic mummers and their leader, the comic poets developed the chorus and the actors of the fifth-century comedy. Attic **Comedy** comedy concerned itself with the present rather than with the legendary past, and consisted of satire leveled at individuals prominent in public life or well-known groups— philosophers, tragedians, jurymen—whose behavior or characteristics might be ridiculed.

The greatest of the comic poets was Aristophanes (446-388). During the Peloponnesian War he wrote many comedies dealing with contemporary affairs, and, on occasion, he openly **Aristoph-** made fun of prominent people in Athens—Pericles, Socrates, **anes** Cleon, Euripides, and others. His attitude was generally conservative; he did not hesitate to express his dislike of democratic leaders and institutions and the sophists by caricaturing them in his plays. After the Peloponnesian War, public sentiment was opposed to free speech on political matters, and Aristophanes turned his attention to more general subjects; parodies of myths and the works of the tragic poets, and satires on social institutions and the foibles of mankind became popular.

In the period between 500 and 362 B.C., three great historians appeared: Herodotus of Halicarnassus, and Thucyd-

ides and Xenophon of Athens. Herodotus (*fl.* 440 B.C.) was
the author of a history of the Persian wars. He saw in the
struggles of the Greeks and the Persians a mighty conflict
Herodotus   between the East and the West, and he tried not only to
describe the actual military operations of the period 499-479
B.C. but also to provide a background by considering the
earlier history of the seventh and sixth centuries. Therefore,
he devoted considerable space to a description of the customs
and origins of the inhabitants of the ancient world, with the
result that his work contains geographic and anthropological
information which makes it much more than a mere history
of the conventional type. Herodotus has been severely criti-
cized for his credulity and his ignorance of military strategy.
On the other hand, his ability to tell a story is unrivaled; furthermore, it must be admitted that it would be difficult to
reconstruct the early history of Greece without the information with which he alone supplies us.

Thucydides (460-395 B.C.) wrote the history of the Pelopon-
Thucyd-   nesian War. His impartiality and his careful analysis of situa-
ides   tions and events have won for him the title of "the first
scientific historian"; he was undoubtedly the greatest historian the ancient world ever produced. Thucydides' remark-
able insight into human nature may be illustrated by a few
quotations:

> The way that most men deal with traditions, even traditions of
> their own country, is to receive them all alike as they are deliv-
> ered, without applying any critical test whatever. . . . So little
> pains do the vulgar take in the investigation of the truth, accept-
> ing readily the first story that comes to hand. . . . The absence
> of romance in my history will, I fear, detract somewhat from its
> interest. . . . I have written my work, not as an essay which is to
> win the applause of the moment, but as a possession for all time.

In spite of his scientific approach, Thucydides did not
neglect the dramatic possibilities of his narrative. His description of the departure of the Syracusan expedition from Athens
and of the final failure of that venture lives forever in the

memories of his readers, and his "Funeral Oration" of Pericles ranks with the greatest works of Greek literature.

Xenophon (*c.* 430-*c.* 350 B.C.), soldier, writer, and pupil of Socrates, is a lesser figure than Herodotus or Thucydides, but **Xenophon** his writings are no less interesting. His *Hellenica* continued the history of Thucydides down to 362 B.C. He was also the author of works on Socrates, the Spartan constitution, Greek economics, and other subjects. He is best known for his *Anabasis*. The *Anabasis* is the account of the unsuccessful attempt of a Persian prince, Cyrus, to overthrow his brother, Artaxerxes II, king of Persia. About 401 B.C., Cyrus led a combined force of native troops and thirteen thousand Greek mercenaries into the very heart of the Persian empire. Cyrus was killed in a battle with his brother's army, and the Greek mercenaries, reduced to about ten thousand men, were left stranded in Mesopotamia. Under the leadership of Xenophon and other able commanders, the Greeks fought their way out of Persian territory by marching north to the Black Sea.

Xenophon was not the only historian who lived in the fourth century, but the works of other writers are available today only in fragments. Ephorus of Cumae, for example, is **Other** known to have written a universal history; Theopompus of **writers** Chios, like Xenophon, continued Thucydides' narrative and also wrote on Philip II, king of Macedon (see below, p. 186). The first biographical writing among the Greeks dates from the fourth century; Xenophon was the author of a quasi-biography of Agesilaus, one of the Spartan kings.

Even as early as the time of Homer, oratory had been highly regarded by the Greeks, but until the closing years of **Oratory** the fifth century B.C. the ability to speak well was more or less considered to be a gift; it did not occur to people that oratory might be studied and cultivated. The rise of democratic government and the increasing importance of the law courts, however, brought home to the Greeks the necessity of learning to express themselves in a creditable manner. Thus, rhetoric and oratory became important features of the sophistic training, the object of which was to enhance the individual's chances of success in public life. Style, diction, and ultimately grammar and syntax were carefully studied; in fact, so much attention was paid to the externals of oratory that fluency and style and diction were considered more essential to a good speech than any ideas which it might contain.

Nevertheless, it was discovered that, while some people could be trained to speak well, others could not master the art. Therefore, about 400 B.C., professional speech writers began to appear; these were skillful men who could not only write good speeches, but also adapt them to the personalities of the people who were to deliver them. Lysias and Isaeus were two of the most prominent and successful men in this field at Athens.

**Profes-
sional
speech
writers**

In the fourth century the professional teachers and writers of oratory became influential enough to take an active part in Greek politics. Greek oratory, as a matter of fact, reached its peak under two major political figures who earned their living from the art: Isocrates and Demosthenes.

Isocrates (436-338 B.C.) was an Athenian who conducted a school for training in rhetoric in his native city. "His reputation as a teacher, however, was more than equaled by his fame as a writer of artistic prose. He brought the florid, periodic style to perfection. He was not content with purity of diction, well-rounded, sonorous periods, and the use of various figures of speech; he gave to his prose the further advantage of rhythms. . . ."[3] In his political views, Isocrates was Pan-Hellenic rather than Athenian. He favored a confederation of Greek states for the purpose of ending warfare among the Greeks themselves and protecting them against their common enemies; particularly, he thought that the Greeks ought to unite in a common attack upon Persia. When they refused to heed his proposals for confederation, Isocrates turned to Philip II of Macedon and urged him to unite the Greeks by force.

Isocrates

Demosthenes (384-322 B.C.), another Athenian and the greatest of the Greek orators, also earned his livelihood by

[3] Edward Capps, *From Homer to Theocritus*, New York, 1901, p. 346.

writing speeches. Unlike Isocrates, however, Demosthenes opposed Macedonian intervention in Greek affairs; he tried to persuade the Greeks to unite to ward off the menace of Philip, and he wrote his famous series of orations, the *Philippics*, in order to arouse the Greeks to action. Demosthenes was more than a rhetorician and a maker of fine speeches, for his orations display great intellectual ability and high ideals.

Demos-
thenes

PHILOSOPHY AND SCIENCE

It is interesting to note the various channels into which Greek intellectual activity was diverted after 500 B.C. In the sixth century the early philosophers had been chiefly mathematicians, astronomers, and physicists, but the fifth and fourth centuries brought important new developments. True, there was a continuation of the work in plane and solid geometry; there were astronomical and calendrical studies; some thinkers advanced the theory of the sphericity of the earth, and others attacked the geocentric conception of the universe; in the fifth century, Anaxagoras, the friend of Pericles, shocked religious conservatives when he claimed that the sun was a huge mass of blazing metal. Nevertheless, the main trends of Greek thought in the fifth and early fourth centuries led away from what we today would term "science." In the century and a half after 500 B.C., Greek philosophy passed through three stages.

Philo-
sophic
trends

1. Roughly speaking, between 500 and 450 B.C., various philosophical schools elaborated, adapted, and altered the ideas that had been advanced in the sixth century. The increasingly abstract and purely speculative character of this thought ultimately led this type of philosophy into a *cul-de-sac*, with the result that in the second half of the fifth century it was largely abandoned and speculation proceeded along new lines.

2. Between 450 and 400 B.C. there was a growing tendency for men to think more about the problems of society, economics, and government, and to pay less attention to the problems of the universe and nature. This new thinking, it

was felt, was more "practical." Certainly, the popular mind was attracted by it; moreover, it is understandable that a man will naturally be more interested in things which relate directly to himself.

3. After 400 B.C., as we shall presently see, ethics, the formulation of "personal" philosophies, speculation concerning ideal forms of society and government, and the systematization of knowledge dominated philosophical thought.

Although the work of the philosophers who were the immediate successors of the sixth-century Ionian school and Pythagoras is important in the history of philosophy, it is not absolutely essential to our purpose here. After Anaximenes, the Greek thinkers struggled with several problems. The motion and change postulated by Anaximander in his theory of the separation of opposites was upheld by Heraclitus of Ephesus, who considered fire to be the prime element and maintained that the universe and all it contains is in a constant state of flux, and that there are continuous generation and decay. The opposite point of view was taken by Parmenides of Elea and his school, who said that change and motion are illusions: what is, always was, and always will be; something cannot be created from nothing, nor can Being become nothing, or not-Being. The Sicilian, Empedocles (495-430 B.C.), combined these divergent views by postulating four elements (fire, water, earth, and air) which united or separated to form all other types of matter; the elements themselves were constant and changeless, and it was their combination or disintegration which gave the impression of change. About the middle of the fifth century, Leucippus and his successor, Democritus, elaborated the atomic theory that was the logical outgrowth of the philosophy of Anaximenes (see above, p. 125). Leucippus considered all material forms to be composed of an infinite number of tiny particles (atoms), continually in motion, uniform in substance, which unite temporarily to form visible objects. In addition, Heraclitus, the Eleatic school, Anaxagoras, and others spoke variously of a single divine wisdom, a God, or a universal mind

The
early
fifth
century

**Stele of Naram-Sin (2550 B. C.)
An Example of Sumerian Relief
Sculpture**

**Babylonian Relief Sculpture
Hammurabi Receives His Law
Code from the Sun God**

Palace and Zikkurat

PLATE I

The Metropolitan Museum of Art

A Sumerian Clay Tablet

The University Prints

**A Sumerian Statue
(King Gudea, 2400 B. C.)**

PLATE II

Rock-cut Temple of Rameses II at Abu Simel

PLATE III

Restoration of the Temple of Amon at Karnak

PLATE IV

Egyptian Painting: Harvest Scene

Egyptian Painting: Musicians

PLATE V

The Metropolitan Museum of Art

Egyptian Painting: Barber at Work

The Metropolitan Museum of Art

Egyptian Painting: Brick-making

PLATE VI

Hittite Sculpture

PLATE VII

The Metropolitan Museum of Art

The Metropolitan Museum of Art

Assyrian Sculpture

PLATE VIII

Minoan Painting

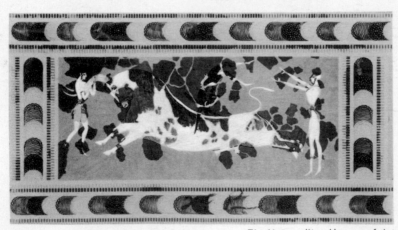

Bull Leaping at Cnossus

PLATE IX

Lion Gate at Mycenae

PLATE X

Egyptian Sculpture
Compare with the early Greek
figures on this page

Apollo of Melos

Hera of Samos

Seated Female Figure

Archaic Greek Sculpture

PLATE XI

The Bettmann Archive

Athenian Red Figure Ware

The Bettmann Archive

Spartan Black Figure Ware

The Bettmann Archive

Athenian Black Figure Ware

The Metropolitan Museum of Art

Athenian Black Figure Ware

PLATE XII

British Museum

Pericles

The University Prints

Socrates

The Bettmann Archive

Plato

The Bettmann Archive

Aristotle

PLATE XIII

Boy with Goose (Alexandrian Style)

Gaul and His Wife (Pergamene Style)

PLATE XIV

The Ara Pacis of Augustus

Reliefs, The Column of
Marcus Aurelius Antoninus

PLATE XV

Arch of Septimius Severus

PLATE XVI

(nous) that was the supreme guiding force in the universe. The materialistic interpretation advocated by the atomists, however, left no room for such ideas.

The only result of all such speculation was the growth of a feeling that no satisfactory conclusion could be reached. Many people took the practical attitude that, even if the philosophers did arrive at a really demonstrable theory, nothing could be done about it. Therefore, men began to turn from their meditations upon "divine" affairs to "human" problems.

The leaders in the new intellectual movement were the Sophists, the itinerant teachers and lecturers, the professional "wise men," who went from city to city giving lecture courses on society, political science, grammar, rhetoric, argumentation, and other subjects. The students of the Sophists were men who wanted a "practical" and "useful" education that would help them in politics and the law courts; for this they were willing to pay their teachers considerable sums of money. In general, the attitude of the Sophists toward established customs and beliefs was one of skepticism, and they regarded the efforts of the philosophers as rather futile and meaningless. The famous Protagoras (*fl. c.* 450 B.C.), for example, preached the relativity of knowledge and said that truth was neither absolute nor eternal; the reality or unreality of anything depended upon its reality or unreality to each individual, and "man is the measure of all things." The Sophists tried to take all knowledge as their province; they had some information on almost every subject, but each Sophist had his own special field for which he was famous.

The Sophists were not well liked by the conservatives in the Greek city-states; the skepticism which sophistic teaching fostered undermined religion, and the individualism encouraged by the Sophists ran counter to the principles upon which the city-state was founded. As a result, the Sophists were frequently driven from cities where the elements in control were hostile to their liberalism. There is a story that the books of Protagoras were burned at Athens about 411 B.C.;

The Sophists

the very word "Sophist" came to have an unfavorable connotation.

It must be admitted that, although many of the Sophists
were popularizers and "half-journalists," some of the foremost of these teachers were brilliant men who performed a
great service in bringing Greek thinking down out of the
clouds and directing intellectual energy into new and profitable channels. Although he was not himself a Sophist—
mainly because he took no money for his teaching—Socrates,
whom we shall now consider, was indebted to the Sophists
for much of the emphasis and method by means of which
he was able to change the course of Greek philosophical
studies.

Socrates
Socrates (469-399 B.C.) stands at the beginning of a new
era in Greek philosophy; it is perhaps too much to say that
he revolutionized Greek thought, but it is certainly true that
both Plato and Aristotle owed much to him. The real Socrates
will probably never be known. None of his writings has been
preserved—if, indeed, he ever wrote anything—and we see
him today chiefly through the eyes of his follower, Plato, who
in his dialogues gives us an idealized picture of the master.
The Socrates of Plato is unlike the Socrates of Xenophon's
Memorabilia, and neither Plato nor Xenophon would subscribe to the unfavorable view of Socrates which Aristophanes
seems to have had. Moreover, the biography of Socrates by
Diogenes Laertius is a miserable hodge-podge in which fact
and fiction cannot easily be distinguished.

In spite of conflicting testimony, however, it is possible to
present some general impressions of Socrates' life and work.
Socrates was an Athenian who came from a "middle-class"
family. He was plain in his tastes, moderate in all things, and
extremely healthy; his pale face, flat nose, bulging eyes, and
thick lips made his physical appearance anything but pre-
possessing. Nevertheless, his conviviality, his homely wit, and
his ability as a teacher attracted many people to him, especially the young men of Athens who sought the intellectual
stimulation that he was able to provide.

Socrates had studied physical science under Anaxagoras, but he came to the conclusion that it was impossible to learn about natural phenomena; therefore he turned to a field that he hoped might prove to be more profitable: the study of society and human relationships. Socrates himself did not profess to have definite knowledge of anything; instead, he pretended to seek information from others. It was his practice to interview people in all walks of life—statesmen, poets, craftsmen, and the like—in order to ascertain their ideas about certain general subjects: justice, truth, courage, piety, democracy, and law.

Socrates' methods

On these subjects "every man fancied that he could give a confident opinion, and even wondered that any other person should feel a difficulty. When Socrates, professing ignorance, put any such questions, he found no difficulty in obtaining an answer, given off-hand, and with very little reflection. The answer purported to be the explanation or definition of a term—familiar, indeed, but of wide and comprehensive import—given by one who had never before tried to render to himself an account of what it meant. Having got this answer, Socrates put fresh questions, applying it to specific cases, to which the respondent was compelled to give answers inconsistent with the first. . . . The respondent then amended his answer; but this was a prelude to other questions —and the respondent, after many attempts to disentangle himself, was obliged to plead guilty to the inconsistencies, with an admission that he could make no satisfactory answer to the original query, which had at first appeared so easy and familiar."[4]

This type of discourse showed clearly the ignorance of mankind in general regarding certain human problems that were of prime importance. Socrates found that definite knowledge was confined to the crafts where the craftsmen knew precisely what they were doing and were able to transmit a knowledge of their work to others; this was in direct

[4] George Grote, *History of Greece* (revised edition), London, 1869, Vol. VIII, p. 235.

contrast to the situation as regards man and society where exact knowledge, even if it were possible, would be difficult to pass on to other people.

Socrates' great contributions to philosophy were the stress which he put upon ethics and his invention of inductive discourse (dialectic). His successors, from Plato onward, followed in his footsteps. Moreover, although Socrates was not himself interested in science, his methods were employed by Aristotle and later scientists with great profit, for his use of general definitions followed by logical classification proved ideal for marshaling scientific facts into clear and concise forms.

Socrates' contributions to philosophy

It is not surprising to learn that Socrates was not universally popular in Athens. He was thought by many to be a Sophist and dangerous to the state. Those who had been subjected to one of his cross-examinations and shown to be hopelessly ignorant naturally became his bitter enemies. For many years his influential friends were able to protect him, but finally he fell a victim to the unsettlement and hysteria which prevailed in Athens after the Peloponnesian War. In 399 B.C. he was indicted for religious non-conformity and for corrupting the youth of Athens. Although at his trial Socrates was able to refute his accusers, he was declared guilty and sentenced to death. It is of interest that the jury which voted on his conviction did so only by the narrowest of margins. Two famous works of Plato are well worth reading in connection with Socrates' trial and execution: the *Apology of Socrates*, which describes the trial, and the *Phaedo*, which is an account of his death.

His death

In the fourth century B.C. the two giants of Greek philosophy, Plato and Aristotle, dominated the stage. Their influence upon their contemporaries was exceeded only by the influence they exerted upon later Greek, Roman, and medieval thinkers. In ethics, politics, science, aesthetics, and nearly every conceivable field the greater part of the effort of subsequent philosophers was conditioned by ideas first put into recognizable form by either Plato or Aristotle.

The fourth century

Plato (428-347 B.C.) had sat at the feet of Socrates. After the death of his master, he traveled to Egypt, Cyrene, Italy, and Sicily. About 387 B.C. he returned to his native Athens **Plato** where he founded a school in the Grove of Academus, an institution which was afterward known as the Academy. Plato employed the discussion methods developed by Socrates, and he continued the search for universal ethical truths. His writings were mostly in the form of dialogues in which Socrates played the part of an interrogator. One of Plato's greatest works is his famous *Republic* in which he set forth his ideas on the ideal form of government. Plato's dream was a Utopian city-state in which the citizens (numbering about 5000) were divided into three classes: workers, warriors, and rulers. The rulers were men of special intellectual abilities who were trained for their task from childhood. This ideal state was, of course, to be economically self-sufficient. Toward the end of his life Plato produced his *Laws*, a work which described a city-state government and organization more practical than the one proposed in the *Republic*.

Plato was not only a magnificent and stimulating philosopher, but he also possessed a fine literary style. Perhaps the most serious criticism which might be made of him is that he looked backward rather than forward. In his political thinking he was not entirely in touch with the trend of his times, and he could not see that the day of the independent city-state was nearly ended. In many ways Plato belongs to the fifth rather than the fourth century; the fact that most of his work was done in the fourth century helps to demonstrate how much that century constituted a transitional period in which there was a mingling of classical Greek culture with the new elements that were to be characteristic of the Hellenistic Age.

Aristotle (384-322 B.C.) spent twenty years as a student in Plato's Academy; then he was appointed tutor to Alexander **Aristotle** the Great, and, finally, about 335 he returned to Athens to open a school of his own in the grove known as the Lyceum. In large part, Aristotle emancipated himself from Plato; his main interest was in studying and organizing in logical form all the knowledge then possessed by mankind. But Aristotle was more than a compiler of facts or an encyclopaedist; through his own observation and thought he was able to add much to the sum total of information available in his own day. His writings on logic (he was the inventor of formal logic), metaphysics, natural history, ethics, rhetoric, and aesthetics help to give some idea of the broadness of his interests and his intellectual power. Aristotle also dealt with political science; he made a careful study of the constitutions of about one hundred and fifty of the Greek states, and he began a philosophical work, the *Politics*, which was not completed when he died. For Aristotle as well as Plato, the city-state was the chief form of government, but Aristotle's views were more practical than those of his predecessor.

The philosophical schools of both Plato and Aristotle, the Academy and the Lyceum, continued to exist after the deaths of their founders. Naturally, both men had followers and imitators who founded schools of their own. In subsequent chapters we shall trace the history of the later progress of philosophy.

One field of Greek science which has not been mentioned thus far is medicine. It is of interest that in the fifth century, when Greek science as a whole was not advancing with any appreciable speed, progress of considerable significance was being made in medicine. The major figure in Greek medicine in this century was Hippocrates of Cos. Hippocrates, a priest of Asclepius (the god of healing), owed much to studies he made in Egypt. As a result of his travels, he was able to free himself from the traditions of magic in medical treatment and to see disease as a natural evil that might be combated by natural methods. He stressed hygiene and maintained that nature is the best physician. The crudeness of his methods, however, were well expressed in his maxim: "Where drugs fail, steel will cure; where steel fails, fire will cure; where fire fails, there is no cure." Hippocrates had many

Medicine

Hippocrates

students; and later physicians, even in the Roman period, were highly dependent upon his writings.

THE CLASSICAL GREEK CONTRIBUTION TO CIVILIZATION

We have now completed our brief survey of classical Greek civilization. We have seen how elements from the civilization of the Ancient Near East were borrowed, adapted, elaborated, and combined with new elements in a new environment, with the resultant formation of a distinctive civilization, that of classical Greece. We shall see, in the succeeding chapters, how classical Greek civilization was spread to non-Greeks, how it was transformed by its new contacts, and how there was created a world civilization, the Hellenistic, which combined culture traits from the Near East, from classical Greece, and (eventually) new elements from the Western Mediterranean world.

To the world civilization of the Hellenistic and Roman periods (and to medieval and modern civilization), the Greeks of the classical age contributed more than any other group. Their language influenced Latin and all the later Indo-European and Semitic languages spoken by the people who were their cultural heirs—our English vocabulary today is rich in Greek roots; Greek literature was read, translated, copied, and imitated—and through the ages the influence of Greek art is apparent to even the casual observer. The science and philosophy of the Hellenistic peoples and the Romans were predominantly an outgrowth from the classical period; this was also true of ideas in the fields of religion, politics, and aesthetics—to cite only a few examples. Even the city-state, although it was no longer the largest of the political units of the new Hellenistic world, was retained and put to good use, for in the empires of the Hellenistic period and in the Roman empire the *polis* became a basic element of imperial organization. In the last analysis, the great empires of the period after 362 B.C. were federations of allied communities (mainly city-states) bound in varying degrees of subjection to a central authority.

The Greek contribution

Moreover, we cannot dismiss the Greeks without a reference to the so-called "Greek view of life" which tended to become an integral part of later thinking. The "Greek view of life" is made up of several elements: the ideal of moderation, and the love of freedom, justice, beauty, and wisdom. Moderation was epitomized by a Greek phrase, "Nothing too much," and a word, *sophrosyne,* which signified sanity, balance, and self-control. The democratic city-state fostered the ideals of freedom and justice; Greek art, because of its sincere attempt to imitate or reproduce nature, could not help but stimulate a love of beauty; and Greek philosophy, by divorcing itself from the supernatural, opened the gates to wisdom.

The concepts of freedom, justice, beauty, moderation, and (in part) wisdom were not unfamiliar to the peoples of the Ancient Near East, as we can see from a perusal of Babylonian, Egyptian, Persian, and other literature; but it was the Greek statement of these concepts that made them known to western Europe. It is not too much to say that these concepts were less familiar to the majority of the Greeks of the classical period than to their successors, for it must never be forgotten that the Greek civilization that existed before 362 B.C. was not widely diffused either vertically or horizontally. In other words, even at Athens, the cultural center of classical Greek civilization, the country people and many of the city proletarians may never have been much affected culturally; finally, there must have been numerous outlying geographic areas in Greece (Aetolia, Arcadia, etc.) where civilization was unknown.

CHAPTER VII

THE HELLENISTIC AGE

THE COMING OF THE NEW ERA

The mainland Greeks, during the bitter years of the early fourth century, had failed to keep pace with the rest of the Mediterranean world; but few Hellenic statesmen who took the trouble to examine the international situation in the period of comparative peace that followed the Battle of Mantinea were sufficiently acute to recognize this vital fact. The intense desire for local independence which had been one of the virtues of the pre-Persian and Periclean Ages had become a vice that was shortly to bring about the complete destruction of any sort of political freedom in Greece. This narrow provincial attitude, long a tradition in the city-states of Hellas and now so out of date, precluded the attainment of the political unity necessary to keep the Greeks predominant in the affairs of the Aegean, for in the new era the nation, and not the *polis*, was to play the leading rôle. *The failure of the polis*

The development of national groups in southern Europe at this time was due largely to the diffusion into the hinterland of the Graeco-Oriental culture of the Mediterranean littoral. Macedonia and Rome, the two most important states thus affected, were destined to figure prominently in the subsequent history of the Greeks and to carry Greek culture to the far corners of the ancient world. More favorably situated, nearer to what was then the center of cultural diffusion, Macedonia reached the high point of her career long before the Romans became interested in affairs outside of Italy; when Rome finally attained the status of a world power, she found Macedonia a decadent nation. *The rise of national states*

Before 350 B.C. Macedonia was a very primitive country; her inhabitants, cut off from the seacoast by the Greek settle-

185

ments in the northern Aegean, were largely a pastoral people.

Although the Macedonians were probably distantly related to the Hellenes, they were classed as barbarians by their more civilized neighbors who lived to the south; only the Macedonian royal family, which traced its descent from Heracles, was accepted in Greek society. The despised Macedonians, however, had many excellent qualities. They were hardy, fond of war, and devoted to their kings; these national characteristics enabled their first great king, Philip II, to transform his people into highly efficient soldiers for whom the Greeks were no match.

Philip II was a man who well understood the Greeks and their politics. With a genius for organization and a great capacity for intrigue, he soon had the disunited and mutually jealous city-states of Greece at his mercy; and step by step, he moved relentlessly toward his goal—the establishment of Macedonian supremacy in Greek lands. At his accession in 359, Philip centralized the Macedonian government and modernized his army. Much-needed revenue was gained by the seizure of gold and silver mines in Thrace. Then came the conquest of the Greek settlements in the northern Aegean, extension of Macedonian influence into Thessaly, and finally in 346 the first foothold in Greece proper, gained when the Thebans sought Philip's aid in settling a quarrel with the Phocians (who had violated the sanctity of Delphi).

With his Thracian gold Philip won many influential Greek statesmen to his side; but some Greek leaders, especially the Athenian Demosthenes, tried desperately to halt the Macedonian advance. Encouraged by the orations (the *Philippics*) of Demosthenes and by generous gifts of Persian gold (the Persians feared that the Macedonians might invade Asia Minor), the Athenians and the Thebans made a vain attempt

to halt the Macedonian intruder. In the Battle of Chaeronea (338) the brilliant charge of the young Alexander won the day for Philip and convinced the Greeks of the futility of resistance. After he had dealt harshly with the Thebans, the Macedonian king had little difficulty in bringing the rest of

Greece to terms. All the city-states (except Sparta) made haste to attend the Hellenic Congress which Philip called at Corinth in 337.

From Philip's point of view the congress was an unquali- **The** fied success. At his suggestion the Greeks entered into an **Hellenic** Hellenic league which was to devote itself to maintaining **League** peace in Hellas. The league became Philip's ally; he was its commander-in-chief, pledged to lead a combined Greek and Macedonian army in an invasion of Persian territory in Asia Minor. A venture of this sort was dear to the hearts of the Greeks; hence the project served to give Philip a temporary popularity in Greece.

Philip, who had seen his great plans succeed with amazing perfection up to this point, was not destined to witness their **Philip's** culmination. In 336, with his advance guard already in Asia **death** Minor, Philip was himself on the instant of departure when he was assassinated by one of his own Macedonians.

ALEXANDER THE GREAT

Alexander, Philip's son, who succeeded him as king of Macedon, is a well-known historical figure. Whether or not he deserved his title of "the Great" has for centuries been a matter for dispute. Some have claimed that Philip was the better man, but the fact remains that few other men have been able to exert so great an influence upon world history as Alexander. A born leader of men, a brilliant general with a flair for the dramatic, in a little over a decade Alexander built up the most extensive empire the world had ever seen.

A king at twenty, Alexander was an unknown quantity to the Greeks; but his sudden and complete destruction of **The** Thebes (after that city had revolted in 335) brought the **attack** **on the** prompt submission of the other city-states. When he proposed **Persian** to carry out his father's plan for a war against Persia, the **empire** Greek allies hastened to provide ships and men. In the spring of 334 B.C. Alexander began the ten-year campaign that was to make him the ruler of the Eastern Mediterranean and the old Persian empire. After a decisive victory over the Persians at the Granicus River, all of Asia Minor soon fell into his hands. In 333 Alexander moved south into Syria; there a ludicrous game of hide and seek with the Persian army in a labyrinth of Syrian mountains finally ended in another Persian defeat at Issus. Darius III, the Persian king, fled ignominiously from the field of battle, and his war chest fell into Alexander's hands with the occupation of Damascus. With this much-needed financial aid the Macedonian forces were able to proceed with the conquest of the Syrian coast. The mighty fortresses of Phoenician Tyre and Philistine Gaza capitulated after prolonged sieges, and in 332 B.C. Alexander entered Egypt where he encountered no resistance. After reorganizing Egypt and founding the city of Alexandria, he returned to Syria. Darius offered to make peace on the basis of the *status quo*, but the young conqueror resolved to follow up his advantage by pushing the attack. Crossing the Tigris and Euphrates and passing into what had once been Assyria, Alexander won another victory over Darius at Gaugamela (331). Darius fled to far-away Media, and Alexander (within four months) gained possession of the three vital cities of Babylon, Susa, and Persepolis.

From Persepolis the invaders moved northward toward Median Ecbatana where Darius had taken refuge. The Persian king did not dare to await Alexander's coming; instead, **Death of Darius** he tried to escape to Bactria, a remote province in the northeast. In swift pursuit of his quarry, Alexander covered four hundred miles in eleven days. The chase ended when the Macedonians came upon the dead body of Darius; the Persian king had been slain by his satrap, Bessus, who planned to seize Bactria for himself.

By right of conquest and by virtue of the death of Darius, **Eastern Persia and India** Alexander was now king of Persia. Rather than turn back to consolidate his conquests, he resolved to push on toward the east to punish Bessus for the murder of Darius. This plan resulted in the reduction of the eastern Persian provinces and the invasion of India (330-326). Alexander wished to proceed farther to the east than the Indus Valley, but his

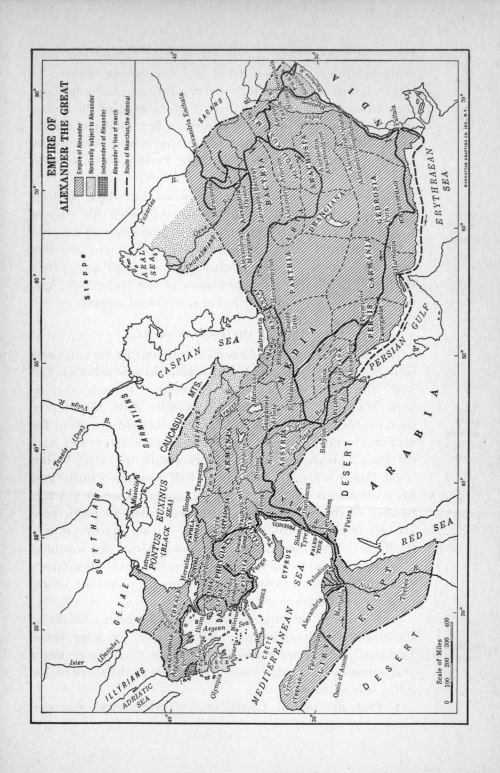

army mutinied; the men, tired of campaigning, wanted to return home. Alexander followed the Indus to its mouth and then turned back toward Babylon; while most of the troops marched across the southern deserts, a fleet under the command of Admiral Nearchus made the return journey by sea through the Indian Ocean and the Persian Gulf. Babylon was reached in 325.

Alexander's death

Alexander planned further conquests, but these projects were forestalled by his death (323). Although his empire soon broke up into a number of parts, the effect of his conquests was to shatter ancient traditions and to pave the way for a new period, the Hellenistic Age (323-146 B.C.). After outlining briefly the political history of the Hellenistic Age, we shall turn to a consideration of its cultural aspects.

POLITICAL HISTORY (323-146 B.C.)

The crisis at Alexander's death

Alexander's empire was his own creation; its various parts were bound together only by the connections which each had with Alexander—no ties connected them with each other or with Macedonia. Thus, when Alexander died, the empire soon disintegrated, for he had made no careful provision for a successor, nor was there any man strong enough to step into his place. Alexander's logical heirs within the Macedonian royal family were his half-witted half brother, Philip, and his posthumous son, the young Alexander. Since in 323 B.C. neither of these heirs was in any way fitted to participate actively in the government, a regency was set up; by 316 B.C. Philip had been assassinated, the young Alexander was held a prisoner by his most implacable enemy, and Alexander's generals had begun to fight one another for possession of all, or parts, of the empire.

The fate of the empire

The struggle for supremacy among Alexander's would-be successors continued for the next thirty-five or forty years. Eventually, his empire was divided into three large states and a number of smaller ones. The origin of the three major states was as follows:

1. Ptolemy, son of Lagus, one of Alexander's younger

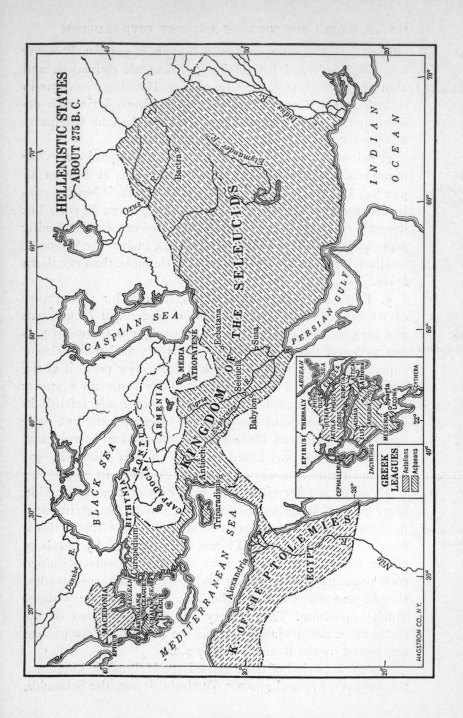

HELLENISTIC STATES
ABOUT 275 B.C.

INDIAN OCEAN

Indus R.

Bactra

Oxus R.

Etymander R.

CASPIAN SEA

KINGDOM OF THE SELEUCIDS

PERSIAN GULF

Ecbatana

MEDIA
ATROPATENE

Susa

Seleucia

Babylon

Tigris R.

Euphrates R.

ARMENIA

Antioch

Triparadisis

MEDITERRANEAN SEA

Alexandria

K. OF THE PTOLEMIES

EGYPT

Nile R.

BLACK SEA

PONTUS

CAPPADOCIA

BITHYNIA

Curopedium

Danube R.

MACEDONIA

AEGEAN SEA

AETOLIAN LEAGUE

ACHAEAN LEAGUE

EPIRUS

GREEK LEAGUES
Aetolians
Achaeans

EPIRUS

THESSALY

AEGEAN SEA

PHTHI-
OTIS

EUBOEA

ATTICA

Athens

OETAEA

PHOCIS

BOEOTIA

AETOLIA

LOCRIS

ACHAIA

ARCADIA

ARGOLIS

Sparta

ELIS

MESSENIA

LACONIA

CEPHALLENIA

ZACYNTHUS

CYTHERA

HAGSTROM CO., N.Y.

The kingdom of the Ptolemies

officers, had become governor of Egypt in 323 B.C. Ptolemy was able to defend his territory against all claimants, and about 306 B.C. he took the title of king. His kingdom came to include Egypt, Cyrene, Cyprus, and southern Syria. His descendants ruled Egypt until 30 B.C.; the famous Cleopatra was the last of the Ptolemaic dynasty in Egypt.

The Seleucid kingdom

2. Seleucus, another of Alexander's companions, after many trials and tribulations founded a dynasty at Babylon in 312 B.C. His descendants, the Seleucids, in their heyday controlled most of the old Persian empire (except Egypt), but dynastic quarrels and the increasing power of neighboring states weakened their kingdom. By 63 B.C., when the Seleucids finally fell before Rome, they held little more than northern Syria.

The Antigonids

3. Two of the most aggressive claimants for the empire of Alexander were Antigonos Monophthalmos (a general) and his son, Demetrius Poliorcetes. Antigonos (between 316-301 B.C.) and Demetrius (between 301-285 B.C.) made almost superhuman efforts to gain control of a major portion of the territory once held by Alexander. They built up a strong navy which commanded the Aegean, they made friends in Greece, and they held Macedon for brief periods; but their opponents—Seleucus, Ptolemy, and others—finally overcame them; Antigonos was killed at Ipsus in Asia Minor in 301 B.C., and Demetrius was captured by Seleucus in 285.

Antigonos Gonatas

This did not terminate the activities of the Antigonids, however, for Antigonos Gonatas, the son of Demetrius, still held the fleet and was in possession of parts of Greece. When Greece, Macedonia, and Thrace were invaded by bands of Gallic marauders (280-277 B.C.), Antigonos Gonatas gained such popularity by defeating and driving out these invaders that he was able to ascend the Macedonian throne without much opposition. The dynasty he established, that of the Antigonids, ruled Macedon until the last king, Perseus, was conquered by the Romans in 167 B.C.

The great period of these three large Hellenistic kingdoms was between 277 and 200 B.C. During this age, the Seleucids,

Ptolemies, and Antigonids engaged in numerous conflicts in which, generally speaking, the Seleucids and Antigonids opposed the Ptolemies. Their actions were dictated by certain fundamental policies.

1. The Ptolemies needed a fleet to hold their territories outside of Egypt. Therefore it was necessary for them to have access to the naval supplies of Asia Minor and the cedars of Lebanon. This brought the Ptolemies into conflict with the Seleucids because (a) the Seleucids wanted access to the Mediterranean through Syria, and (b) they claimed Asia Minor as their territory. As a result, the Ptolemies hotly contested the possession of Syria with the Seleucids, and encouraged the growth of the native kingdom of Pergamum in Asia Minor as a state independent of the Seleucids. *Ptolemaic policy*

To prevent the effective cooperation of the Seleucids and the Antigonids, the Ptolemies stirred up revolts in Greece and fostered movements for Greek independence so that the Antigonids would be kept too busy in Europe to send aid to the Seleucids in Asia Minor. Toward the end of the third century B.C., however, the struggle began to turn in favor of the Seleucids and Antigonids, with the result that the Ptolemies and their Pergamene allies were forced to call upon Rome, the rising state in the west, for aid.

2. The Antigonid control of Greece was in no sense complete. The Antigonids were never strong enough to conquer all the Greeks, yet it was necessary for the Macedonian monarchs to prevent the rise of any powerful Greek movement hostile to Macedon. There were Macedonian garrisons in Athens, Chalcis, and Corinth; but in the Peloponnesus and in central Greece there were strong and independent Hellenic groups. These were the leagues: the Achaean confederation of city-states in the Peloponnesus, and the league of the hill tribes of Aetolia. During the first part of the third century B.C. the Aetolians were friendly with the Antigonids, and the Achaeans were not. The situation was reversed about 230 B.C. when there was a temporary revival of Spartan power which menaced the Achaeans. In desperation, the Achaeans *Antigonid policy*

made an alliance with Macedonia, and the Spartan power was broken. This action of the Achaeans in calling in the Macedonians angered the Aetolians, who felt that it would increase Macedonian predominance in Greece and endanger Aetolian independence. The final result, however, was that, as soon as the Spartans were defeated, the Achaeans reverted to their former anti-Macedonian policy, and both Achaeans and Aetolians then combined to fight the Antigonids.

Philip V

The situation became more complicated when Philip V, the Macedonian king, became the ally of Carthage during the Second Punic War (218-201 B.C.), in which Rome and Carthage struggled for control of the Western Mediterranean. The Achaeans and the Aetolians sided with the Romans; they fought Philip in Greece and thus prevented him from aiding the Carthaginians. After the Second Punic War, the Romans drove Philip from Greece (200-197 B.C.) and in 196 B.C. proclaimed the "freedom of the Greeks."

Rome in Greece

The Aetolians, Achaeans, Pergamenes, and Ptolemies soon discovered that they had made a mistake in inviting the Romans to "help" them, for the Romans began to meddle in the affairs of the Eastern Mediterranean. The Aetolians were the first to regret their friendship with Rome. In the first decade of the second century B.C. they invited Antiochus III, the Seleucid king, to invade Greece and free them from the Romans. In a brief war (192-188 B.C.) the Romans punished both the Seleucids and the Aetolians; the Seleucids were forced to relinquish all claim to Asia Minor, and the Aetolians were made subordinate allies of Rome. Later, when there was a temporary revival of Macedonian influence, the Achaeans sided with the Antigonids against Rome, but once again the Romans were victorious: the Macedonian kingship was abolished, and the Achaeans were severely punished. Finally, a combined Greek and Macedonian revolt (149-146 B.C.) was crushed by the Romans; Macedonia was made a Roman province, Corinth was destroyed, and the Roman governor of Macedonia was given power to supervise Greece very closely.

The increasing strength of the Romans in the Eastern Mediterranean reduced the Seleucids to impotence, and the Ptolemaic kingdom became little more than a Roman protectorate. In 133 B.C. Attalus III, the Pergamene king, recognized the inevitable; he willed his kingdom to Rome, and it was organized as the Roman province of Asia in 129 B.C.

3. It has been said that trade was the life blood of the Seleucid empire. This statement provides a key to Seleucid policies; the Seleucids were like their predecessors, the Babylonians, who were the middlemen in the trade that passed **Seleucid** north and south, east and west, through the Tigris-Euphrates **policy** Valley. As we have seen, the Seleucids desired a western outlet through Syria and Asia Minor; in like manner, Bactria, India, and the Persian Gulf were important to them as eastern outlets.

Unfortunately, in the west the Seleucids had to contend with the Ptolemies and their Pergamene allies. The conflict between the Seleucids and the Ptolemies over the possession of Syria was probably the feature of this struggle that was **Wars in** productive of the greatest trouble to the Seleucids, for, while **Syria** a succession of "Syrian" wars was fought, the Pergamenes were able to consolidate their independent position in Asia Minor, and the eastern Seleucid provinces began to break away (after 250 B.C.).

It will be profitable to consider briefly the history of India and the eastern Seleucid provinces in the period from Alexander's conquests down to about 133 B.C. Alexander had brought most of the Indus Valley under his sovereignty, but in the time of the first Seleucid a native north Indian dynasty, the Mauryas, occupied this territory. The Seleucids, because **India** of their troubles in Syria and Asia Minor, could not actively oppose the Mauryan advance; instead, they followed a policy of appeasement which resulted in the establishment of friendly relations. In this manner, trade with India was assured, and a profitable peace endured for over a century.

On the other hand, affairs in the northeast were less favorable. About 250 B.C., the Parthians, a native group located in the territory between the Caspian Sea and Bactria, declared their independence from Seleucid rule. The Parthian

The Parthians

kings claimed descent from the Persian dynasty which Alexander had overthrown; this nationalistic appeal was not in vain, and ultimately (in the second century B.C.) the Parthians were able to build up a state which controlled the Iranian plateau and drove a wedge between the central Seleucid possessions in Babylonia and the provinces in the east. In the reign of Mithridates I (171-138 B.C.), the first really great Parthian king, the Parthians extended their rule over Media and Babylonia.

The rise of the Parthians in 250 B.C. was very important for the history of Bactria, the northeastern territory of the Seleucid empire. Before the end of the century, Bactria had

Bactria

become an independent state. Its Greek kings, whose dynasty was connected with the Seleucid royal family on the distaff side, ruled over a mixed population of Greek settlers and natives. One ruler, Demetrius (189-167 B.C.), invaded India about 183 B.C. and gained possession of the territory once held by the Mauryas. After his death, his kingdom was divided into two independent parts: Bactria and northern India.

The Greek states in Bactria and northern India continued to exist until shortly after 130 B.C., when barbarians (the Scythians or Sacae) who had formerly lived on the northern borders of Bactria were displaced by pressure from Chinese tribes. The Sacae swept over Bactria and into India and destroyed the Greek kingdoms. At the same time, as we have seen, the Parthians came into the possession of most of the Seleucid empire; the Seleucids had little left but northern Syria.

Other native kingdoms

In the Hellenistic Age there were, in addition to Pergamum, three other native kingdoms in Asia Minor: Armenia, Bithynia, and Pontus. Each of these owed its independence to its remoteness and comparative inaccessibility. Bithynia and Pontus were located on the Black Sea and had at least a veneer of Greek culture, but Armenia was closer to the old

Near East in its outlook. In the first century B.C., as we shall observe later, these native kingdoms came into conflict with Rome.

HELLENISTIC CIVILIZATION

The Hellenistic Age is sometimes defined as a period in which Greek culture became the culture not only of the Greeks, but also of a large body of non-Greeks; the period may thus be distinguished from its predecessor, the Hellenic or classical age, in which Greek culture was almost exclusively the possession of the Greeks. Such a definition is useful, but it may also be misleading. It is undoubtedly true that in the Hellenistic Age Greek culture was diffused in greater or less degree throughout the old Persian empire and into India—some Greek influences even penetrated China; the Western Mediterranean region was also affected. On the other hand, it should not be forgotten that both the Near East (and India) and the Western Mediterranean had cultural contributions to make. Hellenistic civilization was by no means an unadulterated Greek civilization; it was rather a compound of Greek, Oriental, and western elements. Unquestionably, the Greek element was the major one; but the westward flow of culture from the Near East during the Hellenistic Age was almost as strong as it had been during the early years of the Greek Renaissance (in the seventh century B.C.); then, too, with the eastward advance of the Romans (after 200 B.C.), the West began to make its contribution.

The Hellenistic Age

Strictly speaking, in terms of political and military history the Hellenistic Age began with the death of Alexander (323 B.C.) and ended in 146 or 133 B.C. If we consider the Hellenistic Age as a cultural epoch, however, it is more difficult to set up chronological limits. Many of the developments that are characteristic of the period were in evidence at the close of the fifth century B.C., although we might think of the years from the end of the Peloponnesian War to the death of Alexander as forming a period of transition in which the change from Hellenic to Hellenistic culture was taking

The chronological limits of the age

place. Moreover, it is even harder to find a satisfactory date for the end of the Hellenistic Age. What is usually called Roman civilization was, after all, basically and essentially Hellenistic; the really original contributions of the Romans were few in number; for the most part, the Romans played the rôle of adapters, elaborators, and carriers of Hellenistic culture. If one were to accept this view of the Romans in cultural history, he would be justified in saying that the Hellenistic Age came to an end only with the fall of Rome and the beginning of the medieval period.

The most satisfactory solution for this problem is to divide this large cultural epoch into two parts: the Hellenistic Age proper, and the Roman phase. The Hellenistic Age proper coincided with the great period of the Hellenistic monarchies when Hellenistic civilization was centered in the Eastern Mediterranean region. The Roman phase began with the gradual expansion of Rome's political power into the Eastern Mediterranean. At the same time, the Romans were adopting more and more of Hellenistic civilization. The high point of the Roman phase came in the first two centuries of the Christian era when the ancient world was politically unified by the Roman empire and civilization was diffused into Rome's western provinces.

Characteristics of the age   Two related political developments—the decline of the city-state and the rise of empires—were partly responsible for two characteristics typical of the Hellenistic Age: universalism and individualism.

Whereas in the classical period the separatism fostered by the Greek city-states (through their desire for local independence) had been an outstanding characteristic, in the new age the empire of Alexander helped to give rise to the concept of *oecumene,* the unity of the inhabited world. The world **Universalism** was considered the common possession of all human beings; the old distinction between Greek and non-Greek (barbarian) no longer seemed valid. Culture was internationalized: there was a common speech (the *koine,* an adaptation of Attic Greek), people read the same literature and enjoyed the same

art, commerce disregarded political boundaries. The great
Hellenistic kingdoms of Alexander's successors brought vast
areas under single governments, whereas the city-states were
reduced to subordinate political units. Nationalism could not
flourish in the new kingdoms with their diverse populations.
The people of the various parts of these kingdoms were bound
to their rulers by personal ties, but they had no strong feeling
of kinship with the other subjects of the same ruler.

Individualism increased as the importance and significance **Individ-**
of the city-state declined. In the classical period the individual **ualism**
had been subordinated to the state; but in the Hellenistic
Age this was no longer true, for, as we have seen, the Hellenistic kingdoms did not foster nationalism. As a result, personality was allowed a freer scope.

The feeling of world unity, the broadening of political
horizons, the innumerable contacts furnished by international
trade, and the great movement of peoples (the settlement of
Greek colonists in the Near East, the introduction of Oriental **Syncretism**
slaves into the west, and the journeys of travelers and traders)
were all productive of a tendency toward syncretism and also
eclecticism. People were exposed to a host of new ideas in
religion, art, philosophy, and many other fields. In order to
avoid the mental confusion and chaos which the impact of
these new ideas might create, men were forced to turn to
syncretism and eclecticism. The widespread concept of universalism (*oecumene*) impelled people to search for common
denominators for seemingly diverse things. Thus—to cite an
obvious example from the field of religion—the Egyptian
Ammon, the Hebrew Jahweh, the Persian Ahuramazda, and
the Roman Jupiter were all recognized as the foreign counterparts of the Greek Zeus. This led to assimilation and combination (syncretism); in Egypt, for example, the ancient
gods might be worshiped under Greek names: Horus became
Apollo; Thoth, Hermes; Hathor, Aphrodite.

Syncretism was obviously very limited in scope; complete
combination or reconciliation of the ideas and materials **Eclecticism**
available even in a small field was not possible. The next

step was eclecticism, picking and choosing desirable elements or parts from separate organisms and systems. In philosophy or religion, for example, a man might choose individual ideas or practices from a number of systems or beliefs and combine them in a new pattern. This was also done in art and numerous other fields.

The Hellenistic Age was notable for its specialization of activity. In learning, it was no longer possible for one person to take all knowledge for his field. The common fund of knowledge had increased so greatly that it was difficult enough to master a single division of it. This was likewise true of other phases of human endeavor; in industry, trade, art, and even politics, one had to limit oneself.

Last of all, in the five centuries between 300 B.C. and 200 A.D. the ancient world reached the high point of its urbanization. There were more and larger cities than had ever existed before, a situation which was not duplicated until the modern era (after 1500 A.D.).

In its universalism, individualism, syncretism, eclecticism, specialization of activity, and high degree of urbanization, the Hellenistic Age bears some superficial resemblance to the modern era (after 1500 A.D.). Other parallels might be suggested. In the Hellenistic Age there were republics, democracies, federal states, and divine-right monarchies; arbitration and mediation were employed to settle international disputes; capitalism, imperialism, militarism, and communism were to be found; class struggles were not unknown; city life bred romanticism and primitivism in literature; realism, impressionism, and archaism appeared in art.

The Hellenistic world, however, differed from our modern world in that it was almost empty of machines. It is usually said that the place which is today filled by the machine was then occupied by the slave. This is not strictly true, for in the Hellenistic Age the number of free laborers in industry increased. The real point is that because slavery did exist, the free laborer had to compete with it; he had no bargaining power and had to work for the equivalent of slave wages (or

Specialization

Urbanization

Parallels with the modern era

Contrasts

less) or not at all. Thus, labor was cheap. The interesting result was that, although the scientists of the Hellenistic Age made a number of important discoveries and inventions, their work was not turned to any practical use because cheap labor discouraged the development of labor-saving devices.

With the Hellenistic Age ancient civilization reached its climax; the highest point was attained during the Roman phase in the first two centuries of the Christian era. The conquests of Alexander helped to pave the way for a cultural unity which followed upon the heels of an economic unity that had been in the process of formation even before his time; last of all came the Romans who imposed political unity upon a major portion of the ancient world. The cultural interplay which these unities made possible brought ancient civilization into its most complex form. Although it may be argued that the Hellenistic Age was decadent because it produced no Pindar, no Sophocles, no Phidias, and no Plato, the fact remains that civilization (as we have defined it in this book) reached the highest development which it was to attain in ancient times. In the vast number of its culture traits, the complexity of its culture, and the extent of its urbanization, the age was the most civilized in the history of this planet before our own epoch. **Climax of ancient civilization**

GOVERNMENT

The Hellenistic Age was notable for its variety of governmental forms. Athens, Rhodes, and Corinth, as well as many other Greek cities, continued to exist as more or less independent, but politically unimportant, city-states. The monarchy of the Antigonids in Macedonia was only a slightly more sophisticated version of the old Macedonian form of government, not far removed from the primitive Greek monarchy of the Dark Ages. Two new governmental developments of the Hellenistic Age were the great Graeco-Oriental monarchy and the federal state. **Governmental forms**

The Graeco-Oriental (or Hellenistic) monarchy was a combination of Macedonian, Egyptian, and Persian forms. **Hellenistic monarchy**

Alexander himself had recognized the problems involved in ruling a large territory containing diverse national elements in its population. The powers of the ruler, the basis of these powers, the form of governmental organization, and the sources of imperial revenues had to be established. If possible, the various national elements must be fused into a unified whole.

Autocracy

Alexander apparently decided that the ruler of an empire must be an autocrat who governed through an efficient bureaucracy. This was the way of the Near East; it had been followed successfully by his immediate predecessors, the Persian kings and the Pharaohs of Egypt. Furthermore, the ruler must be a god, or else hold his place by divine right. The continuation of the ancient theocracy solved Alexander's

Theocracy

problems in the Near East; he became a god-king in Egypt, and a divine-right ruler in Persia. There still remained, however, the difficulty of finding an absolutist basis for ruling the Greeks and Macedonians. This obstacle Alexander proposed to overcome by requesting the westerners to recognize him as a god. He did not consider himself a god, nor did the Greeks and Macedonians have any illusions about his divinity. His apotheosis was simply a political device. The westerners would not be ruled by a man, but they could salve their consciences by pretending that a man was a god; as a god, he would be above mortal laws and also free to make autocratic demands upon his human subjects.

We do not know whether Alexander planned to unify the governmental organization of his empire. He had begun to build up a bureaucracy before his death, but he retained the existing forms of government in most areas as well as the systems of taxation then in force.

Unity and loyalty

There was, however, one other problem which Alexander did attack: that of creating loyal elements in the imperial population. Throughout the empire, especially in the eastern provinces, he established city-states of the Greek type which were settled by his veterans and Greek and Macedonian colonists. These city-states were intended to serve as garrisons in the conquered regions. It is often said that these settlements were also meant to be centers of diffusion for Greek culture so that the native populations might become Hellenized. Another part of Alexander's program was to conciliate the Persians by appointing them to responsible governmental posts and by encouraging intermarriage between Persians, Greeks, and Macedonians. Alexander rightly recognized the close linguistic and institutional kinship of the three Indo-European-speaking groups as opposed to the masses of Semites who formed the subject population of the Near East, especially in Mesopotamia and Syria. By fusing Persians and westerners he hoped to build up a loyal and substantial ruling class.

Many of Alexander's policies were followed by his Seleucid and Ptolemaic successors. The Ptolemies became Pharaohs, god-kings, following the Egyptian custom. The Seleucids were divine-right monarchs after the custom of the Persians; when a Seleucid king died, however, he was deified, and thus his successor was invested with a semi-divinity as the son or brother of a god. At the courts of the Ptolemies and Seleucids there developed a hierarchy of palace dignitaries; there was also in each of the two kingdoms a fully developed bureaucracy, a pyramid of officials that began at the top with a prime minister and other high officials (military, financial, judicial, etc.) and descended in a horde of minor agents who discharged civil, military, and financial duties. *Alexander's successors*

The imperial armies were composed of Greek and Macedonian mercenaries. These hired soldiers were rewarded with good lands within the empires, and their descendants formed a national militia. Moreover, the Seleucids continued Alexander's policy of colonization by Europeans; traders, craftsmen, and farmers, as well as soldiers, were settled in many newly created city-states. For a few generations the newcomers retained their identity and also their loyalty to their imperial benefactors, but ultimately they became fused with the native populations and their usefulness to the government decreased. *Mercenaries and colonists*

The problems of the Seleucids were different and more difficult than those of the Ptolemies. Whereas the Ptolemies centered their power in Egypt (which was geographically unified and possessed a homogeneous native population) and had an empire which could be easily reached by sea, the Seleucid empire was a far-flung land empire inhabited by peoples of diverse nationalities. The Seleucids could not win the loyalty of all their subjects; neither could they afford an army large enough to hold effectively the extensive regions which they claimed. Consequently, when the Parthians fostered a nationalist revival on the Iranian plateau, the Seleucids had to give way, mainly because they had failed to complete Alexander's plan to fuse the Persians and the Europeans into a ruling class.

The Ptolemies made no attempt to unite the Greeks and Macedonians with the Egyptians. The Greeks and Macedonians were introduced as mercenaries; they formed a caste superior in rank and privilege to the native Egyptians. It is interesting to see how, at the close of the third century B.C., when the Ptolemies had been weakened by their struggles for a Syrian empire, the native Egyptians of the old warrior class were able to win many concessions from their Macedonian rulers. Thus, in a way, Egyptian nationalism proved almost as trying and disastrous to the Ptolemies as the nationalism of Iran to the Seleucids.

The governmental philosophies of the Seleucids and Ptolemies present marked contrasts. The Seleucid government was an agency which provided law, order, and defense; these advantages offered by the Seleucids to their subjects were given in return for value received (revenues in the form of taxes). Trade was probably the greatest source of wealth in the Seleucid empire. Therefore, the governmental policy of the Seleucids was to encourage and protect trade; the larger its volume, the larger the royal revenues which might be derived from commercial taxes. Industry and agriculture were also important. The land of the empire was distributed in various ways: the land owned by the king was called the royal land, and was worked by royal serfs; much land was given to Seleucid nobles who held their estates as feudal lords; temple lands were administered by the priests of various cults and worked by slaves; the city-states founded by the rulers were also granted land, and the mercenaries possessed agricultural holdings (*cleruch* land). Taxes on agricultural produce were paid both in money and in kind.

The attitude of the Ptolemaic rulers was far different. Egypt, for example, was regarded as the private estate of the king, and the whole economic life of the country was organized in such a way as to provide the greatest possible revenue for the government. The land was the chief source of wealth. In theory, all the land belonged to the king; some of it he kept as royal land and rented it out for cultivation by the royal serfs; land given to the nobles was taxed as was the Egyptian *cleruch* land; there was also temple land as in the Seleucid empire. External trade was a state monopoly, and internal trade was taxed. Other state monopolies were salt, the manufacture of papyrus, oils, and linens, the mines, banking, and many other items. With the Ptolemies, state capitalism first appeared on a large scale. The government was a trading company that also controlled the production at home of the things which it sold abroad, for not only did the Ptolemies possess the agricultural surplus of Egypt, but they also operated factories that made papyrus, oils, and linens. Ptolemaic practices of state capitalism and mass production were followed by the kings of Pergamum, their allies.

Ptolemaic policies

State capitalism

While the great Hellenistic monarchies were developing in the Near East, the growth of federal representative government reached its climax in Greece in the Aetolian and Achaean Leagues. The Aetolian League was originally a federation of rural cantons in central Greece. Its governmental organization consisted of (1) a popular assembly of all citizens of the league, (2) a federal council in which each community was represented according to the size of the military contingent it furnished the league, and (3) an inner council elected from the federal council which sat as a per-

Federal government

Aetolian League

manent committee with the league officials. The league officials were a general, a secretary, a board of treasurers, and
other minor officers; all were elected by the assembly. The
individual communities of the league were independent as
far as their local governmental affairs were concerned, but
foreign relations were in the hands of the federal government. The federation also had a uniform system of weights,
measures, and coinage.

**Achaean
League**

The Achaean League was a federation of city-states. It, too,
had a popular assembly with legislative and electoral powers,
but general discussions of policy were sometimes decided by
another body (the synod), a representative group in which
each individual city-state had one vote. The federal council
was composed of delegates from the cities; the number sent
by each city was based on the size of its population. The
Achaean League had as its executive a general; there were
other elected officials whose duties were similar to those of
corresponding officials in the Aetolian League.

From this brief description of the league governments it is
clear that democracy, federation, and proportional representation were not novelties twenty-two hundred years ago.

ECONOMIC LIFE

**New
era of
coloni-
zation**

Although it has never been sufficiently emphasized, the
early Hellenistic Age was for the Greeks a new era of colonization. The growth of a small group of very rich men and a
large group of very poor ones in the Greek city-states during
the fourth century is an indication that Greece, as far as its
economic organization was concerned, had once more become
over-populated; the same thing seems to have been true of
the Greek states in Asia Minor. This situation was relieved
when Alexander and his successors settled thousands of
Greeks as colonists in what had once been the Persian empire.
The Ptolemies rewarded their Greek mercenaries with Egyptian lands, and the Seleucids planted military garrison colonies and organized Greek city-states throughout their empire.

The Hellenistic period brought many other interesting developments. During the early fourth century wages and prices had risen, and this trend was accentuated when Alexander came into possession of the Persian treasuries from which he released vast quantities of gold and silver long hoarded by the Persian kings. The increase of the actual coin in circulation stimulated trade and business enterprise and reduced interest rates; new areas of the ancient world passed from a barter to a money economy. The creation of the Hellenistic kingdoms broke down old trade and customs barriers; the number of coin standards was reduced, a fact which by itself greatly aided the expansion of trade.

Trade was carried on by both land and sea. There was an exchange of goods even with India and (indirectly) with China; in the west, the commerce with Spain, Gaul, and Britain increased. Ships were improved and made larger; harbors, lighthouses, and new roads were constructed. Agricultural products, pottery, metal work, textiles, slaves, books, and hundreds of other items were exchanged in international trade. Alexandria, the city founded by Alexander, soon became the main port of Egypt; from it were exported textiles, perfumes, glass, and papyrus. Parchment, silk, manufactured goods, and agricultural and pastoral products came from Asia Minor. Spanish silver, British tin, Italian cattle and wine, Sicilian grain, Greek olive oil, Sudanese ivory, Russian wheat, and fish from the Black Sea were only a few of the manufactured and raw products drawn from all corners of the ancient world. Key trading cities were Antioch in Syria, Sardes and Ephesus in Asia Minor, Seleucia on the Tigris (near modern Bagdad), Rhodes in the Aegean, Alexandria in Egypt, Tarentum in Italy, Syracuse in Sicily, Carthage in Africa, Gades (Cadiz) in Spain, and Massilia in Gaul.

About 300 B.C. the center of industry and commerce began to shift from Greece to western Asia Minor, Rhodes, and Syria. Greece (except Corinth) had little part in the revived east-west trade through the Mediterranean, and the Asiatic and Syrian cities built up their manufactures to such an extent that the mainland Greeks could not compete with them. In the Western Mediterranean, the old Greek colonies had, of course, been increasing their industrial output for many years; this market was thus lost to the mainland Greeks in the fourth century.

Industry

The industry of the Hellenistic Age was more inclined to mass production and world-wide distribution than that of the classical period. Shops were larger and specialization was more pronounced. State-owned factories for the production of oil, wine, beer, linen, and papyrus in Egypt under the Ptolemies, and similar state-production monopolies in Pergamum illustrate the trend toward mass production for the world trade.

Capitalism

Ancient capitalism reached its fullest development. Financial operations became more complicated. Banks received deposits, honored checks, and issued drafts, loans, and letters of credit. Rich men had multiple investments in commercial and industrial ventures. Speculation was rife; frequent attempts were made to corner the market on certain commodities. The operations of Cleomenes, the Egyptian governor of Alexander, disrupted the wheat market in such a way that a near-famine resulted at Athens.

Agricultural production

In some areas agricultural production was improved and better organized than ever before. The conquests of Alexander had resulted in a new knowledge of and a new interest in plants and herbs; scientific studies in these fields were carried on by the pupils of Aristotle. Reclamation and irrigation projects were common. Fertilizer, the rotation of crops, and attention to stock-breeding were outstanding developments.

SOCIETY

Bourgeoisie

In the thriving economic milieu of the Hellenistic world it was only natural that the bourgeoisie should dominate the social scene, whereas the nobles and the priest class receded into the background. The elaborate houses, extravagant dress, and luxurious appointments of the bourgeoisie were the outward signs of their opulence and power. Undoubtedly, their influence upon government and the determination of governmental policy was much stronger than we suspect. Certainly, the kings of Pergamum prided themselves on being bourgeois monarchs and intermarried with the daughters of wealthy commoners.

The position of the masses, both agricultural and urban, was anything but enviable, and it did not improve as time went on. Slave labor, as we have seen, kept wages low. Moreover, although prices continued to rise after 300 B.C., wages did not; inadequate wages and the increase of unemployment in the urban centers were productive of discontent. Typical of the Hellenistic Age was the large city with its proletarian masses living from hand to mouth, housed in wooden tenements where the dangers of fire and plague were ever present. Long before similar problems became acute at Rome, the Hellenistic cities knew proletarian unrest and resorted to the policy of "bread and circuses." *Urban masses*

Whereas the social conditions of urban life were fairly uniform throughout the Hellenistic world, great regional variation characterized rural life. In Egypt, for example, most of the Egyptian peasants were serfs, bound to the soil and never allowed to leave their native village districts. In addition to the peasants there were the Greek mercenaries and their descendants, free men who enjoyed privileges denied to the peasants. In the Seleucid territories, there were serfs on large crown and private estates, slaves on the estates of the temples, and free farmers elsewhere. Greek and Macedonian colonists, settled in small city-states throughout the empire, also farmed the land as free men. In Greece, the small farmer seems to have held his own, and perhaps he even gained ground during the Hellenistic Age. *Rural masses*

Everywhere, however, whether in the city or the country, the masses were restless and dissatisfied. The rise of the bourgeoisie worsened, rather than bettered the lot of the masses. The gap between the very rich and the very poor widened, and, in widening, it increased social bitterness. Slave, serf, and proletarian revolts were frequent. In the *Discontent* cities, the more vigorous proletarians agitated for the redistribution of wealth and dreamed of setting up communist utopias. In the country, the serfs often deserted their fields, took refuge in the temples, and from their places of sanctuary bargained with the government or the landholders. For the most part, however, the masses succumbed to a feeling of hopelessness. No advance, no reform seemed possible. They sought comfort in religions that promised them an afterlife in which they would live in prosperity and happiness, in which the humble would be exalted and the proud brought low.

Social signifi- cance of the old city-state

The old city-state of the classical Greek period had served an important social purpose by uniting its citizens into a compact social group with common interests. To the individual, the opportunity to identify himself with a large group of his fellows had been productive of a great amount of personal satisfaction. An ordinary person, whose mediocrity would never have allowed him to attain any distinction, took great pleasure in being a member of a distinct society— the same psychology partly explains tendencies toward extreme nationalism today.

In the large new cities of the Hellenistic Age—Alexandria, Antioch, and the rest—the group unity of the old city-state was lacking. In the first place, citizenship in the new cities had neither the duties nor the privileges that it did in the old city-state. Secondly, the inhabitants of the new cities were drawn from many nations and races: there were Greeks, Macedonians, Syrians, Jews, Phoenicians, Persians, and many others. Each national group retained its traditions, religion, and in many cases its language, with the result that each city was composed of irreconcilable factions. "Race" riots were common; the Jews especially were the victims of persecution.

New social groups

The instinctive gregariousness of mankind was not to be denied, however. Craft guilds, religious societies, political clubs, and national organizations began to appear in the large cities. These organizations satisfied in some measure the desire of the masses for human companionship.

RELIGION

With the decline of the city-state, the state cults of the Greek *poleis* likewise waned in influence and degenerated into formalism. The individualism of the age encouraged men to seek personal rather than national or civic gods. Mystery religions and the worship of various eastern mother goddesses (Isis of Egypt and Cybele of Asia Minor) gained swift popularity; in some cases their appeal was based upon their promise of a future life, and in others their devotees were satisfied by the emotional stimulation these cults had to offer. **Trends**

Other influences besides individualism were at work in the field of religion. We have already noted something of the syncretism and eclecticism which were so widespread at this time. It was inevitable, too, that universalism should ultimately encourage beliefs in the existence of one supreme and unique god. Monotheism was already present, of course, in Judaism, and we shall see that Christianity was undoubtedly the product of the conditions which prevailed in the Hellenistic Age (see below, p. 325). **Universalism and monotheism**

Another result of the decline of the old order and the impact of the new era was the growth of uncertainty and skepticism. One of the most popular divinities of the Hellenistic Age was Tyche (Fortune or Chance). Uncertainty, skepticism, and the increase of scientific knowledge led also to agnosticism and complete atheism. At the same time, it is not surprising to find that in an Age of Science people should be attracted by the pseudo-science of the Near East, astrology. **Skepticism**

PHILOSOPHY

Philosophy, as well as religion, was vitally affected by the new conditions of life in the Hellenistic Age. Personal problems of existence assumed such importance in human thinking that the majority of the philosophers abandoned their search for "knowledge" and set themselves to the task of finding bases upon which practical "ways of life" might be **Personal philosophies** built. In general, the new philosophic systems that developed sought one or the other of two seemingly possible goals: happiness, or freedom from unhappiness. Resignation, withdrawal, or conformity was conceded to be the best means of attaining these ends.

Between Socrates and the great Hellenistic schools of philosophy were the transitional philosophies of the Cynics and the Cyrenaics, founded by two of Socrates' disciples. The **Cynics** Cynic school had its origin with Antisthenes, who carried on his teaching at the gymnasium of Cynosarges at Athens. For Antisthenes, virtue was the sole good, and vice the sole evil. Pleasure, comfort, convention, and all externals were to be discarded; man's attention should be focused upon the exercise of virtue, and the inner satisfaction that virtue afforded should be sufficient compensation for anyone.

Aristippus of Cyrene taught that pleasure rather than **Cyrenaics** virtue was the ultimate goal. All pleasures were considered equally good, for they would contribute to happiness. Overindulgence, however, must be restrained by reason.

The philosophy of Skepticism founded by Alexander's contemporary, Pyrrhon, was another interpretation of the teach **Skeptics** ings of Socrates and Plato. The Skeptics denied the possibility of real knowledge; for every argument, an equally valid counter-argument could be advanced. Such a philosophy fostered nihilism in many cases; its alternative effect was agnosticism, as in the case of the later Platonic Academy which became predominantly Skeptic in its thinking.

The transitional schools of the fourth century pointed the way for the two great Hellenistic philosophies that appeared **The two** about 300 B.C. at Athens: Stoicism and Epicureanism. Al **great** though neither the Stoics nor the Epicureans were com **philos-** pletely successful in solving the difficult problems of human **ophies** existence, they did much to help thinking people who could not accept or gain comfort from the religions of the age. The widespread and enduring popularity of Stoicism and Epicureanism is convincing testimony that they met, at least partially, the needs of the men of the ancient world for the next five hundred years.

The founder of the Stoic school was Zeno of Cyprus, who came to Athens about 314 B.C. Zeno met with his disciples at the Stoa Poikile, the Painted Porch, in the Athenian Agora (marketplace); hence, the origin of the term Stoic. **Stoics** The Stoics sought happiness, but their search was not an active one. They said, in essence, "To be happy is to want what you get." Happiness is attained by conforming to the will of God (i.e., the laws of nature). Everything in nature is rational and good. All evils that befall man are necessary evils since they are intended for his education. It is his duty to discover what the laws of nature are; these laws are not necessarily man-made statutes or conventions; even suicide, incest, and cannibalism may be justified in some cases. Inasmuch as the Stoics accepted the existence of a supreme god, albeit an impersonal one, their philosophy tended to take on the aspect of a religion. Moreover, their universalism encouraged them to believe in the brotherhood of man; race, nationality, class, and sex were discarded as criteria for distinguishing one human being from another.

Epicurus of Samos came to Athens about 306 B.C. He maintained that the supreme good was happiness, which he defined as freedom from fear and pain; thus, pleasure is good, and pain is evil. The Epicureans did not deny the existence **Epicureans** of gods, but they did maintain that the gods were not concerned with human affairs, and therefore man need not fear them. One primary aim of the philosophy was to emancipate man from superstition and the fear of death. The atomistic theory of Democritus was employed to prove that birth is simply the result of a combination of atoms, and death nothing more than their separation. Death, therefore, entails no succeeding pain; it merely brings the end of sensation and resembles "eternal sleep." In its purest form, Epicureanism did not exclude sensual pleasures, but it emphasized that such pleasures entail more pain than those of the intellect.

Looking back upon all these philosophies, one gets the

impression that the men of the ancient world had reached a turning point in their attitudes toward life. They were able to see, though dimly, that they were fighting against irresistible forces which they could not hope to harness to their control. One force had been present since the beginning of time: this was nature, the physical world and its unalterable laws of life and death. Another force was culture, the social and economic forms created by man himself. Socrates, Plato, and Aristotle had felt that man could manipulate culture, but the Hellenistic philosophers possessed no such confidence. "Make the best of it," they said; or else "Withdraw." Individualism was a solution—self-sufficiency. Best of all, create a solitude and call it peace.

SCIENCE

From the time of Thales to the end of the fifth century B.C., Greek science went hand in hand with philosophy. Then
came Socrates who turned away from the study of natural phenomena to concentrate upon ethics and pointed the way for Aristotle who finally effected the separation of science and philosophy. In the Hellenistic Age the greatest scientists were not philosophers, although they continued to work in mathematics, physics, and astronomy, fields which had formerly been subject to philosophical study. In addition to the older fields of research, however, the Hellenistic scientists found new worlds to conquer. Aristotle's study of animals created the foundations for the science of zoology, and those who came after him followed paths which led to botany, physiology, anatomy, geology, geography, and many other fields.

The majority of the outstanding Hellenistic scientists lived in the third century B.C., or early in the succeeding century.
Euclid (*fl.* 300 B.C.) organized the study of geometry in his treatise, the *Elements*, which is still used in our schools today. Many students have been forced to recognize the truth of his dictum, "There is no royal road to geometry." This great geometrician also wrote on perspective and music.

Conic sections were exhaustively studied by Apollonius of Perga (*fl.* 230 B.C.). It was he who originated the terms hyperbola, parabola, and ellipse; and if he had pursued his work to its logical conclusion, he would have been the founder of analytic geometry. Apollonius was likewise a devotee of astronomy and seems to have advanced the theory that the planets move in eccentric circles. **Apollonius of Perga**

Aristarchus of Samos (*fl.* 280 B.C.) believed that the earth revolves about the sun; he also attempted to ascertain the relative diameters of the earth, the moon, and the sun. His heliocentric theory, however, did not gain wide acceptance. His ideas were attacked by the second-century astronomer, Hipparchus of Nicaea, and the geocentric theory of the universe was restored to its former preeminence. **Aristarchus of Samos**

Other important scientists were Eratosthenes, the geographer, and the astronomers, Heracleides of Pontus and Poseidonius. Eratosthenes (*fl.* 250 B.C.) produced a map of the world using lines of longitude and latitude; he likewise measured the circumference of the earth, and by a happy accident came within two hundred miles of the correct figure. Heracleides (who lived in the fourth century B.C.) proved that the earth rotates on its axis every twenty-four hours, and Poseidonius (*fl.* 100 B.C.) believed that tides were affected by the moon. **Other scientists**

Most brilliant and versatile of the Hellenistic scientists was Archimedes of Syracuse (*d.* 212 B.C.). His discovery of specific gravity and his wide knowledge of mechanics are well known. He invented a planetarium which demonstrated the movements of the heavenly bodies and explained eclipses. He also computed the value of *pi* by inscribing and circumscribing a circle with regular polygons of 96 sides. Thus he anticipated the invention of the calculus, which has been called (by a phrase which must contain a *double entendre*) the "mathematics of exhaustion." **Archimedes**

Extremely interesting work was done by Strato (*fl.* 300 B.C.), who advanced the theory of the vacuum, experimented with magnets, and investigated the "electric fish," the *narke*. **Strato**

It was the conquest of the Persian empire that provided the impetus for studies in geography and botany at the beginning of the Hellenistic Age. Alexander derived from his tutor, Aristotle, an interest in the collection of data relating to these two fields, and he took with him on his campaigns men whose duty it was to describe the country through which they passed. The *History of Plants* by Theophrastus, Aristotle's pupil and successor, was based largely upon the observations made by Alexander's scientists. Theophrastus became the founder of botany, just as Aristotle had been the founder of zoology.

Theophrastus

In the field of geography, the work of Eratosthenes has already been mentioned. The astronomer Hipparchus also worked in geography, and Poseidonius was the author of a treatise on the ocean. It was perhaps Poseidonius who first suggested that it might be possible to reach India by sailing westward from Spain.

Geography

In view of the extraordinary activity in science during the Hellenistic Age, it is surprising that few scientific discoveries were ever put to any practical use. Even in geography and botany, the knowledge which was available was rarely applied to solve the problems of everyday life. It has already been pointed out that the people of the Hellenistic Age felt no need for labor-saving devices. Then, too, the scientists of that day still followed the philosophic way of thought which ennobled pure science—science for science's sake—and they regarded applied science as beneath their dignity. Archimedes, an extremely clever mechanician, made numerous machines for his own amusement; he thought of them simply as "gadgets" or toys and was usually annoyed when other people suggested that they be employed for practical purposes.

Pure vs. applied science

It was only in the field of medical science that the results of research were turned to the advantage of humanity. In the first half of the third century B.C. three great doctors lived and worked: Herophilus, Erasistratus, and Heracleides of Tarentum. Herophilus and Erasistratus were chiefly inter-

Medicine

ested in the causes of disease, whereas Heracleides concerned himself with its cure. Herophilus was an anatomist who studied the brain and the nervous system. He also discovered the function of the arteries in the circulation of the blood and conducted research on the action of the pulse. Erasistratus founded the science of physiology; his work on the nervous and circulatory systems widened the horizons of the knowledge made available by Herophilus. Whereas Herophilus and Erasistratus opposed the excessive use of drugs, Heracleides took an opposite point of view. Perhaps as early as his time, the juice of the mandragora plant was used as an anaesthetic.

LEARNING

Scholarship came into its own during the Hellenistic Age. As early as the fifth century, the Sophists had begun the scientific study of grammar, rhetoric, and oratory; later, Plato had concerned himself with etymology, and Aristotle's *Poetics* had laid the foundations for literary criticism. As time went on, these interests continued to gain ground. Demetrius of Phalerum (*fl.* 315 B.C.), himself an able orator, wrote a history of oratory. The philosophers of the Aristotelian school wrote scholarly tracts on history, music, art, and literature. The Stoic philosophers studied grammar. The Ptolemaic rulers of Egypt, at the suggestion of Demetrius of Phalerum, founded a great library; the long succession of Ptolemaic librarians at Alexandria were scholars and scientists of the first rank. Zenodotus of Ephesus, the first librarian, made a scientific edition of Homer based upon a study of the available manuscripts. Advances in textual criticism were made by later librarians, Aristophanes of Byzantium (*fl.* 240 B.C.) and Aristarchus of Samothrace (*fl.* 180 B.C). At one period, the scientist Eratosthenes served as chief librarian at Alexandria; the post was also held by the great literary figures, Apollonius of Rhodes and Callimachus (see below).

Connected with the library at Alexandria was the Museum, the "place of the Muses," where numerous scholars and scien-

Scholarship

Librarians of Alexandria

Museum

tists lived and worked supported by the bounty of the Ptolemies. Contemporaries poked much fun at this "hencoop" of the Muses; its learned occupants were regarded by the vulgar as academic trained seals.

Libraries

The Alexandrian library was the largest of its day. In the period of its greatest expansion it contained perhaps 700,000 volumes (papyrus rolls). Other large libraries existed at Pergamum, Rhodes, and Antioch.

LITERATURE

Increased literacy

Compared with its predecessors, the Hellenistic Age was an age of literacy. More people than ever before knew how to read and write, and, moreover, were not averse to employing this knowledge. Writing became a profession which was not unprofitable. A small group of readers constituted a market for literature of high quality and for works on specialized subjects. There was also a much larger reading public that enjoyed light reading and read without much discrimination fables, moralizing tales, dialogues, paradoxes, mythological stories, travel books, and novels.

Menander

The writing of comedy reached its greatest height since the time of Aristophanes in the skillful hands of the Athenian, Menander (*fl.* 320 B.C.), the principal author of the New Comedy, the comedy of manners. Menander enjoyed the reputation of being able to portray life accurately, but we cannot now say whether this reputation was deserved because only fragments of his work have survived. Apparently his plots lacked variety and originality. A common theme is the love of a young man for a girl whose social position is lower than his own; after many difficulties, the lovers finally discover a solution for their problems, and the plays usually end on a happy note. The New Comedy used various type-characters: the drunkard, the braggart, the fool, the soldier, the doctor, and others. Another feature which distinguished it from earlier comedy was that it employed no chorus.

The poetry of the Hellenistic Age was affected by three important influences: the extreme urbanization of the age, its individualism, and a tendency to look backward (which led to archaism). Urbanization was productive of a reaction that appeared in poetry in the pastoral themes of Theocritus (315-250 B.C.). City life almost automatically led to a "back to nature" movement, of which Theocritus with his bucolic idylls, "little pictures" of rural life, was representative. Other noted writers of pastoral poetry were the Greeks, Bion and Moschus. **Pastoral poetry**

Individualism brought the revival of the elegy and the lyric. The third-century Alexandrian poet, Callimachus, employed these forms and also wrote hymns and a short epic. **Callimachus**

Apollonius of Rhodes, the literary rival of Callimachus, attempted to write a long Homeric epic in his *Argonautica*, based upon the myth of the quest of the Golden Fleece. Apollonius' efforts resulted in a very long and very dull poem which justified the dictum of Callimachus: "A big book —a big evil." **Apollonius of Rhodes**

Nevertheless, the archaism of Apollonius is interesting because on the one hand it illustrates the dilemma of the literary men and artists who were faced with the problem of either finding new forms of expression or imitating the great works of the past; on the other hand, it also shows the tremendous respect of the Hellenistic Age for the achievements of the Greeks of the classical period. Callimachus, in experimenting with the short epic, was striking out for himself, whereas Apollonius, in imitating Homer, demonstrated his dependence upon the past and perhaps his inability to create an original poetical form. **Archaism**

Prose works of the Hellenistic Age dealt with oratory, rhetoric, grammar, geography, and the other sciences, as well as history and biography. Regional histories were popular; well-known works of this type are Timaeus' history of Sicily which used Carthaginian sources, Manetho's history of Egypt which was compiled with the aid of Egyptian records, and Berosus' history of Babylon which was based on cuneiform texts. The two greatest historians of the period were Hieronymus of Cardia and Polybius the Achaean. Hieronymus **Prose** (*fl.* 275 B.C.) wrote a history of the period 323-266 B.C., with special reference to the successors of Alexander and their deeds. Polybius (198-117 B.C.) took as his subject the rise of Rome and the Roman conquest of the Greeks. Polybius was an exponent of a broad historical point of view, for he said:

No one, as far as I am aware, has ever attempted to inquire critically when and whence the general and comprehensive scheme of events originated and how it led up to the end. . . . We can no more hope to perceive this from histories dealing with particular events than to get at once a notion of the form of the whole world, its disposition and order, by visiting, each in turn, the most famous cities, or indeed by looking at separate plans of each. . . . He indeed who believes that by studying isolated histories he can acquire a fairly just view of history as a whole, is, as it seems to me, much in the case of one, who, after having looked at the dissevered limbs of an animal once alive and beautiful, fancies he has been as good an eyewitness of the creature itself in all its action and grace.[1]

Short essays were also popular. The *Characters* of Theophrastus, a series of descriptions of human types—the miser, the boaster, etc.—and the essay on the *Art of Shopping* by Lynceus of Samos are good examples of this kind of writing. Then, too, there were travelers' tales, collections of myths, and paradoxes (descriptions of the wonders of nature—an ancient version of our "Believe it or not").

ART

In the Hellenistic period, tendencies that had been present in fourth-century art became more pronounced. The decline of the city-state in Greece meant that artists became dependent for their commissions upon the new Hellenistic monarchies and upon private persons who possessed great wealth. As a result, Greece ceased to be the center of artistic production. Then, too, the new patrons of art—the monarchies and the rich—could not help but exert an influence upon the character of the work that the artists produced. The inspiration

[1] Book I, Chapter IV.

and the idealism which the city-state, as a patron of art, had fostered were replaced by individualism and other personalistic features typical of the new era. Art became "Art"; and although technical knowledge increased, the genuineness and *ethos* of the fifth century disappeared.

In Hellenistic architecture, the favorite styles were the Ionic and Corinthian; experiments were made with composite styles, and the arch was used more frequently. The new structures were larger and more elaborate than those of the classical period. Moreover, although new temples were erected, the number of secular public buildings constructed was much greater. Stadia, gymnasia, colonnades (stoae), theaters, council chambers, and office buildings appeared in every city. The construction of fortifications became a science. Last of all, domestic architecture entered a new era. Houses were larger; they contained more rooms, and they were built with a view to permanence. Architecture

In sculpture, the individualism of the fourth century and the popularity of portraiture continued into the Hellenistic period. Other characteristics of Hellenistic sculpture were symbolism, realism, and, to some extent, impressionism. The eclecticism of the age is also to be seen in its sculpture. In other words, a Hellenistic sculptor might borrow ideas from a number of his predecessors and combine them into a style of his own. The Pergamene sculptors, for example, were greatly indebted to both Praxiteles and Scopas. Sculpture

Lysippos, the official portrait sculptor to Alexander the Great, was the best of the Hellenistic artists in this field. Lysippos' favorite medium was bronze. He was especially well known for his athletic figures, for he excelled in portraying motion. His Apoxyomenos, the statue of an athlete scraping oil from his body, is familiar to everyone. Lysippos, together with Scopas and Praxiteles, exerted a tremendous influence upon Hellenistic sculpture. Lysippos

The three main schools of sculpture in the third century were those of Alexandria, Antioch, and Pergamum. The Alexandrian school, which was influenced by Praxiteles, "Schools" of sculpture

showed impressionistic trends, with its emphasis upon sharp
major details and its practice of merely suggesting other less
important features. The Alexandrian sculptors were fond of
the grotesque and caricature, but they reached their greatest
heights with their *genre* subjects in which old people and
children were realistically portrayed. Pergamene sculpture is
best known through the famous Great Altar and the series of
statues dealing with the Gauls. Everyone is familiar with the
Dying Gaul (sometimes erroneously called the Dying Gladi-
ator). The schools of Antioch and Rhodes were influenced by
Lysippos. The great Colossus of Rhodes, the work of Chares
of Lindus, was one of the Seven Wonders of the ancient
world.

Apelles   Greek painting reached its climax late in the fourth century with Apelles. This painter was famous for his *charis*
(grace), and his portraits were unrivaled in the accuracy and
fidelity with which they depicted their subjects. He painted
the portrait of Antigonos Monophthalmos (the One-Eyed),
a picture of Aphrodite rising from the sea, and many others. A
great art critic of the Roman period said of Apelles: "All
have profited by his innovations, though one of them could
never be imitated; he used to give his pictures when finished
a black glazing so thin that by sending back the light it could
call forth a whitish color, while at the same time it afforded
a protection from dust and dirt, only becoming visible itself
on the closest inspection. In using this glazing one main purpose was to prevent the brilliance of the colors from offend-
ing the eyes. . . ."[2]

One of the important minor arts of the Hellenistic Age
was the making of figurines (little statuettes) of terra cotta
and decorating them with bright colors. The graceful, dainty
terra cottas of Tanagra and Myrina are to be seen today in
almost every good museum.

[2] Pliny, *Natural History*, XXXV, 15, 97.

CHAPTER VIII

THE WESTERN MEDITERRANEAN (to 133 B.C.)

Thus far we have been concerned mainly with the history of civilization in the Near East and the Eastern Mediterranean. We have seen how civilization had its origins in the Near East, how it spread to Greece where it received considerable alteration and elaboration, and how, in the Hellenistic Age proper, a composite civilization was built up in the combined areas of the Near East and the Eastern Mediterranean.

We have yet to consider the climax of these developments, the Roman phase of Hellenistic civilization. This phase began about the middle of the second century B.C., when a new area, the Western Mediterranean, was gradually added to the already existing cultural unit formed by the Near East and the Eastern Mediterranean. The Roman phase reached its climax, its cultural developments attained maturity, in the first two centuries of the Christian era at the time when the whole Mediterranean basin became a political unit, the Roman empire.

The Roman phase of Hellenistic civilization

Before we can discuss this climax of ancient civilization, however, it will be necessary for us to consider the earlier history of culture in the Western Mediterranean. We must trace the westward diffusion of culture from the Near East and Greece, and see how and why the Western Mediterranean area passed from an Age of Primitive Culture to an Age of Agriculture, and finally to an Age of Civilization. In addition, we must pay considerable attention to the phenomenon of the rise of Rome and the development of its institutions. How and why the Romans became the rulers of the ancient world are important questions which necessitate detailed explanation.

Preliminary considerations

The region which we shall call the Western Mediterranean

includes Italy, present-day southern France and eastern Spain, the coast of Africa west of ancient Cyrene, and the western Mediterranean islands, especially Sicily. At the opening of the

Prehistory Age of Agriculture, which may be dated about 5000 B.C. in the Western Mediterranean, this area was populated by Mediterranean man, just as in the case of Crete and Greece; undoubtedly, in the post-glacial period the increasing aridity of north Africa had driven this Mediterranean type into Italy and Spain. Between 5000 and 2000 B.C. the inhabitants of the Western Mediterranean led a quiet agricultural and pastoral existence which underwent no significant alterations. While civilizations arose in the Near East and Crete, and a stream of culture began to flow up the Danube to penetrate central Europe, the Western Mediterranean remained un-affected, for the African desert, the sea itself, and the Alps provided serious obstacles to cultural diffusion.

It was not until the close of the third millennium B.C. that

Transition from the Age of Agriculture to civilization the isolation of the Western Mediterranean began to break down. About 2000 B.C. some Swiss groups moved across the Alps into the Po Valley, and Minoan traders began to come occasionally to south Italy and Sicily. Two hundred years later, bronze-using tribes from central Europe penetrated Italy from the north; by 1500 B.C. Italy had passed into a Full Bronze Age, although "civilization" as we have used the term in this book was not yet established.

The bronze-using peoples who came into Italy during the

The Indo-Europeans middle centuries of the second millennium B.C. spoke Indo-European languages. As a matter of fact, their coming was closely connected with the same general movement that brought the Mycenaeans (or Achaeans) into Greece. In like manner, the next wave of migration among the Indo-Europeans (about 1200 B.C.) which brought the Dorians into Greece and the Phrygians into Asia Minor (and was re-sponsible for the attacks of the sea raiders upon Egypt) was also felt in Italy. Then, too, after 1200 B.C., tribes from west-ern Greece which were displaced by the Dorian invasion crossed the Adriatic and settled along the eastern coast of

Italy and in Venetia. These last arrivals were not Greeks, but they were iron-users, and most of them spoke Indo-European languages.

The first civilized invaders of the Western Mediterranean, however, were (1) the Etruscans, (2) Greeks, and (3) Phoenicians who came slightly later than the Indo-Europeans from the north.

1. Between 1000 and 850 B.C. the Etruscans, a people related to the Lydians, left (or were driven out of) their home in Asia Minor; they came to Italy and settled on the western coast north of the Tiber River in the region which is still called Tuscany. **Etruscans**

2. About 800 B.C. the first Greek traders began to make their appearance in the Western Mediterranean. They were closely followed by colonists from many Greek cities; colonies were established in southern Italy, Sicily, southern France, and northwestern Spain. The areas of Greek colonization were limited by the Etruscans, who were powerful in northern Italy, and by the Phoenicians, who had established a sphere of economic influence in northern Africa and southern Spain. **Greeks**

3. It is difficult to determine when the Phoenicians arrived. There was a tradition that Gades (Cadiz) in Spain was founded by Phoenician traders as early as 1100 B.C.; but certainly the real power of the Phoenicians dates from the foundation of Carthage in north Africa just before 800 B.C. **Phoenicians**

The Etruscans, Phoenicians, and Greeks were important in the history of the Western Mediterranean because they carried their versions of the civilization of the Ancient Near East to the barbarians of the west. For the development of culture in Italy, credit must be given to the Greeks and Etruscans; in Spain both Greeks and Phoenicians were contributors; for the rest of the Western Mediterranean, the Greeks were important in Sicily and southern France, and the Phoenicians left their stamp upon northern Africa. **Importance of the Etruscans, Phoenicians, and Greeks**

The Etruscans were not a large group, but they were able, by virtue of their better weapons and military organization, to conquer the natives of the region in which they settled. **Etruscan civilization**

They established themselves in stone-walled towns through-out Tuscany; each town became a city-state which was inde-pendent of all others. The various Etruscan cities often fought one another; their only real bond was a religious league which held an annual festival and elected a high priest. The Etruscans traded with the Phoenicians and the Greeks, and even with the Egyptians. They brought about an increase of agricultural production by forcing the conquered popula-tion to labor for them in the fields. The Etruscans also manu-factured pottery, terra cottas, and metal products, although their techniques seemed to have been derived from Greek sources. Etruscan writing shows both Greek and Lydian affiliations.

Religion   Etruscan religion was rather gloomy. There was a belief in demons and in human sacrifice; gladiatorial combats were staged as part of certain religious ceremonies. Divination was practiced by observing various signs and portents and examin-ing the entrails of animals. Etruscan gods were usually grouped in threes, or triads; each city had its own particular gods, and there were divinities that were considered the patrons of special crafts. Around each city a sacred boundary, the *pomerium*, was drawn by magical ceremonies.

Conquests   After 700 B.C. the Etruscans began to extend their political influence outside of Tuscany. To the south they advanced as far as Campania where they reached the Greek frontier. Wars were fought with the Greeks, the Samnites (a powerful group of tribes in central Italy), and the Gauls who began to invade the Po Valley about 400 B.C. Eventually the Etruscans were forced to relinquish their holdings in the south and to concentrate on defending the northern frontier against Gallic invasion.

The Greek colonies in the Western Mediterranean soon became very prosperous. The principal Greek cities in Italy **Greek** were Tarentum, Cumae, Sybaris, Croton, Neapolis (Naples), **culture** Locri, and Rhegium; in Sicily were Syracuse, Acragas, Gela, Leontini, Himera, Selinus, and others; in southern France (Gaul) was Massilia (present-day Marseilles). Trade, industry, and agriculture flourished. The Greeks introduced their culture to the natives; Greek architecture, sculpture, pottery, and metal work influenced the native arts and crafts. The Greek alphabet was adopted;[1] the introduction of Greek coinage brought important changes in the economy of the western Mediterranean. The olive and (possibly) the vine were imported from Greece and planted on western soil.

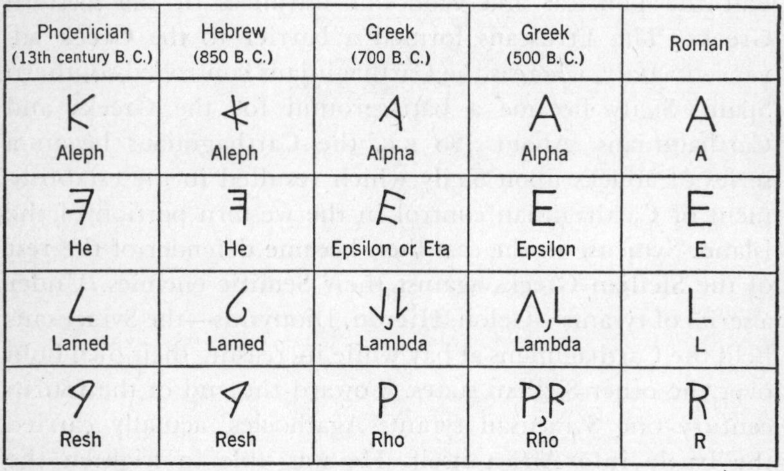

Phoenician (13th century B. C.)	Hebrew (850 B. C.)	Greek (700 B. C.)	Greek (500 B. C.)	Roman
K Aleph	⟨ Aleph	A Alpha	A Alpha	A A
⇥ He	⇥ He	E Epsilon or Eta	E Epsilon	E E
L Lamed	6 Lamed	↓,⎰ Lambda	Λ,L Lambda	L L
9 Resh	⊲ Resh	P Rho	P,P Rho	R R

There were two main Greek alphabets: the Ionic (East Greek) and the West Greek. In the West Greek alphabet ⟨ was employed instead of Γ for · Gamma (g), ⱴ instead of Λ for Lambda (l), and X instead of Ξ for Xi (x) In addition, the West Greek H stood for h instead of for Eta (long e), and Ϙ Koppa (q), was not found in the Ionic alphabet. The double Gamma, Ϝ (w), was used by the Romans as an F instead of a W as it was by the West Greeks.

CHART VI.—Development of the Alphabet.

The Phoenicians continued their commercial activities in the Western Mediterranean until the sixth century, when the Persian conquest of their country caused a break in their western connections. Carthage, the greatest of the Phoenician **Carthage** colonies in the west, then asserted its independence and gained control over the other western Phoenician settlements. Carthage was a city-state like Tyre and Sidon, but its government was republican in form. Most of the power was concentrated in the hands of an oligarchy of merchant princes and large landholders. Therefore, those who determined the

[1] The alphabet used by these western Greeks differed slightly from that used by the Ionic Greeks. The Ionic alphabet is the one employed for writing Greek today; the west Greek alphabet was adopted by the Romans and was transmitted by them to us (see chart VI).

policies of Carthage may be divided into two groups: (1) those interested in trade and industry, and (2) those who had acquired large agricultural holdings. As a result, the policies of the state changed as the commercial group or the land-holders were in the ascendant.

From the middle of the sixth century onward, the Carthaginians and the Etruscans combined forces in an attempt to halt the political and economic advances of the western Greeks. The Etruscans formed a barrier to the Greek advance in Italy, whereas the Carthaginians controlled southern Spain. Sicily became a battleground for the Greeks and Carthaginians. About 480 B.C. the Carthaginians began a series of attacks upon Sicily which resulted in the establishment of Carthaginian control in the western portion of the island. Syracuse in the east then became defender of the rest of the Sicilian Greeks against their Semitic enemies. Under a series of tyrants—Gelon, Hieron, Dionysius—the Syracusans held the Carthaginians at bay while increasing their own hold over the other Sicilian states. Toward the end of the fourth century one Syracusan tyrant, Agathocles, actually carried the battle into Africa itself. He was able to frighten the Carthaginians sufficiently to gain a cessation of hostilities during his lifetime (he lived until 289 B.C.), and he capitalized on his achievements by taking the title of king.

After the death of Agathocles, a group of his mercenary soldiers seized the city of Messana which controlled the straits between Sicily and Italy. By means of this strategic position these former mercenaries (the Mamertini) were able to prey upon the commerce passing through the straits. The piratical activities of the Mamertini soon became so obnoxious that the Syracusans undertook to dislodge them from Messana. Besieged and in danger of capture, the Mamertini appealed for aid both to Carthage and to Rome, the rising state in Italy (265 B.C.). The Carthaginians were only too happy to have an excuse to gain a foothold at Messana, and they quickly sent troops to the city. The Romans, on the other hand, had not been interested in the appeal of the Mamertini; but when

Sicily

The Mamertini

the Carthaginians entered Messana, the Romans became alarmed, for they feared that Messana might serve as a stepping stone for Carthaginian expansion into southern Italy. Consequently, a Roman expeditionary force was dispatched to Sicily for the purpose of driving the Carthaginians from their new position.

Thus it was that the affair of the Mamertini—in itself a minor incident in history—brought Rome and Carthage face to face and precipitated a series of wars in which Rome eventually overcame the Carthaginians and gained control of the Western Mediterranean. Before we can carry this narrative further, however, we must retrace our steps to consider the early history of Italy and of Rome, the city-state which, by 265 B.C., controlled all of peninsular Italy.

ITALY

The influence of environment upon history is well demonstrated in the case of Italy. Italy, like Greece, is a peninsula jutting out into the Mediterranean. The topography is rugged; there are many mountains, valleys, and plains; but, on the whole, Italy is less rugged than Greece. Although Italian topography fostered separatism, the possibility of building up a united state was greater in the Italian peninsula than in Greece. As we have seen, the Adriatic coast of Italy was forbidding, and thus cultural contact with the eastern civilizations was long delayed. On the other hand, it was possible to invade Italy from the south, as was done by Mediterranean man in the prehistoric period, and the country could also be penetrated from the north; many of the Bronze and Iron Age peoples came down over the Alps, and this route was followed by the Gauls after 400 B.C. The plains and valleys of Italy were better adapted to agriculture than were those of Greece; vines, olive trees, and grains grew well on Italian soil. There was an abundance of good timber. In early times the country was best known for its flocks and herds; but especially important for the later development of Italian culture was the fact that copper, tin, clay, and much good

The Italian environment

stone were available in the peninsula; moreover, iron could be secured from the nearby island of Elba.

The Italians

Like the Greeks, the Italian peoples of the historic period were largely the product of a fusion of the Mediterranean stock with the early Indo-European-speaking invaders. The elements provided by the Etruscans, Greeks, and the later Gauls were also of some importance in determining the physical appearance of the Italians. The significant point to be noted, however, is that the Italians of the historic period were a mixed people, and no particular "race" was responsible for what they later achieved.

Italian culture

When the Greeks came to Italy they found many nations and tribes of barbarians living in much the same manner that they themselves had lived in Greece in the Dark Ages. Agriculture and grazing were the chief occupations; there was little trade, and practically no manufacturing. The formation of city-states had begun, the *oppidum*, a town clustered about a fortified citadel, was becoming the political center of its surrounding agricultural territory. The primitive monarchy was being replaced by aristocratic, oligarchic governments; the great landlords dominated the political life of their communities, and the subordination of the peasants was taking place. It should be emphasized that there were many of these nascent city-states in Italy. Those in the central part of the peninsula were stronger than the others, and the Greek colonization of the south had brought commercial and cultural contacts that accelerated their growth.

ROME

Rome

Some distance from the sea, located at a ford of the Tiber River was a little town called Rome, a town destined to become the capital of the ancient world. There was nothing about the town in 750 B.C. that seemed to mark it out for greatness. Its population was not large, and its economic life was not thriving. There was little trade or contact with the outside world; most of the people were either farmers or herdsmen. A number of other city-states in Italy were more populous and more prosperous than Rome. If it had been suggested to a contemporary observer that a single city-state might some day unify Italy, he would not have considered Rome as a possible candidate for that honor. Nor did Rome emerge rapidly from its obscurity. After more than three and one-half centuries (about 390 B.C.) the town, now grown to a small city, achieved its first international recognition when it was sacked by the Gauls. Even then, civilized people in Greece were not exactly sure where or what Rome was. One author referred to it vaguely as a Greek city in Italy.

It is almost impossible to reconstruct Roman history before 390 B.C. The city was too insignificant to merit the attention **Early** of the Greek historical writers, and the Romans had no lit- **history** erature of their own worthy of the name until the late third century. Tradition had it that Rome was founded in 753 B.C., but archaeological excavation has disclosed that the site was occupied shortly after 1000. In the seventh century B.C. Rome became the stronghold of Etruscan robber chiefs who used the city as a base for expansion toward the south. Etruscan kings ruled over the native population; stone fortifications, streets, and sewers were built; the countryside was made agriculturally more productive by drainage projects and the governmental direction of native labor.

About 500 B.C., or possibly even later (the traditional date, however, is 509), there was a revolution at Rome, and the **Roman** Etruscan overlords were expelled. At the same time, appar- **republic** ently, the monarchy was abolished; it was replaced by a republican form of government which resembled very closely that of the early Greek oligarchies. The landed aristocrats, the patricians, were now in control. Their political stronghold was the Roman council of the elders, called the senate. Each year there were elected two chief magistrates, the consuls, who had military, executive, administrative, judicial, and religious functions. The Romans felt that with two magistrates, each enjoying equal power, autocracy was not to be feared. There was an assembly of people, the *comitia curiata*, which, like the Greek *ecclesia*, was composed of that portion of the citizen body available for military service. The essential differences between the new republic and the primitive monarchy were that the king had been replaced by the two consuls, and that these executives were limited in their powers by the senate.

Roman policy

The Romans were not numerous, nor was their army particularly efficient at this time. Like the Assyrians, they were menaced by enemies on almost every side, and they were forced to adopt an aggressive policy in order to defend themselves. This was the real secret of Roman success. They had to conquer or be conquered. When they were victorious, they could not allow their defeated enemies to go free; they had to make them Roman subjects or inferior allies. For over two centuries (500-265 B.C.) the Romans doggedly followed this policy, and when they finally stopped to take stock of their position at the end of the period, they found themselves in control of the whole peninsula. Their history may be summarized as follows:

Expansion (500-265 B.C.)

Shortly after the foundation of the republic, the Romans entered into an alliance with a confederation of their neighbors known as the Latin League. The history of the fifth century B.C. is not clear, but it seems to have been a period of almost continuous conflict with the nearby Italian tribes, a conflict from which Rome and her Latin allies finally emerged victorious in the possession of some new territory. About 390 B.C., the Gauls, who had ravaged Etruria, also sacked Rome; the invaders evacuated the city only after the Romans paid them a large sum of gold. Undaunted by this reverse, the Romans rebuilt their city and improved their army. Shortly after 340 B.C. a war broke out between the Romans and the Latin League; the members of the league felt that Rome was becoming too strong and was taking an unfair proportion of the plunder from their joint conquests. The Latin League was defeated in the war, and its territory and people were incorporated into the Roman state. The conquest of the Latin League was the beginning of really important Roman expansion in Italy. Within the next seventy

ANCIENT ITALY

Scale of Miles

0   50   100   150

ALPS

GAULS

VENETIANS

LIGURIANS

Adige R.

Po R.

ILLYRIANS

ADRIATIC SEA

APENNINES

ETRUSCANS

ELBA

CORSICA

Tiber

Veii

Rome

Ostia

LATIUM

APPIAN

Capua

ITALIANS

Cumae

Naples

Pompeii

Mt. Vesuvius

ITALIANS

Tarentum

Brundisium

GREEKS

SARDINIA

CARTHAGINIANS

TYRRHENIAN SEA

GREEKS

Croton

MEDITERRANEAN SEA

CARTHAGINIANS

ITALIANS

GREEKS

Mt. Etna

Agrigentum

Syracuse

Carthage

SICILY

AFRICA

MEDITERRANEAN SEA

MANHATTAN DRAFTING CO. INC., N.Y.

(From Boak, Hyma and Slosson, *The Growth of European Civilization,*
F. S. Crofts & Co.)

years the Romans conquered the Etruscans, subdued the Samnites—the last native group powerful enough to contest with Rome for Italian supremacy—and overcame the Greeks of the great city of Tarentum (282-270 B.C.).

By 265 B.C. the conquest of the peninsula was complete. About one-seventh of the land south of the Rubicon River was held by the Romans themselves, and the rest belonged to Italian allies who were bound to Rome by treaties which made the Romans the commanders of a powerful military machine.

THE PUNIC WARS

By 265 B.C. the successes of the Romans in Italy had given rise to a spirit of imperialism which grew increasingly strong as the years passed. Rome's only rival in the west was Carthage, and it was almost inevitable that the two states should become enemies. The Romans seemed to think that Carthage constituted a threat to their independence; but it is also likely that the Greeks of southern Italy, who were now the subjects and allies of Rome, desired the destruction of Carthage in order to further their own commercial expansion. Then, too, the Greeks in Sicily—when it became necessary to choose sides—preferred a Roman alliance to one with Carthage. The affair of the Mamertini provided an immediate cause for conflict which led to the First Punic War (264-241 B.C.). The Carthaginians were the losers in the long struggle; they gave up their claims to Sicily and paid Rome a large indemnity. After the war, when civil strife broke out in Carthage, the Romans took advantage of the confusion to seize Sardinia and Corsica, islands long dominated by the Carthaginians.

As in the case of the wars of the Athenians and Peloponnesians in the middle of the fifth century, the First Punic War was not conclusive. The Carthaginians were bitter and revengeful, and the question of supremacy in the Western Mediterranean was still undecided. In preparation for the next war, the Carthaginians strengthened their position in Spain and trained the hardy Spanish natives for disciplined

Rome versus Carthage

First Punic War

Second Punic War

fighting. In the meantime, the Romans had made alliances with the Greeks in southern Gaul and northwestern Spain, thus establishing a sphere of influence that was bound to conflict with Carthaginian expansion in Spain. In 219 B.C. the Carthaginians quarreled with the Spanish city of Saguntum, an ally of Rome, and in the next year the Second Punic War began. The Carthaginian general, Hannibal, carried the war into Italy itself with a daring march through Gaul and over the Alps to the Po Valley. For over a decade, he campaigned throughout the length and breadth of the peninsula. Some of the Greek city-states opened their gates to him, but the Italian allies remained loyal to Rome. Most of the Greeks in Sicily, especially the allied city of Syracuse, went over to the Carthaginian side.

The war lasted from 218 to 201 B.C.; it was fought not only in Italy, but also in Sicily and Spain. At last the Romans moved into Africa and attacked Carthage itself. When Hannibal returned to Africa from Italy, a final decisive battle was fought at Zama in 202 B.C. in which the brilliant Carthaginian strategist was defeated by the Roman general, Scipio Africanus. The terms of peace imposed upon Carthage were very harsh: the Carthaginian navy was wiped out, the Carthaginians were forbidden to go to war without the permission of Rome, and they had to pay a heavy indemnity. The conclusion of the war found Rome in the possession of Spain and all the western Mediterranean islands; by this time the Po Valley had also been added to the Roman domains.

After the conclusion of the Second Punic War imperialism was rampant at Rome. About 200 B.C., when the Ptolemies and Pergamenes appealed to Rome for aid against the coalition of Antigonids and Seleucids, the Romans were delighted at the opportunity to extend their influence into the Eastern Mediterranean. Then, too, the Romans themselves had reason to feel inimical to Philip V of Macedonia. Philip had been the ally of Hannibal, and only the fact that he had been fully engaged by a war with the Greeks had kept him from sending aid to Hannibal in Italy. Moreover, Antiochus III,

Imperialism

the Seleucid king, offended Rome by providing a refuge for Hannibal when he fled from Carthage soon after the end of the Second Punic War. The subsequent defeats suffered by the Macedonians and Seleucids, and the expansion of Rome into the Eastern Mediterranean have already been outlined in Chapter VII. By 146 B.C. Macedonia had been made a Roman province, Greece had lost all but a nominal independence, and the Seleucids had been driven out of Asia Minor. When Attalus III of Pergamum bequeathed his kingdom to Rome in 133 B.C., a base was provided for expansion into the Near East where Rome was already powerful; even at that time Egypt was a Roman protectorate, the Seleucids were confined to Syria and weakened by dynastic struggles, and only the Hellenized native kingdoms of Bithynia and Pontus enjoyed real independence.

Third Punic War

The most striking example of Roman imperialism was provided by the treatment accorded to Carthage. Carthage had become very prosperous after the Second Punic War. Her exports of wine and oil provided serious competition for similar Italian products in the western market. A desire to eliminate this competition and to gain control of the rich land around Carthage led the Romans to seek the termination of Carthaginian independence. In 149 B.C. the Carthaginians were goaded into war. For three years the Romans laid siege to Carthage, and in 146 B.C. the city was finally taken; its walls and buildings were destroyed, and all its inhabitants were sold into slavery.

ECONOMIC HISTORY AND ROMAN POLITICAL INSTITUTIONS

Of equal importance with the external history of Rome is the story of the internal developments that took place in the period between the establishment of the republic and 133 B.C. Perhaps the clearest perspective of Roman economic and political history may be gained if one considers Rome as a city-state of the type we have already observed in Greece. The original monarchical government of Rome was very similar to that which one might have found in almost any Greek

Rome: a Greek city-state in form

state during the Dark Ages, and Rome's subsequent internal economic and political evolution followed the familiar path from oligarchy to timocracy and finally a kind of democracy. The details of this story are not essential to our study, but the general trends ought to be considered. Although some of the events of the early period—the fifth century especially —cannot be determined with certainty, a tentative reconstruction might be made as follows:

After the abolition of the monarchy and the establishment of the republic (about 500 B.C.), the Roman people were divided into two classes: patricians (nobles) and plebeians (commons). These divisions were political and economic as well as social. The patricians were the great landholders; only patricians could be members of the senate or hold the consulship or important religious offices. The plebeians were, for the most part, small farmers. Ineligible for the senate or the consulship, lacking the right of intermarriage with the patricians, the plebeians had little voice in the government. If a plebeian could equip himself for military service, he could participate in the meetings of the *comitia curiata*, the popular assembly; but, as we shall see, this privilege was of little significance at this time.

Patricians
and
plebeians

Between 500 and 450 B.C. the power of the patricians increased. Naturally, the administration of justice was in their hands, and a combination of circumstances allowed the upper class to build up the prestige of the senate at the expense of the popular assembly. As in Greece in the Dark Ages, so in fifth-century Rome, declining returns from agriculture impoverished the small farmer and made it difficult for him to equip himself for the army; consequently, the popular assembly declined. In addition, some of the small farmers gave up their unproductive lands and became tenants on patrician estates; other free men with small holdings found it wise to seek the legal protection (become the clients) of patricians. As a result, the plebeians in the popular assembly became divided into two groups—the tenants and the clients of the patricians on the one hand, and the remaining plebeians on

Increase
of
patrician
power

the other. With the plebeian ranks split in this manner, con-
certed action through constitutional channels was difficult.
The patricians with the support of their tenants and clients
were perhaps even able to outvote the independent plebeians
in the *comitia curiata*.

What happened next is uncertain, but apparently the independent plebeians, excluded from any real participation in
the oligarchic republican government, resolved to build up a
government of their own, a state within a state. Some time
after 500 B.C. the plebeians[2] began to meet together to discuss
matters pertaining to the welfare of their class. When patrician oppression became unbearable, this unofficial assembly
of the plebeians elected four officers called *tribunes of the
people*, one from each of the four Roman tribes.[3] A sacred
oath, sworn by all the plebeians, declared the tribunes to be
sacrosanct—anyone who harmed or disobeyed a tribune was
guilty of sacrilege and could be put to death without trial.
The tribunes, thus protected, became in turn the protectors
of the plebeians against the patrician magistrates, for a tribune could veto (*forbid*) any official action that endangered
a plebeian. The tribunes were the presiding officers of the
unofficial plebeian assembly. The assembly itself, which had
begun as a deliberative body and had added electoral powers
when the tribunes were chosen, soon entered the legislative
field also; the assembly began to pass measures—*plebiscites*
—which were binding upon plebeians.

We do not know whether the patricians took much interest in the plebeian efforts at organization, but the situation
was soon altered. About 450 B.C. there seems to have been a
crisis in the external affairs of Rome which forced the patricians to seek plebeian aid; Rome may have been threatened
by Etruscan reconquest, or her other neighbors may have

*A state
within
a state*

*The
crisis of
450 B.C.*

---

[2] Henceforth, unless otherwise specified, the term plebeian will refer to
the independent plebeians—not to plebeians who were tenants or clients of
the patricians.

[3] At first, as in the case of many Greek communities, the entire citizen body
of Rome was divided into four tribes; in this case, the division was probably
based upon the four wards that comprised the city in the Etruscan period.

endangered her independence. At any rate, the patricians, with plebeian help, were able to weather the storm. Afterward, however, the plebeians demanded increased civic rights as payment for their assistance, and the patricians had little choice but to accede to their requests.

The series of reforms which were now inaugurated gave the plebeians a number of advantages and transformed the Roman government from an oligarchy into a timocracy. **Timocracy** Plebeians were henceforth allowed to hold the consulship and intermarry with the patricians. The law was codified; this initial codification was known as the Law of the Twelve Tables. The patricians formally recognized the veto power of the tribunes, and it was probably at this time that the board of tribunes was increased in number from four to ten. Moreover, the patricians agreed that the plebeian plebiscites, if ratified by the senate, were to become laws binding upon the whole Roman citizen body, patricians as well as plebeians.

One outcome of the crisis of 450 B.C. was the reorganization of the army; the new army became the basis for a new popular assembly—the *comitia centuriata*—which paved the way for timocratic government. In the *comitia centuriata* the citizens were assigned to property classes, and the vote of each class was given a weight proportionate to the wealth of its members. The new assembly elected the consuls and other officials; it was a legislative body, and it also functioned as a court of appeal to which sentences involving the death penalty or a heavy fine might be referred for final decisions.

The settlements made about the middle of the fifth century, however, only temporarily relieved the discontent of the plebeians. After the sack of Rome by the Gauls in 390 B.C., **Plebeian gains** a critical economic situation caused by property losses, financial unsettlement, and the burden of heavy taxes for the rebuilding of the city culminated in new agitation for reform. Shortly after 370 B.C. the patricians were forced to make new concessions. Now it was arranged that at least one of the two consuls elected each year must be a plebeian. Some relief was provided for plebeian debtors whose difficulties were probably the result of the transition to a money economy that was slowly taking place at this time. In addition, land hunger seems to have been a serious question. Since 500 B.C. the Romans had acquired new land by conquest, but the major portion of this new territory had been gobbled up by the patricians. Therefore, an attempt was made to limit the amount of land which an individual might obtain.

Land hunger

It is possible to interpret the subsequent expansion of Rome in the fourth century B.C. as an effort to find a solution for the land problem. It will be remembered that, in the case of the majority of the Greek states, over-population and land hunger had been solved by colonization. This course was not practical in Italy at this late date; hence the Romans were forced to resort to the alternative policy of conquest.

The crisis of 287 B.C.

Nevertheless, dissatisfaction over the debt situation and the land question continued to grow until 287 B.C. (immediately after the close of the Samnite wars), when the most serious of the plebeian revolts occurred. On this occasion the plebeians banded together and threatened to secede from the state unless the patricians yielded to their demands. Once again the patricians were forced to make concessions. A debt moratorium was declared, and new governmental reforms of great significance were instituted.

Democracy

The settlement of 287 B.C. made the Roman government a democracy. All former constitutional distinctions between patricians and plebeians were wiped out. The old unofficial plebeian assembly was reorganized and set up beside the *comitia curiata* and the *comitia centuriata* as a third official assembly. It was called the *comitia tributa* because its organization was based on the tribe.[4] Both plebeians and patricians were eligible to participate in the *comitia tributa*; this

---

[4] As a result of Roman expansion in Italy, new tribes had been created. In 287 there were twenty-seven tribes in addition to the four original ones. The maximum number of tribes, thirty-five, was reached about 240 B.C. Each citizen was assigned to a particular tribe, and membership in a tribe became a badge of citizenship.

body elected the tribunes and could make laws. The legislative measures passed by it were still called plebiscites, but the senatorial power to reject these measures was abolished. The important fact about the *comitia tributa*, however, was that it was a democratic body; each man's vote, regardless of his wealth or social position, was equal in weight to that of any other citizen.

In 287 B.C. the tribunes were given new powers. They were allowed to attend the meetings of the senate, and they could interpose a veto to halt any legislative action in the senate or any of the three assemblies. The tribunes were thus included in the Roman constitutional machinery, and patricians as well as plebeians could now hold the tribuneship. New powers of the tribunes

THE FATE OF THE ROMAN DEMOCRACY

As we have seen, the Roman government of 287 B.C. was a democracy—at least in theory. The constitutional distinction between patrician and plebeian had been eliminated. There was no legal barrier to prevent any man from holding any office, and in the *comitia tributa* the vote of a poor man carried as much weight as that of a rich one. For the second time in the history of the world a large and important state had traveled the rough road from oligarchy to democracy; Athens, of course, had been the first. It is interesting to note, too, that at Rome, as at Athens, the democracy could support itself upon an imperialistic base.

Nevertheless, the theoretical Roman democracy never materialized into actuality, and the Roman government did not advance beyond the timocratic stage. Subsequent developments, both internal and external, were responsible for this rather surprising outcome, and we shall consider them in some detail.

It is not easy to explain the failure of Roman democracy in simple terms. Important factors in its lack of success were the long foreign wars which Rome undertook in the period 282-146 B.C., the social changes occurring during the same General reasons for failure period, and the course followed by Italian economic history after 287 B.C. These factors all contributed to the decline of the old plebeian element (the only group which had the interests of the democracy at heart) and the rise of a new element, a senatorial aristocracy of large landholders (both patrician and plebeian), that wanted to monopolize the government.

Between 282 and 146 B.C. Rome was almost constantly at war with foreign powers. As a result, the attention of the majority of the citizens was concentrated upon external rather than internal affairs, and little attempt was made to consolidate the democratic advance of 287 B.C. More important, perhaps, was the fact that the foreign relations of Rome were handled by the senate; the chronic state of war helped to increase the prestige of the senate, and there was a corresponding decline of the popular assemblies.

The supremacy of the senate might not have had serious results, however, if this body had not been monopolized by a particular social and economic class: the great landholders. A senatorial class, limited in size and hereditary in membership, was built up by these great landholders during the third century B.C. There were several reasons for the growth of a senatorial class. In the first place, a man became a senator by virtue of election to one of the higher governmental offices. Competition for these posts was strong, and the successful candidate was usually the one who could buy the most votes —either by direct bribery, or by winning the good will of the poor citizens by staging magnificent public games or distributing cheap grain. A poor man had little chance of winning an election unless he found a rich backer. From this it will be seen that one important qualification for the senate was the possession of considerable wealth. In the second place, senators were forbidden by law to engage in trade or industry. Since one needed wealth to run for office, few but the wealthy landholders could afford to go into politics; rich traders or manufacturers could not neglect their business enterprises

Power of the senate

Senatorial class

for politics. It was very seldom that any person other than one of the landed gentry made his way into the senate.[5]

Naturally, the senatorial class did not favor democratic government, nor did their general interests harmonize with those of the other citizens of Rome. Democracy might have advanced, however, if it had not been for circumstances which produced the decline and partial extinction of the old plebeian families. The backbone of plebeian resistance to oligarchy had been provided by the sturdy Roman peasants, the small farmers. Unfortunately, during the Second Punic War much of the agricultural land of Italy was laid waste by Hannibal. Moreover, the Roman farmers were called away from their fields to serve in the army, and the land deteriorated in their absence. After the war, many of those who returned to their small farms discovered that they could no longer make a living from agriculture. This was partly due to the condition of the soil, but it was also difficult for the Italian farmers to compete with the low-priced grains which now came from Sicily. Not only was Sicily within the Roman economic sphere, but the island was also a Roman province that paid a tribute of grain to the Roman government, and this grain was sold at Rome much below the market price. The small farmers therefore tended to desert their lands or to sell out to large landholders. The large landholders, on the other hand, found it profitable to plant olive orchards and vineyards, or to establish great ranches, whereas the small farmers did not have the capital necessary for these operations. Italy became a land of large estates worked by tenants and slaves, and in some areas the peasant almost disappeared from the scene.

It is altogether possible that even if the small farmers had not been wiped out by war and economic changes, the Roman democracy might not have functioned, for in order to exercise their political rights of suffrage and legislation, citizens had to be present at Rome, and the lower-class group that was

Agricultural changes

Proletariat

---

[5] Between 233 and 133 B.C. Rome had 200 consuls; 20 senatorial families provided 159 of these officials.

best able to attend the meetings of the assemblies was the urban proletariat of Rome itself. The urban proletariat, as we shall see, became an important political and social group in Rome after 287 B.C., but its devotion to its own peculiar and selfish interests prevented it from accomplishing anything worth while. Actually, it helped to destroy the potential evolution of the democracy.

The proletarian class was composed of the poor citizens and the lower-income groups which might be called a lower middle class (but not a bourgeoisie). These people lived at Rome, and their ranks were swelled by the bankrupt farmers who deserted their lands and came to the capital where they might eke out a precarious existence by selling their votes to the Roman politicians and perhaps finding a day's labor here and there. Added to these (particularly after 200 B.C.) were the new citizens, emancipated slaves and aliens, many of whom were bound to senatorial families as clients. This last group of the proletariat was loyal to the senatorial class rather than to its own, and its vote might be cast in opposition to proletarian interest.

The real interest of the proletarians, however, was not in the welfare of the state or in democracy, but in food and **"Bread** entertainment. As a group they were unpredictable, restless, **and** often riotous, and always hungry for grain and clamorous for **circuses"** amusement at state expense. They constituted a serious problem; and to keep them in some kind of order the policy of "bread and circuses," cheap grain and free entertainment, was introduced. Free grain came later, and the games which accompanied the Roman festivals became more and more elaborate—and more frequent.[6] The proletarians came to feel that the government owed them a living; the power of their votes elected the magistrates and decided legislation, and they felt that they should be paid in some way for performing

[6] The early games had consisted of horse and chariot races. In the third century, however, gladiatorial contests were introduced. The gladiators were especially trained slaves; the Romans seemed to have borrowed the idea from the Etruscans. A variation of the gladiatorial combat was the wild beast hunt which also took place in the arena.

their civic duty of voting. Naturally, they opposed the extension of Roman citizenship to Rome's subjects and allies because they did not wish to share with others the material blessings of Roman suffrage. If more people were admitted into the state as citizens, the votes of the proletarians would have less cash value.

The senatorial class tolerated, yet despised, the proletariat. It was easy enough to buy the proletarian vote in most cases; if matters came to a showdown, the loyal vote of the senatorial clients among the proletariat could be relied upon. Then, too, the tribunes, who were supposed to represent the masses, no longer served their original purpose. Members of the wealthy group, as well as poor citizens, could now hold the tribuneship, and one tribune hostile to the interests of the proletariat could block an action by the use of his veto. ^{Machinery}

Machinery of senatorial control

It might be thought that the increase in the volume of trade and commerce and the growth of industry which Italy experienced after 287 B.C. might have afforded some relief to the small Roman farmers who were forced out of agriculture. Unfortunately, trade and industry were monopolized by Greeks and Italians who were not Roman citizens; although the expansion of industry demanded many more skilled workers, few Romans were qualified for such activities and the new jobs were filled by imported slaves.

Trade and industry

The mention of the new trade and industry brings us to a consideration of a third social and economic class of Roman citizens which appeared after 287 B.C.: the equestrians. The equestrians were wealthy men not of the senatorial class; their census ranking was very high, but they were not officeholders. For the most part, this class grew up during the Punic Wars when enterprising men amassed great fortunes through contracts to supply the Roman armies with food and munitions. Public works contracts also proved lucrative. Later, when Rome acquired her empire outside of Italy, groups of equestrians called *publicani* formed companies which bid for the right to collect provincial taxes; the equestrians would guarantee the state a certain amount, and whatever else they

Equestrian

State contracts

might collect was clear profit. Other equestrian companies obtained contracts to work state mines and to exploit other imperial resources. Once the equestrians built up reserves of capital through these ventures, they were able to invest in trade and industry.

In view of the fact that the equestrian class fed upon state contracts, the class itself was necessarily interested in politics. The equestrians came to resent the senatorial monopoly of the government, and, particularly after 133 B.C., they embarked upon a fierce struggle with the senatorial class for control of the state. It was over the administration of the provinces that the senators and equestrians first clashed; therefore we may turn to a discussion of Roman provincial administration.

EARLY ROMAN PROVINCIAL ADMINISTRATION

When Rome first acquired her empire outside of Italy, her administration of it left much to be desired. The great Roman imperial system which has been so much admired by later generations was the product of a long evolution; in its beginnings it was very crude. The Romans always felt that their empire owed them a living; although their methods of provincial administration were eventually softened and humanized, the ruthless exploitation of the provinces during the republican period cannot be glossed over.

Italian organization

In order to understand the genesis of Roman provincial administration one must first consider the means by which Roman control was extended over Italy. In 265 B.C., the land of Italy could be divided into two categories: (1) the territory which belonged to Rome, and (2) that which belonged to Rome's allies.

Roman territory

1. Within the Roman domain lived the citizens and the subjects of Rome. Among the citizens were those who had full civic rights and those who enjoyed only private rights; the latter group lacked the right to vote and to hold office. The full citizens lived in or near Rome or else in the so-called Roman colonies, small garrison communities established at

strategic points throughout the peninsula. The second class of citizens (those with private rights) were the inhabitants of the communities of the old Latin League or other communities that had been incorporated into the Roman state under special terms.

2. The allies of Rome were divided into two groups: (a) the Latin allies, and (b) the Italian allies.

(a) The Latin allies were, in part, the people of the few **Latin allies** towns of the Latin League that had been spared subjection at the end of the fourth-century conflict between Rome and the league. The rest of the Latin allies were the inhabitants of the so-called Latin colonies. Some of these colonies had been established before the war with the league; they consisted of settlers furnished partly by Rome and partly by the league. After the league lost its independence to Rome, colonies classed as Latin continued to be established by the Romans. The Latin colonies had local self-government, and the colonists could trade and intermarry with the Romans; they were bound to furnish military contingents to aid Rome, and their foreign relations were handled by the Roman government.

(b) The other communities of Italy were the Italian allies **Italian allies** of Rome. Each community had a treaty of alliance with Rome by which it was bound to furnish military aid and to give its foreign relations into Roman hands. Local self-government was retained; trade (and often intermarriage) with Romans was allowed.

The political patchwork which the Romans fostered in **Provincial organization** Italy—the policy of "divide and rule"—was also to be found in the Roman provinces outside the Italian peninsula, although in the provinces it was of a somewhat different character. Each province was an aggregate of three classes of communities: (1) free and federate, (2) free and non-tributary, and (3) tributary.

1. The free and federate communities were the allies of Rome. They retained their own forms of government, paid no tribute, and were bound to aid Rome only in time of war.

2. The free and non-tributary communities paid no tribute, enjoyed local self-government, and were limited only by having surrendered their foreign relations to Rome. It was true, however, that the privileges extended to these communities might be revoked and that the Roman authorities might interfere with their local affairs.

3. The tributary provincial communities were the most common. The inhabitants were Roman subjects; they kept their local governmental institutions, but they were subject to direction by Rome and also had to pay tribute.

The early Roman provincial governors were called *praetors*. It should be explained that a praetor was a Roman magistrate who ranked just below the consuls. Originally the praetorship was essentially a municipal office at Rome. The first praetorship was that of the *praetor urbanus* (city praetor), a judicial official who might also assume the duties and powers of a consul if both consuls happened to be absent from Rome or incapacitated. Somewhat later appeared the *praetor peregrinus* who handled cases involving both Roman citizens and foreigners. When Rome acquired her first provinces about the middle of the third century B.C., new praetorships were established in order to provide provincial governors. After 146 B.C., however, when the number of provinces continued to grow, it was not felt advisable to add to the number of praetors—there were already six. Instead, all the praetors became judicial officials, and men who had served one-year terms as consuls or praetors at Rome were sent to the provinces as proconsuls and propraetors.[7]

The provincial governor, whether a praetor or a pro-

Provincial officials

---

[7] As early as 325 B.C. the Romans had discovered the inconvenience of one-year terms for their chief executives. A consul was supposed to relinquish his authority promptly at the expiration of his year of office. In the case of a crucial military campaign, the Romans might thus find themselves in the proverbial position of changing horses in the middle of a stream if they had to withdraw a successful commander and replace him with one whose ability was an unknown quantity. Therefore, they instituted promagistracies; in other words, the successful commander's term of office might be extended for a definite period beyond the one-year limit. The provincial governships of the proconsuls and the propraetors established after 146 B.C. represented an elaboration of this principle.

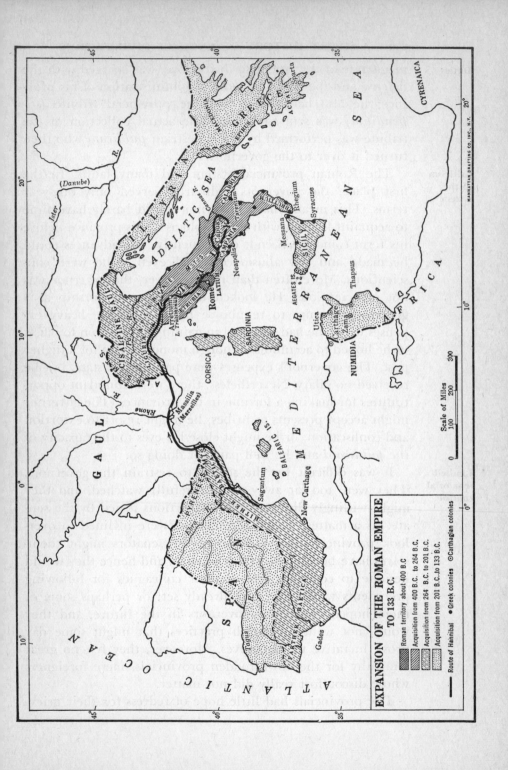

EXPANSION OF THE ROMAN EMPIRE
TO 133 B.C.

Roman territory about 400 B.C
Acquisition from 400 B.C. to 264 B.C.
Acquisition from 264 B.C. to 201 B.C.
Acquisition from 201 B.C. to 133 B.C.
— Route of Hannibal ● Greek colonies ⊙ Carthaginian colonies

Scale of Miles
0   100   200   300

ATLANTIC OCEAN

SPAIN
FARTHER
BAETICA
HITHER
PYRENEES
Gades
Tagus R.
Iberus (Ebro) R.
Saguntum
New Carthage
BALEARIC IS.

GAUL
Rhone R.
Massilia (Marseilles)
CISALPINE GAUL
Po R.
ALPS
Ister (Danube) R.

CORSICA
SARDINIA
Utica
Carthage
Zama
Thapsus
AFRICA
NUMIDIA
CYRENAICA

Rome
LATIUM
CAMPANIA
Neapolis
Tarentum
APENNINES
ETRURIA
UMBRIA
Arretium
L. Trasimene
SAMNIUM
APULIA
CALABRIA
Brundisium
Rhegium
Messana
SICILY
Syracuse
AEGATES IS.

ILLYRIA
ADRIATIC SEA
EPIRUS
MACEDONIA
GREECE
ACARNANIA
Sparta

MEDITERRANEAN SEA

MANHATTAN DRAFTING CO., INC., N.Y.

Duties

magistrate of the type described above, was charged with the defense and the civil and judicial administration of his province; he also had to see that the provincial tribute (*stipendium*) was sent to Rome. The actual collection of the tribute was performed by the equestrian *publicani* who then turned it over to the governor.

Criticism of the system

The Roman provincial system had many faults. In the first place, the governors ordinarily served only one-year terms. This meant that a governor would barely have time to acquaint himself with the problems of his province before his term came to an end; consequently, few advances could be made and few abuses corrected even if he were conscientious. More often than not, however, the governor was not conscientious. He looked upon his governorship as a great opportunity to reimburse himself for the heavy expenses which he had incurred in gaining his election to office, or he hoped to accumulate enough money to run for a higher post. The governor's expenses were paid by the state, but he received no salary. Nevertheless, there were abundant opportunities for making a fortune in the provinces. The governor might accept presents or bribes; he might resort to extortion and confiscation; or he might close his eyes to the rapacity of the *publicani* and be well paid for doing so.

Limited senatorial control

It was difficult for the senate to restrain the governors. They were too far away to be carefully watched, and they might willingly disregard the instructions issued by the senate. As a matter of fact, the senators were inclined to overlook provincial abuses. Some of the senators might themselves have been provincial governors, and hence they would hesitate to condemn one of their colleagues for following precedents which they had already set; or perhaps some of them hoped to become governors in the future, and they would not want to abolish practices that might some day prove lucrative to themselves. Moreover, they felt no great sympathy for the downtrodden provincials, mere foreigners whose discomfort really did not matter.

The provincials had little hope of redress for their grievances. They could send deputations to Rome, but there was only a small chance for reform in such cases. The best course was to find some powerful senator who would act as the patron of their province, some man who had a grudge against the governor and would be glad of the opportunity to prosecute him for maladministration. Occasionally a wayward governor would be tried by the *comitia tributa*, but the percentage of convictions was small. After 149 B.C. a senatorial court was set up at Rome to try cases of extortion; when a governor was tried by a court of his senatorial colleagues, however, the bulk of sympathy was bound to be on his side.

In addition to the maladministration current in the provinces, there was also complaint regarding the system of taxation and tax collecting. Taxes were collected in kind or in money. A fixed sum might be levied upon a province, or the tribute might consist of ten per cent of the annual yield. The former system was hard on the provincials in that a bad harvest might cause great suffering. The *publicani*, moreover, tried to secure as much revenue from a province as was possible, and a compliant governor might allow them to extort fabulous sums. When a province was unable to meet the demands of the *publicani*, these astute business men might then advance loans to the provincials which were to be repaid at exorbitant rates of interest.[8] All in all, the lot of the subjects of Rome in the early period was not enviable.

ROMAN CULTURE BEFORE 133 B.C.

Before 300 B.C. the Romans were largely a simple, hardy nation of farmers whose cultural level was far below that of the more sophisticated Greeks and Carthaginians. The social organization of the Romans closely resembled that of the Greeks of the Dark Ages. The family and the clan were the main elements, and the patriarchal system was even more fully developed than in Greece. The Roman ideal was dignified, austere behavior coupled with great piety. Stress was laid upon devotion to the state. The Romans were tre-

[8] The interest rates varied from 12 to 48 per cent.

mendously conservative; ancestral custom guided them in everything, and any departure from this régime was regarded as in bad taste. The essentially agrarian character of Roman psychology was shown by the fact that they made virtues of economy, endurance, and hard-headed practicality.

Religion   The early religion of the Romans included magical, totemistic, and animistic elements. Great attention was paid to ritual; the Romans did not beg favors of their gods; instead, they made contracts with them. It was not long, however, before the Romans began to borrow from the religions of their neighbors. The Etruscans were early and important contributors: the practice of divination, the idea of the sacred boundary (*pomerium*), and ideas about the gods were borrowed from them by the Romans. The first Roman temples, set on high podia, and early cult images were of Etruscan origin. Etruscan gods were included in the Roman pantheon. Later, another element was added when Greek influences began to invade the religious life of Rome. Greek mythology was important, and the mystery religions were introduced.

Greek influences   The Greek influences to which we have referred came into Rome with greatest force after 300 B.C. when contact with the Greeks of the south and in Sicily began to have its effect. When the Romans extended their sway into the Eastern Mediterranean region, Rome became thoroughly Hellenized. Not only Greek religion and mythology, but also Greek habits and customs, art, literature, and philosophy were adopted, especially by the senatorial and equestrian classes. The old Roman simplicity of life was exchanged for a new luxury and sophistication. Conservative Romans of the old school, like Cato the Censor, tried to stem the rising tide of Hellenism; they inaugurated sumptuary legislation limiting the display of wealth, and they loudly condemned Greek culture in all its social and intellectual aspects, but to no avail. Educated Romans began to learn to read and write Greek, and even Cato took up Greek in his old age.

It should not be forgotten that the composition of the Roman people was also undergoing great changes in this period. The old plebeian stock had been dying out, and the new citizens were non-Romans—Greeks, Etruscans, Italians, Semites, and others—many of whom were the descendants of slaves and conquered peoples who had been brought to Rome. By 150 B.C. it might be said with some justification that the Romans were no longer Romans; hence it is not surprising that under such conditions we should find great cultural changes taking place.

Changes in Roman population

The effect of Greek cultural penetration is shown most clearly in the case of Latin literature. Before 240 B.C. the Romans could hardly have been said to have a literature. There were uses to which writing was put, to be sure, for there were laws, treaties, and other governmental documents as well as religious and business records. Each great clan had pseudo-historical writings in which were recorded the deeds of the ancestors of the clansmen; epitaphs were inscribed on tombs, but there was little else that might be classed as literary composition. The Romans did have poetry and impromptu plays, and oratory was of great importance; nevertheless, this type of expression was transmitted orally and was not ordinarily committed to writing.

Latin literature

In the second half of the third century B.C., the Romans began to create a literature based upon Greek models. In 240 B.C., Livius Andronicus, who had been brought to Rome as a slave from Tarentum many years before, produced a play of the Greek type written in Latin for the Roman games which celebrated the end of the First Punic War. Andronicus' major accomplishment, however, came later when he translated the Odyssey into Latin. A young contemporary of his was Cnaeus Naevius, a native of Rome who wrote tragedies, comedies, and historical plays; he is best known for his epic poem on the First Punic War. At the end of the century came Plautus and Ennius. Plautus wrote over one hundred comedies; his plots were drawn from the works of the famous Greek comedy writer, Menander. Ennius wrote plays based upon Greek models, and also a great epic dealing with Roman history down to the end of the Second Punic War. Ennius and

Livius Andronicus

Cnaeus Naevius

Plautus

Ennius

Plautus were by far the most distinguished of these early writers. The comedies of Plautus were very popular and are still read today; and the epic poem of Ennius, though now lost except for fragments, apparently possessed great literary qualities.

Later writers

In the second century B.C. flourished the tragedians Pacuvius and Lucius Accius, and the comic writer Statius Caecilius. The works of these later writers were more polished and sophisticated than those of their predecessors, but the use—one might say the plundering—of Greek plays was characteristic even of them. The climax of this development of drama in Latin literature was reached in the works of

Terence

P. Terentius Afer (Terence) whose excellence was such that it could not be surpassed by his contemporaries or successors, or appreciated except by a select group of intellectuals.

Cato

The most significant writer of prose in the first half of the second century was Cato the Censor, who wrote on Roman history, on agriculture, and on oratory. Cato was not the first to write Roman history; before him (after 215 B.C.) Quintus Fabius Pictor and others had compiled brief chronicles or annals written in Greek. Cato, however, wrote in Latin, an example which was followed by his contemporaries.

Scipionic circle

Cato, as we have seen, was a reactionary who hated the new Hellenism, and he cordially disliked the liberal intellectuals of the time who were members of the so-called Scipionic circle. The Scipionic circle was composed of a group of men headed by the philhellenic younger Scipio, the adopted grandson of the conqueror of Hannibal. The group included Lucilius, Terence, the orator Laelius, and others, among whom was the Achaean hostage, Polybius, who wrote a great history of Rome in Greek (see above, p. 220).

Rome and civilization

In the broadest sense, the cultural developments which took place in Rome after 300 B.C., especially after 200 B.C., may be characterized simply as the extension of the frontiers of Hellenistic civilization to include the Romans. As creators of civilization the Romans were far less important than the peoples of the Ancient Near East and the Eastern Mediterranean. The rôle of the Romans in cultural history was chiefly that of borrowers, adapters, and (later) carriers of culture. From the Etruscans the Romans borrowed some of their religion, art, and political institutions as well as architecture in stone and the use of the arch. From the Greeks came more culture traits in the field of religion, and an introduction to literature, the fine arts, philosophy, and science. Greek sculpture and painting exerted an increasing influence upon the Romans after the plundering of Greece (171-146 B.C.) when the conquerors brought home Greek art treasures as part of the spoils. About the same time, the Romans began to be attracted by the ethical Greek philosophies, Stoicism and Epicureanism.

It would be most unfair, however, to criticize the Romans for their apparent failure as creators of culture. The major part of this task had been accomplished by others before the Romans had managed to emerge from their Age of Agriculture. In addition, it is only just to point out that, basing their efforts upon the foundations provided by the Graeco-Oriental (Hellenistic) civilization, the Romans later made significant contributions, especially to literature and philosophy. *Cultural rôle of the Romans*

Nevertheless, one ordinarily associates the Romans with the more practical phases of culture, phases in which they made great advances. We shall see later that the Roman forms of municipal government and Roman law were of permanent importance. Roman military organization and science were superior to those of the Hellenistic peoples, and Roman engineering skill, even today, is proverbial. The first of the great Roman roads, the Appian Way (which ran southward from Rome), was built about 312 B.C., and in the years that followed many other highways were constructed. The modern traveler in Italy, France, or Spain can still observe the remains of Roman roads, bridges, aqueducts, and drains; as a matter of fact, many of these structures have fared well in their struggle with time and are still in use. *Roman contributions*

CHAPTER IX

THE LAST CENTURY OF THE ROMAN REPUBLIC

Rome's maritime empire

In 133 B.C. Rome possessed a considerable empire with a large subject population. During the century that followed, additional territory was obtained; the principal acquisitions were in Asia Minor, Syria, Palestine, Cyprus, Egypt, Cyrene, southern France (Narbonese Gaul), central and northern France (Gallia Comata), and Spain. Since most of the territory held by the Romans bordered upon the Mediterranean Sea, that body of water was important to the empire as a unifying factor, for it provided a means of swift and comparatively easy access to all the provinces. One might say that the Roman holdings in this period constituted a maritime empire; the Romans were later to discover—as the Athenians had discovered in the fifth century B.C.—that a maritime empire was less difficult to hold in subjection than a land empire.

Roman competitors

Between 133 and 63 B.C. the Romans were fortunate in that they encountered no really powerful competitors. In this period their only possible rivals were the Seleucids, the Ptolemies, and the kings of Pontus. But the Seleucids were impotent because of dynastic and internal factional strife and the threat of the Parthians on their eastern frontiers, and the Ptolemies had been forced to forswear their imperialism as a result of exhaustion from the Syrian wars of the third century. The kings of Pontus proved vigorous enough, and they were able to stir the Roman provincials in Asia Minor and Greece to revolt; but they were really no match for the military might of Rome.

After 63 B.C., however, when Rome had crushed Pontus and conquered the Seleucids, the Romans found themselves face to face with the Parthians. The Parthians were much more worthy of Roman steel. For nearly three hundred years they threatened the Roman east; if the governmental system **Parthians** of the Roman republic had not been reorganized by Augustus into that of the principate, it is questionable whether the Romans could have continued to hold their eastern provinces.

This brings us to the main subject of our discussion: the **Faults of** fall of the Roman republic. As far as the administration of **imperial** an empire was concerned, the republican system of Rome **organi-** was unsatisfactory. The Romans were trying to govern an **zation** empire by means of a system devised originally for a small city-state. This makeshift arrangement would probably have failed almost immediately if the early Roman empire had been a land empire and if the Parthians and the Romans had come face to face a hundred years earlier. Fortunately, by the time the Romans began to acquire a land empire and to fight the Parthians, the republican system had ceased to exist except in name.

We have already seen how the acquisition of an empire corrupted the Romans and their government, how imperial- **Results** ism worked havoc upon the old Roman morality and ideal- **of im-** ism, and how the struggle to gain territory outside of Italy **perialism** ruined the Roman peasantry. The Roman proletariat, the equestrians, and the senatorial class were, in a sense, the by-products of imperialism. These three classes were now to engage in a struggle for the spoils of empire, a conflict that was to bring the republic to an ignominious end.

In the century of conflict which followed 133 B.C., the participants included not only the three citizen classes, but also **Roman** two other groups: the Italian allies and the Roman army. **factions** The Italian allies sought citizenship and equality with the Romans; shortly after 100 B.C., the Roman army, which had become a distinct professional group, entered politics in order to seek its best interests.

The army, like the proletariat, was ready to sell itself to the highest bidder. This was a development fraught with great political significance, for, whereas before the creation **The army** of a professional army a politician might gain certain ends by **in politics** bargaining with the proletariat to secure votes, much more spectacular results could now be obtained by securing the good will of the army. In dealing with the proletariat, one had to keep fairly close to the constitutional forms and work through established governmental channels. By employing the army, on the other hand, might became right, and it was possible to march straight toward one's goal unhampered by constitutional limitations. When a military leader with political aspirations was thus able to make his own rules of the game, the republican constitution had little chance of survival.

Factional aims

After considering the specific aims of all the groups engaged in the struggle for supremacy in Rome, one is surprised that the republic survived as long as it did. The senators grimly defended their monopoly of the high state offices and the senate; in this way they could hold the vast estates that were the source of their wealth, and they could acquire more land. The senators were greatly embarrassed, however, by their financial indebtedness to the equestrians, for many of them had gone to equestrian capitalists to borrow money for political campaigns and other expenses. The equestrians wanted a free hand in exploiting the provinces, and in order to secure this leeway they had to attack the governmental monopoly held by the senators. The proletariat wanted a living; there was some agitation for land, but many proletarians would have been satisfied to have been supported by the state in some way. At any rate, the proletariat always responded to a promise of cheap or free grain, or a colonization project. In addition, this group was consistently opposed to any extension of citizenship to Rome's allies or subjects; the Roman masses did not want to share their few privileges with anyone. The Italian allies, as we have already observed, would not be content until they had been given equality and citizenship. Last of all, the army desired not only the plunder of conquest, but also pensions; the veteran soldier usually wanted land so that he could retire comfortably when his term of service was over.

These conflicting aims of the various factions were productive of a series of conflicts that began in 133 B.C. with riots in Rome itself and grew in 90 B.C. to civil war in Italy; soon afterward the whole empire became the battleground of the opposing factions. The almost continuous tumult impressed people with the need for reform. It was obvious that something was fundamentally wrong with the Roman system, and various panaceas were suggested for its ills. There were reactionaries who favored a return to senatorial oligarchy; the equestrians sought timocracy; the proletariat, complete democracy (but no enlargement of the citizen body). A few people like Cicero wanted a coalition of senators and equestrians—timocratic or aristocratic (?) government. Julius Caesar, on the other hand, favored autocracy—a dictatorship, or perhaps an absolute monarchy.

Suggested reforms

The whole period (133-30 B.C.) is fascinating not only because of its problems and the remedies suggested for them, but also because of the abundance of striking personalities which the age produced. It is interesting to see, however, that in the midst of the political and social confusion, when wars and civil strife interfered with agriculture, commerce, and industry, the frontiers of civilization continued to advance at a slow pace; in the Western Mediterranean new peripheral areas were penetrated by Hellenistic culture. At Rome itself, in the heart of the maelstrom, significant and lasting contributions were made to literature and intellectual life.

Cultural advance

POLITICAL AND MILITARY HISTORY (133-30 B.C.)

The most striking features of Roman history in the period from 287 to 133 B.C. are the great wars with the Carthaginians and the Hellenistic kingdoms. As a result, the attention of the beginning student of Roman history is often diverted from the contemporary economic developments which were taking place in Rome itself, and the recurrence of domestic strife in Rome in 133 B.C. appears to come entirely without warning. As a matter of fact, trouble at home had been brewing ever since the Second Punic War, a conflict that had wrought

Domestic unrest

great hardships upon the peasantry. Moreover, in the first half of the second century B.C., the increasing avarice of the equestrians endangered the governmental monopoly of the senatorial class to such an extent that a struggle between these two groups was inevitable. The series of long and expensive wars which preceded 146 B.C. was bound to have an effect upon Roman economic life, and it seems likely that after 146 there was a post-war slump that brought matters to a crisis. Undoubtedly this economic depression reacted as un-favorably upon the senators and equestrians as upon the pro-letariat, but the masses were also resentful of the severe con-scription which the widespread conflicts of 149-146 B.C. had necessitated. Then, too, the passage of a law in 139 B.C. establishing the secret ballot might indicate that the senators, if not the equestrians also, had attempted to intimidate the voters. Therefore, in 133 B.C., when the proletariat found a vigorous leader in Tiberius Gracchus, domestic issues were brought into the foreground.

Tiberius Gracchus

Tiberius Gracchus was a young nobleman whose mother, Cornelia, was the daughter of Scipio Africanus. Cornelia was a brilliant, well-educated woman who was ambitious for her sons, Tiberius and Gaius, and had devoted much atten-tion to their upbringing. Tiberius, the elder, had embraced the Stoic philosophy with its emphasis upon the brotherhood of man. Despite his close association with the conservative younger Scipio—his brother-in-law and the recent victor over Carthage in the Third Punic War—Tiberius entertained liberal views and had great sympathy for the common people. He feared the possible results of the increase of slavery, and he wished to find some way to restore the free peasantry, the backbone of the Roman army.

Attempted reforms

In 133 B.C. Tiberius became a tribune. He immediately proposed a plan for the distribution of land to poor Roman citizens, but he incurred the enmity of the senate when he failed to consult that body and tried to push his land act through the tribal assembly. The senate arranged for a con-servative tribune named Octavius to veto the bill. Tiberius, however, was equal to the occasion; he persuaded the assembly to depose Octavius, and, when this was done, the land bill was passed and became a law. The enraged senators maintained that the deposition of Octavius was unconstitutional—it was, at least, without precedent—and they planned to prosecute Tiberius after the expiration of his tribuneship. This prosecution Tiberius hoped to avoid by seeking reelection, a procedure which was also of undetermined legality. The senate then resorted to violence; bands of rioters—the partisans of the senate and those of Tiberius—fought in the streets of Rome. Tiberius and a large number of his followers were slain in the *mêlée*.

For the next decade the senate held the upper hand; but the equestrians, the proletariat, and also the Italian allies were becoming restive. In 123 B.C., Gaius Gracchus, the younger brother of Tiberius and a much more astute politician, became tribune. Gaius obtained the support of the proletariat by reviving Tiberius' land scheme and by securing the passage of bills providing for cheap grain and less severe conscription. He won the equestrians to his side by sponsoring a bill to substitute equestrian for senatorial jurors in the courts which tried provincial officials for extortion; such a change, of course, would give the *publicani* almost a free hand in the provinces, since few senatorial governors would dare to oppose them in the face of almost certain trial before an equestrian jury. Three other bills endeared Gaius to the equestrians: the first gave them the opportunity to collect the taxes of the rich new province of Asia (the former Pergamene kingdom); the second provided for the establishment of two colonies in Italy and one on the site of Carthage in Africa; the third proposed the construction of new roads in Italy. The commercially-minded equestrians were delighted at the prospect of a Roman colony on the advantageous site of Carthage, and the contractors anticipated fat contracts for materials to be used in the new roads.

For two years Gaius was the "uncrowned king of Rome." His popularity with the equestrians and the proletariat was

(margin note: Gaius Gracchus)

The "un-crowned king of Rome"

so great that the senators did not dare to attack him openly. In 122 B.C., he was reelected to the tribunate—a law permitting reelection to this office had been passed a few years before. Then Gaius made his mistake: he antagonized his supporters by advocating citizenship for the Italian allies. About the same time, he left for Africa to be present at the founding of the Carthaginian colony. During his absence his popularity waned, and the senate began to outbid him for proletarian favor. A senatorial land bill of wider scope and greater liberality than that of Gaius was proposed. Moreover, the senate offered to establish not two, but twelve, colonies in Italy. The senators would not consider giving citizenship to the allies, but they offered to modify the conditions of allied military service.

Failure of Gaius

When Gaius returned to Rome he found that his cause had lost ground. He was not reelected to the tribuneship for a third term, and gang warfare broke out between his remaining supporters and the senatorial faction. The greater part of the proletariat had been alienated by his plan to enfranchise the allies and had been won over by senatorial promises. The equestrians felt that Gaius could do them no more favors, and they too abandoned him. The riots in Rome became so disturbing that the senate was given an excuse to declare martial law. Gaius and his friends were hunted down by a senatorial posse; several thousand were killed, and Gaius himself committed suicide.

Jugurthine War

For more than ten years after the death of Gaius Gracchus, the senate ruled unchallenged until senatorial prestige suffered a severe blow in the course of the war with Jugurtha, the African king of Numidia. Jugurtha, whose lack of respect for Roman dignity had led the Romans to invade his country, for three years gained humiliating successes over senatorial commanders. Finally, an investigation of the failure of the Roman forces disclosed bribery and corruption among high officers in the army. In great indignation over the senatorial disgrace, the Romans elected an equestrian, Gaius Marius, to the consulship (107 B.C.), and turned over to him the conduct of the war. Within two years the victorious Marius returned to Rome with Jugurtha as his prisoner.

The triumph of Marius was also a triumph for his class, the equestrian. The senatorial faction was soon pushed further into the background by the new successes of Marius, for he was not long in finding a new field for his talents. We may summarize subsequent events as follows: **Equestrian triumph**

While Marius had been in Africa, the Romans had been thrown into a panic by reports of the movements of barbarian tribes, Celts and Germans, into Narbonese Gaul.[1] Ever since the Gauls had sacked Rome in 390 B.C., the Romans had feared a repetition of barbarian invasion from the north. When Marius came back from the Jugurthine War, he was reelected to the consulship and sent to Narbonese Gaul to repel the expected attack. In preparation, he reformed the army, transforming it into a professional body by allowing men to enlist for a sixteen-year period, thus substituting enlistment for conscription. He trained his troops well, and then inflicted severe defeats upon the barbarians in 102 and 101 B.C. In 100 he returned to Rome to enter upon his sixth consulship. **Celts and Germans**

Marius was primarily a military man. He might have become a political leader, but he had no talent for a career of this type and had to rely upon Roman politicians for aid. He became connected with two demagogues, Saturninus and Glaucia, whose favorite methods were those of mob violence. The activities of these two men were so outrageous that both of them were killed (99 B.C.) as the result of an uprising in Rome; Marius was involved in their disgrace in such a way that he had to retire from politics. **Marius in politics**

Although Marius proved a failure in the political arena and was not able to consolidate the advances which he had made for the equestrian party, he himself is not without significance in the history of Roman constitutional evolution. We have already seen that it was Marius who created the pro- **Significance of Marius**

[1] Narbonese Gaul (southern France) had been made a Roman province about 119 B.C.

264 A SHORT HISTORY OF ANCIENT CIVILIZATION

fessional Roman army, the group which was later to become a
potent force in politics. In addition, he was the first to break
the traditional rule against successive consulships. Because
he seemed to be the only man who could save Rome, Marius
had been allowed to hold the consulship six times in the
period between 107 and 99 B.C. This set a precedent to which
later aspirants for supreme power were able to appeal. The
successive consulships of Marius provide some of the earliest
indications of the dissolution of a tradition that had kept the
republican constitution intact for several centuries.

Although the senators, equestrians, and proletarians were
bitter enemies and each group had its own peculiar aims,
there was one point on which all three were agreed: they
did not want to extend citizenship to the Italian allies. Ever
since the time of Gaius Gracchus the question of Italian en-
franchisement had been avoided; the Romans had concentrated their attention upon domestic politics. A few years
after Marius' disgrace, however, there appeared a reformer
named Marcus Livius Drusus who reopened discussion on the
forbidden topic. Drusus was a tribune who had won the favor
of the senators by his opposition to the equestrians; he also
courted the good will of the proletariat with legislation providing for cheap grain and new colonization. Then, apparently over-estimating his popularity and influence, Drusus
sponsored a bill to enfranchise the allies. It is not surprising
to learn that he was assassinated almost immediately.

The Romans were soon to discover, however, that times
had changed. Whereas, thirty years before, the death of Gaius
Gracchus had closed discussion of the question of Italian
citizenship, now the murder of Drusus had just the opposite
effect. The allies were thoroughly aroused, and they were
determined to obtain some kind of a settlement. Even before
Drusus had introduced his legislation in their behalf, they
had secretly organized their forces. It seems likely that they
held little hope that Drusus would succeed; at any rate, as
soon as he was murdered, they revolted and set up a government independent of Rome. The war between Rome and the

Italian
allies

Social
War

allies (the Social War) was fought in the period between 90 and 88 B.C. As far as the military operations were concerned, the Romans were the victors; but when the war was over, all the allies had been given citizenship—some had been offered civic rights to keep them from joining the revolt, and others had accepted citizenship as the price for laying down their arms. As a result of this war, the Roman citizen body was probably more than quadrupled in size.

Sulla, the most successful Roman general in the Social War, was made consul in 88 B.C. He belonged to the senatorial faction and was a confirmed reactionary. Because of his ability and position, it was only natural that he should be chosen to take the field against Mithradates, the king of Pontus, who had been quietly gaining influence over the Roman provincials in Asia Minor and Greece. In 88 B.C. Mithradates engineered a general uprising of the provincials in Asia Minor in which 80,000 Romans were killed. Emboldened by his success, the mainland Greeks invited Mithradates to cross over into Europe to effect their liberation from Roman rule. Despite the opposition of Marius and the equestrians, which was accompanied by a brief civil war in Italy, Sulla managed to retain the upper hand and subsequently left Italy to expel Mithradates from Greece. Sulla's operations were successful; the Pontic king was driven from Greece, defeated in Asia Minor, and forced to retire to his own small kingdom. *Sulla and Mithradates*

In the meantime, as soon as Sulla had departed from Italy, Marius' party had gained control of the Roman government. Marius himself soon died, but his followers continued in power, instituting a reign of terror in which the senatorial partisans of Sulla in Italy were killed or exiled and their property confiscated. In 83 B.C. Sulla returned to Italy with his veterans of the Mithradatic War. The Marians were driven from the peninsula; some fled to Africa and Sicily, and others to Spain. Only those in Spain escaped immediate punishment; the rest were pursued and destroyed. In Spain, *Marian supremacy*

Sulla's return

however, the brilliant Marian general, Sertorius, held the senatorial forces at bay for over a decade.

In Italy, Sulla was made dictator[2] and given supreme power to enact laws and reconstitute the republic. He devoted much time to the extermination of his enemies. Wholesale massacres of Marians, or of those suspected of being in sympathy with the party, now took place. Long lists of proscriptions were issued which confiscated the estates of Sulla's opponents and set a price upon the heads of fugitive Marians. Then Sulla embarked upon a reactionary program of legislation calculated to establish the supremacy of the senate in the Roman government. The senate was given the veto power over all legislation, and senators were restored to the jury courts. The powers of the tribunes were curtailed; moreover, it was decreed that if a man held the office of tribune, he should be ineligible for election to any higher post. The distribution of cheap grain was forbidden. His work completed, Sulla retired from public life in 79 B.C. and died the following year.

Sulla's reforms

Sulla had tried to turn back the clock of political evolution, but actually he only arrested it momentarily. Too many groups were opposed to his reforms for any chance of permanence in the arrangements he had made. Numerous adherents of Marius were still alive; equestrians who had not been Marians were much dissatisfied with what Sulla had done; and the proletariat was angered by its loss of political power and cheap grain. Just as soon as Sulla died, there were movements to set aside his reforms. By the end of 70 B.C., few vestiges of his legislation remained.

Reaction fails

Nevertheless, Sulla, like Marius, has an important place in Roman constitutional history. Sulla's lengthy dictatorship

Significance of Sulla

---

[2] Under the Roman system, when the state was in great peril, governmental affairs might be placed in the hands of an official called the dictator. The dictator outranked even the consuls, and the appointment of such an official virtually meant the declaration of martial law. The dictator was supposed to resign as soon as the crisis had passed; under any circumstances, his term expired within six months. The extraordinary nature of Sulla's position may be seen in the fact that he held the dictatorship continuously from 82 until he retired in 79.

(82-79 B.C.) provides another illustration of the gradual disintegration of the Roman constitutional tradition. It set a new precedent, and it paved the way for the later absolutism of Julius Caesar. Moreover, Sulla's reforms represented the conservative interpretation of the ills of the Roman government and how they might be remedied.

In the half-century after the death of Sulla, the Roman republic came to an end. In this, the last act of the drama, the leading rôle was played not so much by parties and factions as by individuals. Whereas Tiberius Gracchus, Marius, and Sulla had really been little more than the spearheads of the proletarian, equestrian, and senatorial parties respectively, in the period after 78 B.C. ambitious individuals used the factions as a means to gain personal ends. This statement would not apply to Cicero, but it would certainly be true of Pompey, Crassus, Julius Caesar, Antony, and Octavian. It was not that the various parties were lacking in specific aims, but rather that they lacked the strength to engage in purposeful action. The senatorial party alone possessed sufficient cohesiveness and power to formulate a program and force political leaders to pay some attention to its demands. *Growing importance of individuals in politics*

As a result, this particular half-century is interesting because it is the only period in ancient history in which individuals rather than groups or non-human forces had great power to influence the course of history. A peculiar and unprecedented combination of circumstances was responsible for this phenomenon. The precise point of development that the Roman constitution had now reached, the temper of the proletariat and the other classes, the potential power of the professional army, and a series of external crises were factors which delivered the state into the hands of the ambitious politicians. *Result of peculiar circumstances*

After Sulla, the first strong man to appear was Gnaeus Pompey. As one of Sulla's supporters, Pompey had helped to drive the Marians from Italy and Africa. In 77 B.C. he was sent to Spain to fight the surviving Marians who had joined *Pompey*

Sertorius. This was no easy task, and his work in Spain was not finished until five years later.

Just before Pompey returned to Italy, a serious revolt of slaves and gladiators broke out. The whole Italian peninsula was imperiled. Roman military leaders, on the whole, proved unable to make much headway; the only man who met with

Crassus

any success was Crassus, a wealthy equestrian, who finally broke the back of the rebellion. Pompey entered Italy just in time to intercept a body of the defeated slaves who were trying to escape northward from the peninsula. As a reward for their services, Pompey and Crassus were elected consuls for the year 70 B.C.

In their electoral campaign Pompey and Crassus promised

Consulship of Pompey and Crassus

that the power of the tribunes would be restored and the legislative veto of the senate repealed. These promises were fulfilled. In addition, a great provincial scandal paved the way for a reorganization of the jury courts. A man named Verres, who had served three years as a propraetor in the rich province of Sicily, had openly used his position to amass a fortune of about two million dollars. He was reported to have said that his ill-gotten gains of the first year were for himself, those of the second year for his friends,

Trial of Verres

and those of the third year for his jurors. His Sicilian subjects, however, mustered up their courage and brought suit against him for extortion. They made a wise choice in securing a rising young lawyer named Cicero to prosecute their case. Verres was defended by Quintus Hortensius, who had a great reputation in the courts, but Cicero's brilliant conduct of the trial was too much for his opponents. Verres admitted defeat before the trial was over and went into exile. Cicero's reputation was made, and the whole question of the reform of the courts came before the public. In the subsequent reorganization, it was decided that the juries would henceforth be composed of equal numbers of senators, equestrians, and *tribuni aerarii* (the next lowest census class).

Shortly afterward, the Romans had to find a solution for two pressing problems: piracy had become a serious menace

to trade in the Eastern Mediterranean, and Mithradates of New problems
Pontus had begun once more to meddle in the affairs of the
Near East. Both the pirates and Mithradates had been allies
of Sertorius, the late opponent of Pompey in Spain. Some
attempts had already been begun to punish the pirates, but
they had not been successful. The Roman operations against
Mithradates had fared somewhat better; even so, considerable dissatisfaction had been expressed at Rome over the
conduct of the war.

If the pirates were to be driven from the seas and Mithradates was to be humiliated, the Romans must send out their
most outstanding general, Pompey. The senators mistrusted Pompey and the pirates
Pompey because he had now allied himself with the eques-
trians and the proletariat, a coalition known as the Popu-
lares. Nevertheless, there was no choice, and Pompey became
the recipient of a special command against the pirates. This
special command was created by a law[3] passed in 67 which
conferred upon a general of consular rank supreme power
over the Mediterranean Sea and all Roman territory surrounding it to a distance of fifty miles inland; the appointment was to run for three years. When Pompey was given
this command, he proceeded against the pirates with great
vigor and broke their power within three months. In 66 B.C.
another law was passed which gave Pompey charge of the
war against Mithradates.[4] Within a year's time he had de- Mithra-dates
feated Mithradates and his ally, the king of Armenia. Pompey
spent the years 64 and 63 B.C. in terminating the existence
of the nearly defunct Seleucid empire; Syria was organized
as a Roman province.

While Pompey covered himself with military glory in the
Near East, rich and ambitious Crassus, who had remained in Crassus in Rome
Rome, became more and more envious of the success of his
erstwhile colleague. Crassus, fearing that he himself would

[3] This was the outcome of a bill sponsored by a tribune named Gabinius. It
is usually referred to as the Gabinian Law.

[4] This was the Manilian Law, proposed by the tribune Manilius. One of
the most famous of Cicero's orations, *For the Manilian Law*, was delivered in
support of this measure.

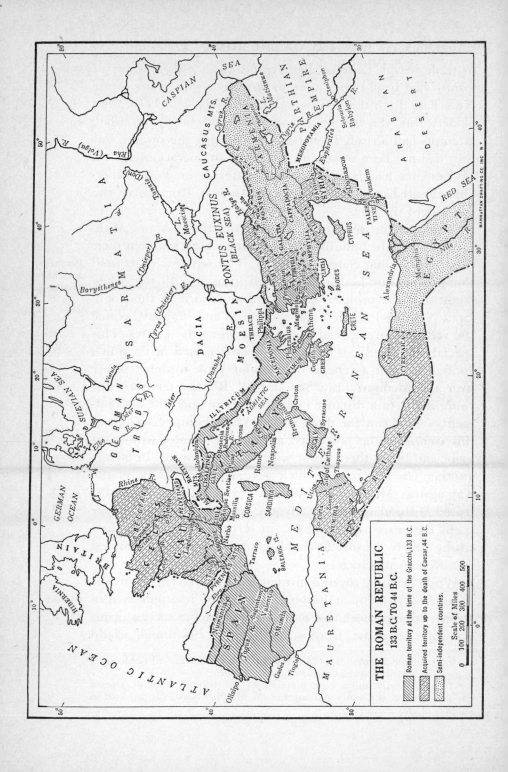

THE ROMAN REPUBLIC
133 B.C. TO 44 B.C.

Roman territory at the time of the Gracchi, 133 B.C.
Acquired territory up to the death of Caesar, 44 B.C.
Semi-independent countries.

Scale of Miles
0   100   200   300   400   500

suffer a political eclipse when Pompey returned to Rome, therefore attempted in several ways to gain control of the situation in Rome. His wealth enabled him to procure the services of a number of young men who seemed to have political promise; one of his henchmen was Julius Caesar, and another was Catiline. One of Crassus' schemes was the annexation of Egypt—he planned to have Caesar appointed **Caesar** to carry out this project, but he failed to persuade the Romans to adopt the plan. Crassus then tried to secure the election of Catiline to the consulship. Catiline ran for office in 64 B.C., but was defeated; one of the victorious candidates was Cicero.

In 63 B.C., when Cicero was consul, Catiline, now repudiated as useless by Crassus, again presented himself as a **Catiline** candidate for election. Defeated a second time, Catiline plotted a revolution, but his plans were exposed by Cicero in the famous Catilinarian Orations. Most of Catiline's fellow conspirators in Rome were arrested and executed; Catiline himself perished in a battle with government forces.

Despite the failure of Crassus to establish himself at Rome, Pompey did not have a free hand when he returned to Rome **Pompey's** late in 62 B.C., for the senators were still opposed to him. **return** What Pompey wanted from the Roman government was a ratification of the political settlement which he had made in the East and pensions for his veteran soldiers, but the senate paid no attention to his demands.

At this juncture, Julius Caesar came to the fore. Caesar, now about forty years old, had thus far led an exciting life— **Caesar** as a member of the Marian party he had narrowly escaped **to the** death at Sulla's hands; he had been married four times; on **fore** one occasion he had been captured by pirates. His political career had been financed by Crassus; he had been praetor in 62 B.C. and a governor in Spain the following year; since 63 B.C. he had been *pontifex maximus*, the head of the state religion. When he returned from Spain in 60 B.C., Caesar was politically strong enough to act independently of Crassus.

He surveyed the Roman situation and evolved a plan of action.

Caesar clearly saw that, as individuals, neither he nor Pompey nor Crassus could accomplish anything in the face of senatorial opposition. Therefore he proposed that he and the other two should pool their political resources. His logic prevailed; Pompey and Crassus became reconciled, and a political marriage was arranged between Julia (Caesar's daughter) and Pompey. The political alliance of Caesar, Pompey, and Crassus thus formed is known to history as the First Triumvirate; it should be emphasized that, although a political monopoly was secured by the triumvirs, their coalition was purely a private affair—a gentleman's agreement—and had no constitutional basis.

The first act of the united leaders was to gain for Caesar an election to the consulship for 59 B.C. As consul, Caesar was able to obtain the ratification of the settlements made by Pompey in the Near East and pensions for his veterans. To the equestrian friends of Crassus were remitted sums amounting to one-third of the total tribute which they had contracted to extract from the province of Asia. For himself, Caesar managed to gain an appointment for five years as proconsul in Cisalpine Gaul (the Po Valley) and Narbonese Gaul.

Passing over the well-known conquest of Gaul which Caesar began in the years 58-56 B.C., we may turn to the next united action of the triumvirs. A meeting of the three leaders was held at Lucca in northern Italy in 56 B.C. in which new plans were laid. Caesar's command in Gaul was to be extended for another five years; Crassus and Pompey were to hold the consulship in 55 B.C., after which Crassus was to go to Syria to undertake a war with the Parthians and Pompey was to have a free hand in Spain and Libya. In the following years, Caesar was able to consolidate his conquest of Gaul and make a punitive expedition into Germany; in 55 and 54 B.C. he also made two unsuccessful attempts to gain a foothold in Britain. Crassus, who had always hoped for military glory, embarked upon his Parthian campaign with great enthusiasm, but unfortunately he was no general: he was defeated and slain in battle by the Parthians in 53 B.C.

The death of Crassus brought the first triumvirate to an end, and shortly terminated any cooperation between Pompey and Caesar. As a matter of fact, the breach between the two men had begun to widen with the death of Julia in 54 B.C. Pompey was now courted by the senatorial faction which feared Caesar's growing popularity. After 55 affairs in Rome itself had been in an uproar. Rival demagogues stirred up urban factions to a point of open warfare in the streets, and in 52 conditions were so chaotic that elections could not be held. To restore order, Pompey was made sole consul and given extraordinary powers. *End of the Triumvirate*

At length, with the encouragement and support of the senate, Pompey broke off his connection with Caesar, and in 49 B.C. Caesar began civil war by invading Italy with his Gallic veterans. Pompey retired to the Greek peninsula where he was defeated by Caesar at Pharsalus in Thessaly in the following year; his flight to Egypt ended in his assassination there as soon as he arrived. *Pompey versus Caesar*

The years 48-45 B.C. were spent by Caesar in stamping out the resistance of the remaining members of the Pompeian party. Caesar followed Pompey to Egypt in 48; there he met the famous Cleopatra and set her upon the Ptolemaic throne in the face of the rival claims of her brothers. The rest of the Near East was pacified in 47 B.C.; the Pompeian forces in Africa were destroyed in 46, and those in Spain in 45.

With these tasks completed, Caesar settled down in Rome to reorganize the Roman government. His intention was to discard the republic and set up a dictatorship—and perhaps, eventually, an absolute monarchy of the Hellenistic type. The powers he received at this time made him the supreme authority in the Roman state. In 46 B.C. he was given the dictatorship for ten years; at the same time he held the consulship. As *pontifex maximus* he controlled the state re- *Caesar as dictator* ligion. He did not hold the office of tribune, but he was given the *power* of that office which allowed him to veto the actions of magistrates and assemblies and made his person sacrosanct. Special laws gave him the right to make war and peace, to nominate and appoint magistrates, to command all the military forces of Rome, and to supervise the coinage. The sum total of these powers placed Caesar above any other official or government body; he could even legislate at his pleasure.

In addition to establishing a dictatorship, Caesar made certain reforms. He tried to bring about uniformity in the municipal governments of Italy by giving the Italian towns city-state constitutions modeled upon that of the city of Rome. He introduced a new calendar, later known as the Julian calendar, which was used by the western world until the sixteenth century A.D.; and he planned the codification of Roman law. The size of the senate was increased, the pay of the army was raised, and provincial taxes were reduced. Caesar was particularly interested in colonization: Corinth and Carthage, two advantageous commercial sites, were re-occupied by Roman colonists. His good judgment in choosing likely sites is shown by the fact that the present cities of Seville, Lisbon, Arles, and Toulouse were either colonized or given municipal charters at his order.

It is true that Caesar was ambitious for power, but his policies may be defended on the ground that something had to be done to end factional strife. The republican system had been unable to do this, and things had gone from bad to worse. Perhaps, if the economic situation had been more favorable, democracy or timocracy might have been restored; but only peace could remedy the economic situation, and, under the circumstances then prevailing, only a dictatorship could bring peace.

If Caesar had lived, his reforms might have been more beneficial than his contemporaries realized. His attempt to secure uniformity in Italy certainly aided the "Romanization" of the peninsula, and his extension of Roman and Latin citizenship to some provincial communities was an initial step toward raising the provinces to equality with Italy. Even if he had established a monarchy, the continued "Romanization" of the provinces might have led back to the restoration of republican government.

Whatever else one may think of Caesar, the fact remains that he was probably even a greater genius than Alexander. His military ability equaled that of the great Macedonian; his powers of organization are established by his deeds, whereas those of Alexander remain problematical. Brilliant, well educated, a fine orator and writer, Caesar left an indelible impression upon the memory of mankind. His private life and his general moral attitudes are less deserving of praise.

Caesar evaluated

It was Caesar's intention to establish a monarchy, or the fear that he would do so, which proved his undoing. There were two things that always aroused and united the Romans: the fear of a Gallic invasion and the threat of monarchy. When it became rumored that Caesar wanted to be king, his opponents of the old senatorial party began to gain ground. On the fifteenth of March, 44 B.C., Caesar was assassinated by a group of conspirators led by Caius Cassius, a Pompeian whom Caesar had pardoned, and Marcus Junius Brutus, rumored to be one of Caesar's illegitimate children.

The Ides of March

Caesar's assassins had planned nothing beyond his death. One might almost say that they expected the republic to restore itself. True, the senatorial class as a whole approved their action, and the proletariat did not immediately condemn them. Nevertheless, there was still the army to be reckoned with in addition to two strong military men: Mark Antony, Caesar's devoted follower who was consul, and Marcus Aemilius Lepidus, Caesar's master of the horse.[5] Antony turned the tide against the assassins when he publicly read Caesar's will which disclosed that Caesar had bequeathed fifteen dollars to every Roman citizen and had ordered some of his property in Rome to be made into a public park. This

Mark Antony

[5] A dictator was always assisted by a subordinate who was called the *magister equitum*, master of the horse.

convinced the proletariat that Caesar had been their friend, and they howled for vengeance. Antony, however, did not yet feel strong enough to take the field against the conspirators; instead, he temporarily made friends with them.

Octavian

Caesar's will also revealed the adoption of his grandnephew Gaius Octavius (Octavian) as his son and heir. Octavian came to Rome in 44 B.C. to claim his inheritance, but Antony, who had already spent Caesar's fortune, ignored him. Octavian was only eighteen at this time and had shown no promise of his future greatness.

Cicero's Philippic Orations

Late in 44 B.C. Antony at last came to an open break with Caesar's murderers, but he found arrayed against him the power of the senate and also that of Octavian, around whom many of Caesar's veterans had flocked. Cicero, too, was outspoken in his enmity and delivered his famous *Philippic Orations* (modeled upon the *Philippics* of Demosthenes) against Antony.

Against such opposition, Antony could make little headway. Then the senate made its great mistake; it antagonized Octavian by failing properly to acknowledge his aid. As a result, Octavian, Antony, and Lepidus joined forces; they soon came into the possession of Rome, Italy, and all the western half of the empire, while the conspirators under Cassius and Brutus held the eastern provinces.

Second Triumvirate

Octavian, Antony, and Lepidus forced the senate to appoint them a "committee of three for the settlement of the republic" (*triumviri reipublicae constituendae*), and thus the Second Triumvirate came into existence (43 B.C.). This triumvirate differed from the first in that it was an official body, established by law, whereas the first triumvirate had been only a private arrangement among Pompey, Caesar, and Crassus. The new triumvirs were to hold their supreme office for five years.

Death of Cicero

The triumvirs now embarked upon a program of proscription, partly out of revenge and partly because they needed money for their troops. One of the first victims was Cicero, who was, of course, bitterly hated by Antony. The great orator met death with courage. It might be said that with him died the republic, for he was the last of Rome's great statesmen who put the republic first and himself second. Cicero had hoped to solve the ills of the republic by a coalition of senators and equestrians; but his program of the "concord of the orders" had aroused little enthusiasm.

In 42 B.C., Antony and Octavian took the field against Brutus and Cassius, who held the Roman East. After a double battle in Macedonian Philippi, Brutus and Cassius committed suicide. This left the triumvirs supreme, except for the resistance provided by Sextus Pompey, the son of Pompey the Great, who had supported the senatorial faction with a strong navy. Subsequent events may be summarized as follows:

Philippi, 42 B.C.

Between 42 and 36 B.C. Antony was engaged in settling the affairs of the east, Octavian held the west, and Lepidus was placed in charge of Africa. Lepidus was gradually pushed further and further into the background during this period, for he was no match for Antony and Octavian. He was useful, however, as a balance wheel, and therefore he was again included in the triumvirate when its powers were renewed for another five years at the end of 38 B.C. The major problem of these years was the disposal of Sextus Pompey; he was finally defeated by Octavian's close friend and general, Agrippa (36 B.C.).

Sextus Pompey

After 36 B.C., affairs resolved themselves into a struggle between Octavian and Antony for possession of the empire. Octavian had never forgiven Antony for what had happened at Rome in 44 B.C. when Antony had squandered Octavian's patrimony and treated him with contempt. This was not the sum total of the difficulty, however, for the fact remained that there was no room in the empire for two supreme rulers. While Sextus Pompey was alive, Antony and Octavian had to remain on friendly terms, but afterward they found themselves natural opponents, and neither was willing to submit or defer to the other.

Antony's popularity with the Romans steadily declined after an unsuccessful Parthian campaign in 36 B.C. Then, too,

**Antony
and
Cleopatra**

Antony had fallen under the influence of the Ptolemaic queen, Cleopatra. He married her in 36, casting off his earlier bride, Octavia, the sister of Octavian. In 34 at Alexandria Antony announced the so-called Donations of Alexandria in which he proclaimed Cleopatra queen of Egypt, Cyprus, Crete, and one of the Syrian provinces; Caesarion, the son of Cleopatra and Julius Caesar, was named joint ruler with her. The two sons she had borne Antony were named kings of other portions of the Near East.

**Actium,
31 B.C.**

Finally, in 32 B.C., Octavian, representing the Roman government, declared war upon Cleopatra—Antony was not named. Antony and Cleopatra assembled troops in Greece for an attack upon Italy; but Agrippa defeated the Egyptian fleet in a naval battle at Actium, off the west coast of Greece, and Antony and Cleopatra took refuge in Egypt (31 B.C.). When Octavian pursued them and arrived the following year, Antony and Cleopatra committed suicide, and Egypt became a Roman province (30 B.C.).

In 29 B.C., Octavian, now master of the whole empire, returned to Rome to begin the task of reorganizing a government and a realm which had been reduced to chaos by a century of civil conflict. In this he was to prove successful, although it took him the rest of his life.

ECONOMIC HISTORY (133-30 B.C.)

**Rome
a financial
center**

After 133 B.C. Rome tended more and more to become the financial capital of the ancient world. Tribute from the far corners of the Mediterranean basin poured into the imperial coffers, and the equestrian capitalists had investments in even the most remote provinces. Despite the presence of pirates in the east, trade seems to have lost little ground; in Italy there was a growth of industry in the first century B.C.

**"Big
business"**

The chief sources of equestrian revenue were moneylending and the state contracts for public works, the exploitation of natural resources in the provinces, and the collection of provincial taxes. Syndicates or stock companies were often formed in which the equestrians and also the senators (working through private agents) might participate. Capital was supplied by the major partners in the company and by small investors who became stockholders. This was truly "big business"; the *publicani* and the *negotiatores* (money lenders) constituted one of the most powerful "pressure groups" in Roman politics.

Although a few equestrians might invest in trade and industry or enter the banking field, these activities were largely **Trade** in the hands of Greeks, south Italians, and Semites (Jews, **and** Phoenicians, and Syrians). These people might be Roman citizens; the Italians and Italian Greeks were made citizens after the Social War, and many who were brought to Italy as slaves later were manumitted and became citizen freedmen, but they could not be classed as truly "Roman."

Most of the manufacturing in Italy was done in small shops that employed only a few slaves or free workers. There were **Manufac-** a modest number of larger establishments—those which **turing in** manufactured pottery, for example—but these were not numerous enough to say that there was mass production in Italian industry. The chief manufactures of Italy were for the home market; they consisted of clothing, furniture, implements, tiles, metal work, pottery, and other necessities; tanning, milling, and baking were also common industries.

Italy's imports far exceeded her exports. The most valuable exports were agricultural (wine and olive oil), but pottery, **Imports** metal work, and Campanian ointments were also exported. **and** Italian imports of grain, slaves, textiles, and luxuries of various kinds over-balanced exports in quantity and value. The chief imported luxuries were wine, spices, precious stones, silks, and glassware, as well as special foods. It is clear that it was not commerce, but the imperial tribute, that helped to keep the economy of Italy on an even keel.

The civil wars and slave rebellions of the first century B.C. interfered with Italian agriculture. The small farms con- **Italian** tinued to decrease in number, whereas the large estates **agriculture** (*latifundia*) increased; the senatorial class usually invested a large share of its imperial earnings in Italian land. Nevertheless, agricultural production was disrupted by the actual military operations of the period and by the frequent changes in landownership resulting from the wholesale confiscations authorized by Sulla, Marius, Caesar, Antony, and Octavian. Grazing fared better than agriculture, as one might expect, since the political disturbances would not affect it to such a great extent. Around the Italian cities, truck gardening became a profitable occupation.

The provinces

In some of the provinces, the economic situation was distinctly unfavorable. In the east, although trade and industry had not seriously declined, the ravages of the Mithradatic and civil wars had left their mark. The destruction of Corinth in 146 B.C. had been a severe blow in Greece, but even worse was the paralyzing effect of the campaigns of Sulla, Pompey, and Caesar. Sulla had ruined Athens in 86 B.C., and the civil wars of Pompey and Caesar had injured Greek agriculture and grazing. In Asia Minor the provincials groaned under the burden of tribute imposed by the victorious Roman parties; it was necessary to borrow money from the equestrians at excessive interest rates in order to meet the payments demanded. Conditions in Africa, Spain, and Gaul in the west were almost as bad.

SOCIETY

The rich

In Roman society there was a great gap between the rich and the poor. Today we know most about the wealthy senators and equestrians who formed only a small group at the top of the social pyramid. Rome had her millionaires and near-millionaires who lived in a luxurious manner in their great town houses in Rome and their numerous villas in the country. The houses of the rich were showplaces which cost fortunes to build or rent. They were filled with sculpture and painting; many works of art had been brought to Rome by the conquerors of Greece; when the supply of original art works was exhausted, Greek sculptors and painters were hired to produce imitations.

Politics and business engrossed the minds of the majority

of wealthy Romans, although there were intellectuals who were interested in philosophy and literature. The typical upper-class education was now of the Greek type with its training in rhetoric, literature, and music; and it was not unusual for men to study oratory and philosophy in the Greek centers of learning—Athens, Rhodes, and others. Some rich men amused themselves by posing as the patrons of artists, literary men, and scholars.

Roman women had always enjoyed considerable freedom, but in the period we are now discussing they were even more emancipated. Divorces and multiple marriages were common; men often married for money or to consolidate political alli- **Women** ances. The old Roman morality among both men and women was so infrequently found in high society that its rare appearance excited comment. Some of the Roman women were well educated and could meet the men on common intellectual ground. Moreover, the influence of women in politics was often important. Certainly, Julia, the daughter of Caesar and the wife of Pompey, helped to make the two men political allies as long as she lived. Antony's wife, the vicious Fulvia, did not hesitate to head an attack upon Octavian.

Not all the Romans of this age were vigorous and purposeful. There were wastrels and spendthrifts who passed their **The** time in search of pleasure. Many people looked upon politics **game of** as a great and amusing game. It was expensive, too. Rising **politics** politicians incurred heavy debts; the borrowing of Caesar, Antony, and others ran into the millions.

Far different from the luxury and ease of the upper classes was the life of the Roman poor who led a precarious existence **The poor** in the slums of the great city. Crowded together in shabby wooden tenements where cleanliness and sanitation were unheard of, the masses lived in almost unspeakable conditions. Often the ill-built tenement structures collapsed or were gutted by fire, catastrophes in which many of the inmates would perish, and the remainder would be left homeless. Always they were under-nourished; work was hard to find, and wages were low. Cheap or free grain, water or a little wine, perhaps fish and a few vegetables, served to keep them from complete starvation. About the middle of the first century B.C., the population of Rome hovered near the one-million mark. At this time 320,000 people (one-third of the population) were receiving free grain. The small shopkeepers and the craftsmen managed to struggle along, but the condition of the ordinary skilled and unskilled workers was one of great insecurity. It is best to leave to the imagination the sordid lives of the wives and children of these men.

Slaves

In the last century of the republic the slave population of Italy reached a new high point. Large numbers of slaves were brought from the territories conquered by the Romans; other people were reduced to slavery when they fought on the losing side in the civil wars. Even these abundant sources were not able to supply the demand. Pirates and slave traders carried off countless thousands every year, and small children might be abducted almost within sight of their parents. Of the Italian population of 14,000,000 in the first century B.C., 4,000,000 were slaves.

Slavery

Slaves were employed in domestic service, industry, agriculture, mining, and ranching. In Roman law the slave was considered not a person, but a chattel; he might be sold or transferred like a horse or cow. His master had absolute power over his life. All freemen were his potential enemies; he was allowed greater or less freedom of movement depending upon the type of work in which he was employed, but escape was not feasible because no freeman would shelter him if he fled from his master. Many of the slaves had once been respected citizens of their home communities in far-off lands; often they were well educated, and in that case they might serve their owners as teachers, secretaries, physicians, or artists. An intelligent and tractable slave might be treated like "one of the family"; he might possibly look forward to manumission at some future date, but even then he would be bound to his former owner by the ties of clientship.

The rural slave population was always restless; out in the country in Italy and Sicily slave revolts were not infrequent.

The savagery of these slaves when they broke out in rebellion is a good indication of their feeling toward their condition of servitude and the kind of treatment they received from their owners. The free population consequently feared the slave uprisings and always put them down with great severity. After all, in the ancient world slavery was a basic element of organized society, and people feared that if the slaves were allowed too much leeway, society itself might crumble. Sometimes an unscrupulous political leader would, in desperation, promote a slave rebellion to further his own ends by promising the slaves freedom in return for their support. Slave revolts

CULTURAL CHANGES AND PROGRESS (133-30 B.C.)

The addition of foreign elements to the Roman population continued to bring about a corresponding change in Roman culture. The various peoples who came or were brought to Italy carried thither the customs, habits, and religions of their own countries. On the whole, we may say that the Roman culture of the first century B.C. could not easily be distinguished from that of other people in the Hellenistic world. The effect of cultural change is clearly shown in Roman religion. In the outlying rural areas the old religions of agricultural Italy might still be found; but in the urban centers Greek, Egyptian, and Oriental cults flourished at the expense of traditional beliefs. The educated Romans turned to philosophy as a substitute for religion—particularly to Stoicism and Epicureanism—whereas the lower classes adopted the imported religions. The state cult of Rome survived because it was so closely bound up with the whole system of government. Few, however, considered the state cult as a religion; it was rather an essential formality. Cultural change

The chief point to remember about the Roman adoption of Hellenistic culture is the eclectic character of this borrowing; the Romans chose what they wanted and made combinations of different elements. This is well illustrated in Roman art and architecture in which the main influences were Etruscan, classical Greek, and Hellenistic. The Romans Roman architecture

employed all three orders of Greek architecture, either sepa-
rately or in composite forms; their favorite style, however,
was Corinthian. They retained the high temple podium of
the Etruscans and made considerable use of the arch. Marble,
concrete, and stucco were favorite building materials. The
first stone theater was built in Rome in 55 B.C. The typical
Roman theater differed from similar Greek structures in
that it had a stage.

**Sculpture
and
painting**

Roman sculpture had both Etruscan and Greek roots.
There was much imitation of classical Greek and Hellenistic
styles, of course; the main Roman contribution was in the
field of portraiture. Painting continued the Greek tradition;
as a matter of fact, it is from the Roman painting of the next
century (from the frescoes of Pompeii and Herculaneum)
that we get our best conception of the character of Hellenistic painting.

Literature

We cannot leave the subject of the last century of the
republic without a few remarks about the literary productions
for which it was noted. The chief poet was a young man
named Catullus who lived in the first half of the first century

Catullus

B.C. Catullus wrote under the influence of the great Alexandrian poets, and he was able to make his Latin as graceful
as their Greek. He wrote much: a short epic, a wedding hymn,
some lyric poems, and a series of love poems; the latter are
famous and well worth reading.

Lucretius

Philosopher, and great poet, too, was Lucretius (99-55
B.C.), who combined his philosophy and poetry in a long work
in which he expounded the ethical and scientific doctrines of
Epicurus. His mission, he felt, was to free men from superstition and the fear of death. Although many of his ideas regarding the causes of physical phenomena were fantastic, we do
find in his work (*De rerum natura*) embryonic ideas which
seem strikingly modern: the atomic theory, the evolution of
species, and an explanation of cultural evolution.

Caesar

Modern students are familiar with Julius Caesar's account
of his campaigns in Gaul and Britain, although, unfortunately, they are seldom fully appreciated by high school Latin

Sallust

classes. Sallust, a contemporary of Caesar, wrote histories of the Jugurthine War, the conspiracy of Catiline, and the decade following the death of Sulla. A series of biographies, principally of famous Greeks, was written by Cornelius Nepos. **Nepos**

Marcus Terentius Varro was a first-century encyclopaedist, a very learned man who wrote more than seventy books. He **Varro** was primarily an antiquarian, but he also wrote on agriculture and the Latin language.

Cicero, the major literary figure of this age, was much more than an orator. True, we have all or parts of more than **Cicero** seventy-five of his orations, but we also have his treatises on rhetoric, political institutions and theory, legal subjects, and philosophy. Most interesting of all Cicero's writings are his letters, about eight hundred of which are extant; they are invaluable for the reconstruction of the life, manners, and history of his age.

In his works called the *Republic* and the *Laws*, Cicero disclosed his theories about the ideal state. He believed firmly **Political** in the Roman republic, but he wished to free it from (what **views** were to him) its obvious imperfections and abuses. His attitude was generally conservative. A coalition of equestrians and senators as a governing class, with little opportunity for democratic government, was the main theme of his program for reconstruction.

Cicero's philosophy represented a combination of the practical elements of Greek philosophy. He inclined toward **Philosophy** Stoicism and the doctrines of the later Platonic school, but he **of Cicero** did not like Epicureanism. In philosophy Cicero contributed little that was new; his main significance was that he helped to popularize Greek philosophical concepts.

In oratory and in prose Cicero was outstanding for his distinctive style. His vigorous, rhythmic, carefully balanced **Cicero's** periodic sentences with their close attention to sense and **style** sound were admired by his contemporaries and his successors. He managed to combine two contemporary trends in style: the Asianic which was rather florid, and the Attic which was severe. Cicero carefully studied the writings of Isocrates and Demosthenes, and he learned something from each.

CHAPTER X

THE CLIMAX OF ANCIENT CIVILIZATION

Octavian

The defeat and death of Mark Antony left only one major political figure upon the stage—Octavian. In control of the army and without any immediate rivals, Octavian's predominance was such that he was able to maintain peace and restore order to a world which had been torn by war and civil strife for over a century. Governmental readjustments were made which insured a political stability that lasted, with only a few interruptions, for the next two hundred years.

Results of the *Pax Romana*

The period of the *Pax Romana*, the Roman Peace, may be said to begin in 29 B.C. with the return of Octavian to Rome; it came to an end with the assassination of Emperor Commodus in 192 A.D. As a result of the generally peaceful conditions prevailing during these two centuries, ancient civilization reached its climax. The largest political unit known to antiquity, the Roman empire, ultimately stretched from the British Isles to Mesopotamia, and from the Rhine and Danube frontiers to the edge of the African deserts. At the same time, the ancient world came to enjoy an economic and cultural unity which included not only the Roman empire but also the Ancient Near East and India. Urbanization reached its peak in the second century of the Christian era, and ancient civilization attained its greatest complexity.

In considering this great cultural epoch, we shall need a description of its social, economic, intellectual, literary, and artistic life, but perhaps it will be most convenient to discuss first the political developments which occurred. Certainly, the subject of the establishment of the Roman imperial system of government and its subsequent evolution is interesting and important, although it should not be over-emphasized at the expense of the non-political features of the age.

OCTAVIAN'S MODIFICATION OF THE ROMAN REPUBLIC

Octavian is usually considered the founder of the Roman empire, i.e., the new system of government which now replaced that of the republic. This should not be understood to mean, however, that he discarded the republican system entirely or that the change was made overnight. We shall presently see that Octavian, for the most part, simply followed certain lines of 'development in the Roman governmental system that had already been clearly marked out since the time of Sulla, or perhaps even earlier. In the second place, it is probably incorrect to assume that Octavian had any definite idea of his final course of action as early as 29 B.C. Unlike Sulla, who wished to go back to the primitive republic, or Caesar, who wished to establish an autocracy, Octavian did not have a fixed program of reform or innovation. It seems more likely that his actions were dictated by circumstances beyond his control, and that certain political settlements which he made as temporary or compromise arrangements subsequently became permanent. Thus, a new system evolved which became further and further removed from the republican tradition and ultimately, three hundred years later, attained the Oriental theocratic form of the Hellenistic monarchy of Alexander and his successors. *Octavian and the Roman imperial system*

It is doubtful whether the change from the republican to the imperial form of government was immediately apparent to Octavian's contemporaries. Let us review the course of events as they must have appeared to the average Roman of the period. *Gradual changes*

Ever since the time of Marius, a succession of internal and external crises had seemed to necessitate temporary departures from the established constitutional traditions of the republic. A series of extraordinary magistracies—the multiple consulships of Marius, the long dictatorship of Sulla, the commands of Pompey against the pirates and Mithradates, the perpetual dictatorship of Julius Caesar, and other political expedients of a similar kind—had been employed to meet difficult situa- *Extraordinary magistracies* tions. The Second Triumvirate was another special bit of machinery devised to tide the republic over the difficulties of the civil war that followed the assassination of Julius Caesar. When Octavian fought with Antony, he possessed some extraordinary powers the exact nature of which is not clear, for it is believed that the triumvirate was terminated after 33 B.C. with the expiration of the second five-year grant of triumviral powers. Perhaps Octavian retained his authority as triumvir; we do know that the senate, the Roman people, and the army swore an oath of loyalty to him.[1]

Octavian continued to hold extraordinary powers until 27 B.C. It was manifestly impossible to return to ordinary republican practice immediately after Antony was defeated in 30 B.C., for reconstruction was needed after the end of the civil war. The army had to be partially demobilized, rewarded for its services, and some veterans absorbed into civilian life. The senate had to be reorganized; Octavian purged it of its non-aristocratic members in 28 B.C. and set the number of the senators at 600.

The "restoration" of the republic

At last, in 27 B.C., Octavian formally returned his extraordinary powers to the senate and the people. In other words, he offered to restore the republican form of government. We shall never know whether this action on his part was sincere, or whether it was merely a political gesture. After all, Octavian still held the consulship and had the loyalty of the army, and his strong position in the state was in little danger of being diminished. Moreover, we can be sure that when he had reorganized the senate in the preceding year, he had been careful to see that no one extremely hostile to himself was included in the reformed body.

New powers of Octavian

In 27 B.C. it must have been clear that the work of reconstruction was not yet complete and that, of all prominent Romans, Octavian was best fitted to finish what he had himself begun. Quite naturally, therefore, he was invested with new powers. The most serious and pressing problems were

---

[1] Moreover, Octavian held the consulship in 33 B.C., probably proconsular power in 32, and the consulship again in successive years from 31 to 23 B.C.

connected with the revision of provincial administration and the defense of the imperial frontiers. As a result, Octavian was given a special proconsular power over Egypt and certain other provinces, mostly on the frontiers, in which the major portion of the Roman army was stationed; older and more settled interior provinces, ten or eleven in number, were to be administered by the senate. Octavian's proconsular power was originally granted for a period of ten years; it was subsequently renewed in varying grants of ten- and five-year terms.

The settlement of 27 B.C. provided the basis of Octavian's power for the next four years. His proconsular command in the provinces gave him virtual control of the army, and his position as consul (even though he had a succession of colleagues) gave him great authority in Rome and Italy. Moreover, since 28 B.C. he had been *princeps senatus*,[2] and thus he was able to guide the deliberations of the senators. Then, too, Octavian had the enthusiastic backing of the rank and file of Roman citizens. His popularity gave him more actual power and authority than his constitutional position could ever confer upon him. Already people in many quarters had begun to think of him as being something more than human. This is well illustrated by the fact that as early as 27 B.C. he was given the title of Augustus (the Revered). After this he was rarely called Octavian, and even now it is customary to refer to him as Augustus, a practice which we also shall follow.

In 23 B.C., Augustus resigned his consulship; he held this office again only at intervals. It has often been suggested that he found certain disadvantages in basing part of his power on the consulship because of the fact that it was necessary to have a colleague in this office. Nevertheless, it might also be pointed out that if it were his intention to preserve cordial relations with the senatorial group and to share the government of the empire with the senate, it would not be politic of him to monopolize this important senatorial office. As a substitute for the consulship, Augustus was given the

Marginal notes: Proconsular power / Consulship / Princeps senatus / Augustus / Further adjustment

---

[2] *Princeps senatus* was the title bestowed upon the most distinguished member of the senate. The *princeps senatus* had the right to speak first of all the senators when the senate was discussing any measure.

full power of a tribune; this had already been done in the case

of Julius Caesar. The point is that neither Caesar nor Augustus became tribunes; they merely held the tribunician power. The recipient of this power had all the powers of a tribune (the right to call the Assembly of the Tribes, the veto power, and personal inviolability—*sacrosanctitas*), but he was freed of the disadvantage of having the other tribunes as his colleagues.

With his proconsular *imperium* in the provinces and his tribunician power at home, Augustus possessed enough power to dominate any ordinary situation in which he might find himself involved; but circumstances arose almost immediately which resulted in an extension of his authority. In 23 B.C., in order that he might deal with an important Parthian embassy, Augustus was given the special right to make war and peace in the name of the Roman state. In 22 B.C., the threat of famine in Rome caused the Romans to place the control of the grain supply in Augustus' hands, and he was also empowered to convene the senate at his discretion. Subsequently, he became a member of each of the four great priesthoods, and in 12 B.C. he was made *pontifex maximus*, the high priest of the Roman state. These religious offices were extremely important because of the close connection of "church and state" in the Roman political organization.

It is not easy to find a name for the new system of government which gradually evolved in Augustus' time. Did Augustus restore the republic? Many of his contemporaries thought so, for they regarded his position and powers as only temporary. Actually, it was impossible to return to the republican system without the recurrence of civil war. At the same time, it had been shown in the case of Julius Caesar that it was equally impossible to break completely with the republican tradition. "Compromise" and "temporize" must necessarily be the watchwords of Augustus.

It has been maintained by some that Augustus established a new form of government—a dyarchy. The dyarchy would consist of the joint rule of Augustus and the senate. The senate was the very backbone of the republican system of organization; moreover, its responsibility for Roman foreign policy and provincial government rested upon ancient foundations. Then, too, the senators constituted the oldest, the most cohesive, and the most influential class within the Roman citizenry. Augustus himself, under a dyarchy, would represent the interests of the equestrians, proletarians, and the army. His proconsular *imperium* emphasized his relationship to the army, whereas his tribunician power made him the representative of the non-senatorial groups, the equestrians and the proletariat. The division of the provinces into two groups—those administered by the senate and those under the control of Augustus—might be looked upon as another example of the joint rule of Augustus and the senate.

On the other hand, it might be said with considerable justification that the Augustan settlement was a modification of the republic in which the executive branch of the government was strengthened by placing a president at its head, a single executive who was not limited, as the consuls were, by dependence upon the senate or by the difficulties inherent in the existence of a colleague who had equal powers. Augustus was often called the *princeps* (first citizen), and we might well call the modified republic the *principate*. **Principate**

The delicate and precise balance necessary for the continued existence of the modified republic or the dyarchy was difficult to maintain because it presupposed an essentially static condition. New internal or external crises would naturally result in the amplification of the powers of the *princeps*, who was already very strong. Moreover, too much depended upon the personality of the *princeps* himself. He must always exercise restraint in order to keep within the bounds of his expressed authority, for his actual authority was much greater than his theoretical constitutional powers indicated. A brief survey of the position of Augustus will demonstrate this point clearly. **The problems of the new government**

As long as Augustus held his proconsular *imperium*, he was really the commander-in-chief of the army, and if he retained

Predominance of the *princeps*

the loyalty of the soldiers, the senators could not depose him. Even if they had not been cowed by the army, the senators were still impotent. Augustus could convene the senate at his pleasure; as *princeps senatus* he could speak first on any subject; by virtue of his tribunician power he could veto the action of the senate or any magistrate. As *pontifex maximus* he could employ his religious powers to influence the conduct of public business. The very composition of the senate itself could be determined by Augustus; he could raise equestrians to senatorial rank; senatorial candidates for the magistracies had to obtain his permission to run for office; if necessary, he could assume the consulship and revise the rolls of the senate by virtue of the consular power of the *lectio senatus*.

Weakness of the older magistrates

Although theoretically the consuls and other high officials possessed powers which might have enabled them to hamper Augustus' actions, it was unlikely that they would attempt to do so. Then, too, few men who did not have the approval of the *princeps* would ever attain high offices. Last of all, the *princeps* was a long-term magistrate, whereas few of the other officials held office for more than a year at a time.

Bureaucracy favors the *princeps*

Another foundation for the predominance of the *princeps* was provided by the growth of the imperial bureaucracy. In provincial administration, in the administration of the city of Rome, and in the care of public works, the high officials were senators, but the real work was done by equestrians and freedmen who were the natural allies of the *princeps*. Even more to the point is the example of the imperial prefectures, offices filled only by equestrians. The bodyguard of the *princeps* (the praetorian guard), a small army of 9000 men commanded by equestrian prefects, was stationed just outside Rome. The important province of Egypt was governed by another equestrian prefect. In Rome itself, the police and fire brigade was commanded by the Prefect of the Watch, and the grain supply was administered by another prefect; both these officials were equestrians. From this it will be seen that the bureaucracy was not only dominated but also really belonged to the *princeps* and not to the senate. As the empire increased in size, so did the bureaucracy, and the power of the *princeps* was thus amplified.

Those who thought that the principate of Augustus was to be only a period of transition which would lead back to the real restoration of the republic should have received some warning from what is called the "problem of the succession." This provides another example of a temporary arrangement that grew into a permanent one. The developments connected with it may be summarized as follows:

Problem of the succession

Augustus was seldom in good health; one of his most serious illnesses occurred in 23 B.C. and he was near death. Even before 23, he had realized that his life might be cut short at any time. In those early days, while the peace of the empire still rested upon insecure foundations, Augustus felt that chaos might result if he were to die and leave no one to step into his place. His logical understudy must be one who bore the name of Caesar or who was connected with the imperial family in some way.

Ill health of Augustus

Marcellus, Augustus' nephew, was his first choice for a successor. Marcellus was given Julia, Augustus' daughter, in marriage, and he was allowed to hold high state offices. In 23 B.C., however, when Augustus was ill, Marcellus was obviously too young and inexperienced to take command if Augustus died. Therefore, the signet ring of the *princeps* was given to his trusted general and friend, Agrippa, in that crucial period. Soon afterward Marcellus died, and Augustus began to favor Agrippa. Julia now married Agrippa, and he was given the proconsular *imperium* and the tribunician power; he thus became a colleague of Augustus.

Marcellus

Agrippa

In 12 B.C. Agrippa died. His successor was Augustus' stepson, Tiberius, who consequently received Julia, the proconsular *imperium*, and the tribunician power. Although Augustus later turned away from Tiberius and began to push Gaius and Lucius Caesar, the two sons of Agrippa and Julia, to the fore, the early deaths of the two young men forced Augustus to rely once more upon Tiberius. When Augustus himself finally died at a ripe old age, it was Tiberius who bore

Tiberius

the name of Caesar, held the proconsular and tribunician powers, and stood ready to carry on the work of the first *princeps*.

It is possible to see, in this series of events, the growth of an idea. It is altogether probable that, in the case of Marcellus and again of Agrippa, Augustus felt that the danger of civil war had not passed. Before Agrippa died, however, we may suspect that Augustus had decided that the principate must endure as a governmental form. His subsequent understudies were therefore regarded as heirs to his position.

The growth of an idea

Once firmly established, the principate could proceed only in one direction—toward autocracy. The power of the *princeps* increased, and that of the senate waned. Three centuries after the time of Augustus, the principate reached its final and logical form in the Oriental monarchy of Diocletian. ⟩⒀

The autocratic trend

POLITICAL HISTORY AND THE EVOLUTION OF THE PRINCIPATE
(14-192 A.D.)

Although the personalities of the emperors who succeeded Augustus are interesting, our real concern must be with the general political developments of the period from 14 to 192 A.D. These developments may be explained in terms of two factors; the struggle of factions within the empire, and the natural evolution of the principate toward autocracy. Thus, we may treat the political history of the imperial period as we did that of the republic.

During the republican era—at least, down to the death of Sulla—we found that various parties or factions were largely responsible for the political vicissitudes of the Romans. The senatorial class, the equestrians, the proletariat, the army, and the allies all had special aims which they tried to achieve or special privileges which they sought to protect. The Social War, of course, eliminated the allies from the picture, and the growing political importance of the army gradually decreased the power of the proletariat. The other factions survived and continued to be significant in determining the course of imperial history. In addition to the senatorial class,

Republican factions

Imperial factions

the equestrians, and the army, there were new groups of importance on the scene: the praetorian guard and (at a late date) the provincials.

One of the reforms of Augustus was to draw a sharp line between the senatorial and equestrian classes. A senator had to have property valued at one million sesterces ($50,000). Membership in the order was hereditary provided the property qualification could be filled. If it could not, the prospective senator would be demoted to equestrian status. On the other hand, a rich equestrian might hope to gain admission to the senatorial class by a promotion from the *princeps*. The senators were not only members of the senate; they also served as provincial governors, consuls, and other high state officials in civil and military life.")⁴ **Senatorial order**

Equestrians had to possess property valued at 400,000 sesterces ($20,000). Free birth and good character were also qualifications for membership in the order. Admission was controlled by the *princeps*. The equestrians filled minor state offices, and they were the holders of the great prefectures which the *princeps* never intrusted to senators. **Equestrian order**

The government of the empire was thus placed on what was, in a way, a timocratic basis. It was largely wealth, rather than ability, which determined class membership. Unfortunately, the division of the classes on the basis of wealth did not help much in breaking the unity of feeling and purpose within the senatorial class itself. The equestrians who were promoted to the senatorial group soon forgot their equestrian sympathies and adopted the point of view of their new colleagues. The senatorial class continued to have a program; it wished to retain its governmental powers and resented any arrogation of authority by the *princeps*. As late as the second century A.D., many of the senators were still vigorous in their opposition to the principate, which they maintained was almost irreconcilable with liberty. **Timocracy**
Senatorial aims

The equestrians resented the high position of the senators, and still hoped for equality with them. Consequently, the equestrians were the natural allies of the *princeps* in his **Equestrian aims** continuous, though rarely open, struggle with the senate. As time passed, the equestrians made steady gains, especially as a result of the growth of the imperial bureaucracy.

The army

The potentially most powerful faction under the empire was the army; but the fact that the *princeps* was its commander-in-chief and the high military offices were held by the senators naturally made the army, on most occasions, the tool of either the *princeps* or the senators. There were, however, other occasions on which the army chose its own leaders, and then civil war resulted. Ordinarily, the emperors were careful to see that the army was well disciplined—and also well paid. Thus, it was seldom a disturbing element before 192 A.D.

Praetorian guard

The praetorian guard was a picked group of Italian soldiers. The men had little sympathy for the regular army, and when they entered any situation at all, it was for the selfish interests of themselves as a group. The close connection of the praetorian guard with the *princeps* meant that the attitude of the guardsmen was sometimes anti-senatorial, especially since their commander was an equestrian.

The provincial factor

In the early republican period, the city-state Rome had conquered Italy and the citizens of Rome had ruled the Italians. After the Social War, when the Italians were made citizens, it was the Italians (all the Roman citizens of Italy) who ruled the great empire bordering on the Mediterranean. In other words, Italy was a distinct area which enjoyed privileges not accorded to the provinces. During the first century A.D., however, many Romans migrated to the provinces, and numerous communities in the provinces were given Roman citizenship. Naturally, the Roman citizens who dwelt in the provinces acquired regional interests. They began to resent the favored position of Italy; they wanted their own provinces to be placed on an equal footing with the peninsula. As the provinces increased in economic strength (see below, p. 314), their political influence became stronger, and eventually they stood on the same level with Italy. This rise was only gradual, however. It was quite apparent in the second century A.D., although regionalism and decentralization did not attain their greatest importance in politics until the third century.

Keeping in mind the aims of the various factions and the natural tendencies of the system of government known as the principate, we may now turn to a summary of the events and developments of the period from 14 to 192 A.D. This period may be divided chronologically as follows: (1) the Julio-Claudian period (14-68 A.D.), (2) the period of the first civil war (68-69 A.D.), (3) the Flavian period (69-96 A.D.), and (4) the era of the Good Emperors (96-192 A.D.). Imperial periods (14-192 A.D.)

The Julio-Claudian Period (14-68 A.D.).—At the death of Augustus, his stepson Tiberius held the proconsular *imperium* and the tribunician power. Tiberius convened the senate, and the senate ratified the acts of Augustus, deified him, and, after some hesitation, asked Tiberius to continue as *princeps* in the place of Augustus. Thus, a precedent was established. A succession of emperors then followed: Tiberius (14-37 A.D.), Gaius (37-41 A.D.), Claudius (41-54 A.D.), and Nero (54-68 A.D.). All these men belonged to the closely related Julian and Claudian clans; their dynasty is therefore known as the Julio-Claudian. The Julio-Claudians

The Julio-Claudian emperors were generally popular with the common people and the army because they were related to Julius Caesar and Augustus. Moreover, their administration was such that the provincials found little reason to complain. The senators, on the other hand, came to hate the Julio-Claudians bitterly. This animosity was caused partly by the friction inevitable in the dyarchal system, but mostly by the personal faults of the emperors themselves. Conflicts within the dyarchy

Tiberius realized the delicacy of his position. At first, he was careful to follow the course already laid out by Augustus. He showed his good will toward the senate by allowing the senators themselves to elect those magistrates of senatorial rank who had previously been elected by the assembly. As Tiberius grew older, however, he became morose and suspicious; and at the same time the senators began to chafe Tiberius against the restrictions imposed upon them by the system of the principate. When several plots against Tiberius were discovered, he began to make use of informers and spies who warned him of real and also imaginary conspiracies. Treason trials were held with increasing frequency, and many senators were convicted.

When Tiberius finally died in 37 A.D., the Romans (including the senators and the army) turned hopefully to his young and popular grandnephew, Gaius (Caligula). Caligula, however, soon became insane. In the ensuing reign of terror, many were executed or murdered at the command of the mad emperor who bestowed the consulship upon his favorite horse, proclaimed himself a god, made faces at himself in a mirror for light amusement, and bewailed the fact that no great fires, earthquakes, or other catastrophes ever occurred to brighten his dull existence.

Caligula

In 41 A.D. Caligula was murdered by a member of the praetorian guard. In jubilation, the senators proclaimed the restoration of the republic, but the praetorian guard had other plans. The praetorians naturally were vitally interested in the continuation of the principate. Therefore, they forced the senate to accept their imperial nominee, Claudius, the uncle of Caligula and nephew of Tiberius.

Claudius

Claudius, who was crippled and at one time considered mentally deficient, proved himself a careful and conscientious administrator. He was never very popular with the senators, and he did not increase his slight hold upon their affections when he chose to rely upon the only friends and confidants of his unhappy youth, his freedmen. Claudius installed his freedmen as heads of new governmental departments of finance, correspondence, petitions, investigation, and records. These key positions in the nascent bureaucratic system were, in the second century A.D., to evolve into important ministries and secretariats.

Nero

Nero, the stepson of Claudius, became *princeps* in 54 A.D. after Claudius was poisoned (probably by Nero's mother). The new emperor was young, popular, affable, and highly regarded by the senate during the early years of his reign. For five years he allowed himself to be guided by his advisers who favored close cooperation with the senators. After this, however, Nero struck out for himself and became autocratic, extravagant, and antagonistic toward the senate. He devoted much of his time to music and the theater and allowed his praetorian prefect, Tigellinus, and his freedmen to run the government. The embittered senators began to conspire his overthrow. After the great fire in Rome in 64 A.D., the heavy taxes imposed by Nero in order to rebuild the city and pay for his other expenditures aroused widespread opposition. A revolt broke out in Gaul which spread to Spain where the governor, a senator named Galba, was proclaimed emperor (68 A.D.). In a panic, Nero committed suicide. `` *16*

The First Civil War (68-69 A.D.).—Galba, who was favored by the senate and the praetorian guard, was brought to Rome Civil war and installed as *princeps*. In the confusion, however, the army got out of hand and began to assert itself. The legions on the lower Rhine hailed their commander, Vitellius, as emperor. Galba's incompetence lost him the support of the praetorian guard who now murdered him and set Otho, another senator, in his place (69 A.D.). Vitellius advanced upon Italy. Otho was defeated by him and committed suicide; Vitellius then became *princeps* by force of arms. Within a short time, the Danubian legions and those in the Near East revolted from Vitellius and declared for Vespasian, the principal commander in the Near East. Before the end of the year 69 A.D. Vitellius was overthrown and Vespasian was master of the empire.

The Flavian Period (69-96 A.D.).—Vespasian was the founder of a new dynasty which is called the Flavian because The of the name of his clan. Vespasian himself ruled from 69 to Flavians 79 A.D. He was followed by his elder son, Titus (79-81 A.D.), and his younger son, Domitian (81-96 A.D.).

Vespasian was an equestrian by birth. He bore the senate little affection and made it clear that he was the real ruler Vespasian of the empire. The senators were powerless against him because he had the support of the army, and his son, Titus, was commander of the praetorian guard. Vespasian was a good administrator. By means of rigid economy and new taxes he wiped out the billion-dollar deficit accumulated by Nero. He also completed the rebuilding of Rome as well as the pacification of the provinces.

Titus

Titus was a popular spendthrift and a good soldier, but his reign was cut short by his early death in 81 A.D. He was remembered chiefly for the two great catastrophes that occurred while he was *princeps*: the eruption of Vesuvius which buried Pompeii and Herculaneum (79 A.D.), and another great fire in Rome (80 A.D.).

Domitian

Domitian, the most autocratic of the Flavians and the most unpopular, insisted upon being addressed as *dominus et deus* (Lord and God) and made no attempt to cooperate with the senate. His poor generalship cost him the support of the army. Last of all, the expense of his wars against the Germans and the Dacians (see below, p. 306) and the cost of rebuilding Rome after Titus' fire were productive of financial difficulties. The target of several senatorial plots, he was finally slain as the result of a conspiracy that had the cooperation of the praetorian guard.

The Good Emperors (96-192 A.D.).—From 14-96 A.D., as we have seen, there was constant friction between the senators and the *princeps*. The senators themselves were never quite powerful enough to overthrow a *princeps*, but they could always, as a last resort, gain the support of the praetorians or the army. After the death of Domitian, however, a certain equilibrium was attained, and a better understanding existed between the emperors and the senate down to about 180 A.D. However, we shall see that the senate gradually lost ground until the situation during the reign of Commodus (180-192 A.D.) paralleled that in the reign of Domitian.

New understanding between senate and princeps

Nerva

The *princeps* chosen to succeed Domitian was an elderly senator named Nerva who, although tolerated by the praetorians, was really the nominee of the senate. Nerva took an oath never to put a senator to death; he also recalled the political exiles of the Flavian period and punished the informers who had flourished under Domitian. Many people, however, were disposed to worry about the age and infirmity of the new emperor. The restlessness of the army and the praetorians aroused forebodings of a civil war like that which had followed after the death of Nero. Furthermore, no arrangements had been made for the succession. All these problems were solved early in 97 A.D. when Trajan, a Spaniard and a competent general, was adopted by Nerva and given the proconsular *imperium* and the tribunician power. When Nerva died in 98 A.D., after a brief reign of less than two years, Trajan succeeded him without opposition.

Trajan (98-117 A.D.) enjoyed great popularity with both the senate and the army. He, like Nerva, took an oath never **Trajan** to harm a senator; in return, he received strong senatorial support. The army favored Trajan because of his vigorous policies of foreign conquest (see below, p. 306). He was always remembered as the *Optimus Princeps*.

Just before Trajan died, he adopted his cousin Hadrian. Hadrian was acclaimed emperor by the army, and his ap- **Hadrian** pointment was ratified by the senate. His reign (117-138 A.D.) was generally peaceful, although growing tension between the *princeps* and the senate might be observed. Hadrian treated the senate with outward respect, but a number of his reforms reduced this body to a subordinate position. His division of Italy into four judicial districts presided over by imperial nominees (*juridici*) struck directly at the traditional senatorial control over the peninsula and also had the effect of reducing Italy to the level of the provinces. Moreover, Hadrian began to rely upon the equestrians to assist him in governmental administration, and opportunities for civil service careers for those of equestrian rank were increased. Hadrian also replaced the freedmen in the great imperial secretariats with equestrians. These offices, which had originated in the reign of Claudius, now acquired greater prestige.

Antoninus Pius

In the year of his death Hadrian adopted an elderly senator who became the next emperor, Antoninus Pius (138-161 A.D.). The reign of Antoninus was notable for its internal peace and freedom from foreign conflicts. As a concession to the senate, Antoninus abolished the Italian judicial system that Hadrian had established.

Marcus Aurelius and Lucius Verus

The two adopted sons of Antoninus, Marcus Aurelius and Lucius Verus, succeeded him in 161 A.D. as co-emperors. Marcus Aurelius, the elder *princeps*, was much more competent than Verus and assumed the major part of the responsibility of government. Hence, Verus' death in 169 A.D. did not lead to any significant changes in the administration of the empire.

The reign of Marcus Aurelius

There was no conflict between Marcus Aurelius and the senate, even though the emperor did not take the customary oath regarding the senators, and even though he did restore Hadrian's *juridici* in Italy. It was his misfortune to have to engage in a series of foreign wars with the Parthians and with the barbarians who were pressing upon the Danubian frontier. The wars were very expensive; at one time, the barren condition of the treasury forced the emperor to sell many of his personal belongings at public auction in order to carry on the war against the barbarians. Earlier, the army upon its return from the Parthian campaigns had brought back a plague which swept over the empire and left thousands dead in its wake.

The Good Emperors

Marcus Aurelius was the last of the so-called Good Emperors, the line of rulers which had begun with Nerva. The Good Emperors had, on the whole, kept peace with the senate and given the empire the benefit of careful, conscientious government. The army and the praetorian guard had been kept under strict discipline. Down to the time of Marcus Aurelius, prosperity had been evident throughout the empire except in Italy and Egypt (see above, pp. 301 ff.). An increasing number of provincial communities had received grants of Roman citizenship.

This happy age came to an end during the reign of Com-

modus, the son of Marcus Aurelius, who had been made co-   Commodus
emperor with his father in 177 A.D. and succeeded him in
180. A nearly empty treasury, a dissatisfied army, and an
incompetent emperor soon brought disaster. The senate was
antagonized and the praetorians were alienated. Commodus
seems to have become insane, for, among other things, he
identified himself with Hercules and renamed Rome the
"Colony of Commodus." He was well on the way toward
equaling the exploits of Caligula or Nero when the praetorians assassinated him in 192 A.D.

IMPERIAL EXPANSION

The generally unsettled conditions of the first century B.C.
had given the Romans little opportunity to consolidate the   The task of Augustus
territory which they acquired (principally through the cam-
paigns of Pompey and Julius Caesar). Thus, it became the
task of Augustus to organize the empire and to find defensible frontiers which would help to eliminate the necessity
of maintaining a large army, for a large army was expensive
and also dangerous to the state.

In addition to adding Egypt to the empire, Augustus completed the conquest of northwestern Spain and the organi-   The frontiers
zation of Caesar's Gaul, but he made no attempt to retain
Britain since Caesar had never really secured a foothold
there. Augustus believed in employing natural boundaries as
frontiers, but in the Near East it was difficult to find any line
to separate the Roman and Parthian empires. This problem
was solved by using the vassal kingdoms of Armenia, Cappadocia, and Commagene as buffer states; the same thing
was done in northwestern Africa, the vassal kingdom of
Mauretania protecting the Romans from the desert tribes.

In the north, Augustus found the entire length of the
Danube useful as a boundary, and he incorporated all the   The Danube, the Rhine, and the Elbe
territory south of it into the empire—with the exception
of Thrace which was not made a province until 46 A.D. For
the frontier line running from the north down to the Danube,
the Romans had a choice between the Rhine and the Elbe.

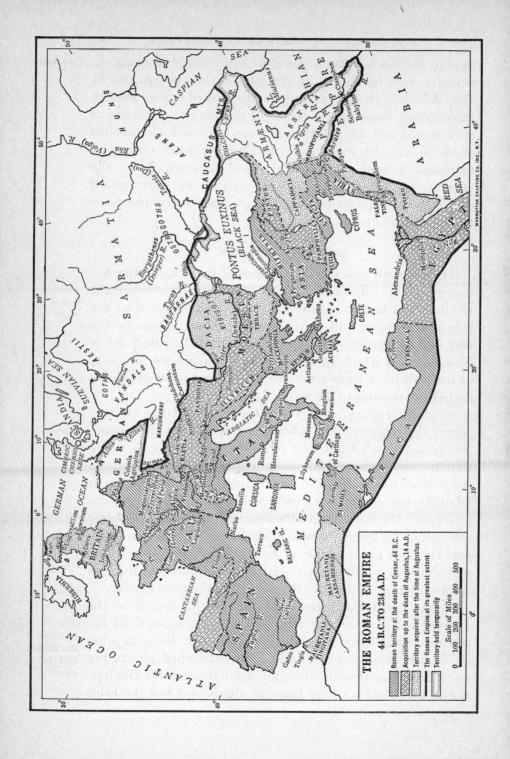

THE ROMAN EMPIRE
44 B.C. TO 234 A.D.

Roman territory at the death of Caesar, 44 B.C.
Acquisition up to the death of Augustus, 14 A.D.
Territory acquired after the time of Augustus
The Roman Empire at its greatest extent
Territory held temporarily

Scale of Miles
0   100 200 300 400 500

For all practical purposes, the Romans already possessed the Rhine boundary, but it was clear that an Elbe-Danube line would make a shorter frontier to defend. Therefore, Augustus resolved to obtain the Elbe line by the conquest of the German territory between the Rhine and the Elbe. The advance into Germany was made, and Augustus was almost on the point of success in 9 A.D. when his general, Varus, and three legions were ambushed and cut to pieces by the Germans in the Teutoberg Forest. This serious loss brought the abandonment of the Elbe line; henceforth, the Rhine was the boundary.

Until the accession of Claudius, there were no important changes in the empire except that Cappadocia and Commagene were reduced to provincial status by Tiberius, and Caligula annexed the kingdom of Mauretania. Claudius, however, not only made Thrace a province, but also undertook the conquest of Britain. **Alterations (14-54 A.D.)**

It is doubtful whether the conquest of Britain was a necessary step. From the military point of view, the English Channel was a much better frontier than any the Romans found in Britain. Economically, the cost of conquest and occupation could never be paid from British tribute. On the other hand, any emperor who conquered Britain was likely to be popular because he would appear to be completing the work of Julius Caesar. Moreover, many argued that the reduction of Britain was the final logical step in the conquest of Gaul. Numerous Gallic malcontents, especially the Druid priests, had taken refuge in Britain, and they were constantly stirring up the Gauls who were Roman subjects. At any rate, Claudius sent Roman forces into Britain in 43 A.D. A foothold was gained in the south, and the Romans expanded their holdings during the next half-century. **Conquest of Britain**

The Flavian emperors continued Augustus' search for defensible frontiers. The famous general Agricola, the father-in-law of the historian Tacitus (see below, p. 333), campaigned in northern Britain. The most successful move of the Flavians, however, was the shortening of the northern European fron- **The Flavian policies** tier by drawing a diagonal line from Mainz on the Rhine almost over to Vienna on the Danube. This eliminated the deep salient which cut down into present-day Switzerland.

Trajan and the Dacians

From Domitian Trajan inherited the knotty problem of the Dacians, the people who lived north of the Danube in what is today Roumania. Their marauding expeditions into Roman territory had been a constant source of annoyance in Domitian's reign, and Trajan resolved to punish them. It was clear that the conquest of Dacia would give Rome a province which would be hard to defend, but the fertile land and the gold of the Dacians may have provided some incentive for conquest. It is also possible that Trajan wished to occupy his restless soldiers and at the same time gain popularity with the majority of Roman citizens. Whatever his motives, Trajan defeated the Dacians and took their lands for Rome (101-106 A.D.).

The period of greatest expansion

Under Trajan, the Roman empire reached its greatest territorial extent. Trajan not only conquered Dacia, but he also annexed an Arabian kingdom that lay to the east of Syria and Palestine (106 A.D.) and almost acquired the Parthian empire. War between the Romans and Parthians began in 114 A.D. when the Parthians took possession of Armenia. Trajan reconquered Armenia, overran Mesopotamia and Assyria, and penetrated Babylonia to the Persian Gulf. A Jewish revolt in the Near East, however, forced Trajan to retrace his steps from Parthia in 116 A.D., and his death in the following year prevented the consolidation of his Parthian conquests.

Hadrian's policies

Hadrian abandoned the Parthian territory which Trajan had gained, and he returned Armenia to its former position as a vassal kingdom. He probably felt that in military and financial strength the empire was incapable of controlling such extensive regions in the east. Hadrian's general policy was one of strengthening the frontiers by adequate fortifications. He fortified the Flavian Rhine-Danube sector, and during his reign the famous wall was built across northern England from the Tyne to Solway Firth. During the reign of Antoninus Pius, the British frontier was moved north to the Clyde-Firth of Forth line.

There was no further expansion. The period of Marcus Aurelius, which was marked by bitter struggles with the Parthians and the tribes north of the Danube, demonstrated clearly that the Romans would be most fortunate to retain what they already possessed—a fact that became even more evident in the next century.

The end of expansion

IMPERIAL GOVERNMENT

The Roman empire was an aggregation of urban and rural communities which enjoyed a large measure of local self-government; these communities were grouped into provinces and bound to Rome by varying relationships. At the beginning of the principate there were thirteen provinces; by the death of Augustus, twenty-eight; and in the time of Hadrian, forty-five. The imperial expansion which we have just described was partly responsible for this increase in number; but many provinces were divided and subdivided to form new provinces so that the task of the governors would be easier and the danger of large-scale revolts lessened.

Communities and provinces

The administration of the provinces was divided between the *princeps* and the senate. The eleven provinces under the care of the senate were headed by senatorial governors (ex-consuls and ex-praetors) who all had proconsular powers. The general arrangements were much as they had been under the republic, and the revenues from these provinces went into the senatorial treasury at Rome, the *aerarium Saturni*.

Senatorial provinces

The provinces that were administered by the *princeps* were, in general, those most recently acquired and those in which military forces were stationed. These so-called imperial provinces were governed by different types of officials. Egypt, for example, had an equestrian prefect. Small provinces might be under an equestrian procurator, but most of the imperial provinces were governed by imperial legates with propraetorian powers. The legates were assisted by fiscal and military

Imperial provinces

officials. Revenues from the imperial provinces eventually found their way into the central treasury at Rome, the *fiscus*.

Taxation

The direct taxes in the provinces consisted mainly of a poll tax paid by those who were not Roman citizens, and land and property taxes which were assessed on the basis of a census taken periodically. A fixed sum might be levied annually upon the senatorial provinces, but in the imperial provinces the tribute was a percentage of the annual yield. Indirect taxes consisted of customs duties, a tax on the manumission of slaves, and possibly a sales tax. Food, supplies, and materials might be requisitioned from the provincials for the support of the military forces within a given province; this was called the *annona*. The *publicani*, or sometimes individual contractors called *conductores*, collected the indirect taxes. Direct taxes in the senatorial provinces were collected by the *publicani* until about the time of Hadrian, but in the imperial provinces the agents of the emperor were responsible for tax collection from the beginning of the principate.

Improved administration

On the whole, the administration of the provinces was on a much higher plane in the imperial period than it had been during the republican era. Although there continued to be some graft and extortion, the attitude of the government was well expressed by Tiberius when he warned a governor that it was the duty of a good ruler "to shear his flock, not to skin it."

Classes of provincial communities

The old classification of communities within the provinces —free and federate, free and non-tributary, and tributary— persisted. In addition, Roman and Latin colonies were planted in the provinces, and many of the older urban centers in the west were granted Roman or Latin citizenship. Those communities which were urbanized enough to have some form of municipal government were the key points in the provinces. Eventually, the Roman government hoped to attach all rural areas to nearby municipalities, and therefore the growth of towns and cities was encouraged in outlying regions; in the more settled areas, rural territory was turned over to the cities for administration.

Municipal organization varied throughout the empire. In the east, the Greek *polis* with its magistrates, council, and assembly was the prevailing type. In the west, the Italian municipal system as reorganized by Julius Caesar provided the model. The western municipalities each had a local senate (*curia*) whose members, the *decuriones*, were men of considerable property. The magistrates were the *duoviri* (two men whose functions somewhat resembled those of the consuls at Rome) and the *aediles*, two other officials who were chiefly treasurers and market commissioners. In both the east and the west, municipal government was on a timocratic basis; it was the rich who held the high offices and had the responsibility of government, whereas the poorer citizens had less and less opportunity to express themselves. During the second century A.D., the municipalities lost much of their opportunities for self-government because their financial inefficiency necessitated the interference of the emperor, either through the provincial governor or through special appointees called *curators*.

Municipal organization

The municipalities were extremely important as centers of cultural diffusion. Their growth greatly aided the "Romanization" of Spain, Gaul, and Britain as well as northern Africa. They are interesting to the cultural historian not only because of this particular function, but also because of the survival of their form of government down to the modern period; this was especially true in Spain, and the Spaniards subsequently transplanted it to the New World.

Cultural significance of municipalities

ROMAN LAW

In early Rome, before the middle of the fifth century B.C., the patrician priests had the guardianship of customs and laws, and the patrician magistrates dispensed justice. After the codification of the Law of the Twelve Tables about 450 B.C., a basis for future expansion was provided. The ancient laws were put into definite form, and new laws could be

The early period

added as the occasion arose. Then, too, as we shall presently see, there was the important question of the interpretation of the law.

During the republican period, the laws (*leges*) were made by the Assembly of the Centuries. At first the plebiscites of the plebeian assembly were binding upon the whole citizen body only when approved by the senate; but after 287 B.C. this approval was no longer needed, and plebiscites passed by the Assembly of the Tribes had the force of law. The decrees (*senatus consulta*) of the senate did not produce much in the way of legislation in the republican period because they dealt chiefly with constitutional matters.

Lawmaking under the republic

The real development of Roman law came through its interpretation. This was due to the work of the praetors and the juristic writers (*prudentes*). We have already seen that the city praetor dispensed justice among the citizens of Rome, and the *praetor peregrinus* performed the same function when the citizens of Rome and foreigners were concerned. Each praetor, upon assuming office, issued a statement (edict) in which he explained the principles that would govern his decisions during his year of office. It was recognized that strict adherence to the letter of the laws might result in injustice, and the praetor tried to act according to the spirit of the laws instead. In the case of the *praetor peregrinus* especially, it was found that Roman law could not be applied to foreigners, and it was thus necessary to discover certain common principles in the laws of Rome and those of foreign states. As a result, a universal body of law, a *jus gentium* (law of nations), was created.

Interpretation

The praetor's edict

The *prudentes* were professional jurists who studied and wrote about the law and legal procedure. Their advice was sought, and their opinions had considerable influence upon subsequent legal interpretations. The first *prudentes* appeared about 200 B.C.

Prudentes

In the imperial period, of course, the assemblies declined; by the second century A.D., they no longer made laws. The decrees of the senate, on the other hand, increased in impor-

Imperial lawmaking

tance because it was through them that the *princeps* frequently expressed his will. In addition to this, the *princeps* also issued edicts (proclamations), decisions, rescripts (answers to questions from officials and private citizens), and mandates (orders to officials) which came to have the force of law.

Eventually, the codification of Rome imperial law was undertaken. In the second century A.D., under Hadrian, the praetor's edict was codified, and the imperial edicts were codified two centuries later in the time of Theodosius (438 A.D.). The final codification in the *Corpus Juris Civilis* by Justinian was carried out between 529 and 535 A.D. Of the four parts into which the *Corpus* was divided, the first (Institutes) dealt with the principles of the law, the second (Digest) contained written opinions of the great jurists, the third (the Code) included the decrees of the emperors, and the fourth (the *Novellae*) was reserved for new laws.

Codification

CHAPTER XI

THE CLIMAX OF ANCIENT CIVILIZATION
(Continued)

Prosperity

The period of the *Pax Romana* was characterized by the most widespread prosperity and most flourishing economic activity the ancient world had ever known. With the exception of certain areas which will be specified later, agriculture, trade, and industry reached new levels of production. The increased volume of trade everywhere led to the growth of new cities as well as the increase of populations in the older urban areas; commercial advances were likewise paralleled by an amplification of industrial production. The progress of urbanization naturally brought with it a more complex and more widely diffused civilization.

Roman phase of Hellenistic civilization

This was the Roman phase of Hellenistic civilization. To the Hellenistic base were added the contributions which the Western Mediterranean had to make, principally the Roman adaptations and elaborations of culture traits that had been borrowed from the peoples of the Eastern Mediterranean. New contacts with the Near East, India, and even the Far East were productive of cultural borrowings which were added to the general store of culture traits, and much of this borrowed finery was modified and adapted to meet the needs of the Occident.

Characteristics of "Roman" civilization

The civilization of the first two centuries of the Christian era possessed all the characteristics that we have already associated with the Hellenistic civilization. We shall have occasion to observe specific examples of the universalism, individualism, syncretism, eclecticism, and specialization which were present in this age. We have already mentioned urbanization as a characteristic, and it will also be shown that a

312

movement of peoples occurred which might be characterized as colonization.

ECONOMIC LIFE

It is probably a fair question to ask whether the *Pax Romana* was responsible for the economic prosperity of the first two centuries A.D., or whether the economic prosperity of that period produced the *Pax Romana*. The correct answer appears to be that the peace which the reign of Augustus gave the Roman world provided the necessary impetus and opportunity for economic growth, and that the favorable economic conditions that immediately resulted gave the empire a stability which for many years could not be upset by mere political ruptures and changes.

Pax Romana and prosperity

Looking at the economic life of this period as a whole, we may note certain developments as being especially important. In the first century A.D., Italy reached its commercial and industrial peak. In the meantime, the western provinces gradually built up their trade, industry, and agricultural production to a point where, even before 100 A.D., they were fast becoming economically independent of Italy. In the second century, these provinces freed themselves from Italian dominance, with the result that Italy fell into a subordinate position in world economic affairs. In the second century, too, the eastern provinces (even including Greece) became more prosperous than they had been since perhaps 100 B.C. The one exception to this rule in the east was Egypt which began to feel the full effects of the ruthless economic exploitation practiced there by the Roman government; the Egyptian situation was also aggravated by a succession of "low Niles" which curtailed agricultural production. From this will be seen the necessity of emphasizing strongly the fact that conditions during this period of two centuries were anything but static. On the contrary, there was a gradual, but very definite, change in almost every aspect of economic life and activity; the general situation which prevailed at the end of the period was far different from that of the time of Augustus.

Economic changes

As far as the trade of the Roman empire was concerned, it had two aspects: internal and external. The internal trade grew by leaps and bounds in the early period of the *Pax Romana*. The suppression of piracy by the imperial fleet, the reduction of customs barriers, the uniform system of imperial coinage, and the general improvement of communications and facilities for transportation all contributed to this development. The Roman army was employed for widespread road-building in all the provinces, harbors were improved, and much use was made of inland waterways, especially in Gaul and Britain.

During the first century A.D., Italy was the chief distributor of manufactured goods to the western provinces. Italy herself produced wine, olive oil, pottery, glassware, and metal work which she exchanged for the grain, hides, metals, foodstuffs, and raw materials of Spain, Britain, Gaul, and Africa. Then, too, the Italians were the middlemen in the trade between the provinces of western Europe and the Near East.

Toward the end of the century, however, there was a growth of domestic manufacturing in Gaul, Britain, and Spain that seriously curtailed Italy's exports to the west. The Gauls and the Britains, in particular, began to make their own pottery, glass, woolens, and metal products. Italy soon felt the effects of an unfavorable balance of trade, a condition further aggravated by the fact that Italian wine and olive oil had to face the increasing competition of similar products from Gaul, Spain, and Africa.

Gaul, Britain, and Spain were all noted for their cattle, horses, sheep, and wheat; metals, too, were important. The British exports included also slaves, dogs, oysters, pearls, and woolen cloth. Spain produced such additional products as flax, honey, fish, oranges, lemons, and figs; the steel of Toledo was already famous. North Africa was mainly an agricultural and pastoral area which exported fruits, vegetables, horses, and cattle as well as wheat, olive oil, and wine.

In the Roman east, economic conditions gradually improved, becoming very favorable during the second century

A.D. Greece produced wine and olive oil; the Greek city of Patras was known for its linens; Corinth regained its old prosperity as a trading center and was also a leading manufacturer of terra cotta lamps. Trade and manufacturing were highly significant in the coastal cities of Asia Minor, whereas in the interior agriculture and grazing flourished. The exports of Asia Minor were metal and textile products, parchment, timber, and stone. As the middlemen in the trade between the Parthians and Arabs on the one hand and the Roman empire on the other, the merchants of Syria continued to find trade profitable. The steel of Damascus and the glassware, dyes, woolens, and linen of Phoenicia were also valuable exports.

The Roman east

We know most about economic conditions in Egypt because of the thousands of papyrus documents that have been recovered from the ruins of Egyptian cities and villages of the Roman period. It has been estimated that the Roman government extracted from Egypt a revenue of about twenty million dollars a year in addition to the five million bushels of wheat annually sent from that country to Rome. Egypt was, of course, a tremendously rich country which produced grains, vegetables, legumes, and fruits of various kinds. Moreover, the Egyptians manufactured vegetable oils, textiles, papyrus, glass, pottery, jewelry, perfumes, and cosmetics. Finally, Alexandria was a commercial center which served as a terminus for the major portion of the great external trade that was built up between the Roman empire and Arabia, India, and east Africa.

Egypt

Unfortunately, Roman greed and mismanagement ruined Egypt, the most valuable of all the Roman possessions. Most of the carefully planned state capitalism of the Ptolemies was abandoned for a policy which allowed Roman citizens as well as the Roman government to plunder the country. In Egypt, the Roman government levied more than fifty different agricultural taxes which were paid in kind, as well as money taxes on trades and professions. There were internal and external customs duties and numerous special levies and

Exploitation

assessments. Last of all, more than two hundred miscellaneous taxes are known to have been levied in Egypt.

External trade

Returning once more to the subject of trade, we may consider the external commercial relations of the Roman empire. This external trade formed part of a great body of commerce that was carried on over a vast area stretching from the British Isles to the China Sea. In the west, Britain and Gaul traded with Ireland, Scotland, Scandinavia, and Germany. Roman merchants crossed the Danube to carry their wares into central Europe; the conquest of Dacia by Trajan had been preceded by Roman economic penetration. The Black Sea region and southern Russia had been in commercial contact with the Mediterranean world since the sixth century B.C. From the cities of northern Africa, caravan routes ran southward into the Sahara, and traders and explorers from Egypt went up the Nile past the cataracts and into Nubia and equatorial Africa.

Trade with the east

Most interesting, perhaps, is the subject of trade between the Romans and the east. The commercial relations between the Eastern Mediterranean and India had, of course, attained great significance during the Hellenistic period. In the time of Augustus, most of the Indian trade passed through the hands of Arabian middlemen who transported goods overland to Syria. Augustus managed to arrange it so that Roman merchants might sail from the Red Sea ports of Egypt to the cities of southeastern Arabia. Subsequently, an all-water route from the Red Sea ports to India replaced the earlier route; the geographer Strabo (see below, p. 335) reported that about one hundred and twenty ships a year made this voyage.

The Roman government at various times entered into commercial treaties with the Parthians with the idea of furthering trade not only with Mesopotamia, but also with the Far East, particularly China, because one of the main routes from Syria to China passed through Mesopotamia, across Iran to Bactria, and thence through Turkestan to China itself. Another route ran from Bactria to the Caspian and from there to the Black Sea. In the trade between Syria and Mesopotamia, the great caravan city of Palmyra on the edge of the Arabian desert was highly important. We shall later see that Palmyra became rich and powerful enough to take advantage of Roman weakness in the third century A.D. and to maintain an independent political existence for a brief period.

From India the Romans imported cotton, spices, precious stones, ivory, rare woods, indigo, rice, and sugar; from Arabia came spices, frankincense, and myrrh; from China, principally silk and furs. In return, the Romans exported metals, amber, textiles, and glass. Thus, it is clear that one may draw a parallel between the trade relations of the Orient and Occident as they existed in (1) the first two centuries A.D. and (2) the period between the Crusades and the voyages of Columbus and Vasco da Gama. In both cases the trade between Orient and Occident was essentially a luxury trade; the high cost of transportation, the substantial profits demanded by the middlemen of the Near East, and the numerous customs barriers erected between the east and the west all helped to make goods which were relatively cheap in the countries of their origin very expensive when they reached their final destination. Moreover, the balance of trade distinctly favored the east. Oriental exports were mostly of light weight and small bulk, whereas Occidental exports were, in general, both heavy and bulky; the advantage of the Orientals in overland trade is therefore quite plain. Then, too, the fact that the Orientals wanted most of all the metals of the west, especially gold and silver, meant that the west was being gradually drained of its media of exchange; it has been estimated that five million dollars in gold and silver were lost by the Romans to the Orientals every year. Consequently, the Oriental-Occidental trade was doomed to temporary extinction, and the loss of the precious metals not only made it increasingly difficult for the Romans to trade with the Far East, but also became a contributing factor in the economic decline within the Roman empire itself.

The only solution to this commercial problem was the discovery of all-water routes to the Far East. The Romans did

Imports and exports

Trade problems

Need for all-water routes

open up an all-water route from Egypt to India; this was probably one reason for the decline of the Parthian empire. On the other hand, the trade with China continued to be an overland trade, and it was not until the time of Columbus and Vasco da Gama that the Europeans were able to provide a satisfactory answer to this question.

Economic organization

Large companies or corporations for either commercial or manufacturing ventures were rare among the Romans and their subjects. Individuals or families and their employees or slaves handled the majority of business projects. Most manufacturing was done in small shops, although there were some large establishments which produced pottery, metal work, glassware, or bricks and tiles. The growth of large commercial and industrial firms was to a great extent discouraged by the developments of the second century when, for example, domestic manufacturing increased in the western provinces. This provincial industry existed mainly to satisfy the demands of the local markets, and the bulk of the trade also became regional. Each city and its surrounding agricultural area tended to become an economic unit, a situation which was to be found in the eastern as well as the western provinces.

Finance and investment

The large fortunes of the age were made either in trade or in money-lending. The banking practices of the Hellenistic Age (see above, p. 208) were adopted in the west; and as trade and industry grew, banking operations expanded and became more complex. Roman capital was invested not only in Italy, but also in the provinces. Land investments in the provinces were favored by the senatorial class, whereas the equestrians put their money into provincial industry and trade. Many Roman families abandoned Italy and settled in the provinces. In fact, the Roman migration from Italy was so great that we may be justified in calling the period a new age of colonization.

Agriculture

Everywhere, with the exception of Italy and Egypt (and possibly Greece), agriculture was in a flourishing condition. In the Near East, agricultural serfdom was retained. In Europe, however, serfdom had not yet appeared. Free men worked small farms in the western provinces, and the large estates were cultivated by tenants. The imperial lands (the personal property of the emperor) were managed by overseers (*conductores*) who rented small plots to free tenants (*coloni*).

In Italy, toward the end of the first century A.D., the effects of the agricultural competition of the western provinces began to be felt. The government found it necessary to aid the small farmers with loans, and the owners of large estates had to change their methods. Slave labor in Italian agriculture declined. The cessation of civil war and the comparatively few imperial conquests of the principate cut off an important source of slaves. As a result, the prices for agricultural slaves became almost prohibitive, and tenants had to be substituted for slaves on the great landholdings. *Italian agriculture*

SOCIAL LIFE

In some ways, the society of imperial Rome resembled that of the Hellenistic period; in other ways, there were marked dissimilarities. For example, both periods saw the rise of an opulent and powerful bourgeoisie which gloried in luxury and ostentation; at the same time, the condition of the proletariat became more and more desperate. On the other hand, the Hellenistic period had no group to parallel the Roman senatorial class; the Hellenistic aristocracy was a class of newcomers which lacked the confidence that blue-blooded ancestors imparted to the Roman senators. Then, too, in imperial Roman society the freedmen were more numerous and more influential than they had been in the Hellenistic Age. *Roman and Hellenistic society compared*

At the peak of the Roman social pyramid was the imperial court, composed of the relatives and close friends of the emperor, the influential senators, and the high-ranking equestrian officials. Very near to the *princeps* were the members of his household, his freedmen, and, occasionally, his slaves. The habits and customs of the court varied with the personalities of the emperors and their wives; the austerity of *The imperial court*

Augustus, the debauchery of Caligula, or the vulgarity of Vespasian certainly had some influence upon the behavior of those who surrounded them.

Senatorial class

As members of an ancient ruling class and a very wealthy one, most of the senators were extremely conscious of the social responsibilities which tradition laid upon them. They guarded their prerogatives jealously and met with biting sarcasm the attempts of the newly-rich business men of equestrian and freedman status to acquire "culture" in one generation. Surrounding the senators were their clients, impecunious, fawning, sycophantic. Early in the morning the clients assembled at the house of their patron—the struggling artists or poets, the poor relations, the freedmen, the decadent gentility. There the great man received them and their pitiful compliments with a gracious word or a cold stare, depending upon his own personal reaction to the state of the weather

Clients

or the adequacy of his breakfast. The clients accompanied their patron as he went about his business in the city, breaking a path for him through the crowds, and applauding his speeches (if he made any) on art, literature, or public policy. Later, they returned home with him, and each received a small gift of food or money. In addition to providing economic support to his clients, the patron also acted as their legal representative.

Equestrians

The equestrians were the business men, the merchants, the industrialists, the bankers, and the contractors. As we have seen, posts were open to them in the imperial civil service, and an equestrian might hope to be made a senator. Many freedmen rose to equestrian status. Like the members of any bourgeois society, the equestrians tried to copy the manners and customs of those above them on the social scale, often with ludicrous results.

The city masses

The city masses were composed of the small traders, artisans, workers, slaves, and the unemployed. Living conditions in the great urban areas might be described as unattractive; this would be putting it very mildly considering the crowded tenements, the poor food, and the lack of sanitation which were only minor discomforts to those accustomed from infancy to a proletarian existence. Nevertheless, many people preferred life in the city to life in the country, for urban life could be, on occasion, exciting and amusing. The gladiatorial combats and beast hunts in the amphitheater, the chariot races in the circus or stadium, the triumphal processions and religious festivals, the fires, riots, and street fights far surpassed any entertainment available in the rural areas. As in the Hellenistic period, clubs and societies were important. There were associations of traders, artisans, and other professional men; these organizations were known as *collegia*—they were *Collegia* not guilds or unions, for their aims were only social. The majority of these organizations—whether *collegia*, religious clubs, or burial societies—were extremely democratic: free men, freedmen, and slaves all mingled together on equal terms.

The new cities of the west were miniature Romes. They *Western* had their temples, theaters, amphitheaters, public baths, and *cities* municipal games and festivals. In prosperous times the rich citizens vied with one another for civic offices. In almost every city there were state-supported schools, libraries, and hospitals. The older cities of the east retained their Hellenistic *Eastern* way of life and their Greek city-state customs and organiza- *cities* tion. Great cities, like Alexandria and Antioch, changed very little. Corinth grew into a commercial metropolis, whereas Athens became a rather quiet university town.

An outstanding characteristic of the period was its increasing humanitarianism and social consciousness. The state and the municipalities provided money for schools and hospitals, *Humani-* fed the poor, and tried to care for under-privileged children. *tarianism* In Rome, at least a quarter of the population received free grain, and the emperors made periodic donations of money to the populace. In the time of Nerva, the so-called *alimenta* was instituted in Italy; the government loaned money to small farmers, and the interest on these loans was given to the Italian municipalities to be used for the support of needy children. Private philanthropy was probably even more extensive than that carried on by the state. Also interesting is the fact that slavery became less harsh; the slaves seem to have been treated with greater consideration, and manumission was made easier to secure. The difficulty of obtaining slaves and their resultant high cost may have had something to do with this changed attitude.

Migration and travel

We have already noted the exodus of Romans from Italy to the provinces. There was also considerable movement among the non-Roman elements in the empire; traders and artisans from the Near East and Eastern Mediterranean moved into the west; Greeks, Syrians, and Phoenicians were to be found everywhere. Last of all, since it was relatively easy to journey by land or sea to almost any point in the Roman empire, travel increased in volume. Certain areas enjoyed a fine tourist trade; everyone who could afford it wanted to see Athens, Corinth, Delphi, and "Troy." In Egypt, people visited the pyramids, the Colossus of Memnon, and the temples of Karnak and Luxor; few ever forgot the sight of the priests feeding the tame crocodiles of the Fayum.

RELIGION AND PHILOSOPHY

Trends in religion and philosophy

The first two centuries A.D. show clearly the effects of universalism, individualism, syncretism, and eclecticism upon religion and philosophy. All these forces contributed to the evolution of Christian doctrine, and they also influenced the major developments in Stoicism. Individualism, in particular, was especially important in decreasing the attention paid to state and municipal cults which could not offer the personal satisfactions that could be gained from the mystery religions, Christianity, or philosophy.

Imperial cult

The strongest and most tenacious of the official religions was the imperial cult. During the republican period, the conquered peoples in Greece and the Near East had instituted the worship of the goddess Roma. At various times in the first century B.C., this cult included the worship of prominent Romans—Sulla, Pompey, and Julius Caesar. In the time of Augustus, the cult of Roma and Augustus became popular in

the east and later spread to the western provinces; in a modified form, it existed in Italy also. Thus, the basis was laid for
the evolution of a ruler cult of the Hellenistic type. When
Augustus died, he was proclaimed a god by the senate, and
Tiberius, as his successor and adopted son, was regarded by
the provincials as more than human. Later emperors, particularly Caligula, Domitian, and Commodus, desired deifica-
tion in their own lifetimes, but they only outraged Roman
public opinion. In large part, the worship of the living emperor in the provinces was a political fiction, a means of
demonstrating loyalty to the ruler by the adoration of his
statue and the performance of a sacrifice or by pouring a
libation to him.

The most popular religions were the mystery cults with
their elaborate rituals and their promises of immortality. The **Mystery**
Egyptian cult of Isis continued to gain converts; about 100 **religions**
A.D., a new competitor, Mithraism, an outgrowth of Zoroastrianism, entered the field. Mithras, the chief deity, was the
god of light, the chief general of Ahuramazda in the war
against the powers of darkness and falsehood. Because of its
militant nature, Mithraism was popular with the Roman army
where it gained the majority of its converts. Mithraism and
Christianity became rivals, and they had much in common.[1]

The period as a whole witnessed a return to superstition.
At least, this is the impression which is given by the popu- **Super-**
larity of astrology, oracles, and fakirs who professed to work **stition**
miracles. Perhaps, however, it is only that we have more information about this age than its predecessor. On the other hand,
if we may accept the available evidence, it is possible to explain the reversion to superstition as a reaction to rationalism.
People wanted desperately to believe something. Moreover,
the world as it appeared through the eyes of a rationalist
was not a pleasant place; most people did not want to see the
world in its naked reality, and therefore they preferred to
blind themselves with emotion and turn to faith in something

[1] A list of the common elements may be found conveniently in A. A. Trever,
History of Ancient Civilization, New York, 1939, Vol. II, pp. 596-597.

unseen but infinitely better than what the rationalist could see.

Even philosophy had to surrender to and compromise with these escapist tendencies. The mysteries of Pythagoreanism were revived, and the most successful of the Neo-Pythagorean teachers were mystics and miracle workers. Stoicism became more and more a monotheistic religion, and the materialistic Epicurean philosophy continually lost ground.

The principal philosophical teachings of the age, as advanced by the Stoics and Cynics, aimed at moral regeneration. Stoicism emphasized self-control, self-examination, rational conduct, and the social obligations of the individual. One must seek to follow the "will of God." The most influential of the Stoics was Epictetus (50-120 A.D.) who had many followers. Marcus Aurelius, emperor and philosopher, recorded his own thoughts in his *Meditations*, a valuable source for the intellectual trends of the period. Eclecticism is clearly shown in the elements of Epicureanism which appear among the Stoic doctrines of the *Meditations*, and universalism is demonstrated more than once, particularly when Marcus Aurelius calls himself "a citizen of the world."

Changes in philosophy

Moral regeneration

CHRISTIANITY

We have still to speak of the most important religious phenomenon of the age—the origin and development of Christianity. The beginnings of the Christian faith may be dated, of course, in the reign of Tiberius. The faith subsequently gained many converts; by the middle of the second century A.D., there were thousands of Christians scattered throughout the Roman Empire. Most of them lived in the cities, and they were to be found in largest numbers in the Near East.

Perhaps the clearest perspective of the position of Christianity in the ancient world may be gained if we consider it as it must appear to some hypothetical modern scholar who is not himself a Christian. From such a point of view, certain things are apparent. First of all, Christianity was a mystery

Christianity a product of its age

religion based upon Judaism, but its theology contained a number of basic ideas that were also to be found in Oriental religions which were contemporary with it and likewise in Stoic philosophy. In other words, Christianity appears as the product of a special time and place, a development that was conditioned by a particular social, economic, and intellectual environment.

A number of modern scholars believe that Christianity originated as a reform movement within Judaism itself. The Jews of that day were divided into a number of sects which maintained differing interpretations of Judaism. Moreover, thousands of Jews had left Palestine during the Hellenistic Age and their descendants were living in many cities of the Roman empire, especially in Antioch, Alexandria, Ephesus, Corinth, Athens, and Rome. These Jews who lived away from Palestine had been exposed to much Greek, Oriental, and Roman influence, and they naturally incorporated many non-Jewish ideas into their religion. These ideas were not in harmony with the theology that had been developed by the priest class at Jerusalem, for official Judaism had become a rigid and formalized religion. In their program of reform, Jesus and his followers attacked this formalism; they stressed the fact that mere formalism was barren, that it was the spirit rather than the letter of the laws which was important. This was the principal reason for the hostility of the priest class toward Jesus; in addition to this, the fact that Jesus made certain criticisms of the rich and openly favored the masses aroused the antagonism of the propertied classes.

A reform movement within Judaism

After the death of Jesus, his followers were forced to abandon their plans to reform Judaism. Orthodox Jews not only resented Christian criticism, but they also accused Jesus of violating the Mosaic code by practicing magic (because of the miracles) and they cast off the Christians as polytheists (because the Christians proclaimed Jesus a god). As a result, the Christian missionaries began to teach among the Gentiles and the Hellenized Jews, where they met with great success.

Failure of the reformists

As soon as the Christian faith spread beyond the borders of Palestine, it was exposed to the influence of religious and philosophic ideas prevalent in the Roman world as a whole, and Christian doctrine was enhanced and modified by the inevitable processes of syncretism and eclecticism. This is another way of saying that the Hellenized Jews and the Gentiles who were converted to Christianity brought into the faith many of their own beliefs.

Subsequent developments

The success of Christianity was due to several factors. In the first place, it was not a new and radical religion at all; instead, it represented a restatement of many attractive ideas of the past. The idea of a savior god who died, yet lived again, and made possible the redemption of his followers was common to the earlier Oriental fertility cults and the Greek mystery religions. Brotherly love, forbearance, and disregard for temporal matters had been preached by the Stoics for centuries. The Messianic prophecy, Mosaic law, and monotheism formed the principal Jewish heritage of Christianity.

Reasons for the success of Christianity

Secondly, while the inspiring mythology of the Christians and the great imaginative appeal of their religion attracted converts, the very amorphous character of early Christian theology allowed the faith to adapt itself to its environment. In addition, the lack of positive dogma in the early years gave the opponents of Christianity little basis for attacks based on theological grounds.

We have noted previously, in discussing Hellenistic philosophy (p. 214), that men had come to feel that they were fighting a losing battle against the overwhelming strength of the forces of nature and the crushing weight of civilization in its social and economic aspects. The philosophers had finally advised people "to make the best of it." The Christians went a step further. They said, "What happens here on earth really does not matter. Live a Christian life, and you shall find your just reward in heaven."

With its simplicity, its emotional appeal, and its promise of a better life to come, Christianity was better fitted than any other faith or philosophy to satisfy the needs of the weary millions of a decaying civilization. It is highly significant that the majority of the first Christian converts came from the lower ranks of society, the slaves and the proletarians, groups among which increasing hopelessness engendered by the harsh economic system had been prevalent since Hellenistic times. As the economic decline of the ancient world became more apparent, particularly in the third century A.D., the bourgeoisie and the aristocracy, too, sought the refuge which Christianity offered.

For three centuries, the Christians were persecuted by the Roman government and by private individuals. This was **Persecution** largely because the Christians were misunderstood. As members of a secret society, they were naturally suspect. They were accused of practicing human sacrifice, incest, and atheism. The charge of atheism arose from the fact that the Christians refused to worship pagan gods and had no cult statues. Non-Christians regarded some of Jesus' doctrines or utterances as subversive and aiming at the destruction of private property and the family; certain well-known pronouncements of Jesus regarding the family and the rich were interpreted by pagans as being anarchistic and communistic. Moreover, the Christians were confused with the Jews; the pagans could see little, if any, difference between the two groups. Anti-Semitism had been present in the ancient world since the Hellenistic period, and the Christians, as well as the Jews, suffered because of it.

In the eyes of the government, the Christians were neither good nor loyal citizens. Their disregard for the affairs of this world aroused the hostility of the state, and the fact that they refused to perform the ceremonies of the imperial cult brought down upon them the suspicion that they were not loyal to the emperor.

The generation of Christians which lived after the death of Jesus felt little need of planning for the future, for they **Growth of** expected his second coming at any moment. As time went **organization** on, however, and it was apparent that the millennium would not arrive immediately, definite organization and planning began to take place.

The various Christian communities, especially in the urban areas, soon took the form of religious societies modeled on the *collegia*. For financial and administrative purposes, each community elected boards of officials from the members of their respective congregations: there were the overseers (bishops), the elders (presbyters) who had spiritual duties, and the deacons who looked after the material welfare of the congregation.

During the second century A.D. there were further changes. The board of overseers gave way to a single bishop who was the president of the board of elders. The bishop presided at religious ceremonies and, with the assistance of the deacons, managed the finances of the community. It was also his task to impose discipline and to settle disputes that might arise between members of the congregation. Naturally, the bishops of important metropolitan centers—Antioch, Alexandria, and Rome, for example—were more influential than those of other communities.

Priest class
At the same time, the elders gradually evolved into a definite priest class with special functions and prerogatives. As the ceremonies of worship were elaborated and a fixed ritual developed, the business of the priests became more and more specialized, and a dividing line was drawn between clergy and laity. The laity were called upon to provide financial support for the clergy; when, about 150 A.D., a man named Montanus spoke out against the growth of a priest class, he was promptly branded as a heretic.

LITERATURE

Increased literacy
The Roman phase of Hellenistic civilization was characterized, like the Hellenistic Age proper, by an increasing literacy. Two developments, the rise of the bourgeoisie and the establishment of numerous state-supported and privately endowed schools, were responsible for the widespread knowledge of reading and writing. Thus, more people engaged in

literary production, and they were encouraged in this by the growth of a large reading public. Of special interest is the productiveness of those of equestrian and freedman status, the members of groups which rose to new economic and social heights in the late republican and early imperial periods.

The literature of the great age of ancient civilization was bilingual (people wrote either in Greek or Latin, or both), and it was basically Hellenistic. In Latin literature, there was a continuation of forms developed in the republican period, but, after all, the republican literature was also basically Hellenistic. As we shall presently see, however, a few new forms appeared. ^{**Literature basically Hellenistic**}

The character of Roman imperial literature was somewhat limited or influenced by two factors: the power and prestige of the *princeps*, and the necessity for subsidization. Political oratory and the writing of political pamphlets and contemporary history—literary activities which had flourished in the latter days of the republic—now declined simply because it was not wise to offend the government by offering political criticism or by writing or talking too freely about current issues. Even under comparatively liberal regimes, such as those of Augustus, Nerva, Trajan, and the other "Good Emperors," writing on political subjects was much restrained. ^{**Imperial influences**}

The difficulties of manuscript production, of marketing literary works, and the lack of copyrights made it hard for authors to make a living despite the large audiences which popular writers might have. Most authors, therefore, unless they were financially independent, had to find a rich patron. ^{**Patronage**} Subsidization inevitably affected the character of the literature produced. An author would have to be careful not to offend his patron, and many times he would have to turn out work at the latter's order; under such conditions, it was not easy for an author to do the best work of which he was capable.

The principate of Augustus was a great period in Roman literary history—it is usually referred to as the Golden Age. It is important not only for itself, but also because it is, in ^{**Golden Age**}

a sense, the culmination of the literary developments of the republic and the point of departure for Roman imperial literature.

Virgil

Virgil (70-19 B.C.), the author of the Aeneid, is the best known of the Augustan poets. The Aeneid, although written in imitation of Homer, is more sophisticated than the Iliad and Odyssey; unlike them, it breathes the spirit of nationalism, a feeling inspired by the Roman empire in its triumphant and most optimistic period. Virgil also wrote the *Eclogues*, pastoral poems based upon those of the Alexandrian Theocritus, and the *Georgics*, a didactic poem intended to encourage agriculture and glorify Italy.

Horace

Horace (65-8 B.C.), a writer of refined and sophisticated poetry, is remembered chiefly for his *Satires, Epistles,* and *Odes.* The poetic form, the satire, had been developed in the second century B.C. by Lucilius (p. 254); in the skillful hands of Horace, it now reached its high point. The *Epistles* are moralizing letters in poetic form which extol virtue, wisdom, restraint, and simplicity, the traditional Greek view of life. The *Odes* employ Greek lyric meters and are based on Alcaeus and Sappho rather than Catullus and the Alexandrians.

Minor poets

Love elegies in the style of Catullus and the Alexandrians were written, however, by the Augustan poets Tibullus (54-19 B.C.), Propertius (50-15 B.C.), and Ovid (43 B.C.-17 A.D.). Ovid, the greatest poet of this triumvirate, published his love poetry in two books, the *Amores* and the *Heroides.* He was subsequently banished from Rome because his highly provocative and immoral *Ars Amatoria* (Art of Love) was offensive to Augustus. After this, Ovid composed his calendar of Roman festivals, called the *Fasti.* Before his banishment, he completed what some consider his best work, the *Metamorphoses*, a series of poems on Greek myths.

Livy

The voluminous history of Rome by Livy (59 B.C.-17 A.D.) was also a product of the Augustan period. Livy lacked the critical scholarship that characterized the work of Polybius, and his excessive patriotism makes it necessary to judge his work as literature rather than history. Roughly contemporary with Livy were Pompeius Trogus, who wrote on Philip of Macedon and Alexander the Great, Diodorus of Sicily, whose *Historical Library* (written in Greek) dealt with universal history, and Dionysius of Halicarnassus, whose *Roman Antiquities* (also in Greek) covered Roman history. **Other historians**

Other writers of note were Seneca the Elder, a teacher of oratory and rhetoric, Verrius Flaccus, who dealt with Roman antiquities and the early Latin language, and Vitruvius, who wrote on architecture. Vitruvius' work is a valuable source of modern information regarding Greek and Roman architectural theory and engineering knowledge. **Seneca the Elder, Flaccus, and Vitruvius**

During the half-century after the death of Augustus, the production of Greek and Roman literary works seems to have remained at the same level as far as volume is concerned, although the quality of the writing is often inferior. From the time of Vespasian down into the second century A.D., however, there is an increase in production (particularly under the liberal second-century emperors and as a result of the prosperity of the period), and many great poets, historians, biographers, and other writers appear on the scene; this is the period known as the Silver Age of Latin literature. **Silver Age**

With this chronological background in mind, we may now survey the literary developments which took place in various fields from the death of Augustus down to the reign of Commodus.

Virgil had given great impetus to the writing of epic, and he had numerous followers and imitators. A Spaniard named Lucan (39-65 A.D.) was the author of an epic, the *Pharsalia*, which dealt with the civil war between Julius Caesar and Pompey. In the Flavian period, Silius Italicus composed an epic poem on the Second Punic War; the epics of Statius were based upon the ancient myths of Thebes and the Trojan War, and Valerius Flaccus wrote an *Argonautica* (in Latin) in imitation of Apollonius of Rhodes. **Epic poetry**

The satires of Horace provided inspiration for those of Persius (34-62 A.D.), and in the reign of Trajan the brilliant satirist of the Silver Age, Juvenal, attained his greatest peak. **Satire**

The Spaniard, Martial, who wrote during the Flavian period, is well known for his satirical epigrams which present social life in Rome in a most unfavorable light.

Seneca the Younger

Seneca the Younger, philosopher, dramatist, and the tutor of Nero, was a major figure during the reigns of Claudius and Nero. His philosophical works, based upon Stoic philosophy, were widely read in his own and later times. He also wrote nine tragedies for which Euripides was his chief model. Seneca's plays, however, were not suitable for stage presentation, although they could be recited or read with some profit.

Fiction

Of considerable interest is the development of prose fiction during this age. Petronius, the aristocratic arbiter of fashion in Neronian society, was the author of a novel called the *Satyricon*. It is the story of the adventures of three lively and unscrupulous gentlemen on their travels in southern Italy. One of the best-known episodes is the Dinner of Trimalchio, a description of a banquet given by a newly rich freedman who sought to put on airs.

Petronius

Apuleius

Lucius Apuleius, who came from a Roman colony in Numidia, wrote a fantastic mystical and satirical novel called the *Metamorphoses*, or the *Golden Ass*. It deals with the adventures of a young would-be magician who wished to transform himself into a bird, but changed himself into a donkey by mistake. In the *Metamorphoses*, Apuleius included a number of incidental stories of Greek origin.

Chariton

The oldest extant Greek novel, *Chaireas and Callirrhoe,* is dated about 150 A.D. Its author was a man named Chariton, about whom nothing is known. The plot of this novel is not particularly complex, but the story moves with some rapidity and contains enough melodrama and romance to make it compare fairly well with some modern light fiction of the same type.

Lucian

An ancient author whose work is timeless in its ability to interest and amuse is Lucian, a Greek who lived in the second century A.D. Lucian wrote satirical dialogues in which he poked fun at philosophers, rhetoricians, miracle workers, sophists, historians, and many others.

It is not until the beginning of the Silver Age that historians of real stature appear. A contemporary of Vespasian was Josephus, the Jewish historian, who wrote in Greek on the history of his people. Josephus was neither accurate nor critical in his use of sources, but his work is interesting nevertheless. **History**

Josephus

The outstanding historian of the age is, of course, Tacitus, who was born in 55 A.D. and died in 116. Most of his writing was done during the reign of Trajan, when it was possible for him to express himself more freely than he could, for example, in the reign of Domitian. In two works, the *Annals* and the *Histories*, Tacitus wrote the history of the period from 14 to 96 A.D. Ironic and embittered, he presented a most unfavorable picture of the Julio-Claudian and Flavian emperors. His sympathies were entirely with the senators, his own class. In spite of his obvious bias, however, Tacitus may well be called the Latin counterpart of Thucydides. In addition to his historical works, he wrote on orators, a description of the people of Germany, and a biography of his father-in-law, the general Agricola. **Tacitus**

Next to Tacitus stands Arrian (*c.* 95-175 A.D.), who wrote in Greek the best extant history of the campaigns of Alexander; he entitled it *The Anabasis of Alexander*. Arrian also committed to writing the teachings of the philosopher Epictetus. **Arrian**

The great biographers of the second century A.D. were Suetonius (*fl.* 120 A.D.) and Plutarch (46-120 A.D.). Suetonius wrote in Latin the scandalous and interesting *Lives of the Twelve Caesars*, the biographies of Julius Caesar, Augustus, and the succeeding emperors down to Domitian. He wrote with his public in mind and never sacrificed a good story to the cause of accuracy. Suetonius was also the author of the *Lives of Illustrious Men*, short biographies of Roman literary figures. **Biography**

Suetonius

The *Parallel Lives* of the Boeotian, Plutarch, is probably the best-known biographical work of antiquity. Plutarch made comparisons of the lives of famous Greeks and Ro- **Plutarch**

mans—Alexander and Julius Caesar, and other similar figures—and produced a series of biographies which make fascinating reading. His ability to tell a good story and his
sense of humor help one to overlook his moralizing and his
inaccuracies. Plutarch also wrote the *Moralia*, a group of
essays the content of which is generally philosophic.

Oratory   Oratory and rhetoric received considerable attention during the Silver Age. In the Flavian period lived Quintillian, a
Spaniard, who wrote the *Education of the Orator*; this dealt
not only with oratory and education but also with literary
history and criticism. The famous Greek orator and moralist,
Dio Chrysostom, was a contemporary of Quintillian; another
well-known Greek orator, Aristeides, flourished in the succeeding generation. Fronto, orator, rhetorician, and tutor of
Marcus Aurelius, graced the court of Hadrian.

Pliny the Younger, the friend of Tacitus and Suetonius,
Pliny the is one of the literary figures about whom we are best in-
Younger   formed. He composed a panegyric, a laudatory oration, in
honor of Trajan, but his real fame rests upon his many letters
that he wrote for publication in the manner of Cicero. The
letters were addressed to close friends and to men prominent
in public life. One group of the letters was written to Trajan
when Pliny was governor of Bithynia. These letters are especially valuable to us today because of the information they
give us about provincial government in this period.

Scholarship in the imperial period aimed chiefly at pre-
Scholarship serving and making known the knowledge amassed in preceding ages. In the second century A.D., for example, appeared the *Attic Nights* of Aulus Gellius, a hodgepodge of
essays on learning, language, philology, law, and natural history. At the same time a number of lexicographers were com-
piling lists of rare Greek and Latin words and their definitions. The work in science, as we shall presently see, followed a similar path.

The first Christian writings appeared in the Flavian period.
Christian The letters of the apostle Paul were collected, and the gospels
literature of Mark, Matthew, Luke, and John were composed between

70 and 100 A.D. Many books later relegated to the apocrypha were written by Christians during the second century. Moreover, Christian apologists began to defend their religion against pagan attacks in essays and dialogues. The New Testament itself, of course, did not attain its final form until about 370 A.D.

SCIENCE

The first half of the first century A.D. witnessed the appearance of two works on geography: one in Greek by Strabo, and the other in Latin by Pomponius Mela. Strabo's work is the most complete treatise on geography that has survived from ancient times. It is a description of the entire known world of his day; much of his information was drawn from older writers, but he himself traveled in some of the regions which he described. The geography by Pomponius Mela is chiefly important for its description of the western Roman empire and because it is the first book on the subject written in Latin.

Geography

Pliny the Elder (23-79 A.D.), the uncle of Pliny the Younger, was an enthusiastic scholar and scientist who not only combed earlier writings for information, but also liked to acquire knowledge by actual observation and experiment. As a matter of fact, his intellectual curiosity was the cause of his death, for he attempted to observe too closely the eruption of Vesuvius in 79 A.D. The demise of this great scholar is described in one of his nephew's most famous letters. Pliny the Elder was the author of the *Natural History*, a huge compendium of facts about the natural world which included geography, astronomy, the physical sciences, and even the history of Greek art.

Pliny the Elder

In the second century Ptolemy and Galen flourished. Ptolemy was an astronomer and geographer whose works had great influence upon his contemporaries and the scholars of the Middle Ages. Galen was the author of a medical encyclopaedia which summarized the medical knowledge of the past

Ptolemy and Galen

and provided a useful source of knowledge for later generations.

Brief mention might be made of a few other writers of the imperial period. In the Julio-Claudian age, Columella of Spain wrote a treatise on agriculture, and Celsus wrote in Latin on medicine. Under Domitian, the soldier and administrator, Frontinus, composed his *Strategems* on military science and his *Aqueducts* which described the system of the Roman water supply. Last of all, the Greek Pausanias, in the latter half of the second century A.D., produced his *Tour of Greece*, a guidebook to the interesting monuments and buildings in the various Greek cities.

ART

The Roman architect was always hampered by inability to obtain an adequate supply of the best building materials. Italian marble, for example, was very good, and marble could be imported from Greece; but the expense of transportation and the heavy demand for materials made it necessary for the Romans to use their best stone sparingly. As a result, they placed considerable dependence upon brick, concrete, and inferior kinds of stone, using fine marbles only in the most conspicuous places; sometimes a building was covered with a veneer of thin marble slabs. Because of the problem of materials, the Roman architects had to develop their engineering skill to a high point and to exercise the greatest ingenuity.

The Romans continued to use columns and half-columns for façades and exterior decoration, but they came to rely heavily upon the arch, the barrel vault, and the dome, mainly because these structures did not necessitate the use of high grades of stone. Roman architecture was also distinguished by its monumental character, its use of composite styles, and its predilection for lavish decorative relief sculpture.

Although the Romans built temples, stoae, libraries, and theaters, they also introduced new structural types: basilicas, baths, amphitheaters, and triumphal arches. The basilica was an elaboration of the stoa; it was a colonnaded hall covered by vaulting, and was used primarily as a law court. This was the architectural form out of which the Christian church evolved. The baths were huge buildings with a complex of **Baths** rooms; a bath usually contained a large court for exercise, a dressing room, a room which was kept very warm to induce perspiration, a hot bath, and a cold plunge. The larger baths might include libraries, lounging rooms, and lecture halls. The amphitheaters were oval in shape, like our football **Amphi-** stadia, and they contained tier upon tier of seats with ramps **theaters** and stairways rising to a height of several stories. Triumphal arches were decorated with sculptured reliefs and panels as **Triumphal** well as columns. **arches**

Almost every emperor sponsored a comprehensive building program in Rome, and quite often, especially in the second **Public** century, these programs were paralleled by public works **works** projects in the provinces. It was the reigns of Augustus, Nero, the Flavians, Trajan, and Hadrian, however, that saw the greatest activity in construction. Famous imperial buildings were the Pantheon of Augustus' friend, Agrippa, the Colosseum of Vespasian, the Tomb of Hadrian, and the baths constructed by Nero and Titus. It will be remembered that, under Hadrian, the city of Athens experienced a building boom: the temple of Olympian Zeus was finally completed, and the Arch and Library of Hadrian were constructed. It was not only the desire for ostentation and display that encouraged the emperors in their public works projects, but also their concern over unemployment. The story of how Vespasian rejected a labor-saving device for erecting columns because there were already too many people out of work well illustrates the latter point.

The achievement of the Romans in the field of decorative sculpture is not to be despised. The reliefs on the Altar of **Decorative** the Augustan Peace, on the Arch of Titus, and on the Column **sculpture** of Trajan and that of Marcus Aurelius are often considered superior to Hellenistic reliefs. The spiral bands of relief on the Column of Trajan present graphic episodes from that emperor's Dacian campaigns, and they provide us with a useful source for a period which is lacking in written sources.

Portraiture   The substantive sculpture of the Romans met with its greatest success in the field of portraiture. On the whole, the sculptured portraits of the Roman imperial period are not idealized; rather they are realistic and rarely complimentary. This is also true of the portraits of the emperors which appear on the coins—we see these rulers as they actually appeared to contemporaries.

Painting and mosaic   The paintings and mosaics, particularly those found in the ruins of Pompeii and Herculaneum, show the technical skill with which the Roman artists were able to handle these Hellenistic media.

CHAPTER XII

THE DECLINE OF ANCIENT CIVILIZATION

The climax reached by ancient civilization in the second century A.D. was followed by a gradual decline in the course of which the political, economic, and cultural unity of the ancient world slowly disintegrated until, by 600 A.D., it had ceased to exist. Western Europe reverted to what was almost a new Age of Agriculture, although in the Eastern Mediterranean the Byzantine empire managed to keep alight the flickering torch of ancient culture. *(Decline after the second century A.D.)*

We speak of the "fall of Rome." It was more than that—it was the fall of ancient civilization.

There was no sudden collapse. Ancient civilization, a complex structure reared to a great height by the toil of ages, subsided slowly, almost imperceptibly, like the ruins of some deserted mud-brick city. Contemporaries saw a changing world, full of invasion and civil war, far different from the quietude and security of the *Pax Romana*. People were vaguely conscious of the economic decline, the intellectual sterility, and the artistic stagnation. The pagans sighed wistfully for "the good old days," but the Christians were more optimistic and looked ahead for something that was "just around the corner." *(No sudden collapse)*

It is now our final task to consider this period of decline and to find answers for two questions:

1. What happened?
2. Why?

THE PRELUDE TO ANARCHY (192-235 A.D.)

After the murder of Commodus late in 192 A.D., a senator named Pertinax was invested with the imperial purple, but he was deposed within three months by the dissatisfied prae-

A new
period of
civil war
(192-196
A.D.)

torian guard (193 A.D.). The principate was then auctioned
off by the praetorians to the highest bidder, a wealthy man
named Didius Julianus. In the meantime. however, the army
began to take matters into its own hands. The British legions
wished to see their commander, Albinus, on the throne;
the forces along the Danube favored their general, Septimius
Severus; and the army of the east nominated Niger, the governor of Syria. Severus, who was nearest Rome, overthrew
Julianus (193), defeated Niger (194), and finally put Albinus
out of the way (196).

Septimius
Severus
(193-211
A.D.)

Septimius Severus, an equestrian from Africa, frankly based
his power upon the support of the army. The soldiers were
given good pay and special privileges, and the senate was
pushed into the background. The civil service was opened
to army officers. The praetorian guard, which had been composed exclusively of Italians, was henceforth recruited from
provincial soldiers. New opportunities were afforded the
equestrian class in the army, provincial administration, and
the civil service. The senate lost its control over Italy when
judicial affairs in Rome and within a radius of one hundred
miles of the city were placed in the hands of the city prefect
and the rest of Italy was transferred to the jurisdiction of the
praetorian prefect.

Worn out by campaigns against the Parthians, the northern
barbarians, and the Scotch highlanders, Septimius Severus

Caracalla
(211-217
A.D.)

died at York in Britain in 211. His sons, Caracalla and Geta,
succeeded him, but Caracalla soon murdered Geta and became sole emperor (211-217 A.D.). Caracalla, who fancied himself a second Alexander the Great, spent much time away
from Rome fighting expensive wars. He was about to invade
Parthia when he was murdered by his praetorian prefect,
Macrinus.

Caracalla had continued his father's favorable policy
toward the army. This had given him a certain measure of
popularity, but his costly campaigns had necessitated heavy
taxes and inflation of the currency which aroused economic
discontent. Caracalla is remembered chiefly for his famous

Antoninian Constitution (decree) which extended Roman citizenship to all but one minor class of free men within the Roman empire (212 A.D.). This was no philanthropic gesture, but a carefully considered move to increase the number of those subject to certain taxes and municipal services.

Macrinus, who succeeded Caracalla, reigned for only a short time before he was overthrown by the family of Septimius Severus' Syrian wife, Julia Domna. Her grandnephew, Bassianus, better known as Elagabalus, won the favor of the army and was placed upon the throne. A sexually perverted religious fanatic, he reigned wildly and kept Rome in an uproar for five years (217-222 A.D.) before he was assassinated. _{Elagabalus (217-222 A.D.)}

Alexander Severus, the cousin of Elagabalus, became *princeps* at the age of fourteen. He was never more than a figurehead, for the real power was exercised by his domineering mother, a few high officials, and the senate. This situation, however, the army refused to tolerate. In 235 A.D. the soldiers murdered Alexander and his mother, and proclaimed as emperor Maximinus, a general of Thracian origin. _{Alexander Severus (222-235 A.D.)}

ANARCHY (235-285 A.D.)

The murder of Alexander Severus was followed by a half-century of near-chaos. In these fifty years there were no less than twenty-six different emperors; only one of them died a natural death. Civil and foreign wars, invasions, revolts, usurpations, and conspiracies were almost without number in this tumultuous period. The army could not be disciplined; the barbarians crossed the frontiers at will. In 227 A.D. the Parthian empire had gone down into oblivion before the onslaught of a Persian revival which elevated a new dynasty, that of the Sassanids. Zoroastrianism became the national Persian religion; it provided a powerful unifying force within the new empire and also served as a prop for the authority of the Persian king. Naturally, the new Persian nationalism demanded the restoration of the ancient boundaries of the empire of Cyrus and Darius, and this led to attacks upon Roman territory in the Near East. About the middle of _{Political chaos}

the third century A.D., the general confusion was increased by a new plague from the east that swept westward over the Roman empire.

Political anarchy was productive of economic disruption. Internal and external warfare, accompanied by a revival of piracy and brigandage, hampered trade, cut down the industrial output, and injured agriculture. The imperial treasury was always empty. High pay and frequent donatives to the soldiers to keep them from revolting or to encourage them to it, the cost of foreign wars, and poor financial management prevented any accumulation of government funds. This situation was met by increasing taxation and inflation of the currency. High taxes and inflation were bad enough for business, but there was also the steady withdrawal of the precious metals from the empire through the Oriental trade and the hoarding of gold and silver because of the inflation. The decrease of the amount of gold and silver in circulation was in itself sufficient to paralyze trade.

Economic disruption

As the power of the central government became weak, the political unity of the empire broke up. An independent Gallic empire existed between about 258 and 274 A.D., and in the east the vassal kingdom of Palmyra was, for all practical purposes, free of Roman control from 260-272 A.D. At one time, the Palmyrenes exercised authority over the Asiatic provinces and Egypt.

The brief independence of Gaul and Palmyra

The threefold division of the empire was, in many ways, a good thing. It gave the emperors at Rome a chance to reorganize their forces and rebuild their power. They were temporarily relieved of the problems and expense of defending Gaul and the east; it was a much-needed breathing spell.

The tide began to turn in favor of Rome when a new emperor ascended the throne in 270 A.D. This was Aurelian, a capable soldier and a good administrator. Aurelian enjoyed the respect of the army and was thus able to reestablish discipline. By 274, he had managed to overthrow Palmyra and restore Gaul and Britain to the empire. His reform of the currency helped to improve the economic situation. He

Aurelian (270-275 A.D.)

anticipated the later solution of Roman governmental problems when he attempted to set up an autocracy. Aurelian was assassinated in 275 A.D., but his good work was not completely undone. Ten years later it formed the basis for the stabilization of the empire by Diocletian.

AUTOCRACY

The chaos of the third century brought the principate to an end, just as the civil wars of the first century B.C. had destroyed the republic. A new order arose upon the ruins of the old, and the whole fiction of the dyarchy was abandoned for an openly autocratic government in which the emperor was the sole source of authority. The concentration of all power in the hands of one man, the dream of Julius Caesar, became a reality.

The end of the principate

It is one of the paradoxes of Roman political history that, the more widely citizenship and political privileges were extended, the less the Romans as a whole were able to participate in their government. After 287 B.C., when the theoretically democratic system had been established, the simultaneous growth of an empire had increased the power of the senate and the equestrians at the expense of that of the masses; the extension of citizenship to the allies in Italy was really the death sentence of the popular assemblies at Rome. The principate, of course, saw the emperor and the senate sharing a theoretical division of powers. As long as the senators were Italians, this form of government came fairly close to achieving its professed aims; but when citizenship was extended to provincials and provincial senators appeared, the senate began to lose ground to the *princeps*. The establishment of an autocracy was the final and logical step. In other words, the city-state Rome could govern Italy and Italy could rule an empire, but when all the subjects of Rome were made citizens they had to be ruled by an emperor.

The political paradox

Two emperors, Diocletian (284-305 A.D.) and Constantine (310-337 A.D.), gave the new autocratic system its form. Diocletian, through the numerous changes which he instituted

The founders of the autocracy

during his reign, contributed more to the building of the autocracy than Augustus to that of the principate, but even Diocletian did not disdain to use materials provided by his third-century predecessors. His political and economic reforms represent the natural culmination and crystallization of third-century developments. It was then the function of Constantine to modify, adapt, and elaborate Diocletian's work.

The philosophy of autocracy

The philosophy of the new government was simple. The empire had narrowly escaped extinction during the course of the turbulent half-century before Diocletian's accession. Political and economic stabilization were essential if the empire was to be saved. Factional strife must be wiped out. The army must be disciplined and the senate subordinated. The State must take precedence over any faction or any individual, and the state was now identified with the emperor. The emperor stood alone at the head of the government; he directed the administration through the bureaucracy; he made the laws and dispensed justice; he was the commander-in-chief of the army and represented the state in its dealings with foreign powers; he even had the authority to regulate economic life.

Divine rule

The emperor could not base his rule upon the consent of those whom he governed or receive his authority from any human agency, the senate or the army. Diocletian proclaimed himself a god. He was thus bound by no human laws, and his subjects addressed him as Lord (*Dominus*), as slaves addressed their master. Constantine was also worshiped as a god by his pagan subjects, but his political alliance with the Christians necessitated a different basis for authority. For the Christians, he was the ruler whom God had ordained. Thus, when Christianity came to be the state religion, the emperor was thought to rule by divine right. This was a much better solution for the problem of autocratic authority than that of Diocletian. To thinking people, the idea of a god-king was merely a political fiction, but no one would dare to question the emperor whom God had chosen as his representative on earth.

Neither of these new governmental theories was especially novel. The patesis of the Sumerian city-state had been earthly representatives of the gods, and the Egyptian Pharaohs had been gods on earth; the Ptolemies and the Seleucids had continued to use these ideas, and in the new Persian monarchy (established in 227 A.D.) the emperor ruled by divine right. Although Diocletian proclaimed himself a god, he borrowed much from the Oriental monarchy of his Persian contemporaries in the way of kingly vestments and jewels, ceremonies and court etiquette, and the establishment of a hierarchy of palace dignitaries.

Diocletian realized that, from both a military and an administrative point of view, one man could not rule the empire. He therefore elevated his general, Maximian, to the position of co-Augustus (emperor) with himself; Diocletian took the eastern half of the empire, and Maximian the western. This arrangement was not entirely satisfactory, however, and in 293 A.D. two additional but subordinate rulers called Caesars were appointed. The empire was then divided into four parts. Constantius (the father of Constantine), the Caesar subordinate to Maximian, ruled Gaul and Britain; Maximian, the co-Augustus, had Italy, Spain, and Africa; Galerius, the Caesar subordinate to Diocletian, watched over the Danubian provinces and the Balkans, and Diocletian took the east as his special region. The empire now had four capitals: Diocletian centered his administration about Nicomedia; Galerius, Sirmium; Constantius, Lugdunum (Lyons); and Maximian had his headquarters at Milan. In this manner, Rome ceased to be the capital of the empire, and the senate was reduced to the position of a municipal council.

Diocletian continued to be the supreme ruler; he was always regarded as the senior Augustus, and Maximian never questioned his preeminence. The authority of the Caesars was based upon grants of the *imperium* and the tribunician power; Maximian adopted Constantius, and Diocletian

Administrative division: the tetrarchy

Galerius. Moreover, Constantius married Theodora, the daughter of Maximian, and Galerius married Valeria, Diocletian's daughter. All proclamations, decrees, and laws were issued in the name of all four rulers and were supposed to be enforced in all parts of the empire.

Prefectures Diocletian, Maximian, Galerius, and Constantius each had a praetorian prefect. As a result, the four divisions of the empire were called prefectures. The prefectures were sub-**Dioceses** divided into thirteen groups of provinces called dioceses, each of which was ruled by an official called a *vicarius*. Under Diocletian, the provinces were broken up into smaller units in order to lessen the danger of revolt and increase the effi-**Provincial** ciency of administration. Where there had been only 45 **subdivision** provinces in the time of Hadrian, there were 101 under Diocletian. Moreover, the provincial governors had only civil powers, the command of military forces being turned over to special officers.

The Like Augustus, Diocletian had to face the problem of the **succession** succession. He planned to have the Caesars elevated to the rank of Augusti when he and Maximian retired in 305 A.D. and to have new Caesars step into the places of Galerius and Constantius. This was done, but the plan soon failed because Constantius died in 306 before adequate arrangements for future successions were completed. Civil war ensued; by 310 A.D. there were five Augusti and no Caesars.

Constan- Without going into the details of the period after 305 A.D., **tine** we may note that finally Constantine, the son of Constantius, became sole Augustus (324 A.D.). He adopted most of the political reforms of Diocletian, but he also made some changes. The four prefectures were retained, but the prefects lost their military functions and became civil administrative officials. The high army officers were henceforth the Master of the Horse and the Master of the Foot (infantry). Constantine solved the problem of the succession by making his sons Caesars.

The senate We have already noted how Diocletian eliminated the senate from the governmental picture by moving the capital of the west from Rome to Milan. The senate, however, had been nearly defunct even before Diocletian came to the throne. During the course of the third century, equestrians had gradually replaced senators in military posts and provincial governorships. Carus, the emperor who preceded Diocletian, had not even asked the senate to ratify his acclamation as emperor by the army. Diocletian himself staged the ceremonies of his own accession at Nicomedia. The senate, however, continued to exist at Rome even when the western capital was moved from Milan to Ravenna. A second senate was set up in Constantinople (Byzantium) when Constantine transferred his government thither in 330 A.D.

Nevertheless, the senatorial class did not go out of existence. It became a landholding aristocracy under the autocratic regime, and it was modified by the admission of a number of persons who would have been equestrians under the principate. From this class came the high officials of the bureaucracy and the advisers of the emperor. **The senatorial class**

The centralization of government, the revision of provincial administration, and the changes in the economic order (which we shall presently discuss) under Diocletian were productive of an increase in the size and complexity of the imperial bureaucracy. The departments of government were headed by great ministers, each of whom worked through a host of subordinate officials. The bureaucracy offered fine positions and opportunities for great careers. Naturally, graft and corruption accompanied the growth of the bureaucracy. As might be expected, contemporaries who were not in the imperial service complained bitterly about the evils of bureaucracy. **Bureaucratic growth**

In addition to making his political reforms, Diocletian also found it necessary to attack certain economic problems which had arisen during the third century. His stabilization of political life and his victories over the barbarians and the Persians had done much to improve economic conditions, but other more direct steps seemed to be advisable if the economic life of the empire were to be kept on an even keel. **Economic reforms**

Diocletian's reform of the currency and the building program which he instituted were not without precedent. His attempt to regulate prices and wages through his famous Edictum Pretium of 301 A.D. was novel, but it was a failure. He was more successful in his revision of the system of taxation. Whereas money taxes were now levied upon senators, the propertied classes of the municipalities, and tradesmen,

Taxation the taxes on land were paid in kind. Land, cattle, and agricultural labor throughout the empire were divided into units of equal tax value. The land unit was called the *iugum*, and varied in size according to the quality of the soil and the type of crops it produced. A certain number of cattle also constituted a *iugum*, and the tax was levied at the same rate as on a *iugum* of land. Labor was taxed by the *caput*; one man or two women became the basic unit of reckoning in this case.

Partly as a result of third-century developments and partly

Economic castes because of these reforms, legal restrictions came to be placed both upon the economic freedom of Roman citizens and even upon their personal freedom. A rigid system of economic castes developed. Henceforth, membership in these castes became hereditary; a man could not change his status even if he wanted to.

In agriculture we have already had occasion to note the

Serfdom growth of large estates which were worked by tenant farmers. The scarcity of agricultural labor led both the government (on the imperial estates) and the large landholders to bring pressure upon the tenants to remain on the land. Diocletian's taxation system made such steps even more necessary. Finally, it was Constantine who legally reduced the agricultural workers to serfdom and bound them to the soil. This system, which was ultimately derived from Egypt, was thus extended to the whole empire.

Membership in the *collegia* becomes hereditary Traders and artisans suffered the same fate as the agricultural workers. As early as the second century A.D. it had been customary for the government to make use of the associations of merchants and the trade guilds. The *collegia* of merchants had been intrusted with state contracts to supply their native cities with foodstuffs. In the course of the third century such services were made compulsory. Likewise, the craft guilds had been responsible for certain civic duties; one guild might constitute a fire brigade, another might have other responsibilities, and so on. At any rate, by the fourth century, membership in these organizations was made hereditary; the merchants and artisans and their sons not only were bound to enter their ancestral professions, but were also forbidden to leave their native towns and cities.

Even the wealthy class of the municipalities now suffered regimentation. The officeholders in the municipalities had always been drawn from the men of property who were also liable for the public services that the Greeks called liturgies (the Roman *munera*). Under Diocletian and Constantine, this municipal aristocracy was transformed into a caste, the *curiales*. The *curiales* of each municipality were then made **The** responsible for the collection of taxes within their city and *curiales* its surrounding countryside. If they could not collect the amount assessed, they had to make up the difference themselves. They were forced to remain in their native cities, and they enjoyed no more freedom of movement than the serfs or the members of the *collegia*.

The political and economic stabilization which Diocletian and Constantine were able to effect through the creation of **Political** the autocracy and the new economic system delayed the col- **and** lapse of the Roman empire for about a century. The whole **economic** theory of the new organization was that conditions would **delayed** remain, or would be forced to remain, static. This, of course, was an impossibility.

In the years that followed, the economic decline continued. Perhaps the increasing cost of government and national defense was more than the empire could bear. Perhaps the inefficiency of the great bureaucracy was one of the chief faults of the system.

At any rate, the political unity that had been the Roman empire disintegrated. In 395 A.D., the empire was formally

The "fall
of Rome"

split into two parts, and the two sons of the Emperor Theodosius became rulers of independent kingdoms, one in the
west and one in the east. The western Roman empire went
down before barbarian assaults in the fifth century, but the
Greek-speaking Byzantine empire in the east, centered at
Constantinople, remained in existence until 1453 A.D.

THE REASONS FOR THE DECLINE OF ANCIENT CIVILIZATION

The preceding pages have briefly summarized the developments in the Roman world after 192 A.D. It now remains
for us to consider the reasons for the political disintegration
and for the cultural and economic decline which began even
before political unity was disrupted.

General
aspects
of the
problem

In modern times there have been numerous attempts to explain the phenomenon of the decline of ancient civilization
that is usually called the "fall of Rome." The "fall of Rome"
in the strictest sense was the collapse of Roman world dominion. Actually, this was but one phase of the cultural
decline; it might even be called a manifestation of it. Most
of the explanations which scholars have offered thus far have
confused cause and effect, although it is true that an effect
which results from one cause may in turn become the cause
of another effect. There is also the danger of selecting a
single cause as being responsible for the whole decline; mature consideration will show that a number of factors, rather
than a single one, were important.

Theories

It is safe to say that theories attributing the decline of
ancient civilization to moral degeneracy, race suicide, "failure
of nerve," and miscegenation are patently absurd and may
be dismissed without further comment. The barbarian invasions, it is true, administered the *coup de grâce* to the
Roman empire, but it is now recognized that the barbarians
were able to cross the frontiers only because of the internal
weakness of the empire. Some have sought the reason for the
decline in political or military factors—the lack of democracy, the development of the autocracy, the inability of the
army to defend the empire, or the great political influence

which the army acquired—but these things are superficial, or, at best, results rather than causes of decline. The argument that the fall of Rome was due to social conflict or class warfare is plausible, but some scholars feel that the evidence is insufficient to supply adequate proof for the theory; then, too, the theory has the additional disadvantage of attributing the decline to a single cause. Last of all, the blame cannot be laid upon the rise of Christianity, since the Christian attitude was prompted by the causes which were also responsible for the decline; one might even say that Christianity provided an answer to the problems that the decline presented to those involved in it.

No one theory of the reasons for the decline of ancient civilization has gained universal acceptance, and probably there will never be one that will satisfy everyone. At any rate, it is not within the province of this book to undertake this task, although some suggestions might be made on the basis of what we have seen of the operation of the process of cultural evolution.

The whole problem of the latter days of ancient civilization has two main aspects. First of all, it is necessary to explain why a tendency toward stagnation and a lack of creativeness should appear in the art, literature, science, and philosophy of the ancient world before the beginnings of the actual decline of political and economic complexity. Secondly, one must consider the possible causes of the decline itself. *The real problems*

Cultural Stagnation.—The stagnation of art, literature, and philosophy seems to arise from the fact that, as far as certain lines of development were concerned, terminal points were reached. Perfection of some techniques in sculpture, for example, had been attained as early as the time of Praxiteles; the climax of painting came with Apelles. The same thing happened in philosophy and literature. One could not out-Plato Plato or write better satires than Horace had written. There was only one Homer and one Virgil. Apparently, when development in any field reached a certain point, men did not *"Dead ends"* have the ability to go farther and they had to content themselves with imitation and repetition.

Creativeness and Its Decline.—Even though certain lines of development might reach terminal points, there was still the possibility of escape from blind alleys through the exploration of side avenues, or, what was less likely, the discovery of new lines to follow. Thus, terminal barriers were avoided again and again in the period before 200 A.D., but in the process new "dead ends" were reached, and the number of possible escapes was constantly being diminished.

Creativeness, however, is largely dependent upon stimulation received from outside contacts. It was no accident that the civilization of antiquity suffered a decline in its creativeness when a cultural unit of great extent came into existence in the second century A.D. As we have seen, this culture area spread from the British Isles to India. It was surrounded by peripheral cultures of lesser degrees of complexity. These peripheral cultures had little to contribute to the civilization of the larger area; they could only borrow from it. The only possible source of stimulus for ancient civilization was China, and that was too far away to provide many fruitful contacts.

On the other hand, ancient civilization itself was of such complexity that there were innumerable opportunities for the combination and elaboration of its culture traits. Thus, for a time, one might say that the civilization could feed upon itself. Eventually, however, two factors closed this door. They were: (1) the necessity for specialization of activity, and (2) the overwhelming complexity of the civilization itself.

It is clear that the more complex civilization became, the greater became the necessity for specialization. The inevitable result was that, when a man attempted to master one field, he had to limit his contacts with other fields. If he did manage to master his field, there still remained the problem of making a contribution to it. Contributions could be made only with the greatest difficulty unless stimulus could be

Escape from "dead ends"

Creativeness and stimulation

Cultural unity

Cultural complexity

Specialization

derived from other fields, but the demands of specialization made this almost impossible.

Let us suppose, however, that an exceptional person did master his field and had time left for outside contacts. He must then, consciously or unconsciously, resort to syncretism and eclecticism in order to glean something useful from the complexity that surrounded him. This complexity had attained such proportions, however, that it defied human understanding. Intelligent selection of ideas from the mass of material available was beyond the power of most individuals, and the whole process of selection assumed the character of a lottery.

The difficulties of syncretism and eclecticism

The suggestions offered above may provide the explanation for the lack of "progress" or "evolution" in the philosophy, literature, and art of the second century of the Christian era. It partially explains why scientific research of a creative character was retarded, but in the case of science we must remember that the incentive provided by the practical application of knowledge was lacking in the ancient world. Ancient science, which was almost entirely theoretical, was only a form of "scholarship." Consequently, like philosophy and literary scholarship, it tended to become static.

The most promising line of development which was opened up was Christianity. Christianity was, of course, the result of the combination and elaboration, the syncretism and the adroit selection, of older ideas. Under its stimulus, art, literature, scholarship, and philosophy were eventually diverted into new channels. Science, however, did not benefit from the new religion, since the Christians had no use for it.

Christian advance

The attainment of "dead ends" and the stifling of the creative impulse halted progress, but there was not necessarily a cultural retreat simply because the forward movement had stopped. On the contrary, if the political and economic situation remained favorable, all existing culture traits could be retained. It is not surprising that respect for the past and an interest in the preservation of culture should be characteristic of the first and second centuries A.D. Compila-

"Preservation" replaces creation

tions of ancient knowledge, commentaries, and summaries began to occupy the attention of those who in earlier periods might have been creators of culture.

The actual decline of culture, on the other hand, came with political and economic disruption. As the cities began to melt away in the west, culture became less complex, and many culture traits were discarded because they were useless in an agricultural society. Moreover, when Christianity supplanted paganism, the trappings of paganism were cast aside. Thus, even within the Byzantine empire of the east, which was far more urbanized than the west in the medieval period, much of the culture of classical antiquity was rejected because no place could be found for it in the Christian scheme of things.

The Economic Decline.—It has been emphasized throughout this book that the complexity of a civilization depends upon (1) the extent of its urbanization, and (2) what it may have inherited from its predecessors. We have also seen that the life blood of a city is its trade; in turn, trade usually fosters industry. From this it is clear that if we wish to learn why ancient civilization declined, we must learn what happened to its trade and industry.

Looking backward over the path we have traveled, we may observe an interesting economic phenomenon. In the beginning, the Near East was the commercial and industrial center of the ancient world. There was a flourishing trade within the area of the Near East itself, and also there was trade with the peripheral areas.

The external trade of the Near East merits our consideration because it presents an economic situation which was typical in the ancient world. This trade of the Near East and its peripheral areas consisted largely of the export of manufactured goods to the peripheral areas in return for raw products. As a result of this trade, cities began to appear in the peripheral areas. Industrial production developed in these cities. Ultimately, the cities of the periphery became

Margin notes:

Decline of culture

Urbanization and accumulation

The importance of trade and industry

Economic history: the Near East

commercial and industrial centers which supplied new peripheral areas.

The Aegean region was one of the peripheral areas of the Near East. We have seen how the Greeks became traders **Greece** and manufacturers and how they exchanged their industrial products for the raw products of their colonists and the barbarians who lived around the Mediterranean and the Black Sea. After a time, the colonies of the Greeks and the towns of the barbarians grew into cities which became centers of production and distribution for more remote areas.

The whole process was repeated in the case of Italy. Italy, developed mainly through trade with the Greeks, became the **Italy** economic center of the Western Mediterranean in the first century B.C. Through trade with Italy, Gaul and Britain were stimulated to economic advance. Toward the end of the first century A.D. they were rapidly becoming urbanized and were building up their industries. The climax was reached in the second century.

This, however, was the end of the long series of developments that had begun hundreds of years before in the Near **The west** East. Except for Scandinavia, Germany, and the New World (which was unknown), there was no peripheral area with which the west could trade. Germany and Scandinavia had little that the western provinces desired, and there were transportation difficulties as well. The result was that the western provinces became largely self-sufficient. They could supply their own agricultural and pastoral products; their **Self-** industries, because of the lack of a large foreign market, **sufficiency** were geared to the needs of the domestic market. Ultimately, this fostered an economic decentralization which led naturally to political separatism.

Although the western provinces might be able to hold their own because of their self-sufficiency, Italy and Greece were less fortunate. The city-states of mainland Greece which **Economic** had grown to economic maturity through trade with their **decay in** colonies were not agriculturally self-sufficient. When the **Greece and** colonies attained industrial independence, the Greek city- **Italy** states lost their sources of prosperity, and economic and political decline resulted. Italy suffered the same fate when the western provinces became industrially self-sufficient and began to raise their own grapes and olives.

The Near East more fortunate

The situation in the Near East was much different. The Near East was agriculturally self-sufficient, and its total area, though more or less naturally unified, was large enough to make possible a profitable internal trade. In addition, there was the trade with the Far East and India in which the peoples of the Near East continued to act as middlemen in the distribution of Oriental products to the west. It is therefore clear that, even though the economic structure of the west might collapse, the Near East would still retain a measure of its prosperity. This explains, of course, why the Byzantine empire survived long after the fall of the west.

Relation of economic to political decline

The Political Decline.—The collapse of Roman world dominion had as its underlying causes the economic developments described above. Roman political power was centered in Italy; it cannot be a coincidence that Italy's economic decline which was accompanied by the attainment of self-sufficiency in the western provinces was followed in the third century A.D. by the temporary establishment of an independent Gallic empire and the rise of the kingdom of Palmyra in the self-sufficient Near East.

The restoration of imperial unity by Aurelian shows that the third-century manifestations of separatism were premature, but the chaos of the period accelerated the economic regression that naturally followed the end of commercial and industrial expansion in the West. The attempt of Diocletian and Constantine to maintain an economic *status quo* might have delayed the collapse even longer than it did if the bureaucracy had functioned efficiently, but the final result was inevitable.

The cost of the autocracy exceeds its income

The emperors of the period of the autocracy had to defend the frontiers and keep internal order. This necessitated a costly military force. Funds for the army had to be raised by increased taxation. The collection of taxes called for the expansion of the bureaucracy, which in turn increased the cost of government. The major portion of the taxes had to be raised in the prosperous sections of the empire: the western provinces and the Near East. The rest of the empire could contribute very little. Moreover, it was only in the Near East that there existed what might be called a real taxable surplus. In other words, it was only in the Near East that profits were made in amounts large enough to bear the burden of heavy taxation. The western provinces could "break even," but an additional tax burden would destroy their profits, and then decline would follow. In effect, what happened was that the government took not only the interest (the taxable surplus) but also part of the principal (the working capital of trade, industry, and agriculture). We may therefore conclude that the cost of keeping out the barbarians and maintaining internal unity was more than the Roman empire could afford to pay. The Near East (the Byzantine empire) had the resources to defend itself, and thus it survived and retained its independence.

It is not pleasant to linger in the sad twilight of antiquity amid the ruins of a past which had seemed full of promise for the future. Yet the survivors of the catastrophe, for the most part, spent little time in wailing and lamentation. Encouraged by the promises of their new Christian faith, they set about building a new world, and most of them were happy in their work. *The end of the ancient world*

Even though the men of the medieval period drew heavily upon the resources provided by their pagan forefathers, it was truly a new world which they created. Within the Mediterranean basin the murmur of Greek and Latin was heard but faintly through the clamor of strange barbarian tongues. The old landmarks stood in their accustomed places, but they seemed strangely unfamiliar. The walls of Athena's Parthenon echoed but hollowly the praises of the Virgin Mary, and the gibbering "saints" who fasted atop the ruinous columns of other pagan temples must have angered the ghosts of the now-dead "immortals" of Olympus. The real tragedy, however, was that beneath the sands of Egypt and in the dark recesses of the monasteries most of the accumulated wisdom of the Near East, Greece, and Rome lay for centuries unused, neglected, and forgotten.

BIBLIOGRAPHY

The following bibliography is in no sense complete. It represents merely a list of easily accessible works which might be consulted by the student.

GENERAL WORKS

Cambridge Ancient History, edited by J. B. Bury and others (Cambridge and New York, 1923-39, 12 vols.).

Toynbee, A. J., *A Study of History* (Oxford, 1934, 3 vols.).

TEXTBOOKS

Boak, A. E. R., *History of Rome to 565* A.D. (2nd ed., New York, 1929).

Botsford, G. W., *Hellenic History,* revised by C. A. Robinson, Jr. (New York, 1939).

Bury, J. B., *A History of Greece to the Death of Alexander the Great* (2nd ed., London, 1913).

Caldwell, W. E., *The Ancient World* (New York, 1937).

Cary, Max, *History of Rome* (London, 1935).

Laistner, M. L. W., *A Survey of Ancient History to the Death of Constantine* (Boston, 1929).

Laistner, M. L. W., *Greek History* (Boston, 1932).

Perkins, C., *Ancient History* (New York, 1936).

Rostovtzeff, M. I., *A History of the Ancient World* (Oxford, 1926-27, 2 vols.).

Sanford, E. M., *The Mediterranean World in Ancient Times* (New York, 1938).

Smith, C. E., and Moorhead, P. G., *A Short History of the Ancient World* (New York, 1939).

Trever, A. A., *History of Ancient Civilization* (New York, 1936-39, 2 vols.).

Turner, R. E., *The Great Cultural Tradition* (New York, 1941).

THE ORIGIN AND RISE OF CIVILIZATION

Boas, F., *The Mind of Primitive Man* (New York, 1924).

Burkitt, M. C., *The Old Stone Age* (New York, 1933).

Childe, V. G., *Man Makes Himself* (London, 1936).
Childe, V. G., *The Bronze Age* (London, 1930).
Hooton, E. A., *Up from the Ape* (New York, 1932).
Kroeber, A. L., *Anthropology* (New York, 1923).
Linton, R., *The Study of Man* (New York, 1936).
MacCurdy, G. G., *Human Origins* (New York, 1926, 2 vols.).
Vendryes, J., *Language* (New York, 1925).

THE ANCIENT NEAR EAST

Albright, W. S., *The Archaeology of Palestine and the Bible* (3rd ed., New York, 1935).
Barton, G. A., *Archaeology and the Bible* (New York, 1927).
Breasted, J. H., *Ancient Records of Egypt* (Chicago, 1906-07, 5 vols.).
Breasted, J. H., *A History of Egypt* (2nd ed., New York, 1912).
Chiera, E., *They Wrote on Clay* (Chicago, 1939).
Childe, V. G., *New Light on the Most Ancient Near East* (New York, 1934).
Cowley, A. E., *The Hittites* (Oxford, 1926).
Delaporte, L., *Les Hittites* (Paris, 1936).
Delaporte, L., *Mesopotamia* (New York, 1925).
Erman, A., *A Handbook of Egyptian Religion* (New York, 1907).
Erman, A., *The Literature of the Ancient Egyptians* (London, 1927).
Hall, H. R. H., *The Ancient History of the Near East* (8th ed., London, 1932).
Harper, R. F., *Assyrian and Babylonian Literature* (New York, 1901).
Hertzler, J. O., *The Social Thought of the Ancient Civilizations* (New York, 1936).
Herzfeld, E., *The Archaeological History of Iran* (London, 1935).
Huart, C., *Ancient Persia and Iranian Civilization* (New York, 1927).
Jastrow, M., *The Civilization of Babylonia and Assyria* (New York, 1915).
Johns, C. H. W., *Babylonian and Assyrian Laws, Contracts and Letters* (New York, 1904).
Luckenbill, D. D., *Ancient Records of Assyria and Babylonia* (Chicago, 1926-27, 2 vols.).
Mackay, E., *The Indus Civilization* (London, 1935).

Marshall, J., *Mohenjo-Daro and the Indus Civilization* (London, 1931, 3 vols.).

Moret, A., *The Nile and Egyptian Civilization* (New York, 1927).

Olmstead, A. T., *History of Assyria* (New York, 1923).

Olmstead, A. T., *History of Palestine and Syria* (New York, 1931).

Sykes, P. M., *A History of Persia* (3rd ed., London, 1930, 2 vols.).

Woolley, C. L., *The Sumerians* (Oxford, 1929).

Woolley, C. L., *The Development of Sumerian Art* (London, 1935).

GREECE AND THE EASTERN MEDITERRANEAN

I. Before 1000 B.C.

Baikie, J., *The Sea Kings of Crete* (4th ed., London, 1926).

Bell, E., *Prehellenic Architecture in the Aegean* (London, 1926).

Burn, A. R., *Minoans, Philistines, and Greeks* (New York, 1930).

Casson, S., *Ancient Cyprus* (London, 1937).

Evans, A. J., *The Palace of Minos* (London, 1921-35, 4 vols.).

Glotz, G., *The Aegean Civilization* (New York, 1927).

Hall, H. R., *Aegean Archaeology* (London, 1915).

Hall, H. R., *The Civilization of Greece in the Bronze Age* (London, 1928).

Myres, J. L., *Who Were the Greeks?* (Berkeley, 1930).

Nilsson, M. P., *Homer and Mycenae* (London, 1933).

Pendlebury, J. D. S., *The Archaeology of Crete, An Introduction* (London, 1939).

Rose, H. J., *Primitive Culture in Greece* (New York, 1925).

Swindler, M. H., *Ancient Painting* (New Haven, 1929).

II. 1000-362 B.C.

Anderson, W. J., Spiers, R. P., and Dinsmoor, W. B., *The Architecture of Ancient Greece* (New York, 1927).

Burn, A. R., *The World of Hesiod* (London, 1936).

Burnet, J., *Early Greek Philosophy* (London, 1930).

Bury, J. B., *The Ancient Greek Historians* (London, 1909).

Buschor, E., *Greek Vase-Painting* (London, 1921).

Calhoun, G. M., *The Business Life of Ancient Athens* (Chicago, 1926).

Ferguson, W. S., *Greek Imperialism* (New York, 1913).

Fowler, H. N., and Wheeler, J. R., *A Handbook of Greek Archaeology* (New York, 1909).

Freeman, K., *The Work and Life of Solon* (London, 1926).

Gardner, E. A., *A Handbook of Greek Sculpture* (London, 1915).

Glotz, G., *Ancient Greece at Work* (New York, 1926).

Glotz, G., *The Greek City and Its Institutions* (New York, 1930).

Gulick, C. B., *The Life of the Ancient Greeks* (New York, 1902).

Hasebroek, J., *Trade and Politics in Ancient Greece* (London, 1933).

Laistner, M. L. W., *A History of the Greek World from 479 to 323 B.C.* (London, 1936).

Linforth, I. M., *Solon, the Athenian* (Berkeley, 1919).

Richter, G. M. A., *The Sculpture and Sculptors of the Greeks* (New Haven, 1930).

Robertson, D. S., *A Handbook of Greek and Roman Architecture* (Cambridge, 1929).

Robin, L., *Greek Thought and the Origins of the Scientific Spirit* (New York, 1928).

Ure, P. N., *The Greek Renaissance* (London, 1921).

Ure, P. N., *The Origin of Tyranny* (London, 1922).

Weller, C. H., *Athens and Its Monuments* (New York, 1913).

Whibley, L., *A Companion to Greek Studies* (4th ed., London, 1931).

Wright, W. C., *A Short History of Greek Literature* (New York, 1907).

Zimmern, A. E., *The Greek Commonwealth* (5th ed., Oxford, 1931).

III. 362-146 B.C.

Bevan, E. R., *A History of Egypt under the Ptolemaic Dynasty* (London, 1927).

Bevan, E. R., *The House of Seleucus* (London, 1902, 4 vols.).

Bury, J. B., and others, *The Hellenistic Age* (London, 1923).

Cary, M., *The Legacy of Alexander: A History of the Greek World from 323 to 146 B.C.* (London, 1932).

Dickens, G., *Hellenistic Sculpture* (Oxford, 1920).

Ferguson, W. S., *Hellenistic Athens* (New York, 1911).

Jouguet, P., *Macedonian Imperialism and the Hellenization of the East* (New York, 1928).

Körte, A., *Hellenistic Poetry* (New York, 1929).

McEwan, C. W., *The Oriental Origin of the Hellenistic Kingship* (Chicago, 1934).

Macurdy, G. H., *Hellenistic Queens* (Baltimore, 1932).

Rostovtzeff, M. I., *The Social and Economic History of the Hellenistic World* (Oxford, 1941, 3 vols.).

Tarn, W. W., *Hellenistic Civilization* (2nd ed., London, 1930).

Tarn, W. W., *The Greeks in Bactria and India* (Cambridge, 1938).

Wilcken, U., *Alexander the Great* (New York, 1932).

ROME AND THE WESTERN MEDITERRANEAN

General

Abbott, F. F., *The Common People of Ancient Rome* (New York, 1911).

Abbott, F. F., *Roman Political Institutions* (3rd ed., New York, 1911).

Duff, J. W., *A Literary History of Rome* (3rd ed., London, 1927, 2 vols.).

Frank, T., ed., *Economic Survey of Ancient Rome* (Baltimore, 1933-40, 5 vols.).

Frank, T., *Economic History of Rome* (2nd ed., Baltimore, 1927).

Homo, L., *Roman Political Institutions from City to State* (New York, 1929).

Louis, P., *Ancient Rome at Work* (New York, 1927).

Platner, S. B., and Ashby, T., *A Topographical Dictionary of Ancient Rome* (Oxford, 1929).

Sandys, J. E., *A Companion to Latin Studies* (3rd ed., Cambridge, 1925).

Before 27 B.C.

Anderson, W. J., and Spiers, R. P., *The Architecture of Ancient Rome* (New York, 1927).

Botsford, G. W., *The Roman Assemblies* (New York, 1909).

Fowler, W. W., *Social Life at Rome in the Age of Cicero* (New York, 1909).

Greenidge, A. H. J., *Roman Public Life* (New York, 1911).

Hadas, M., *Sextus Pompey* (New York, 1930).

Holmes, T. R., *The Roman Republic and the Founder of the Empire* (Oxford, 1923, 3 vols.).

Homo, L., *Primitive Italy and the Beginnings of Roman Imperialism* (New York, 1926).

Marsh, F. B., *A History of the Roman World from 146 to 30 B.C.* (London, 1935).

Pais, E., *Ancient Italy* (Chicago, 1908).

Peet, T. E., *The Stone and the Bronze Ages in Italy and Sicily* (Oxford, 1909).

Randall-MacIver, D., *Italy Before the Romans* (Oxford, 1928).

Scullard, H. H., *A History of the Roman World from 753 to 146 B.C.* (London, 1935).

Strong, E. S., *Art in Ancient Rome* (New York, 1928, 2 vols.).

Whatmough, J., *The Foundations of Roman Italy* (London, 1936).

After 27 B.C.

Abbott, F. F., and Johnson, A. C., *Municipal Administration in the Roman Empire* (Princeton, 1926).

Arnold, W. T., *The Roman System of Provincial Administration to the Accession of Constantine the Great* (3rd ed., London, 1914).

Arragon, R. F., *The Transition from the Ancient to the Medieval World* (New York, 1936).

Baynes, N. H., *The Byzantine Empire* (London, 1926).

Bouchier, E. S., *Life and Letters in Roman Africa* (London, 1913).

Bouchier, E. S., *Spain under the Roman Empire* (London, 1914).

Bouchier, E. S., *Syria as a Roman Province* (London, 1916).

Buchan, J., *Augustus* (New York, 1937).

Chapot, V., *The Roman World* (New York, 1928).

Charlesworth, M. P., *Trade-Routes and Commerce of the Roman Empire* (2nd ed., Cambridge, 1926).

Collingwood, R. G., *Roman Britain* (2nd ed., Oxford, 1932).

Cumont, F., *The Oriental Religions in Roman Paganism* (London, 1911).

Dill, S., *Roman Society from Nero to Marcus Aurelius* (2nd ed., London, 1905).

Dill, S., *Roman Society in the Last Century of the Western Empire* (2nd ed., London, 1905).

Duff, A. M., *Freedmen in the Early Roman Empire* (Oxford, 1928).

Friedländer, L., *Roman Life and Manners, the Early Empire* (New York, 1908-13, 4 vols.).

Gibbon, E., *The History of the Decline and Fall of the Roman Empire*, ed. by J. B. Bury (London, 1900-02, 7 vols.).

Halliday, W. R., *The Pagan Background of Early Christianity* (Liverpool, 1925).

Hammond, M., *The Augustan Principate in Theory and Practice During the Julio-Claudian Period* (Cambridge, 1933).

Harnack, A., *The Expansion of Christianity in the First Three Centuries* (London, 1904-5, 2 vols.).

Haverfield, F. J., *The Romanization of Roman Britain* (4th ed., Oxford, 1923).

Henderson, B. W., *Five Roman Emperors: Vespasian, Titus, Domitian, Nerva, Trajan*, A.D. *69-117* (Cambridge, 1927).

Henderson, B. W., *The Life and Principate of the Emperor Hadrian*, A.D. *76-138* (London, 1923).

Holmes, T. R., *The Architect of the Roman Empire* (Oxford, 1928-31, 2 vols.).

Lot, F., *The End of the Ancient World* (New York, 1931).

Marsh, F. B., *The Reign of Tiberius* (Oxford, 1931).

Parker, H. M. D., *A History of the Roman World from* A.D. *138 to 337* (London, 1935).

Rostovtzeff, M. I., *The Social and Economic History of the Roman Empire* (Oxford, 1926).

Scramuzza, V., *The Emperor Claudius* (Cambridge, Mass., 1940).

Strong, E. S., *Roman Sculpture from Augustus to Constantine* (New York, 1907).

Winspear, A. D., and Geweke, L. K., *Augustus and the Reconstruction of Roman Government and Society* (Madison, 1935).

INDEX

Doric order, 130
Drama, 169 ff.
Druids, 305
Drusus, Marcus Livius, 264
Duoviri, 309
Dyarchy, 290-291
Dyes, 64
Dying Gaul, 222

East Greek alphabet, 227
Eastern Mediterranean, 83 ff.
Eastern Roman Empire, *see* Byzantine
    Empire
Ecbatana, 188
Ecclesia, 101, 102, 111, 157
Eclecticism, 199-200, 211, 312, 353
Economic life, primitive, 9 ff.; Age of
    Agriculture, 13 ff.; Age of Civiliza-
    tion, 17 ff.; Babylonia, 33-34; Indus,
    43-44; Egypt, 46-47, 51-52; Hittite,
    61; Minoan, 86; Greek, 100 ff.,
    109 ff., 145-149; Hellenistic, 206-
    208; Roman, 236-241, 278-280, 313-
    319, 342, 348, 354-355
    See also Capitalism; Trade, etc.
Edict, praetor's, 310
Edictum Pretium (Edict of Prices),
    348
Education, 80, 117-118, 152-153
Egypt, 16, 17, 24, 26, 30, 32, 45 ff.,
    205 ff., 271, 277, 315, 342
Egyptian, writing, 23-24, 57-58; civ-
    ilization, 45 ff.
Elagabalus, 341
Elam, 68
Elbe, 305
Eleatics, 176
Electricity, 215
Elegy, 127
Emancipation of slaves, 37, 150, 282,
    322
Empedocles, 176
Empire, 35; Egyptian, 49; Assyrian,
    66 ff.; Persian, 75 ff.; Athenian,
    139 ff.; of Alexander, 187 ff.; Hel-
    lenistic, 190 ff.; Roman, 286 ff.
Ennius, 253
Environment, influence of, 12, 27, 29;
    Babylonian, 33; Egyptian, 45-47;
    Assyrian, 66; Greek, 97 ff.; Italian,
    229
Ephialtes, 155
Ephors, 119

Ephorus, 173
Epic poetry, 126-127, 219, 330, 331
Epictetus, 324, 333
Epicureanism, 212-213, 255, 284, 324
Epicurus, 213, 284
Equestrians, 245 ff., 257-258, 294 ff.,
    320, 340
Erasistratus, 216-217
Eratosthenes, 215, 216
Erech, 35
Erechtheum, 163
Eridu, 35
Esarhaddon, 42
Esquimaux, 27, 29
Ethics, 52, 79-80, 175 ff., 212
Ethos, 166, 167, 221
Etruria, 137, 225
Etruscans, 225-226, 252
Euclid, 214
Euphrates, 13, 16, 17 *passim*
Euripides, 170-171, 332
Evolution, physical, 2-8; of brain,
    4 ff.; cultural, 8 ff., 27, 97; of writ-
    ing, 22-24; political (Greek), 97,
    100 ff., 116 ff., 154 ff.; (Roman),
    236 ff., 286 ff.
Extraordinary commands, 269, 287

Fabius Pictor, 254
Fasti (of Ovid), 330
Fertility cults, 41, 62
Fire, 2, 8, 10, 29
Fiscus, 308
Fist axe, 9
Flint, 8, 9, 16
Fortifications, 93, 165, 221
Fortune (Tyche), 211
Fossil men, 3, 7, 8
Freedmen, 298, 319
Frieze, 130, 163
Frontiers, Roman, 304-307
Frontinus, 336
Fronto, 334
Fulvia, 281

Gabinian Law, 269
Gades (Cadiz), 64, 225
Gaius, *see* Caligula
Galba, 299
Galen, 335
Galerius, 345-346
Garden culture, 12
Gaugamela, Battle of, 188